MS-DOS Power User's Guide

Volume I

MS-DOS® Power User's Guide

Volume I
(Second Edition)

Jonathan Kamin

SAN FRANCISCO • PARIS • DÜSSELDORF • LONDON

Cover art by Thomas Ingalls + Associates
Book design by Jeffrey James Giese
Chapter art by Liberty Batol

ABM is a trademark of Franklin Telecom, Inc.
HomeBase and PowerMenu are trademarks of Brown Bag Software.
dBASE, dBASE III, dBASE III PLUS, and Framework II are trademarks of Ashton-Tate, Inc.
SideKick and SuperKey are trademarks of Borland International.
PC Tools is a trademark of Central Point Software.
Computer Thaumaturgy is a trademark of Computer Thaumaturgy, Inc.
Corona PC is a trademark of Corona Data Systems, Inc.
Epson is a trademark of Epson America, Inc.
Disk Optimizer is a trademark of Softlogic Solutions, Inc.
DPath+PLUS is a trademark of Personal Business Solutions, Inc.
SmartKey and SmartPath are trademarks of FBN Software.
FastBack is a trademark of Fifth Generation Systems.
IBM PC, PC/AT, PC/XT, QuietWriter, and ProPrinter are trademarks, and IBM is a registered trademark, of
International Business Machines Corporation.
ITT is a registered trademark of ITT Corporation. ITT Xtra is a trademark of ITT Corporation.
KeepTrack is a trademark of The Finot Group.
Mace Utilities is a trademark of Paul Mace Software, Inc.
QDOS II is a trademark of Gazelle Systems.
Ready! and ThinkTank are trademarks of Living Videotext, Inc.
Lotus, 1-2-3, and Symphony are trademarks of Lotus Development Corporation.
WordStar is a registered trademark of MicroPro International.
MS and MS-DOS are trademarks, and Microsoft is a registered trademark, of Microsoft Corporation.
Okidata and Microline are trademarks of Okidata Corporation.
The Norton Utilities is a trademark of Peter Norton Computing.
Polytron, PolyKey, PolyWindows, and PolyWindows DeskPlus are trademarks of Polytron Corporation.
QSPOOL and QSWAP are trademarks, and Quadboard and QuadMaster III are registered trademarks, of
Quadram Corporation.
ProKey is a trademark of RoseSoft Inc.
WordPerfect is a trademark of WordPerfect Corporation.
XTree is a trademark of Executive Systems, Inc.
SYBEX is a registered trademark of SYBEX, Inc.

SYBEX is not affiliated with any manufacturer.

Every effort has been made to supply complete and accurate information. However, SYBEX assumes no
responsibility for its use, nor for any infringements of patents or other rights of third parties which would
result.

Library of Congress Card Number:
ISBN 0-89588-473-9
Manufactured in the United States of America
10 9 8 7 6 5 4 3 2 1

To David Greene, Joshua Orkin, and Arnold Stoper,
who helped get me into this mess

You sing it till you learn it.
—Anonymous

ACKNOWLEDGEMENTS

No book of this size and complexity is created without the contributions of numerous people. Dr. R. S. Langer and Carole Alden were present from the beginning to support the book through its formative stages and to help give it coherence, focus, and a sense of direction. Dianne King helped bring the second edition into being.

The technical information assembled in this book was not easily unearthed. Joe Campbell proved a goldmine of information on the fine points of the inner workings of MS-DOS and the PC family of computers. The section on nationalizing the computer could not have been written without the assistance of Linda Devan and Nick Savage of IBM. Other technical points were contributed by Richard Allen King, Dick Andersen, Matthew Holtz, Neil Strock, Martin Waterhouse, and Rosemary Morrisey.

Many software products are mentioned in this book. Thanks are due all those who contributed products for review or gave technical support when needed: Ken Woog of Franklin Telecom; Michael Brown, David Pease, and Catherine McGreevey of Central Point Software; Steve Rosemary and Stan Brin of Software Research Technologies; Doug Root of Polytron Corporation; Suzanne M. Dickson and many others of Fifth Generation Systems; Dennis Murray and Jason of Brown Bag Software; many people at Borland International; Bill Templeman and Holden Aust of Paul Mace Software; Kelly Horan of MicroPro International; Tim Huff of Peter Norton Computing; and others at RoseSoft, Inc., Quadram Corporation, Tall Tree Systems, and Living Videotext.

In addition, many on the staff of SYBEX contributed to making the ideas tangible: Fran Grimble supervised the project, contributing significantly to the organization of the new edition. Copy editor Jon Strickland ensured that all changes meshed smoothly with the existing text. Joel Kroman and Dan Tauber tested all the programs, commands, and professions of truth within an inch of their lives, for which they deserve your eternal gratitude as well as my own. John Kadyk and Maria Mart word-processed the manuscript; Olivia Shinomoto typeset it; Winnie Kelly proofread the typeset galleys; Liberty Batol provided an attractive layout; Michelle Hoffman was responsible for the screen reproductions; and Bret Rohmer and Jeff Green oversaw the production process.

The following people also made important contributions to the first edition: Karl Ray, Dave Clark, Olivia Shinomoto, Ray Keefer, and Cheryl Vega of Sybex; Marilyn Smith, free-lance editor; Tori Case of Living Videotext; and Beverly Johnson of ITT.

Finally, my wife Nancy has earned my eternal gratitude for keeping a significant portion of the universe running on course while I was involved in this work.

TABLE OF CONTENTS

5: INTRODUCTION TO BATCH FILE PROGRAMMING

6: ADDING POWER TO THE BATCH LANGUAGE

11: ADVANCED FILE MANAGEMENT

14: SENSIBLE HARD DISK MANAGEMENT

15: RECOVERING LOST FILES AND BAD DISKS

I N T R O D U C T I O N

MS-DOS is the most popular operating system for computers using the 8088, 8086, 80286, and 80386 microprocessors—in other words, the IBM PC and its various clones, compatibles, and extensions. This set of programs tells the microprocessor how to communicate with the computer's peripheral devices and how to run programs. (From the point of view of the microprocessor, such taken-for-granteds as disk drives, serial and parallel ports, and memory are peripheral devices.) Without an operating system, the computer can do almost nothing. Replace one operating system with another, and you give your computer a different set of preconceptions.

DOS includes much more than the simple commands everyone needs to know in order to copy files and disks and perform basic file-management chores. Indeed, it includes most of the facilities needed to let programmers write the most sophisticated applications programs.

The MS-DOS Power User's Guide, Volume 1 will not teach you how to use your computer for the first time. Neither will it teach you the inner workings of your hardware nor the ways in which DOS communicates with it. However, it will introduce all the facilities of MS-DOS and PC-DOS that you can employ to control your computer. You do not need any technical background to use the techniques presented here. All you need is a willingness to experiment. (A bit of programming experience wouldn't hurt, however.)

The current edition covers all versions of MS-DOS and PC-DOS from 2.1 through 3.3. It has been completely revised and updated to cover the latest software releases and hardware configurations.

The book is more or less in two parts. Chapters 1 through 9 provide a review and tutorial of the facilities built into DOS. Chapters 10 through 17 discuss specific applications of the tools and techniques presented in the first part.

Chapter 1, *What Is MS-DOS?*, gives a brief history of the evolution of this operating system, to provide a context for discussion. Also noted are the relationship between MS-DOS and BASIC, MS-DOS and PC-DOS, and various releases of the operating system.

Chapter 2, *Disks, Files, and Directories*, gives a complete overview of its subject. The structure of various types of disks is examined in detail. The properties of files are explained, along with details on naming them and using file names in DOS commands. Commands to create and use tree-structured directories are also discussed at length.

Chapter 3, *Your DOS Toolkit*, introduces the DOS editing keys; the EDLIN line editor; DEBUG, the programming editor; and the ANSI.SYS device driver. Chapter 4, *Worthy Additions to Your Toolkit*, discusses some commercially available software packages. These programs can help you overcome the deficiencies of DOS to perform functions that perhaps should have been included but were not.

Chapters 5 and 6, *Introduction to Batch File Programming* and *Adding Power to the Batch Language*, present a complete tutorial on DOS's built-in programming language. This language can be used to automate a wide variety of tasks. Also discussed are ways to extend the language. The techniques introduced in these chapters are used throughout the rest of the book.

Redirection is DOS's method of altering the flow of information inside your computer. Pipes and filters let you change the information as it moves. Chapter 7, *Redirection, Pipes, and Filters*, teaches you how to use these techniques.

Chapter 8, *Configuring Your System*, and Chapter 9, *Customizing Your Screen and Keyboard*, teach you all you need to know to allow your computer to make the best use of your hardware, run smoothly, and conform to your preferences. Chapter 9 includes a tutorial on the powerful ANSI.SYS device driver, which gives you a great deal of control over the appearance of your screen.

Beginning the application section, Chapter 10, *Creating and Enhancing DOS Commands*, gives you practice in applying the principles introduced in Chapters 5 and 6. Batch and BASIC programs are introduced that allow you to customize many DOS commands to perform specialized tasks. As an advanced exercise, we use DEBUG to make modifications to COMMAND.COM, the central command processor.

Chapter 11, *Advanced File Management*, presents some little-known ways to use the COPY command and tips on sharing files among applications. The centerpiece of this chapter is a BASIC program to perform various housekeeping tasks on selected files of your choice.

Chapter 12, *Advanced Directory Management*, explains the technical structure of directory entries. It includes a complete discussion of file attributes and how to control them to your advantage. You will learn to change directory information by directly altering the data as it is recorded on disk.

Chapter 13 introduces *RAM disks*—portions of memory that behave like disks. You will learn what they are good for, how to set them up, and how to use them. Chapter 14 gives extensive pointers on setting up hard disks for efficient use. It also presents ways of automating your hard disk backup procedures so that you don't lose data.

Chapter 15, *Recovering Lost Files and Bad Disks*, tells you how to salvage lost files. The few tools provided by DOS are explained in detail. Some commercially available software products that go considerably further are also discussed.

Chapter 16, *Getting More from Your Printer*, tells you how to use DOS's PRINT command and how to use a spooler for printing while performing other tasks. You will also learn how to control your printer's type styles without using BASIC programs.

With DOS 3.0, it became possible to configure your computer to use default settings and keyboard layouts for various languages and nationalities. Chapter 17, *Nationalizing Your Computer*, explains how to do so, noting the differences in each release of DOS.

Finally, a group of appendices present reference material. Appendix A is a series of diagrams for 14 of the nationalized keyboard layouts discussed in

Chapter 17. Appendix B presents reference tables of ANSI escape sequences. Appendix D lists sources of software mentioned in the book. Appendix E provides an overview of DOS's networking features. Appendix H is a series of ASCII tables, including all displayable characters in the standard and international character sets; control characters; extended ASCII codes for key combinations and special keys; and box and border characters.

Other appendices contain several special features. Appendix C is the source code for programs to make batch files accept input. Appendix F is a patch file to allow WordStar 4.0 to create true ASCII files. Appendix G is a script file to create a keyboard for drawing boxes and borders.

HOW TO ENTER
THE PROGRAMS IN THIS BOOK

Five type of program listings are presented in this book:

- ▲ Batch programs
- ▲ Display screens (help screens and menus)
- ▲ BASIC programs
- ▲ Macro files
- ▲ Assembly-language programs

We'll discuss the requirements for entering the various listings, then explain the typographical, syntax, and naming conventions used in the book.

Batch Programs

Most of the programs in this book are batch files, which are programs that automate the execution of DOS commands. We will be working with some quite elaborate batch files. The text in batch files *must* consist of the standard ASCII characters (the standard alphanumeric characters, and the symbols that you can type from the keyboard), or DOS will not be able to execute them. For a complete list of ASCII characters, including the extended ASCII character set (ASCII codes 128 through 255), see Table H.1 in Appendix H.

Tools for Creating ASCII Text Files   The simpler files can be entered using the COPY CON command, which is explained in Chapter 3. However, this command is inadequate for the longer, more complex files.

DOS's resident line editor, EDLIN, although clumsy, is adequate for entering and editing all of the batch files and help screens in the book. With it, you can enter the Escape character and any necessary control and graphics characters. Its use is also explained in Chapter 3.

Most word processors or text editors can create ASCII text files, but some cannot include graphics characters in their files. Several word processors that do have all the necessary capabilities are reviewed in Chapter 4.

How the Programs Are Listed   The batch files and help files all appear in separate, boxed listings. In these listings, each line is preceded by a number, which is followed by a colon and a space. *Do not type in these line numbers and colons!* They are merely for reference in text, as well as for your reference when you are entering the programs. (There are times when additional spaces have been included deliberately at the beginning of a line. You can insert these spaces with the spacebar or the Tab key.)

Control Characters   When control characters are discussed in text, they are referred to by name; for example, Ctrl-S, Ctrl-C, or Ctrl-[. In program listings, they appear as the character preceded by a caret mark:

^S ^C ^[

How you enter them depends on the program that you use to create the listing. Some word processors cannot accept any such codes, as they use these characters as commands. Some of them will accept only a few of the control characters, while still others will accept all of them. For details, consult the appropriate sections of Chapters 3 and 4. If the software you use is not discussed there, consult its manual.

The Escape Character   The Escape character (ASCII 27) is a special control character, equivalent to Ctrl-[. When the Escape character is required in a program listing, it appears either as ^[or as a ← (its graphic representation in Table H.1). It precedes most codes sent to the printer and codes known as *ANSI escape sequences*, which are explained fully in Chapter 9 and listed for reference in Appendix B.

Again, how you enter this character depends on the software you are using. Generally, if you can insert a control character into a file by preceding it with a command key (such as Ctrl-P in WordStar), you can insert an Escape character either by following the command key with Ctrl-[or with the Esc key.

Testing the Results

Even the most careful typist sometimes makes mistakes. A typographical error in a program listing, even in a simple batch file, can cause unexpected results. Therefore, unless you are sure of what you are doing, *type the programs exactly as they appear.*

It is essential that you test each program after you type it in to be sure that it behaves correctly. Try each one out on a disk full of expendable files (I'd suggest creating such a disk for the purpose). If you modify the programs, be sure to test your modifications on files that you can afford to lose.

Hint: Most of the batch programs in this book begin with the command ECHO OFF. This tells DOS not to display each command before it is executed. When you are testing a program, it is a lot easier to locate an error if every command *is* displayed before it is executed. Therefore, when testing a program or a program modification, place a colon (or the word REM) before the ECHO OFF command. The form

    :ECHO OFF

or

    REM ECHO OFF

prevents the statement from being executed. When you are sure that the program is behaving correctly, edit the file to remove the colon or the REM.

Display Screens

The display screens we'll be creating are also ASCII text files. In addition to the standard ASCII characters (0 through 127), they include graphics characters from the extended ASCII character set (codes 128 through 255). These characters are used principally to create lines for borders and separators.

The display screens appear in the same format as the batch programs—with line numbers, colons, and spaces—and the same rules apply to typing them in.

In some cases, you will find more than one version of a display screen: one consisting of simple text; one with special codes added for video attributes such as boldface and inverse video, which can be displayed on a monochrome screen; and one with codes added to create a color display. The latter two types of screens require that you have the ANSI.SYS device driver installed in your CONFIG.SYS file. For a full discussion of the ANSI.SYS device driver, see Chapter 9. For an explanation of the CONFIG.SYS file and its uses, see Chapter 8.

The graphics characters in the listings for the display screens are the actual characters that should appear on the screen. Table H.4 in Appendix H lists the ASCII codes of the border characters.

Entering Graphics Characters You can insert the graphics characters with the COPY CON command, in EDLIN, and in many commercial word processors and text editors by holding down the Alt key, typing the digits of the decimal ASCII code on the numeric keypad, and then releasing the Alt key. For example, to enter the double horizontal line character, which has the ASCII code of 205, you would hold down the Alt key, type 2 0 5 on the numeric keypad, and then release the Alt key. With some software you must also hold down the Shift key.

The software you use, therefore, must have some sort of graphics mode. Entering these characters will be even easier if your software has either a built-in macro processor or a search-and-replace mode. With a macro processor, you can assign the graphics characters to specific keys and type them directly. If your software has a graphics mode but not a macro processor, you can use a RAM-resident macro processor for the same purpose. Chapter 4 discusses several macro processors in some detail.

Hints on Entering the Display Screens Here are a few suggestions to simplify typing in the display screens if your word processor does not handle graphics characters easily:

▲ For the graphics characters, you might enter an asterisk (*) in place of the horizontal double lines, an at sign (@) in place of the vertical double lines, and a dollar sign ($) in place of the single horizontal lines. Then globally search and replace the asterisks with ASCII 205, the at signs with ASCII 186, and the dollar signs with ASCII 196. To make the replacements, use the Alt-key technique.

▲ Type the text first. When you have it laid out as you want it to appear, add the border in typeover mode.

▲ Alternatively, if your software can copy lines and has a typeover mode, you can create the border patterns first, copying a line containing the vertical borders enough times to create a big enough box, and then fill in the text in typeover mode.

▲ If you want to use one of the versions of the help screen that includes ANSI escape sequences, first type in the all-text version so you can be sure that the layout is correct (the escape codes distort the appearance of the display). Then switch to insert mode to add the escape sequences. To make your work still easier, after you enter each new escape sequence, mark and copy it to the other locations where you want it to appear.

▲ If you have a macro processor, assign each of the graphics characters to a key. For vertical lines, assign the graphics character, a cursor-down, and a cursor-left, to a single key. You can then draw the vertical line just by pressing that key repeatedly.

BASIC Programs

You do not have to understand the BASIC language to use the BASIC programs listed in this book. You just have to type them in exactly as they appear (*including* the line numbers). However, if your version of BASIC is nonstandard in some way, or if you make errors, you may want to consult a friend who knows BASIC, a users' group, or your manual for hints as to what went wrong.

The easiest tool to use for typing in the BASIC programs is the BASIC editor. To load the BASIC editor that comes with your version of DOS, type

BASICA

Each numbered line is a separate line. The information on it is not recorded until you press Return. If you edit a line of a BASIC program, your changes will not be recorded until you press Return.

One big advantage of the BASIC editor is that it will automatically sort the lines into numerical order. Thus, if you forget a line, you can type it in with the correct line number wherever you happen to be in the listing, and it will appear in the right place when you list the program with the LIST command.

When you are entering or editing a BASIC program, it remains entirely in memory until you save it to disk. To save a BASIC program, type

> SAVE "FILENAME"

BASIC will automatically include a .BAS extension. To save to a drive other than the default drive, include the drive specifier inside the quotation marks.

You can also type in a BASIC program in a text editor, a word processor, or EDLIN. The only requirement is the same as the one that applies to batch files: the resulting files must be ASCII text files. You can include graphics characters within quotation marks as text to be displayed, but your software must not append graphics characters to the ends of words or lines, or BASIC will not be able to interpret the commands correctly.

When you use the LIST command to view a BASIC program in the BASIC editor, all commands and keywords will appear in uppercase letters. However, you do not need to type them in that way—BASIC will convert them for you. This is not true of any text that appears within quotation marks.

You may want to use both the BASIC editor and a word processor to create these programs. This is no problem, but it requires that you save the programs with a special syntax. When saving a program from the BASIC editor, type

> SAVE "FILENAME.BAS",A

The A at the end tells BASIC to save the file as an ASCII text file, which can be read by most word processors. This is especially useful if you want to use advanced word-processing features such as search-and-replace, which are not available in BASIC. For further information about using the BASIC editor, consult your computer's BASIC manual.

Macro Files

Also included in the book are files of keystroke macros for use with the macro-recording programs described in Chapter 4. These files, like the batch files, are numbered for reference purposes only. The macro files are all tailored specifically for SuperKey. However, the similarities among files used by SuperKey, SmartKey, ProKey, and several other programs are great enough that you may be able to use the programs as listed, with no modification at all. Consult your macro-recorder's manual for the changes needed to make these files readable by your program.

Whenever special macro commands are used, they are explained in text, so that you can convert them to the format required by your software.

Assembly-Language Listings

Chapter 6 includes two short assembly-language programs to type in. The disassembled listings of the compiled code are presented in the form of *script files*. Type in these files as listed, follow the instructions in the book, and DEBUG will create the programs for you.

In addition, assembler source code for these programs appears in Appendix C. If you have a macro assembler, you can type the listings from this appendix. Just follow the instructions in the remarks at the beginning of each program to assemble it.

If You Don't Want To Type In the Listings

If you'd rather not type in the listings, all the programs that appear in this book, along with a few free utility programs that are in the public domain, are available on disk. To obtain a copy of the disk see the order form on the last page of this book.

TYPOGRAPHICAL, SYNTAX, AND NAMING CONVENTIONS

All file names, DOS commands, and BASIC commands appear entirely in uppercase letters, although they may be typed in uppercase, lowercase, or both.

The file name *FILENAME.EXT* is a generic name, representing any file. If several file names are used as part of a command, the form

FILE1.EXT FILE2.EXT . . .FILEN.EXT

is used.

When sample syntax is given for a command, anything in square brackets is optional, and anything in italics is generic. Thus, for example, when you see the command

CHKDSK [*drive*]

you must type

CHKDSK

and you may optionally follow it by a drive specifier, such as A: or B:. Do not type the word *drive*. You must always press Return after entering a command.

Throughout the book, marginal symbols will help you find important information. The symbol

points out information regarding a specific release of DOS or a particular hardware configuration. It always appears with a notation as to the relevant version. The symbol

indicates a hint that will smooth out a process or make some technique easier to use. The symbol

denotes a warning regarding something to avoid—an undesirable result of a technique or command, or a mistake that's easy to make.

THE SYSTEM ASSUMED BY THIS BOOK

In order to use this book effectively, your computer system should have at least the following components:

▲ DOS 2.0 or later

▲ The BASIC programming language

▲ At least 512K of system memory

▲ Two or more disk drives, including either two floppy disk drives, or one floppy disk drive and a hard disk

- ▲ A printer
- ▲ A monitor, with an appropriate card
- ▲ A macro-recording program

If you have a color monitor, you will find hints on ways to make use of it throughout the book. Although the issues of extended memory (beyond 640K), networking, and telecommunications are touched on only lightly, you may nonetheless find some helpful suggestions about these functions.

WHAT IS
MS-DOS?

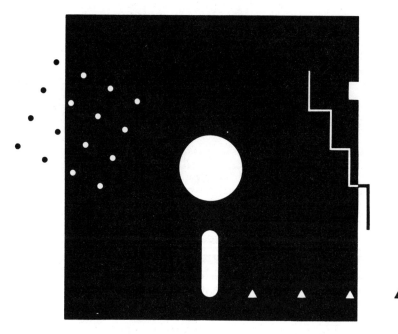

C H A P T E R

1

▲   ▲   ▲

Y OUR COMPUTER'S disk operating system (DOS) is a collection of files
and programs that controls every aspect of the flow of data between
your computer, your disks, and your other peripheral equipment. The
system not only manages your hardware, but interacts with every program you use to ensure that it functions smoothly and effectively with
your hardware.

Because DOS is relatively well designed, you can run many application programs on your MS-DOS-based computer with only a minimal
knowledge of DOS. Once you have set up your system so that the various hardware elements know how to communicate with each other, and
you have learned how to copy, rename, and erase files and format and
copy disks, you could get by with no further knowledge of DOS.

But if you are reading this book, you obviously want more from your
computer than these few processes require. You want your computer to
behave according to *your* needs, not according to the assumptions of
whoever happened to write your software.

MS-DOS, with its more than 40 commands, gives you a great deal of
power over how your computer behaves. It includes elements to serve the
needs of the most advanced programmers. But even if you are not a programmer, you can learn enough about DOS to bend that stubborn collection of chips and circuits to your will. This book will teach you how.

You will learn how all of those previously invisible processes take place and how to control them to your advantage. You will find out how to use the more obscure commands, as well as discover the hidden power of the commonplace ones. By the time we are finished, you will know everything you need to become a true power user of MS-DOS.

THE PARTS OF DOS

DOS is, first of all, a *disk* operating system. It must be loaded from a disk before your computer can do anything (the only exceptions are the IBM PC and some compatible computers, which will come up in an abbreviated version of the BASIC programming language if DOS is not present). When you boot your computer with a system disk, it reads the first sector on the disk, the *boot record*. (You will learn more about the boot record in Chapter 2.) This is a short program that tells your computer to load two hidden files, called the *system files*. These two programs then take control of the computer. They remain in the computer's memory until you turn the computer off or reset it with Ctrl-Alt-Del.

They immediately look for a file named CONFIG.SYS. If there is one, the system files configure your computer using the specifications contained in that file. (You will learn all about the CONFIG.SYS file in Chapter 8.) Next they load COMMAND.COM, DOS's *command processor*. This file, like the system files, generally remains in memory. However, another program occasionally needs some of the memory in which it is stored. If this happens, you must reload COMMAND.COM when the other program is finished.

DOS has two types of commands: internal and external. The *internal* commands are included as part of the COMMAND.COM program. You have access to these commands whenever a DOS prompt is displayed on the screen. Your application programs probably make use of these commands as well.

The *external* commands are less frequently used. They are in the form of separate programs on the DOS System Disk. To use these commands, the programs that they invoke must be present on a disk in the computer.

VERSIONS OF MS-DOS

MS-DOS first took form when IBM asked Microsoft to produce a disk operating system for its new PCs. IBM adapted the Microsoft product to its machines and released it as PC-DOS, so that for some time PC-DOS was the only version of MS-DOS on the market. Thus, in the discussion of the generations of MS-DOS that follows this section, all versions below 2.0 refer to PC-DOS. Nevertheless, we refer to these versions as MS-DOS, since they are implementations of the master system produced by Microsoft.

As manufacturers of PC compatibles have released their own machine-specific versions of MS-DOS—ITT DOS, Compaq MS-DOS, and so on—PC-DOS has become one of many versions of the master MS-DOS released to manufacturers by Microsoft. Some of these MS-DOS releases are stripped-down versions of the master release, containing only the bare minimum of commands needed to run the computer. Other manufacturers have added enhancements to the package. Some have additional external programs. Others have commands that display a menu when you fail to specify a required parameter. Still others may display many messages and warnings as they operate. Most of these implementations, however, make no changes to the basic operations of MS-DOS, so that you may be able to use different implementations interchangeably without noticing any differences between them.

Keep in mind that Microsoft does not directly support or market any version of MS-DOS. In this book, therefore, the term MS-DOS refers to a master version of MS-DOS, which is the basis for all released versions. This version is released to computer manufacturers, but is theoretically unobtainable by ordinary users except from computer manufacturers. (In actual fact, I bought a copy of MS-DOS 3.2, in Microsoft's typical blue box, off the shelf at a neighborhood computer store.) The term DOS refers collectively to all versions—or all versions with a given release number—including PC-DOS. When a different specific name, such as PC-DOS, is used, it refers to one computer manufacturer's released version of DOS.

THE GENERATIONS OF MS-DOS

Although there were several precursors to MS-DOS, they need not concern us. For our purposes, we can consider the history of these operating systems as beginning with the release of the first version of the IBM PC. Generally, each new release of DOS has accompanied a change in hardware design—specifically in disk drive design.

Version 1.X

Version 1, which was released three times, was originally designed to operate with single-sided floppy disk drives. In contrast to the later versions, the date and time functions were in separate programs, rather than part of the group of files that remained in memory, and files were not marked with the time, only the date. The first release, version 1.0, had some serious bugs in the two versions of the BASIC programming language included in the package, and it did not handle serial communications effectively. Version 1.05 fixed the bugs in BASIC.

Version 1.1 functioned with double-sided drives for the first time. It also contained the following additions:

▲ Time and date functions for the resident portion of DOS

▲ Time-stamping of files

▲ Verification and file-concatenation options for the COPY command

▲ An improved MODE program to handle serial communications and provide for port reassignment and configuration

▲ The EXE2BIN program, of use mainly to programmers

Version 2.X

It was with version 2.0 that MS-DOS came into its own. PC-DOS 2.1 was an adaptation for the PC*jr* and half-height disk drives. It corrected a few bugs, but is otherwise indistinguishable from version 2.0. This is why these versions are often referred to collectively as version 2.X.

The principal change in version 2.X is the addition of commands and programs to manage a hard disk drive. Besides the external programs FDISK, BACKUP, RESTORE, and TREE, several new internal commands were added, all dealing with tree-structured directories:

MKDIR (MD)	Make a new directory
CHDIR (CD)	Change the current directory
RMDIR (RD)	Remove a directory
DIR /P	Show directory in pages
DIR /W	Show file names only, in wide format

Version 3.0

Version 3.0 of MS-DOS has numerous additions and enhancements. The third generation of MS-DOS is designed to work with the faster processor chip and high-density drives of the AT series of computers. Other facilities have been added to allow the user to configure the keyboard and the style of the date and time display for different languages. A GRAFTABL program, which permits the display of graphics characters on graphics screens, makes it possible to display those foreign-language characters with ASCII codes higher than 127.

Another new feature involves file-sharing and block-locking, so that files can be shared by several users at the same time, without the risk of a "deadly embrace" locking up the system. Finally, it includes software to create a RAM disk in a portion of memory. (The assembly-language code to create this program has been present in several generations of the DOS manual, but only with version 3.0 was it actually made available on disk.)

Version 3.1

Two significant additions were made to version 3.1. First, enhancements were added to many commands to make them compatible with local-area networks. Second, two new commands, JOIN and SUBST, were added to allow the user to reassign drives to directories and to combine directories. These features make it easier to use software that was not designed with tree-structured directories in mind.

Version 3.2

As with all previous revisions of DOS, DOS 3.2 was created to deal with a hardware change. In this instance, there were two: double-sided, 3½-inch, 720K capacity disks, such as are used on some laptop computers, and external disk drives. DISKCOMP, DISKCOPY, and FORMAT have been extended to operate effectively on 3½-inch disks.

In addition, several other commands have been enhanced. The FORMAT command will no longer function without parameters, to reduce the chance of formatting the default drive by accident. The ATTRIB command, which in earlier releases of DOS 3.X set or cleared the read-only bit of the attribute byte, can now also set or clear the archive bit.

The SELECT command (present in some versions of 3.2 only) will format a floppy disk, copy the DOS files onto it, and establish default nationality formats and keyboards.

DOS 3.2 also includes two new external file-management commands, XCOPY and REPLACE. These commands, which are discussed in Chapter 11, allow fast and selective copying of files. They provide many options not available with the COPY command.

In addition, MS-DOS 3.2, but not PC-DOS 3.2, includes the APPEND external command. (IBM included the APPEND command with its network software, but not with DOS.) This command creates a search path for data files as well as program files. There were also minor enhancements to other commands.

Version 3.3

Version 3.3, released with IBM's PS/2 series of computers, includes many new commands for dealing with the new hardware. Most obviously (as usual), the FORMAT, DISKCOMP, and DISKCOPY commands can now address another storage medium—1.44 megabyte, 3½-inch disks like those on the PS/2 computer. There are special files for addressing new types of screens. In addition, a complex system has been introduced for selecting foreign-language character sets and keyboards. The MODE command has been enhanced to handle serial communications at 19,200 baud and address up to four serial ports. Previous versions of DOS could only go as high as 9600 baud and could address only two serial ports. Finally, the APPEND command is now available in PC-DOS as well as in MS-DOS.

MS-DOS AND PC-DOS

MS-DOS seems to have become more or less standardized with version 2.11, which is almost identical to PC-DOS 2.1. The version numbers in the above discussion that are lower than 2.11 are all PC-DOS version numbers. Non-IBM versions of MS-DOS may indicate their relationship to this standard release with suffixes, such as MS-DOS 2.11, revision G, or revision 2.1. Unless the version number is 3.0 or higher, however, you should assume that your version of MS-DOS is some form of DOS 2.X.

Some manufacturers have released a version 3.0 or 3.1 of MS-DOS. These versions are to all intents and purposes equivalent to PC-DOS 3.0 and 3.1.

Virtually everything in this book was tested on an IBM PC using PC-DOS 2.1 and 3.1; an ITT Xtra using ITT DOS 2.11, revision 2.1; a Corona PC using Corona MS-DOS 2.11; and an AT clone using the master MS-DOS 3.2, and PC-DOS 3.2 and 3.3. If some aspect of a program or an operation does not behave as described here, please check your DOS manual—your version of a DOS command may have a somewhat different syntax or different messages.

MS-DOS AND BASIC

Generally, each major revision of DOS has been accompanied by a new release of the BASIC programming language. Programs written in BASIC 2.0 will run with DOS 3.X, but the converse may not be true. Many versions of BASIC released with MS-DOS 2.11 do not recognize path names, path commands, or file names that include path names.

Another difference concerns the SHELL command, which allows you to exit temporarily to DOS from within BASIC. This command, although present in IBM BASIC 2.0, was not documented until version 3.0. It is not present in all MS-DOS versions of BASIC 2.0.

COMPATIBILITY AMONG VERSIONS

As a rule, programs written to run with earlier versions of DOS will run with later versions. However, they will not take advantage of all the options included in later versions. On the other hand, there is no guarantee that programs written to run under later versions of DOS will run with earlier versions. Indeed, few programs today will still run with DOS 1.X, although most will run with DOS 2.0 or later. (DOS 3.X will not work on some computers.)

The DOS programs themselves are generally *not* compatible with other releases of DOS. Running the external programs from, say, DOS 2.1 while your computer is operating under the control of DOS 3.1 will probably result in the error message

Incorrect DOS version

So will the opposite arrangement. The external programs in the various DOS releases are tailored to match the characteristics of the system files and COMMAND.COM, which have changed significantly from one release to the next. Therefore, you should not try to mix different versions of DOS.

Whether one manufacturer's version of DOS will run on another's machine is significantly more problematic. If your computer is 100 percent IBM-compatible, you can probably use any release of PC-DOS that you like, as well as the version of MS-DOS supplied by your computer's manufacturer. If its compatibility is less than 100 percent, you can expect occasional trouble and unpredictable results.

One element that is definitely *not* compatible is the IBM BASIC programming language and other MS-DOS versions of BASIC. IBM PCs include a subset of BASIC in ROM (which is why they come up in BASIC if DOS is not loaded). The extended BASIC included on the PC-DOS disk (BASICA) is designed to use the routines present in the BASIC ROM. If you try to use IBM BASIC on a machine that does not have the BASIC ROM, your system will crash.

Most MS-DOS packages include a BASIC called GWBASIC or XBASIC. To ensure that software developed for the IBM PC's BASICA will be compatible, they may also include a BASICA program. This is simply a short loader program that loads the full, extended BASIC language. If you have a BASIC of this type, you can safely erase BASICA and change the name of XBASIC or GWBASIC to BASICA.

WHICH DOS VERSION IS CURRENT?

It would appear on the face of things that DOS 3.3, and only DOS 3.3, is the current version. However, it depends on the company that manufactured your computer. As noted, the version of DOS supplied by your manufacturer may be a subset, a superset, or an unaltered version of MS-DOS. But it is a particular release of MS-DOS that forms the basis of your computer's version. Many manufacturers have adapted one release for their hardware, and will not upgrade to the later versions. For example, even though DOS 3.1 may have been packaged with your computer, you may not be able to use DOS 3.2 or DOS 3.3. For different computers, DOS version 2.1, 3.1, 3.2, or 3.3 may be the latest version.

Microsoft, the developer of MS-DOS, does not support any version directly. Nor will they warrant that any given release will run on any particular computer. The company expects you to call your dealer or the computer manufacturer for help and advice.

IBM supports both version 2.1 and version 3.3 of PC-DOS, since version 2.1 is sufficient for IBM PCs and XTs. PC-DOS 3.0 through 3.2 are regarded as obsolete, even though 3.1 and 3.2 still work perfectly well.

DISKS, FILES, AND DIRECTORIES

C H A P T E R

2

I N THIS CHAPTER, we'll look at disks and their directories in detail and
review their relationship to files. You'll learn what goes onto a DOS disk,
how it is laid out, the form it takes, and how it is organized. This will help
you to successfully access and modify the contents of disks directly.

Ultimately, what goes onto a disk, like everything else in a computer,
is nothing but a series of on-bits and off-bits, or 1-bits and 0-bits. However, it is the arrangement of these bits, and the bytes they form, that
makes all the difference.

Certain parts of a disk are reserved by the operating system for specific
purposes. Both their contents and the way they are arranged are determined by the options you use with the FORMAT command.

THE FORMAT COMMAND
AND ITS OPTIONS

The FORMAT command rearranges the random magnetic impulses on
the disk—or the data that are already recorded—into a series of tracks
and sectors. The total number of tracks and sectors and the arrangement of those that the operating system reserves for its own use depend
on the *format* of the disk. This in turn is determined in large part by the
options you specify when formatting the disk.

The FORMAT command is *downward-compatible*. In plain English, this means that the FORMAT command in any given generation of DOS allows you to format a disk that will be compatible with earlier generations of DOS. (To a large degree, the converse is also true: disks formatted in earlier versions of DOS can be used with later versions. The principal exception seems to be in transferring a later version of the operating system to the disk.) Thus, DOS 2.X includes options for both single-sided and double-sided disks with either eight or nine sectors per track, and each release of DOS 3.X includes options for the new type of disk it addresses as well as for earlier types.

The number of sectors on the disk affects the amount of data it can hold, since each sector holds 512 bytes. A double-sided, eight-sectored disk holds 320K, while a double-sided, nine-sectored disk holds 360K. There is also some additional room, not available to the user directly, that DOS uses for its own purposes.

DOS 3.X

DOS 3.0 through 3.3 also include options to deal with the AT's 1.2 megabyte drive, and DOS 3.2 and 3.3 have additional options for 3½-inch disks. You can specify these options as parameters for the FORMAT command, as summarized in Table 2.1.

As a rule, if you use DOS 2.X (or 3.X on anything but an AT or AT-compatible computer), you will format your disks as double-sided with nine sectors per track, which is the default format for PCs and XTs. (Unless otherwise specified, this discussion assumes that you are using the default format for your version of DOS.) However, you might choose a different format depending on the type of disks and drives that you are using. If you format a high-density disk in a high-density drive, the FORMAT command without parameters will give you the desired result. You can also format a regular double-density disk in a high-density drive by using the /4 switch. You may have trouble reading or writing to a disk formatted in this manner, because the tracks are only half as wide as normal.

You can, if you are brave, format a double-density disk in a high-density drive *without* the /4 switch. You will probably end up with a disk having 80 tracks, each track containing 15 sectors of 512 bytes each (the normal configuration for a high-density disk). However, as many as

PARAMETER	FORMAT RESULT	PURPOSE
/1	Single-sided	DOS 1.0; (when used with /8 switch) early PCjrs
/8	8 sectors per track	DOS 1.1
/9	9 sectors per track	DOS 2.0 and above
/B	8 sectors per track, can be made a boot disk with any version of DOS.	Makes a distribution compatible with disk with all versions of DOS.
/4 (version 3.X only)	Regular double-density	Allows a regular double-sided diskette to be formatted in a high-density drive.
/T:nn (version 3.3 only)	Specifies number of tracks	Use with /N switch to format 720K disks in 1.44MB drives, or 320 or 360K disks in 1.2MB drives.
/N:n (version 3.3 only)	Specifies number of sectors per track.	Use with /T switch to format 720K disks in 1.44MB drives, or 320 or 360K disks in 1.2MB drives.

Table 2.1 ▲ *Disk-Formatting Options.*

two-thirds of the sectors may be marked as unusable. The amount of usable storage you get by this method depends very much on the brand of high-density drive in your computer. Needless to say, you cannot expect such a disk to be readable in any other drive.

You should have no need for the other options listed in Table 2.1 unless you plan to share your disks with users of earlier versions of DOS. If you do, take note of the following guidelines:

▲ DOS 1.0 requires single-sided formats with eight sectors per track.

▲ DOS 1.1 requires eight sectors per track, but can read both single-sided and double-sided disks.

▲ If you are a DOS 3.X user and want your disk to be bootable under DOS 2.X, you *must* use the /B or the /8 parameter, even though this will restrict the disk to eight sectors per track.

▲ If you use the /B parameter, you cannot add a volume label to your disk, and you should not specify the /8 parameter, as it is assumed by the /B parameter.

There are two additional parameters that you can specify with the FORMAT command. One adds a *volume label* to the disk, and the other makes the disk bootable.

 Warning: There is a bug in PC-DOS 3.1's version of the /B switch. It reserves only 9K for the hidden system files. Thus, if you copy a file before you use the SYS command, there will not be enough room for the system files to be copied contiguously to the first part of the disk. Therefore, the disk will not boot.

Volume Labels

DOS 2.X was the first version that allowed you to specify a volume label for your disks. This is largely a matter of convenience, but it can be a great convenience.

To give a disk a volume label in DOS 2.X, you *must* use the /V parameter when you format a disk:

FORMAT B:/V

When you specify this parameter, as soon as the formatting process is complete, you are prompted with

Volume label (11 characters, ENTER for none)?

If you press the Enter key, no volume label will be entered. When you display the directory, the first line of the display will then read

Volume in drive B has no label

Alternatively, you can type in a name of up to 11 characters, including spaces and any characters that are valid in a file name except periods. (Volume names do not follow the standard FILENAME.EXT format.) However, some versions of DOS are less forgiving than others, permitting only alphanumeric characters and the underscore character.

If you have given a volume label to a disk, the first line of the display will read something like

Volume in drive B is 123-DATA #5

or

Volume in drive C is MY SYSTEM

If you name your disks, you can use the VOL command at any DOS prompt to see quickly which disk is in a drive. Type

VOL [*drive*]

You will see just the first line of the normal directory display, showing the volume label or the message that the volume has no label.

The CHKDSK command will tell you the volume name of the disk you check, along with the date and time you entered the volume name, as in the following example:

Volume TEST DISK created Jun 16, 1987 11:35a

DOS 2.X

In DOS 2.X, you can assign a volume label *only* by using the /V switch with the FORMAT command. You cannot add a label at a later time. Once you have labeled a disk, you can change the label only by somewhat devious means, which we'll go into in Chapter 12.

DOS 3.X/MS-DOS late releases

DOS 3.X, and some late releases of MS-DOS 2.11 (especially if they have a revision number higher than 1 following the version number) allow you to change an existing volume label or to enter one after the disk has already been formatted. To do so, use the external LABEL command, followed by the drive specifier and the volume name. Don't put any spaces between the drive letter colon and the label text. If you attempt to change the volume name using the VOL command in any version of DOS, you will see the error message

Invalid drive specification

Making the Disk Bootable

The last option of the FORMAT command transfers the operating system to the newly formatted disk. It is invoked by adding the /S parameter to the FORMAT command:

FORMAT B:/S

This command transfers the two hidden system files IBMBIO.COM and IBMDOS.COM (and, in most versions of DOS, COMMAND.COM) to the newly formatted disk. The first two files remain permanently in memory once the computer is booted. You can use both the /S and /V options in a single command.

MS-DOS

If you use MS-DOS rather than PC-DOS, the transferred files may have slightly different names, depending on which manufacturer's version you are using. Most commonly, they are called IO.SYS and MSDOS.SYS, but other names are also used.

Because the system files are hidden files, you will not normally see them in a directory listing. However, you can tell that they are present by using the CHKDSK command. When the CHKDSK command has finished its work, it displays a status message, which may include a line in the form

NNNNN bytes in *N* hidden files

An alternative way of making a disk bootable is by using the SYS command. With a disk that includes the external SYS.COM program in the default drive, type

SYS *drive*

where *drive* is the drive containing the disk to which you want to transfer the system. Because the SYS command does not transfer COMMAND-.COM to the destination disk, you will have to copy it using an additional COPY command.

When you try to transfer the system, you may see the message

No room for system on destination disk

This may occur for several reasons. Most commonly, it is because the specific part of the disk that the system files must occupy is already filled. If the disk was formatted using the same version of DOS that you are now trying to transfer, you have two choices. You can either format a new disk with the /S switch and copy all the files from your old disk onto it, or remove specific files from the destination disk.

To use the latter approach, you must find out which files appear first *physically* on the disk. These are not necessarily the first files listed in the directory. In Chapter 12, you'll learn how to identify these files. You must then erase them. If you still need them, you can first copy them to new files on the same disk under another name. Finally, after the system is transferred, you can give the copies their original names.

If this technique doesn't work, it's probably because your disk was formatted using a larger version of the operating system than the one you are now trying to transfer. In the next section, you will see several examples of a *boot record*. The boot record includes the name of the version of DOS that formatted the disk and the names of the system files it uses. Thus, if you are now using, say, MS-DOS 2.1, and the disk was formatted using PC-DOS 2.1, the boot record will look for the files IBMBIO.COM and IBMDOS.COM, while your DOS attempts to transfer IO.SYS and MSDOS.SYS.

You can sometimes use the SYS command to make the distribution disk of an application program bootable. This depends on whether the manufacturer allowed room on the disk for the system files. If this is so and the boot record is appropriately flexible, or if the disk was formatted with the /B switch, you will be able to make the disk bootable. Otherwise, you will get the *No room for system on destination disk* message.

THE PARTS OF A DISK

The following discussion pertains to normal double-sided, double-density floppy disks formatted using DOS 2.0 or later. Any differences from other types of disks will be discussed at the end of the section.

The back of the disk—the side without the label—is the first side, and it is called side 0. The front is side 1. The tracks on the disk are numbered from 0 to 39.

The sectors are numbered following different schemes, depending on the purpose. The ROM BIOS numbers the sectors on each track from 1 to 9, starting over at sector 1 on side 1. However, for many purposes (including DOS's), the sectors on a disk are numbered using a different scheme. These *logical*, or *relative*, sectors are numbered consecutively, starting with 0. BIOS side 0, track 0, sector 1 is thus DOS sector 0. DOS then continues numbering on the opposite side; thus, after numbering sectors 1 through 8 on side 0, track 1, DOS starts with BIOS side 1, track 0, sector 1 as DOS sector 9. The first sector on track 1, side 0 (the second track) is 18, the first sector on track 2, side 0 is 36, and so on. As you will see in Chapter 12, you must use the DOS numbering system when you want to read a disk sector in DEBUG.

DOS accesses the data on the disk in *clusters* of two sectors each, or 1K. It reads the sectors into a buffer in memory, so that, as long as a given cluster is in use, it is immediately available to your program. You can set the number of clusters to be retained by using the BUFFERS= command in your CONFIG.SYS file, as explained in Chapter 8.

The Boot Record

DOS sector 0 (BIOS side 0, track 0, sector 1) is called the *boot record*. The main function of the boot record is to start your computer. It contains the names of the hidden system files, some basic disk error messages, and a short program to load the system files into memory.

The boot record also contains a great deal of information about the disk, including

- ▲ The version of DOS used to format the disk

- ▲ The number of bytes per sector

- ▲ The number of sectors per cluster, per track, and per disk

- ▲ The number of sectors at the beginning of the disk reserved for the system's purposes

- ▲ The number of copies of the file allocation table (normally 2) and its size in sectors

- ▲ The maximum number of entries the root directory can hold

- ▲ The total number of sectors on the disk

- ▲ The number of sides

Figure 2.1 shows the boot record of a disk formatted by PC-DOS 2.1, as displayed by DEBUG at memory location 21D5:1000. The version number is indicated in the upper-left corner of the right-hand column (as you can see, version 2.1 is, to most intents and purposes, identical to version 2.0). For comparison, Figures 2.2, 2.3, and 2.4 show the boot records of disks formatted in PC-DOS 3.3, master MS-DOS 3.2, and Corona MS-DOS 2.11, respectively.

You may find it strange that the version number displayed on the boot record does not always match the release number of the version of DOS that it comes from. The reason is that DOS is not just an operating system, but also includes a collection of ancillary programs. A manufacturer may issue a new release of DOS without actually modifying the three system files. Thus, the version number in the boot record is the number of the disk operating system itself, rather than that of the complete release.

The File Allocation Table

Following the boot record are four sectors reserved for two copies of the *file allocation table* (or FAT, as it is often called). This is a map of the disk, keyed to the file names in the directory. It includes information concerning which sectors are unusable, which ones are in use, and which ones are available.

```
21D5:1000   EB 2C 90 49 42 4D 20 20-32 2E 30 00 02 02 01 00   .,.IBM  2.0.....
21D5:1010   02 70 00 D0 02 FD 02 00-09 00 02 00 00 00 00 00   .p..............
21D5:1020   0A DF 02 25 02 09 2A FF-50 F6 0F 02 CD 19 FA 33   ...%..*.P......3
21D5:1030   C0 8E D0 BC 00 7C 8E D8-A3 7A 00 C7 06 78 00 21   .....|...z...x.!
21D5:1040   7C FB CD 13 73 03 E9 95-00 0E 1F A0 10 7C 98 F7   |...s........|..
21D5:1050   26 16 7C 03 06 1C 7C 03-06 0E 7C A3 03 7C A3 13   &.|...|...|..|..
21D5:1060   7C B8 20 00 F7 26 11 7C-05 FF 01 BB 00 02 F7 F3   |. ..&.|........
21D5:1070   01 06 13 7C E8 7E 00 72-B3 A1 13 7C A3 7E 7D B8   ...|.~.r...|.~}.
21D5:1080   70 00 8E C0 8E D8 BB 00-00 2E A1 13 7C E8 B6 00   p...........|...
21D5:1090   2E A0 18 7C 2E 2A 06 15-7C FE C0 32 E4 50 B4 02   ...|.*..|..2.P..
21D5:10A0   E8 C1 00 58 72 38 2E 28-06 20 7C 76 0E 2E 01 06   ...Xr8.(. |v....
21D5:10B0   13 7C 2E F7 26 0B 7C 03-D8 EB CE 0E 1F CD 11 D0   .|..&.|.........
21D5:10C0   C0 D0 C0 25 03 00 75 01-40 40 8B C8 F6 06 1E 7C   ...%..u.@@.....|
21D5:10D0   80 75 02 33 C0 8B 1E 7E-7D EA 00 00 70 00 BE C9   .u.3...~}...p...
21D5:10E0   7D E8 02 00 EB FE 2E AC-24 7F 74 4D B4 0E BB 07   }.......$.tM....
21D5:10F0   00 CD 10 EB F1 B8 50 00-8E C0 0E 1F 2E A1 03 7C   ......P........|
21D5:1100   E8 43 00 BB 00 00 B8 01-02 E8 58 00 72 2C 33 FF   .C........X.r,3.
21D5:1110   B9 0B 00 26 80 0D 20 26-80 4D 20 20 47 E2 F4 33   ...&.. &.M  G..3
21D5:1120   FF BE DF 7D B9 0B 00 FC-F3 A6 75 0E BF 20 00 BE   ...}......u.. ..
21D5:1130   EB 7D B9 0B 00 F3 A6 75-01 C3 BE 80 7D E8 A6 FF   .}.....u....}...
21D5:1140   B4 00 CD 16 F9 C3 1E 0E-1F 33 D2 F7 36 18 7C FE   .........3..6.|.
21D5:1150   C2 88 16 15 7C 33 D2 F7-36 1A 7C 88 16 1F 7C A3   ....|3..6.|...|.
21D5:1160   08 7C 1F C3 2E 8B 16 08-7C B1 06 D2 E6 2E 0A 36   .|......|......6
21D5:1170   15 7C 8B CA 86 E9 2E 8B-16 1E 7C CD 13 C3 00 00   .|........|.....
21D5:1180   0D 0A 4E 6F 6E 2D 53 79-73 74 65 6D 20 64 69 73   ..Non-System dis
21D5:1190   6B 20 6F 72 20 64 69 73-6B 20 65 72 72 6F 72 0D   k or disk error.
21D5:11A0   0A 52 65 70 6C 61 63 65-20 61 6E 64 20 73 74 72   .Replace and str
21D5:11B0   69 6B 65 20 61 6E 79 20-6B 65 79 20 77 68 65 6E   ike any key when
21D5:11C0   20 72 65 61 64 79 0D 0A-00 0D 0A 44 69 73 6B 20   ready....Disk 
21D5:11D0   42 6F 6F 74 20 66 61 69-6C 75 72 65 0D 0A 00 69   Boot failure...i
21D5:11E0   62 6D 62 69 6F 20 20 63-6F 6D 30 69 62 6D 64 6F   bmbio  com0ibmdo
21D5:11F0   73 20 20 63 6F 6D 30 00-00 00 00 00 00 00 55 AA   s  com0.......U.
```

Figure 2.1 ▲ *The Boot Record of a Disk Formatted by PC-DOS 2.1.*

```
57BA:0100  EB 34 90 49 42 4D 20 20-33 2E 33 00 02 01 01 00   .4.IBM  3.3.....
57BA:0110  02 E0 00 60 09 F9 07 00-0F 00 02 00 00 00 00 00   ...`...........
57BA:0120  00 00 00 00 00 00 00 00-00 00 00 00 00 00 00 12   ................
57BA:0130  00 00 00 00 01 00 FA 33-C0 8E D0 BC 00 7C 16 07   .......3.....|..
57BA:0140  BB 78 00 36 C5 37 1E 56-16 53 BF 2B 7C B9 0B 00   .x.6.7.V.S.+|...
57BA:0150  FC AC 26 80 3D 00 74 03-26 8A 05 AA 8A C4 E2 F1   ..&.=.t.&.......
57BA:0160  06 1F 89 47 02 C7 07 2B-7C FB CD 13 72 67 A0 10   ...G...+|...rg..
57BA:0170  7C 98 F7 26 16 7C 03 06-1C 7C 03 06 0E 7C A3 3F   |..&.|...|...|.?
57BA:0180  7C A3 37 7C B8 20 00 F7-26 11 7C 8B 1E 0B 7C 03   |.7|.. .&.|...|.
57BA:0190  C3 48 F7 F3 01 06 37 7C-BB 00 05 A1 3F 7C E8 9F   .H....7|....?|..
57BA:01A0  00 B8 01 02 E8 B3 00 72-19 8B FB B9 0B 00 BE D6   .......r........
57BA:01B0  7D F3 A6 75 0D 8D 7F 20-BE E1 7D B9 0B 00 F3 A6   }..u... ..}.....
57BA:01C0  74 18 BE 77 7D E8 6A 00-32 E4 CD 16 5E 1F 8F 04   t..w}.j.2...^...
57BA:01D0  8F 44 02 CD 19 BE C0 7D-EB EB A1 1C 05 33 D2 F7   .D.....}.....3..
57BA:01E0  36 0B 7C FE C0 A2 3C 7C-A1 37 7C A3 3D 7C BB 00   6.|...<|.7|.=|..
57BA:01F0  07 A1 37 7C E8 49 00 A1-18 7C 2A 06 3B 7C 40 38   ..7|.I...|*.;|@8
57BA:0200  06 3C 7C 73 03 A0 3C 7C-50 E8 4E 00 58 72 C6 28   .<|s..<|P.N.Xr.(
57BA:0210  06 3C 7C 74 0C 01 06 37-7C F7 26 0B 7C 03 D8 EB   .<|t...7|.&.|...
57BA:0220  D0 8A 2E 15 7C 8A 16 FD-7D 8B 1E 3D 7C EA 00 00   ....|...}..=|...
57BA:0230  70 00 AC 0A C0 74 22 B4-0E 07 00 CD 10 EB F2   p....t"........
57BA:0240  33 D2 F7 36 18 7C FE C2-88 16 3B 7C 33 D2 F7 36   3..6.|....;|3..6
57BA:0250  1A 7C 88 16 2A 7C A3 39-7C C3 B4 02 8B 16 39 7C   .|..*|.9|.....9|
57BA:0260  B1 06 D2 E6 0A 36 3B 7C-8B CA 86 E9 8A 16 FD 7D   .....6;|.......}
57BA:0270  8A 36 2A 7C CD 13 C3 0D-0A 4E 6F 6E 2D 53 79 73   .6*|.....Non-Sys
57BA:0280  74 65 6D 20 64 69 73 6B-20 6F 72 20 64 69 73 6B   tem disk or disk
57BA:0290  20 65 72 72 6F 72 0D 0A-52 65 70 6C 61 63 65 20    error..Replace
57BA:02A0  61 6E 64 20 73 74 72 69-6B 65 20 61 6E 79 20 6B   and strike any k
57BA:02B0  65 79 20 77 68 65 6E 20-72 65 61 64 79 0D 0A 00   ey when ready...
57BA:02C0  0D 0A 44 69 73 6B 20 42-6F 6F 74 20 66 61 69 6C   ..Disk Boot fail
57BA:02D0  75 72 65 0D 0A 00 49 42-4D 42 49 4F 20 20 43 4F   ure...IBMBIO  CO
57BA:02E0  4D 49 42 4D 44 4F 53 20-20 43 4F 4D 00 00 00 00   MIBMDOS  COM....
57BA:02F0  00 00 00 00 00 00 00 00-00 00 00 00 00 00 55 AA   ..............U.
```

Figure 2.2 ▲ *The Boot Record of a Disk Formatted by PC-DOS 3.3.*

The FAT takes the form of a series of *linked lists*. Specific bits in the FAT represent each sector on the disk. If the sector is not in use or is a bad sector, the bits that represent it contain that information. If a sector is part of a file, however, the bits representing a given sector contain the address of the location in the FAT representing the next segment of a file. If the sector is the last one in a file, the bits representing that sector contain information to that effect.

If you were to read a FAT sector in DEBUG, it would appear as meaningless gibberish, unless you were familiar with the method by which DOS encodes the information. The interpretation of bits in the FAT is beyond the scope of this book. Both *The MS-DOS Handbook*, by Richard Allen King (2d ed., SYBEX, 1986) and *The Peter Norton Programmer's Guide to the IBM PC* (Microsoft Press, 1985) explain this information in detail. However, some illustrations may help to clarify how the FAT works.

```
57BA:0100   EB 34 90 4D 53 44 4F 53-33 2E 32 00 02 01 01 00   .4.MSDOS3.2.....
57BA:0110   02 E0 00 60 09 F9 07 00-0F 00 02 00 00 00 00 00   ...`...........
57BA:0120   00 00 00 00 00 00 00 00-00 00 00 00 00 00 00 0F   ...............
57BA:0130   00 00 00 00 01 00 FA 33-C0 8E D0 BC 00 7C 16 07   .......3.....|..
57BA:0140   BB 78 00 36 C5 37 1E 56-16 53 BF 2B 7C B9 0B 00   .x.6.7.V.S.+|...
57BA:0150   FC AC 26 80 3D 00 74 03-26 8A 05 AA 8A C4 E2 F1   ..&.=.t.&.......
57BA:0160   06 1F 89 47 02 C7 07 2B-7C FB 8A 16 FD 7D CD 13   ...G...+|...}..
57BA:0170   72 66 A0 10 7C 98 F7 26-16 7C 03 06 1C 7C 03 06   rf..|..&.|...|..
57BA:0180   0E 7C A3 3F 7C A3 37 7C-B8 20 00 F7 26 11 7C 8B   .|.?|.7|. ..&.|.
57BA:0190   1E 0B 7C 03 C3 48 F7 F3-01 06 37 7C BB 00 05 A1   ..|..H....7|....
57BA:01A0   3F 7C E8 94 00 B0 01 E8-A9 00 72 19 8B FB B9 0B   ?|........r.....
57BA:01B0   00 BE D5 7D F3 A6 75 0D-8D 7F 20 BE E0 7D B9 0B   ...}..u... ..}..
57BA:01C0   00 F3 A6 74 18 BE 76 7D-E8 61 00 32 E4 CD 16 5E   ...t..v}.a.2...^
57BA:01D0   1F 8F 04 8F 44 02 CD 19-BE BF 7D EB EB A1 1C 05   ....D.....}....
57BA:01E0   33 D2 F7 36 0B 7C FE C0-A2 3C 7C A1 37 7C A3 3D   3..6.|...<|.7|.=
57BA:01F0   7C BB 00 07 A1 37 7C E8-3F 00 A1 18 7C 2A 06 3B   |....7|.?...|*.;
57BA:0200   7C 40 50 E8 4D 00 58 72-CF 28 06 3C 7C 76 0C 01   |@P.M.Xr.(.<|v..
57BA:0210   06 37 7C F7 26 0B 7C 03-D8 EB D9 8A 2E 15 7C 8A   .7|.&.|.......|.
57BA:0220   16 FD 7D 8B 1E 3D 7C EA-00 00 70 00 AC 0A C0 74   ..}..=|...p....t
57BA:0230   21 B4 0E B3 FF CD 10 EB-F3 33 D2 F7 36 18 7C FE   !........3..6.|.
57BA:0240   C2 88 16 3B 7C 33 D2 F7-36 1A 7C 88 16 2A 7C A3   ...;|3..6.|..*|.
57BA:0250   39 7C C3 B4 02 8B 16 39-7C 8A EA D0 CE D0 CE 80   9|.....9|.......
57BA:0260   E6 C0 8A 0E 3B 7C 80 E1-3F 0A CE 8A 36 2A 7C 8A   ....;|..?...6*|.
57BA:0270   16 FD 7D CD 13 C3 0D 0A-4E 6F 6E 2D 53 79 73 74   ..}.....Non-Syst
57BA:0280   65 6D 20 64 69 73 6B 20-6F 72 20 64 69 73 6B 20   em disk or disk
57BA:0290   65 72 72 6F 72 0D 0A 52-65 70 6C 61 63 65 20 61   error..Replace a
57BA:02A0   6E 64 20 73 74 72 69 6B-65 20 61 6E 79 20 6B 65   nd strike any ke
57BA:02B0   79 20 77 68 65 6E 20 72-65 61 64 79 0D 0A 00 0D   y when ready....
57BA:02C0   0A 44 69 73 6B 20 42 6F-6F 74 20 66 61 69 6C 75   .Disk Boot failu
57BA:02D0   72 65 0D 0A 00 49 4F 20-20 20 20 20 53 59 53   re...IO      SYS
57BA:02E0   4D 53 44 4F 53 20 20 20-53 59 53 00 00 00 00 00   MSDOS   SYS.....
57BA:02F0   00 00 00 00 00 00 00 00-00 00 00 00 00 00 55 AA   ..............U.
```

Figure 2.3 ▲ *The Boot Record of a Disk Formatted by MS-DOS 3.2.*

Figure 2.5 shows a portion of a directory displayed in The Norton Utilities Advanced Edition. Figure 2.6 shows the first sector of the FAT of the same disk, displayed by the same program. This display translates the binary coding into decimal cluster numbers. Notice that, in the column marked *Cluster* in Figure 2.5, IBMBIO.COM starts in cluster 2, and IBMDOS.COM starts in cluster 10. In Figure 2.6, you will see that the first position, representing cluster 2, contains a 3. The consecutive positions, through the eighth, each contain the address of the next cluster. The ninth position, which represents the last cluster in the file, contains the mark

<EOF>

representing the end of the file. Similarly, each cluster representing IBMDOS.COM contains the address of the next sector, up through the

```
21D5:1000  E9 A2 00 43 44 53 20 32-2E 30 33 00 02 02 01 00   ...CDS 2.03.....
21D5:1010  02 70 00 D0 02 FD 02 00-09 00 02 00 00 00 00 00   .p..............
21D5:1020  00 00 00 14 DF 02 25 02-09 2A FF 50 F6 00 02 CD   ......%..*.P....
21D5:1030  19 00 00 0D 0A 44 69 73-6B 20 62 6F 6F 74 20 66   .....Disk boot f
21D5:1040  61 69 6C 75 72 65 00 0D-0A 44 69 73 6B 20 65 72   ailure...Disk er
21D5:1050  72 6F 72 00 0D 0A 4E 6F-6E 20 73 79 73 74 65 6D   ror...Non system
21D5:1060  20 64 69 73 6B 00 0D 0A-52 65 70 6C 61 63 65 20    disk...Replace
21D5:1070  64 69 73 6B 65 74 74 65-20 61 6E 64 20 64 65 70   diskette and dep
21D5:1080  72 65 73 73 20 61 6E 79-20 6B 65 79 0D 0A 00 49   ress any key...I
21D5:1090  4F 20 20 20 20 20 20 53-59 53 4D 53 44 4F 53 20   O      SYSMSDOS
21D5:10A0  20 20 53 59 53 FA 8C C8-8E D8 8E D0 BC 00 7C C7     SYS........|.
21D5:10B0  06 78 00 24 7C A3 7A 00-FB 2B C0 CD 13 73 0A CD   .x.$|.z..+...s..
21D5:10C0  1B BE 33 7C E8 08 01 EB-FE A1 16 7C F6 26 10 7C   ..3|.......|.&.|
21D5:10D0  03 06 0E 7C 03 06 1C 7C-A3 03 7C B8 20 00 F7 26   ...|...|..|. ..&
21D5:10E0  11 7C 33 D2 8B 0E 0B 7C-F7 F1 0B D2 74 01 40 8B   .|3....|....t.@.
21D5:10F0  C8 03 0E 03 7C 89 0E 13-7C 89 0E 31 7C 0E 58 05   ....|...|..1|.X.
21D5:1100  50 00 8E C0 2B DB A1 03-7C E8 AB 00 B8 01 02 E8   P...+...|.......
21D5:1110  94 00 73 06 BE 47 7C EB-7B 90 BE 8F 7C 2B FF B9   ..s..G|.{...|+..
21D5:1120  0B 00 FC F3 A6 75 6A 83-C7 15 B9 0B 00 F3 A6 75   .....uj........u
21D5:1130  60 0E 58 05 70 00 8E C0-B0 00 2B DB 80 3E 23 7C   `.X.p.....+..>#|
21D5:1140  00 7E 2B 98 F7 26 0B 7C-03 D8 A1 13 7C E8 67 00   .~+..&.|....|.g.
21D5:1150  A0 18 7C 2A 06 22 7C 98-01 06 13 7C 50 53 28 06   ..|*."|....|PS(.
21D5:1160  23 7C B4 02 E8 3F 00 5B-58 73 D1 E9 51 FF CD 11   #|...?.[Xs..Q...
21D5:1170  25 C0 00 D1 E0 D1 E0 86-E0 75 01 40 40 8B C8 F6   %........u.@@...
21D5:1180  06 20 7C 80 75 02 33 C0-8B 1E 31 7C EA 00 00 70   . |.u.3...1|...p
21D5:1190  00 BE 54 7C CD 1B E8 36-00 BE 66 7C E8 30 00 B4   ..T|...6..f|.0..
21D5:11A0  00 CD 16 E9 89 FE 8B 16-20 7C 8A 2E 08 7C 8A 0E   ........ |...|..
21D5:11B0  22 7C FE C1 CD 13 C3 2B-D2 F7 36 18 7C 88 16 22   "|.....+..6.|.."
21D5:11C0  7C 2B D2 F7 36 1A 7C 88-16 21 7C A3 08 7C C3 8A   |+..6.|..!|..|..
21D5:11D0  04 0A C0 74 0A B4 0E BB-07 00 CD 10 46 EB F0 C3   ...t.......F...
21D5:11E0  20 41 75 74 68 6F 72 3A-20 50 65 72 20 48 6F 6A    Author: Per Hoj
21D5:11F0  6D 61 72 6B 20 35 2F 31-31 2F 38 34 00 00 55 AA   mark 5/11/84..U.
```

Figure 2.4 ▲ *The Boot Record of a Disk Formatted by Corona MS-DOS 2.11.*

23d, which contains the end-of-file indicator. The next position marks the beginning of COMMAND.COM, which continues through cluster 36. Thus, the 35th position also contains an end-of-file mark.

The positions that follow this each contain an end-of-file mark. This is because they represent files less than one cluster in length. In fact, they represent subdirectories. You will note in Figure 2.5 that the DOS, BATCH, and UTIL directories occupy clusters 36, 39, and 40. Thus, the positions representing these clusters contain end-of-file marks. (Clusters 37 and 38 contain subdirectories to the DOS directory, which is why these cluster numbers do not appear in Figure 2.5.)

Several utility programs will display a graphic representation of the FAT as a map of the disk's sectors and will illustrate the location of particular files within it. Figure 2.7 shows a map of the FAT displayed by the PC Tools utility program.

When DOS finds bad sectors on a disk, either when you format the disk or when you use the CHKDSK program, it reserves the addresses in

```
┌─ Root dir ══════════════════════════════════════════ Directory format ═┐
│ Sector 123 in root directory                              Offset 0, hex 00│
│                                                              Attributes    │
│ Filename Ext    Size    Date      Time    Cluster  Arc R/O Sys Hid Dir Vol│
│                                                                            │
│ IBMBIO   COM    16369   5/06/87   3:25 pm     2        R/O Sys Hid         │
│ IBMDOS   COM    28477  12/30/85  12:00 pm    10        R/O Sys Hid         │
│ JK'sTurb oAT            3/18/87  12:00 pm          Arc                  Vol│
│ COMMAND  COM    23791   3/18/87  12:00 pm    24                            │
│ DOS                     3/18/87  12:00 pm    36                    Dir     │
│ BATCH                   3/18/87  12:00 pm    39                    Dir     │
│ UTIL                    3/18/87  12:00 pm    40                    Dir     │
│ FRAMEWK                 3/18/87  12:00 pm    46                    Dir     │
│ FASTBACK                3/18/87  12:00 pm    47                    Dir     │
│ AUTOEXEC BAT      281   6/08/87  10:46 am    76                            │
│ CONFIG   SYS      193   6/23/87   8:50 am   184   Arc                      │
│ ABMCLOCK COM     5086   1/08/87   5:22 pm    71                            │
│ ANSI     SYS     1651   7/07/86  12:00 pm    74                            │
│ ANSI43   SYS     1651  11/26/86   4:11 pm    75                            │
│ AUTOEXEC BAK      317  12/15/86   4:30 pm  1737                            │
│ AUTOEXEC CAR      325   6/12/87   9:13 am  8356                            │
│                                                                            │
│                        Press Enter to continue                            │
│1Help  2Hex  3Text  4Dir  5FAT  6Partn  7       8       9Undo  10QuitNU    │
└────────────────────────────────────────────────────────────────────────┘
```

Figure 2.5 ▲ *A Directory Sector Displayed in The Norton Utilities Advanced Edition.*

```
┌─ FAT area ══════════════════════════════════════════════ FAT format ═┐
│ Sector 1 in 1st copy of FAT                          Cluster 2, hex 0002│
│                                                                          │
│   3      4     5     6     7     8     9 <EOF>   11    12    13    14    │
│  15     16    17    18    19    20    21    22    23 <EOF>   25    26    │
│  27     28    29    30    31    32    33    34    35 <EOF> <EOF> <EOF>   │
│<EOF> <EOF>    41 <EOF> <EOF> <EOF> <EOF> <EOF> <EOF> <EOF> <EOF> <EOF>   │
│<EOF> <EOF> <EOF> <EOF> <EOF> <EOF> <EOF> <EOF>    81    82 <EOF>   84    │
│<EOF> <EOF> <EOF> <EOF> <EOF> <EOF>    67    68 <EOF> <EOF> <EOF>    72    │
│<EOF> <EOF> <EOF> <EOF> <EOF> <EOF> <EOF> <EOF>    81    82 <EOF>   84  85  86│
│<EOF>    88 <EOF>    90    91    92    93    94    95    96    97    98    │
│<EOF>   100   101   102 <EOF>   104   105   106   107   108   109   110   │
│ 111    112   113   114   115   116   117   118   119   120   121   122   │
│ 123    124   125   126   127   128   129   130   131   132   133   134   │
│ 135    136   137   138   139   140   141   142   143   144   145   146   │
│ 147    148   149   150   151   152   153   154   155   156   157   158   │
│ 159    160   161   162   163   164   165   166   167   168   170 <EOF>   │
│ 171    172   173   174   175   176   177   178   179   180 <EOF> <EOF>   │
│ 185      0 <EOF>   187 <EOF> <EOF> <EOF>   190   191   192   193   194   │
│ 195    196   197   198   199   200   201   202   203   204   205   206   │
│ 207    208   209   210   211   212   213   214   215   216   217   218   │
│ 219    220   221   222   223   224   225   226   227   228   229   230   │
│                                                                          │
│                        Press Enter to continue                          │
│1Help  2Hex  3Text  4Dir  5FAT  6Partn  7      8      9Undo  10QuitNU     │
└────────────────────────────────────────────────────────────────────────┘
```

Figure 2.6 ▲ *A FAT Sector Displayed in The Norton Utilities Advanced Edition.*

the FAT of the entire track on which the sectors are located as unusable, and no data will be written to that track.

As a rule, unless you are an assembly language programmer, you should do nothing to the FAT because you could lose files or totally trash your disk. There are two copies of the FAT precisely because it is so vital.

The FAT is used by the CHKDSK program to verify the integrity of your disks. It follows each chain of disk addresses to be sure that they are

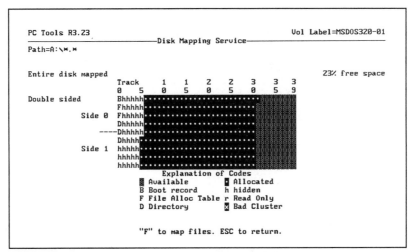

```
PC Tools R3.23                                              Vol Label=MSDOS320-01
                              ─Disk Mapping Service─
Path=A:\*.*


Entire disk mapped                                         23% free space
                    Track    1   1   2   2   3   3   3
                    0    5   0   5   0   5   0   5   9
Double sided        Bhhhhh
                    Fhhhhh
        Side 0      Fhhhhh
                    Dhhhhh
     ----Dhhhhh
                    Dhhhh
        Side 1      hhhhh
                    hhhhh
                    hhhhh
                         Explanation of Codes
                     █ Available         ▫ Allocated
                     B Boot record       h hidden
                     F File Alloc Table  r Read Only
                     D Directory         ▓ Bad Cluster

                     "F" to map files. ESC to return.
```

Figure 2.7 ▲ *A File Allocation Table Map as Displayed by PC Tools.*

part of the file to which they are assigned. If you use the /F switch with
the CHKDSK command, any sectors that the FAT shows as allocated to
files, but which are not part of any files listed in the directory, are written to new files on request. These files have names of the form

    FILE*NNNN*.CHK

where *NNNN* is a series of consecutive numbers beginning with 0000.
The directory entries for these files will always appear in the root directory, so you know where to look for them. If you look into these files,
either by using the TYPE command or DEBUG, you may find that they
are files that you previously erased. This seems most likely to occur
when you have to exit a program improperly—for example, when your
computer freezes, and you have to reboot while a file is open. In any
case, when you know the contents of the files, you can either rename
them appropriately or get rid of them safely, freeing more space on your
disk for data.

The Directory Sectors

Disk sectors 5 through 11 are reserved for the disk's root directory. Each
sector has room for 16 entries, which means that you can have up to 112
files in the root directory. If your disk has a volume name, it takes up one
entry in the directory. So does each hidden file and the name of each
subdirectory.

Subdirectories are treated just like any other file and may appear anywhere on the disk. Therefore, they can be of any length; additions to a subdirectory merely result in a longer file being saved on the disk.

If you refer back to Figure 2.5, you'll notice that consecutive entries in the directory do not necessarily represent consecutive files on the disk. If a file is erased, the name of the next file written will appear in the directory where the erased file's name appeared. However, the file may not be in the same position on the disk as the erased file. This point will become important when you learn to modify directory entries.

The Data Sectors

The rest of the disk is used for storing files. As far as DOS is concerned, all files—whether programs, data, device drivers, or whatever—are simply chains of bytes laid out sequentially (although data files with fixed-length records can be used as random-access files).

When a file is written to disk, writing begins at the first available cluster (which comprises two sectors). DOS writes in consecutive sectors, but it skips over any sectors that are in use and continues writing the file in the next unallocated cluster. I say "unallocated" rather than empty because it is quite possible that there will be some old data in unallocated clusters. DOS does not actually erase files; it merely deallocates their clusters. Thus, if a file has been modified many times, it may be broken into many short, non-contiguous segments. Such a file will take much longer to read than a contiguous one because DOS will have to move the drive head all over the disk as it searches for the parts.

The next unusual feature of the data sectors is the numbering scheme. DOS uses clusters rather than sectors so that it has a uniform standard for dealing with the various disk formats. As noted, each cluster is normally 1K, or 1024 bytes; however, larger clusters are usually used on hard disks, and the size of a cluster can generally be adjusted on a RAM disk. There are 354 data clusters on a disk. The first data sector (sector 12, right after the last directory sector), for reasons that are entirely obscure to me, is considered the first sector of cluster 2, not cluster 1. There does not appear to be a cluster 0 or cluster 1. The directory sectors include an indication of the first cluster of each file, and the FAT is mapped out in clusters as well, not sectors. However, if you want to view the data in a file directly by using the utility programs or DEBUG, you have to ask for a sector, not a cluster.

You therefore need a formula to tell you which sectors are in which clusters. For a high-density disk, where the clusters each contain one sector, it's relatively easy. You subtract the number of reserved sectors from the cluster number to get the sector number.

For disks with more than one sector per cluster, the formula to find the sector number for a given cluster is

$$\text{sector} = ((\text{cluster} - 2) \times \text{cluster-size}) + (\text{reserved sectors} + 1)$$

For a double-sided, double-density disk, this works out to

$$\text{sector} = (\text{cluster} \times 2) + 8$$

Thus, for example, if you want to look at a file whose starting address is cluster 325, you have to ask for sector $(325 \times 2) + 8$, or 658.

Hard disks have either four or eight sectors to a cluster. The size of the FAT is proportional to the size of the disk. Therefore, you may have to experiment to find the correct formula for locating sectors using a given cluster number. RAM disks are even less predictable, since they are configured by software, and you can often set the sector and cluster size yourself.

In determining these numbers, or in locating particular clusters, you may find some of the utility software discussed in Chapter 4 especially useful.

The Location of the System Files

Despite appearances, all data clusters may not be equal. If the disk is to be a system disk, the hidden system files *must* appear immediately following the directory sectors. Since the size of these files is not the same for all versions of DOS, you may not be able to update the DOS on a disk with the SYS command. If the space used by the current system files is less than that required for the version that you want to place on the disk, you will see the message

No room for system on destination disk

For reference, Table 2.2 shows the starting address and length of the system files for the last five versions of DOS.

OTHER DISK CONFIGURATIONS

All disks formatted by DOS begin with a one-sector boot record, followed by two copies of the FAT and a root directory. The exact size of these items, however, varies with the storage medium.

DOS VERSION	IBMBIO.COM		IBMDOS.COM		COMMAND.COM
	Size	Location	Size	Location	Size
	(K)	(Clusters)	(K)	(Clusters)	(K)
2.X	4	2–6	18	7–24	18
3.0	9	2–10	19	11–38	22
3.1	10	2–11	28	12–39	23
3.2	16	2–17	28	18–45	24
3.3	22	2–23	30	24–53	25

Table 2.2 ▲ *The Size and Location of the Operating System Files.*

Table 2.3 compares the various disk configurations with respect to reserved sectors, root directory size, and amount of data storage available. Note that the actual data storage area is somewhat smaller than the nominal size reported by CHKDSK. The difference is made up by the directory sectors, which are reserved by DOS, but are still included in DOS's report of the number of bytes that are free.

Single-Sided Disks

Floppy disks may be formatted as single-sided using the /1 switch. Additionally, you can specify the number of sectors per track as either eight or nine by using the /8 or /9 switch, respectively. Single-sided disks have 512-byte clusters, each comprising a single sector. Their FATs are one sector each, and their root directories can hold up to 64 entries.

DOS 1.1 Disks

Double-sided disks formatted by DOS 1.1 or formatted with the /B switch (or the /8 switch without the /1 switch) have eight sectors per track and nominally store 320K. They have one-sector FATs, but otherwise their format is similar to a standard double-sided disk.

High-Density Disks

 ATs and compatibles

DOS computers with a high-density, 5¼-inch drive can use both regular double-density disks and high-density disks. A high-density drive

	DISK FORMAT						
	1S2D8S	1S2D9S	2S2D8S	2S2D9S	2SHD9S	2SHD15S	2SHD18S
NOMINAL CAPACITY	160K	180K	320K	360K	720K	1.2MB	1.44MB
BOOT SECTORS	1	1	1	1	1	1	1
FAT SECTORS	2	2	2	4	10	14	18
DIRECTORY SECTORS	4	4	7	7	7	14	14
DIRECTORY ENTRIES	64	64	112	112	112	224	224
DATA CLUSTERS	313*	351*	315	354	708	2,371*	2,814*
DATA KBYTES	156.5	175.5	315	354	708	1,185.5	1,407

* One 512-byte sector per cluster

Table 2.3 ▲ *Disk Storage Capacity.*

normally has no trouble reading from or writing to a double-density disk. You can format such a disk in a high-density drive by using the /4 switch. If you do, however, the tracks will be half the normal width for double-density disks. Therefore, you may have trouble reading or writing to them in a regular double-density drive.

A true high-density disk has 80 tracks, with 15 sectors per track on each side. High-density disks thus can hold much more data than double-density disks. Therefore, more space is allocated both for directory entries and for the FATs.

DOS 3.2, 3.3

Two configurations of 3½-inch, high-density disks are available for DOS computers: 720K disks, which have been common on laptop computers for some time, and 1.44MB disks, introduced with the IBM Personal System/2. Both use one-sector clusters. To use the former, you must have DOS 3.2 or later; to use the latter, you must have DOS 3.3. Of course, you must also have the appropriate disk drive.

On 720K disks, there are 80 tracks per side, with 9 sectors per track. Because of the higher storage capacity, the FATs are larger than on standard double-sided disks. See Table 2.3 for further details.

On 1.44MB disks there are 80 tracks per side, with 18 sectors per track. The FAT and the root directory are proportionally larger.

Hard Disks

Hard disks consist of one or more *platters*, each of which has two sides. The sides are numbered consecutively, beginning with 0. Each usable side has its own read/write head.

With multiple platters, a third dimension is introduced into the logical numbering scheme. On a hard disk the equivalent tracks on both sides of all platters are grouped together into *cylinders*. Thus, the first cylinder comprises track 0 of every one of the hard disk's storage surfaces. Each track on each side of a platter normally has 17 sectors, but some manufacturers may divide tracks differently. Sector (and cluster) numbers are assigned to all the sectors in one cylinder before beginning the next cylinder.

Like all other DOS disks, hard disks have a one-sector boot record. The space allocated for the FAT and the root directory, as well as the number of sectors in a cluster, varies with several factors, including

- ▲ The total storage capacity of the disk

- ▲ The size of the partition assigned to DOS rather than other operating systems

- ▲ The version of DOS with which it was formatted

The physical (BIOS) side 0, track 0, sector 0 is reserved for the *partition table*. This is where DOS stores the following information:

- ▲ Which portion of the hard disk is assigned to each operating system

- ▲ Which operating system is assigned to each portion

▲ Which, if any, of the partitions will boot the system

The rest of the first physical track is also reserved.

If the entire disk is assigned to DOS, all of the first cylinder will be used for the three reserved areas. As a rule, clusters consist of four or eight sectors and store either 2K or 4K, respectively.

The allocation pattern for hard disks varies greatly. I examined two 10MB hard disks, both entirely allocated to DOS. One had 10 sectors for the FATs and 32 for the root directory. The other had 12 sectors for the FATs and 38 for the root directory.

To find out the number of sectors in a hard disk's cluster, display a directory and note the number of "bytes free" on the last line of the directory. Now write a small file—just a few characters. Display the directory again, and note the number of bytes free. Subtract this number from the first number. The result is the number of bytes in a cluster. Divide this number by 512 to get the number of sectors. See Chapter 15 for more information about hard disks.

RAM Disks

A RAM disk is a segment of the computer's memory that has been con-figured by software to emulate a floppy disk. Since "reading" a RAM disk merely transfers data electronically from one segment of memory to another, these disks are especially fast and a great boon to users of disk-intensive software.

RAM disks, just like more palpable disks, always start with a one-sector boot record, the FAT, and an area reserved for the root directory. The soft-ware normally sets up these reserved areas and then partitions the rest of the memory assigned to the disk into sectors. Many RAM disk software packages allow you to specify the number of entries the directory can hold, the size of a sector, and the number of sectors in a cluster.

An entire sector is allocated to a file when as little as one byte is used. Therefore, different combinations of sector size and number of sectors per cluster are useful for different purposes. For example, if you are work-ing with a large number of short files, a cluster size of 128 bytes will allow you to store a great many more files on a RAM disk than will a cluster size of 1K.

See Chapter 14 for more information about RAM disks.

FILES

Now that you know how storage media are set up, it's time to turn our attention to files. All files have certain characteristics:

- ▲ They have names of up to eight characters.

- ▲ Their names may have an extension of up to three characters.

- ▲ They consist of a series of consecutive bytes of data which can be read by the computer.

Reserved File Names and Characters

You cannot use file names that are the same as the DOS device-driver names. You also cannot use the names of internal DOS commands as the names of executable files (programs). (In Chapter 10, you will learn how to create an exception to this rule.) The names of the reserved device drivers and their functions are listed in Table 2.4.

DEVICE NAME	FUNCTION
AUX	Whatever device is attached to the first serial port; also known as COM1
COM1	The standard name for the first serial port; depending on your hardware, you may also have a COM2. DOS 3.3 allows for a COM3 and COM4 as well.
CON	The console, or keyboard as an input device and screen as an output device
LPT1	The first printer; you may have up to three, with the others designated LPT2 and LPT3.
NUL	An empty file or device; also called the "bit bucket," since anything written to it is thrown away
PRN	Another name for the first printer
PRT	Yet another name for the first printer, in some versions of DOS
USER	In some versions of DOS, an alternative version of COM1

Table 2.4 ▲ *Reserved Device Names.*

There are also some characters that may not be used in file names because they are used to send specific kinds of information to DOS. The reserved characters are listed in Table 2.5. Except for those listed in the table, virtually any other character can be used in a file name. You will learn in Chapter 12 how to create file names with illegal characters, but such files cannot be recognized by DOS, and therefore they cannot be opened.

Although you may type file names in uppercase or lowercase characters, they are always in uppercase characters as far as DOS is concerned. They appear on disk in uppercase and are always displayed in uppercase in directory listings.

Wild Cards

DOS has two *wild-card characters:* the asterisk and the question mark. These characters allow you to issue commands that will affect a group of files. The asterisk substitutes for all remaining characters in a file name or extension, and the question mark represents a single character. Thus

    .

represents all non-hidden files in a directory. As you may see in certain error messages, this shorthand is automatically translated by DOS to

    ????????.???

substituting one wild-card question mark for each character.

The wild-card question mark, when placed at the end of a file name or extension, will substitute for a nonexistent character. (It will also substitute for a nonexistent character if it appears right after the period, thus including files with no extension and files with one-character extensions.) Suppose, for example, you have a series of files with the following names:

    CHAPMAN.BAT
    CHAPPED.BAS
    CHAPEL.BAR
    CHAPTER.BA
    CHAPTER1.BAK

RESERVED CHARACTER	FUNCTION
.	Used to separate a file name from its extension.
\	Used to separate directory names from subdirectories and from the names of the files on them.
< and >	Used to redirect input and output.
¦	Used to separate items in a pipeline.
* and ?	Wild-card characters used to specify groups of files.
/ or -	Used to indicate *switches* for certain commands (different versions of DOS use one or the other of these characters).
:	Used as part of a drive specifier.
,	and space Used for separating entries on command lines.
+	Used for concatenating files

Table 2.5 ▲ *Reserved Characters.*

If you issued a DEL command with a wild-card pattern in the form

CHAP???.B?

it would erase only the file name CHAPTER.BA. The same would happen if the wild-card pattern were

CHAP????.B?

because the B? pattern would still not include three-character extensions. However, if you used a wild-card pattern in the form

CHAP???.BA?

all the files except CHAPTER1.BAK would be erased. The pattern

CHAP????.BA?

would erase all of the files. Of course, so would

CHAP*.BA*

File Name Extensions

Certain conventions are observed in using file name extensions; some are required by your computer and others are merely common usage. Knowing about these conventions will give you some insight into what various types of files contain and how your computer will treat them. Table 2.6 lists the most common file name extensions, along with their meanings. You can, of course, create a text file and give it a .COM or .EXE extension, but this will only make mischief. It is much safer to learn what the standard extensions mean and respect the conventions.

In addition to the extensions listed in Table 2.6, many programs create files with other extensions; for example, dBASE II and III create files with a .DBF extension, VisiCalc uses .VC, Framework uses .FW, Framework II uses FW2, Lotus 1-2-3 uses .WKS or .WK1, Symphony uses .WRK, and Symphony 1.1 uses .WR1.

When a program is written, its code is first created as source code, with the extension appropriate to the programming language. When the program is compiled, the resulting file will have the extension .OBJ or .COD. This file is then sent through the linker, which may create

EXTENSION	MEANING
.ASM	Source code for an assembly-language program
.BAK	Backup copy of a text file created by WordStar, EDLIN, the SideKick Notepad, and many other text-processing programs
.BAS	Source code for a BASIC program
.BAT	A batch program, consisting of a series of commands that can be executed by DOS
.BLD	A program to be loaded as a binary file by the BASIC BLOAD command
.BIN	A binary file
.COB, .CBL	Source code for a COBOL program
.COD	Object code listing generated by some compilers
.COM	Executable program, stored as an image of the program as it appears in memory

Table 2.6 ▲ *Common File Name Extensions*

EXTENSION	MEANING
.DAT	Data file
.DIF	Data Interchange File; a special type of ASCII text file for sharing tabular data (as from a spreadsheet program) with other programs; used especially by VisiCalc, but can also be created by many other programs
.DOC	Extension used by some word processors for their document files; also used for documentation files to public-domain software
.EXE	Executable program, but one which is relocated to a specific memory location after loading, unlike a .COM file
.FMT	Formatting specifications used by a word- processing program; display screens command file created and used by dBASE III and dBASE III Plus
.FOR	Source code for a FORTRAN program
.LIB	Library files used by a compiler
.LST	Printable listings of programs, often created by compilers; also used by some word-processing programs when a file is "printed to disk"
.MAP	A map of program linkages created by linker programs
.OBJ	Object code files generated by some compilers
.OVR, .OVL	Overlay file, containing code to be swapped into and out of memory by a program, as needed
.PAS	Source code for a Pascal program
.PGM	Program file; equivalent to an overlay file; or uninstalled version of an executable file
.PIF	Program Information File, used by Microsoft Windows and some other programs
.SYS	A device driver to be loaded into the computer by the CONFIG.SYS file, or the CONFIG.SYS file itself
.TMP	Temporary work file
.TXT	Text file; used by some word processors
.$$$	Temporary work file; pipeline file in DOS 2.X

Table 2.6 ▲ *Common File Name Extensions. (continued).*

intermediate .LST and .MAP files and then an executable version with the .EXE or .COM extension. Some programs with the .EXE extension can be passed through the external DOS program EXE2BIN, which will convert them into .COM files.

ASCII Files

Some text files are of a special type known as *ASCII text files*, or *DOS text files*. Like all computer files, the contents of these special types of files are stored as a series of bytes, each of which has a value from 0 to 255. However, in an ASCII text file, each byte represents its equivalent character in the ASCII code. As a general rule, such files contain only the characters represented by ASCII values 0 through 127. These codes include the control characters, the uppercase and lowercase English letters, numbers, punctuation marks, and the special symbols, such as + = & \ ¦, that you can type on your computer's keyboard.

The control characters Ctrl-J (ASCII 10), Ctrl-M (ASCII 13), and Ctrl-Z (ASCII 26) have special significance in ASCII text files. In such files, each line is terminated by a *newline*—a combination of a carriage return and a line feed, represented by Ctrl-M and Ctrl-J, respectively. Text following a newline is displayed or printed on a new line, beginning at the left margin (although some printers behave a bit differently). Ctrl-Z is the end-of-file marker. When DOS encounters a Ctrl-Z in a text file, it will not display anything in the file past that point.

In addition, some of the control characters can be used to control other aspects of the computer. Some of them are used in serial communications. For example, Ctrl-L sends a form feed to most printers. The Escape character (ASCII 27) generally precedes special instructions to a printer and is also used in conjunction with the ANSI.SYS device driver to control the keyboard and screen.

Characters with ASCII values above 127 also can be included in an ASCII file. You can include some of the graphics or foreign-language characters if you would like them to be displayed. The important point, however, is that, unlike programs, the byte values in ASCII files represent characters, rather than executable instructions to the computer. When you create batch files, you must be sure that the commands include only the lower 127 ASCII characters, unless the instruction is to display the contents of a line on the screen, or DOS will not understand them. If you create your batch files in WordStar, for example, the program may convert some of the characters in the file to those with an

ASCII value 128 higher than the value of the character that you typed. When DOS encounters these characters, it will not recognize them. Neither will you if you look at these files without using WordStar.

Processing Order

The file name extension has some effect on which programs will be executed. When DOS sees a command on the command line, it first looks in COMMAND.COM to see if the command is one of the internal commands. Next, it searches for a file with the name specified on the command line and a .COM extension. If one is found, it will be executed. If not, the search continues for a file with the same name and an .EXE extension, which will be executed if found. If there is none, it searches for a similarly named file with a .BAT extension. If the command is neither an external command, nor a file name with any of these extensions, DOS displays the message

Bad command or file name

One result of this search pattern is that executable files with the same name as an internal command will never be executed. A second consequence is that a .BAT file with the same name as a .COM or .EXE file will never be executed if it is in the same directory.

Viewing the Contents of Files

DOS gives you two tools for viewing the contents of files directly—the TYPE command and the DEBUG program. The TYPE command displays the contents of a file on the screen. If the file is not an ASCII text file, however, you probably won't be able to see it this way. If it's a WordStar file, you'll be able to see it, but you will not be able to read it because of the character substitutions. If it's an executable file, you will probably see a few lines of graphics characters and hear some beeps, and the display will halt as soon as a byte with the value of 26 (equivalent to Ctrl-Z) is encountered. In addition, many programs store their data and text files with a great deal of additional formatting information. These types of files, too, will not display properly with the TYPE command.

To view a file that contains such formatting information, you need a program that will not balk at control characters. Such programs generally display the contents of a file in *hexadecimal format*—a format in which the values of the bytes are represented by base-16 numbers. This is especially convenient for programmers because numbers up to 255 (the highest number that can be encoded in an eight-bit binary number, or a byte) can be represented in two digits. Unfortunately, it's less convenient for normal humans. In the next chapter, I'll give you a short course on reading hexadecimal numbers.

One program that creates such a *hex dump* is the DEBUG program included with DOS. To view a file in DEBUG, type

DEBUG *FILENAME.EXT*

DEBUG will load the program into the computer's memory. Next, type D (for *dump* or *display*), and you will be shown eight lines of characters. On the left side of the screen are two four-digit hexadecimal numbers. These represent the address in memory where the displayed data appear. They are in the standard DOS address format, in which the number to the left of the colon represents a segment of 64K of memory, while the number to the right represents the *offset*—the number of bytes (in hexadecimal) from the start of the 64K block—of the data in the first column of the center area. The center area contains rows of 16 hexadecimal numbers, separated into two groups of eight by a hyphen. In the right-hand column, any bytes that have values from 32 to 126 are represented by their ASCII equivalents. Thus, if there is text in the file, you may be able to read it. (Incidentally, this is a way of snooping out existing, but undocumented, commands in program files.) Figures 2.1 through 2.4 are examples of the display created by DEBUG.

Every time you press D, the next 128 bytes (eight lines of 16 characters) will be displayed. If the file is not a text file, however, and you are not familiar with the file format, you may not know when you have reached the end of the file, as DEBUG will continue displaying the next 128 bytes of memory whether or not it is part of the file. When you are through looking at the file, press Q to issue the QUIT command.

DIRECTORIES

DOS keeps track of files using *disk directories*. Disk directories are entries on a specific portion of a disk that contain binary-coded information for the following items:

▲ The file name

▲ The file name extension

- ▲ The length of the file in bytes
- ▲ The date that the file was last created or modified
- ▲ The time that the file was last created or modified
- ▲ The location of the file's starting point
- ▲ Information about the file's attributes

The last two items do not appear when you display a disk directory. You learned how DOS keeps track of a file's location earlier in this chapter. File attributes are discussed in detail in Chapter 12.

Viewing Directories

To view the default disk directory, all you have to do is type

DIR

at any DOS prompt. The DIR command also has several options. You can view a directory on a disk other than the default disk by typing the drive specifier after the DIR command. If your directories are long, DIR has two other options, or *switches*. The command

DIR [*drive*] [*path name*] **/P**

will show the file in *pages*. The display will stop when the screen is full, and DOS will prompt you to press a key to continue the directory. The command

DIR [*drive*] [*path name*] **/W**

displays directories in *wide* format. In this format, five file names and their extensions are displayed on each line, without any information about the files. Note the use of *path name* in the command lines above; you'll learn about path names in the next section.

Tree-Structured Directories

To simplify navigation around hard disks, which can hold literally thousands of files, DOS versions 2.0 and above allow you to create *tree-structured directories*. These are simply directories that have other directories, called *subdirectories*, subordinate to them. The main directory on a disk is called the *root directory*. The directory of a standard double-sided disk can have up to 112 entries. Other types of disks may allow more or fewer entries. Subdirectories, however, can have any number of entries.

Every subdirectory has a name. The rules governing subdirectory names are identical to those governing file names. However, in practice, most people do not assign extensions to subdirectory names.

Although subdirectories were conceived mainly as a tool to simplify hard-disk management, they are equally useful for high-density floppy disks, which can hold many files.

They can also be helpful in organizing files on floppy disks. Some hard disk backup systems copy the files in usable form, so that they do not have to be restored before you use them. With such a system, it is useful to have subdirectories on your floppy disk backups that correspond to those on your hard disk. In addition, you might want to create subdirectories on a standard floppy disk if you are backing up several software packages on a single floppy disk, or if you are keeping several groups of related files, such as the word processor, spreadsheet, and database files for a project, on a single disk.

One big advantage of using subdirectories is that DOS treats them as though they were completely separate directories. Thus, you can maintain multiple copies of a file on the same disk under the same name as long as they are in separate subdirectories. DOS will not permit you to have two files with the same name in the same directory. Another advantage is that you can copy files from one subdirectory to another.

Basic Directory Syntax

DOS commands dealing with directories use a syntax slightly different from that of other DOS commands. There are three principal commands, all similar in form. Each has a long and a short version (just as RENAME and REN, or ERASE and DEL, are equally effective):

▲ MKDIR or MD creates a new subdirectory

▲ RMDIR or RD removes an existing subdirectory

▲ CHDIR or CD logs onto a different directory

These commands all have the following characteristics:

▲ Generally speaking, the command is followed by the name of a directory, preceded by a backslash (\), with the following exception.

▲ When referring to a directory subordinate to the current one (a *child* of the current directory) they should *not* be preceded by a backslash, with the following final exception.

▲ If the root directory is current, a backslash is optional before a directory name one degree subordinate to the root.

▲ The root directory is always referred to by a backslash (\). It cannot have any other name.

▲ If the directory name in a directory command *is* preceded by a backslash, there need not be a space between the command and the directory name; for example, the following command lines will all create a directory called NEWDIR which is one degree subordinate to the root (a child of the root), no matter what directory is current.

MKDIR \NEWDIR
MKDIR\NEWDIR
MD \NEWDIR
MD\NEWDIR

On the other hand, both

MKDIR NEWDIR

and

MD NEWDIR

will create a directory called NEWDIR which is subordinate to the *current* directory. If the current directory is the root, the NEWDIR directory will be a child of the root.

The specification of all the subdirectory information needed to execute a command from your present location is called a *path name.* Thus, to refer to a file on the \NEWDIR directory if the root directory is current, you can use the path name NEWDIR. To refer to it when another directory is current, use the path name \NEWDIR.

You can have subdirectories nested several levels deep. However, this is generally not a good idea, because you can easily lose track of your files.

The directory one level higher than the current directory is called the *parent directory.* It appears in a directory listing as two periods. The current directory appears as a single period, as in the following example:

. <DIR> 3-18-87 4:46p
.. <DIR> 3-18-87 4:46p

These two entries appear at the beginning of every subdirectory listing.

You can use these directory names in commands. For example, the command

COPY C:. B:

will copy all the files in the current directory of drive C to drive B. If you use this form, you will notice that as the copying proceeds, each file name will be preceded by the symbols

.\

To use the file names from our previous example, the screen would display the following:

.\CHAPMAN.BAT
.\CHAPPED.BAS
.\CHAPEL.BAR
.\CHAPTER.BA
.\CHAPTER1.BAK

Similarly, to make the parent directory your current directory, you can use the special syntax

CD ..

DOS 3.X

In DOS 3.X, no space is required before either a single or double period.

DOS 2.X

In DOS 2.X, a space is required before a single or double period, with one exception. If the root directory is current, and you want to use a command with a single period, you cannot use a space before the period.

You can refer to all the files on a directory *other* than the current one just by using the path name. Thus

DEL *PATH*

is the same as

DEL *PATH**.*

You can always log onto the root directory with the command

CD

Changing the Default Directory   The command to change the default directory is CHDIR or CD. The syntax is the same as that for creating a subdirectory. You can make a subdirectory on any disk current by prefacing the path name with a drive specifier. For example, if your current drive were A, and you typed the command

CD C:\\NEWDIR

a command of the form

COPY *FILENAME.EXT* C:

would copy the specified file from drive A to the NEWDIR subdirectory of C. The command

DIR C:

would list the files in the NEWDIR subdirectory.

To move to a directory subordinate to the current directory, type CD followed by the name of the directory you want to move to. If it is subordinate to your current directory, you should not enter the path name with an initial backslash. Alternatively, you can always log onto a directory by specifying its complete path name from the root. Suppose, for example, that you had the set of directories shown in Figure 2.8 on your disk. To move from SECOND2 to SECOND3 you could type either

CD SECOND3

or

CD \\SECOND\\SECOND2\\SECOND3

You need not enter the space before the first backslash.

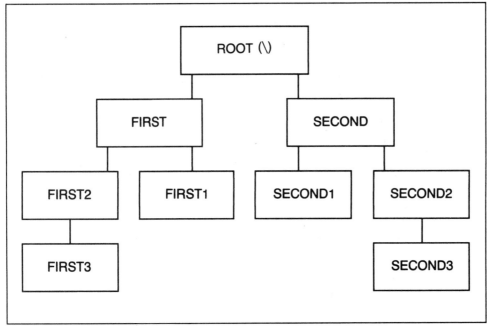

Figure 2.8 ▲ *A Sample Directory Tree.*

There is a special syntax for moving to a parallel subdirectory of a common parent. It involves going through the parent directory, calling it with the .. syntax. To move from FIRST to SECOND, for example, type

CD ..\SECOND

To move from SECOND1 to SECOND2, type

CD ..\SECOND2

These commands mean, "Move to the specified subdirectory of the current directory's parent."

Removing Subdirectories The command to remove a subdirectory is RMDIR or RD. Again, the syntax is the same. The only limitations are that you cannot remove a subdirectory under the following conditions:

- ▲ If it is the current directory on its drive
- ▲ If it contains other subdirectories
- ▲ If it contains files

To get around the first condition, simply change directories. In the second case, you must remove the subdirectories. If the third condition exists, you can log onto the directory and type

> **DEL *.***

or, using the path syntax, type

> **DEL *PATH**.***

where *PATH* is the name of the subdirectory and of any other subdirectories between it and the current directory. This won't work with hidden or read-only files, however. In order to remove such a file, you must first change its attribute to normal, as discussed in Chapter 12.

Renaming Subdirectories You cannot rename subdirectories using DOS. For this reason, you should give some thought to the names that you give to directories. If you don't like the name of your directory, the only way you can change it through DOS is to create a new directory with the name that you want, copy all the files from the old directory, delete them from the old directory, and remove the old directory. There are, however, utilities that will rename directories, and you can rename directories using DEBUG, as explained in Chapter 12.

YOUR DOS
TOOLKIT

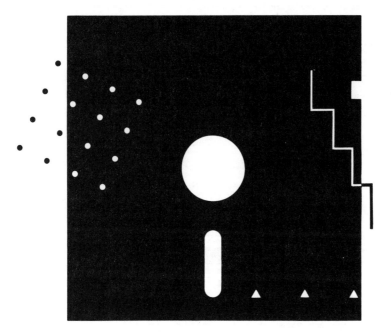

C H A P T E R

3

▲ ▲ ▲

W HEN YOU ARE ENHANCING YOUR SYSTEM (which is what this book
is all about), you need some tools to work with. The command processor
(COMMAND.COM) includes a number of commands that allow you
to automate your computer's operation to a large degree through the
creation of *batch files*, which we'll discuss extensively in Chapter 5.
However, to create these files and to complete the other tasks that we'll
perform, you'll need some other tools. DOS provides two of them: a
very limited line editor called EDLIN and an all-purpose, though limited, debugger, called DEBUG. In this chapter, you'll get an overview of
their basic commands. For a more thorough tutorial, see *Peter Norton's
MS-DOS Guide* (Brady, 1987), or *Running MS-DOS*, by Van Wolverton
(Microsoft Press, 1986). We'll also review the DOS editing keys and
describe a simple technique for creating text files.

Another program included with DOS that we'll be exploring in some
detail is ANSI.SYS, which, when properly installed, gives you a great
deal of control over the behavior of your keyboard and screen. We'll
take a brief look at it here and explore it in detail in Chapter 9.

THE DOS EDITING KEYS

There are several keys that can be used with DOS to edit text on the command line. These keys function in EDLIN and DEBUG, as well as at the DOS prompt. Table 3.1 summarizes the DOS editing keys.

Whenever you type a command terminated with a carriage return, DOS creates a template of it. You can edit the completed command

KEY	EFFECT
F1 or cursor-right	Copies one character from the template to the new line.
F2 *char*	Copies all characters from the template to the new command line up to but not including the character *char*.
F3	Copies all remaining characters from the template to the new command line.
F4 *char*	Copies all characters from *char* on in the template to the new command line.
F6	Inserts an end-of-file marker (Ctrl-Z).
F7	Inserts ASCII 0 (Ctrl-@, or null).
Ins	Toggles between insert and overwrite mode. The command line is normally in overwrite mode; pressing Ins allows you to insert characters at the current location of the cursor without affecting the template.
Del	Skips a character in the template for each press of the key.
Esc	Cancels the current command line without affecting the template. Does not return to DOS prompt.
Ctrl-C or Ctrl-Break	If Return has not been pressed, has the same effect as Esc. If Return has been pressed, cancels the command currently being executed, which will already be in the template buffer.
Backspace or cursor-left	Deletes the last character on the command line.

Table 3.1 ▲ *DOS Editing Keys.*

with the editing keys. Perhaps the most useful of these keys is the F3 function key. This key recalls the entire previous command (without the final carriage return), so that you can edit it before reentering it. Similarly, the F1 function key and the cursor-right key both recall the previous command, but they display only one character at a time.

You cannot type over existing characters on the command line; both the Backspace and cursor-left keys erase characters to the left. However, you can insert, delete, or replace characters on the line. To insert one or more characters, press the Ins key, then type the new characters. When you are finished inserting, press F3 to recall the rest of the command. For example, suppose that you wanted to enter the command

 COPY EXAMPLE.TXT B:

but had left out the second E in EXAMPLE. To correct the command, hold down the F1 or cursor-right key until the command line reads

 COPY EXAMPL

Then, press Ins, type E, and press F3 to recall the rest of the command.

Similarly, you could press the Del key to delete one character at a time, then press F3 to restore the remainder of the line. If you find you have deleted too many characters, it may be easiest to use the Backspace or cursor-left key to delete all the characters from the end of the line to the beginning, or else press Ctrl-C to cancel the command, and start over. Your changes do not affect what DOS remembers until you press the Return key.

Two more keys allow you to copy part of the template. The F2 key, sometimes referred to as the *copy-to* key, can be used to copy all of the command up to a specified character. Suppose that after copying our example file, you wanted to copy another file named EXAMPLE2.LST. You could press F2 L, and the command line would show

 COPY EXAMP

You could then enter the rest of the command. Why not press F2 E? Because then the command line would only display

 COPY

The copy will stop at the first instance of the specified letter.

Similarly, the F4 key functions as a *skip-to* key. It skips over all of the command up to the specified character. Suppose now that after copying EXAMPLE.TXT, you wanted to copy NEWFILE.TXT. You could press

F2 E to reenter COPY (or, more easily, hold down the cursor-right key until the word COPY appeared on the command line followed by a space), type NEWFIL, press F3, and the command line would read

COPY NEWFILE.TXT B:

I have generally found that it's easier to enter and correct commands by using just the cursor-right, Ins, and Del keys.

There are a few other special editing keys. In EDLIN, but not in DOS, the F5 key can be used to copy a line to the template without executing it. F6 enters a Ctrl-Z, the end-of-file mark for text files, and F7 enters a Ctrl-@ (ASCII 0, or null). Esc cancels the current command line and moves the cursor to near the end of the following line. If you press Return at this point, you will empty the template. However, if you do not, you can begin a new command line, with full access to the characters in the template. (We'll see a special use for Esc on the command line in Chapter 6.) As mentioned earlier, Ctrl-C cancels the command on the command line without entering it.

About the only point at the DOS prompt that these keys are truly useful is when you make a mistake of one character in a command or when you need to copy part of a command. You may want to copy part of a command, for example, when you're installing a program onto a hard disk. Generally, the first two tasks are to create a directory and then to make it the current one. To do this, you normally type the following commands:

MD \NEWPROG
CD \NEWPROG

You could, instead, enter

MD \NEWPROG

Then type C and press F3. Similarly, you could use a copy of part of a command when you want to move a file from one disk or directory to another. You would first enter the COPY command, then type DEL (followed by a space), and hold down the F1 or cursor-right key until the entire file name is entered, pressing Return before the destination drive specifier appears.

None of the changes you make to a command line with the editing keys affect the command in the template until you press Return. If you terminate the command with Ctrl-C, you can start over. Moreover, if you backspace to the prompt, you can reedit the command in the template at any time before executing it.

Although these keys are of limited value when you're entering DOS commands, they can actually be quite useful in EDLIN and DEBUG, where you may need to make a minor change to a rather long line or a complex command.

THE COPY CON COMMAND

Many of the programs in this book are in the form of ASCII text files. You can use DOS's editor, EDLIN, or some sort of a full-screen editor to type in these files, but you don't actually need a special program. DOS's COPY CON command will do the job.

The syntax of the COPY CON command is

COPY CON *FILENAME.EXT*

where *FILENAME.EXT* is the name of the file that you want to create. DOS will then display a promptless screen, on which you can type a line at a time. You can edit each line until you press Return, at which point you begin a new line and can no longer move back to the previous line. When you are finished, press F6 to insert a Ctrl-Z, the end-of-file mark (if you have redefined your function keys, you can just press Ctrl-Z). Then press Return, and what you have typed will be copied to the file that you specified.

Say, for example, that you want to create a file called THISFILE, whose text reads

Get back to work!

To create this file, you would type

COPY CON THISFILE
Get back to work!
^Z

After you enter the final carriage return, DOS will display the message

1 File(s) copied

and THISFILE will appear on your default directory. What you have really done is copy the input from the keyboard (CON, for console device) to the specified file.

Unfortunately, this method has some severe limitations:

▲ If you see that you have made a mistake on a previous line, your only choice is to start over from scratch (as with virtually all DOS commands, you can abort the process by pressing Ctrl-C or Ctrl-Break).

▲ You cannot use this method to edit an existing file. You can over-write an old one, but again, if there's a mistake in a file that you have saved, your only choice is to type it in from scratch. That's the kind of drudgery we use computers to avoid!

▲ You cannot enter an Escape character.

As you'll learn in Chapter 6, you can overcome some of these problems with a cut-and-paste utility. And for typing in a quick-and-dirty, two-line batch file, the COPY CON command is perfectly adequate. You can even use the DOS editing keys. But as your files become longer and more complex, you will definitely want to use a more sophisticated tool, such as a full-screen text editor.

You can also use COPY CON to send the text you type to a device rather than a file. Thus, for example, you can send a line of text to the printer with the command

COPY CON PRN

As with copying to a file, you can continue to type until you press Ctrl-Z. When you do, the screen will display the message

1 File(s) copied

and the text will be sent to the device you have specified.

INTRODUCTION TO EDLIN

DOS provides you with a rather limited and recalcitrant line editor, EDLIN. If you choose, you can use it to type in ASCII text files, but you will undoubtedly find its limitations rather confining over the long run. EDLIN is most useful for creating and editing batch programs.

EDLIN's biggest limitation is the fact that it is a line editor, not a full-screen text editor. You can work on only one line at a time. However, it does have several great advantages over the COPY CON technique. First, you can edit existing files. Second, EDLIN will save the previous version of your file with the extension .BAK, so that, if your revised version comes out worse than the original, you can return to the earlier version. Third, it allows you to insert any of the escape and control characters, including all of the graphics characters.

To invoke EDLIN, type

EDLIN *FILENAME.EXT*

where *FILENAME.EXT* is the name of the file that you want to create or edit. If the file already exists, you may see a message

End of input file

This means that the entire file has been read into memory. If the file is long, part of it will remain on disk, and no message will be displayed. (You'll learn how to retrieve the rest of the file in the section on EDLIN file commands.)

If the file is a new one, you will see the message

New file

Either message will be followed by an asterisk, which is EDLIN's prompt. Table 3.2 summarizes the EDLIN commands.

Inserting Text

Since EDLIN is a line editor, almost all EDLIN commands must be preceded by one or more line numbers. There is one exception: if you are creating a new file, you must enter the Insert command:

I

You will then see

1:*

All EDLIN commands are entered with a single-letter abbreviation, in either uppercase or lowercase. You may, but need not, enter a space after a comma or before the command letter. The asterisk now indicates the current line. You can enter up to 253 characters of text on a line. Of course, a line of more than 80 characters will wrap on the screen. (Indeed, since the line number, colon, and asterisk are indented several columns from the left, the line will wrap before you type 80 characters.)

COMMAND	PURPOSE
line-number	Displays the specific line and allows you to edit it.
	Displays the current line and allows you to edit it.
*number-of-lines*A	Appends lines from the file on disk to the end of the file.
*range-start,range-end, target[,number-of-times]*C	Copies the specified range before the target line the specified number of times.
D	Deletes the current line.
*[range-start],range-end*D	Deletes the specified range of lines; if no starting line is specified, deletes from the current line to the end of the range.
E	Ends editing and writes file.
*line-number*I	Inserts lines, beginning before the specified line number.
L	Lists 23 lines, beginning with the current line.
*line-number*L	Lists the specified line.
*range-start,range-end*L	Lists the specified range of lines.
*range-start,range-end, target*M	Moves the specified range of lines to the point before the target line.
*[line-number]*P	Displays successive 23-line segments of the file, beginning with the specified line number, making the last line displayed the current line.
Q	Quits editing, but does not write file.
*[range-start][,range-end]*R *original*Ctrl-Z*replacement*	Replaces the original text with the replacement text.
*[range-start][,range-end] [?]*S*search-text*	Searches for the specified text within the specified range of lines.
target-line T*FILENAME.EXT*	Copies the specified file into the current file before the target line.
*number-of-lines*W	Writes the specified number of lines from the beginning of the file to disk to make room for additional text.

Table 3.2 ▲ *EDLIN Commands.*

Unlike most word processors, however, EDLIN will break at the eightieth screen column, whether or not you are in the middle of a word. Moreover, once you have gone on to the next physical line on the screen, you cannot backspace past the left margin, even though you may still be on the same logical (numbered) line.

To end a line, press Return. The next line number will appear, followed by a colon and the asterisk. To stop inserting, press Ctrl-C.

To edit a line, enter its number. It will be displayed in its entirety, and the asterisk will appear to indicate the current line. If you create one line, quit, and enter edit mode, your screen might look like Figure 3.1.

You can either type entirely new text on the line or edit it with the DOS editing keys. If you use the F1 or cursor-right key to space over to the point at which you want to make a change, be careful that you do not go past the end of the screen line that you want to edit. Once you go past the end of a line on the screen, you can't go back to it.

Relative Line Numbers

When entering EDLIN commands, you may use either absolute or relative line numbers. Absolute line numbers refer to specific lines, and

```
C:\>EDLIN TEMP.TXT
New file
*I
        1:*This is the first line of my new file.
        2:*^C

*1
        1:*This is the first line of my new file.
        1:*_
```

Figure 3.1 ▲ *Text Entry in EDLIN.*

relative line numbers refer to a range relative to the current line. Entering a period will allow you to edit the current line.

Relative line numbers can use plus or minus signs to indicate their relationship to the current line. For example,

   −5, +5 *command*

will act on all the lines from five lines before the current line to five lines after. If you enter

   , +5 *command*

the command will act on the current line and the five lines following it. Similarly,

   −5, *command*

will act on the current line and the five lines preceding it. If you enter a command without a line number or range, it will usually affect only the current line.

Displaying Your File

There are two EDLIN commands for displaying a file: L for list and P for page. If you type L (assuming that you are editing an existing file or have already typed some text into your new file), EDLIN will display 23 lines (which it suspects is a screenful, based on the assumption that none of the lines wrap), starting with the current line. If your lines are longer than a single screen line, some of them will probably scroll off the top of the screen.

You can specify the lines to display by entering their line numbers. For example,

   3L

will display line 3, and

   3,20L

will display lines 3 through 20.

If you use the P command, EDLIN will display the subsequent 23 lines each time that you press P, and the last line displayed will become the current line.

Deleting Lines

To delete a single line, type the line number followed by D. To delete a range, type the starting and ending line numbers of the range. For example,

3D

will delete line 3, and

3,7D

will delete lines 3 through 7. When you delete lines, all the subsequent line numbers are adjusted. If you want to delete lines at several points in the file, you should either display the file after each deletion or start deleting from the highest line number to be sure that you are addressing the correct lines.

Moving and Copying Lines

To move lines from one point in the file to another, specify the starting line of the range to be moved, the ending line of the range, and the number of the line before which you want the moved line to appear. Even if you are moving only one line, you must still specify the starting and ending line. To move line 3 so that it appears before line 12, for example, you would type

3,3,12M

The Copy command works exactly like the Move command, except that you may also specify the number of times that the line is to be copied.

Entering Control Characters and Graphics

Some of the control characters can be entered directly in a file. To issue a beep in a batch file you are writing, for example, type

ECHO ^G

where you enter the Ctrl-G by pressing the keystroke combination. Some of the control characters cannot be entered in this fashion. To enter these characters, press Ctrl-V, followed by the character whose control equivalent you want to enter. If the character is a letter it must be entered in uppercase. To enter an escape character, enter Ctrl-V[.

DOS 3.0, 3.1

In the DOS 3.0 and 3.1 versions of EDLIN, unlike virtually every other program in existence, control characters are represented on the screen by the letter *followed*, rather than preceded, by the caret mark, e.g., G ^ .

You can enter graphics by holding down the Alt key while entering the ASCII code of the graphics character that you want from the numeric keypad.

Searching For and Replacing Text

The Search command, issued by S, requires three parameters. The syntax is

starting-line, ending-line[?]Stext-to-find

If you do not specify the range, the search will proceed from the current line to the end of the file in memory. If you do not specify text to find, EDLIN will search for whatever text you last specified. The command will locate only instances in which the case of each letter in the specified text matches that in the file.

If the text is found, the line is displayed, and EDLIN displays the prompt

OK?

If you answer Y or press Return, the search stops. If you answer N, it continues. If you continue after the last instance, the message

Not found

appears.

To replace text, the syntax is

starting-line,ending-lineRold-text ^ Znew-text

File Commands

If your file is too large to fit in memory, you must write some of the text in memory back to the file and then read some of the subsequent text into memory. The syntax of the Write command is

>*number-of-lines*W

The syntax of the Read command is

>*number-of-lines*A

where A stands for Append.

You can also merge a file on disk to the one in memory by using the Transfer command. The syntax is

>*target-line*T*FILENAME.EXT*

where *target-line* is the line number before which you want the text from the file to appear.

Saving the Edited File

When you are through editing, make sure that you are not on a numbered line (press Ctrl-C if you are), and type E. The edited file will then be written to disk. The original version will still exist under the original file name with the extension .BAK. If you want to stop editing without saving the file, use the Quit command. Again, make sure that you are not on a numbered line, then press Q. EDLIN will respond with

>Abort edit (Y/N)?

Pressing anything but Y will leave you where you left off.

INTRODUCTION TO DEBUG

DEBUG can be used to display the contents of a disk sector, a segment of memory, or the contents of a file. In later chapters, we'll use DEBUG to edit COMMAND.COM, to recover a lost file, and to write a couple of short programs. For now, we will just get an overview of its use.

A Short Course in Hexadecimal Counting

Any work you do in DEBUG *must* be done in hexadecimal notation. Hexadecimal is a numbering system with 16 as its base instead of 10. Hexadecimal (or *hex*, as it is commonly called) is generally used by programmers because it can represent the contents of any eight-bit binary number in only two digits.

To use DEBUG, you should be able to convert from hexadecimal to decimal and back. If you have SideKick, or another desk-accessory program with a converting calculator, such as Homebase or Desk Set Plus, you can use its calculator for this purpose (in SideKick enter a decimal number, press H, and the number will be converted to hex; enter a number in hex, press D, and it will be converted to decimal). HomeBase's calculator will also perform these conversions. If you don't have such a program, you can use the ASCII table in Appendix H for reference. Table H.1 presents every ASCII value in both decimal and hexadecimal form, and the table includes all values up to 255 (FF hex), which is the highest value that a single byte can represent.

In hexadecimal notation, numbers up to 9 are exactly the same as in decimal. The decimal numbers 10 through 15 are represented by the letters A through F. You therefore have to get used to the fact that in hex, the number written as 10 is the equivalent of 16 decimal, 11 is the equivalent of 17, 20 is the equivalent of 32, etc. You do not "carry" a number to the next column until the previous column has reached F, or 15 decimal.

Table 3.3 shows the 16 digits used in the hexadecimal system, along with their decimal and binary equivalents. The binary equivalents are shown as they would be represented in eight-bit bytes. The table also includes some higher values. Careful consideration of the information in Table 3.3 will help to familiarize you with the relationship between the three numbering systems.

All data in DEBUG are displayed at particular *addresses* in memory. MS-DOS's addressing system divides memory into *segments* of 64K, or 65,536 bytes. The addresses are displayed in two parts. At the very left edge of the screen is a four-digit hex number (up to FFFF) representing the beginning of the memory segment. This is followed by a colon and another four-digit hex number, which represents the number of bytes from the beginning of the segment (also called the *offset*). To see an example of this type of display, you can quickly look ahead to Figure 3.2.

Invoking DEBUG

There are two ways to invoke DEBUG. Simply typing DEBUG will display a blank line with a hyphen, which is DEBUG's prompt. You can then explore memory locations or load a disk sector into memory. The

DECIMAL	HEXADECIMAL	BYTE REPRESENTATION
0	00	00000000
1	01	00000001
2	02	00000010
3	03	00000011
4	04	00000100
5	05	00000101
6	06	00000110
7	07	00000111
8	08	00001000
9	09	00001001
10	0A	00001010
11	0B	00001011
12	0C	00001100
13	0D	00001101
14	0E	00001110
15	0F	00001111
16	10	00010000
17	11	00010001
20	14	00010100
25	19	00011001
26	1A	00011010
31	1F	00011111
32	20	00100000
48	30	00110000
64	40	01000000
80	50	01010000
96	60	01100000
112	70	01110000

Table 3.3 ▲ *Decimal and Binary Equivalents of Hexadecimal Digits.*

DECIMAL	HEXADECIMAL	BYTE REPRESENTATION
128	80	10000000
144	90	10010000
255	FF	11111111
256	100	00000001 00000000
4095	FFF	00001111 11111111
4096	1000	00010000 00000000
32767	7FFF	01111111 11111111
32768	8000	10000000 00000000
40960	A000	10100000 00000000
61440	F000	11110000 00000000
65535	FFFF	11111111 11111111

Table 3.3 ▲ Decimal and Binary Equivalents of Hexadecimal Digits (continued).

other way is to type

DEBUG *FILENAME.EXT*

which will load DEBUG and place the named file into the first available chunk of free memory. Again, however, all you will see is the hyphen.

Like EDLIN commands, all DEBUG commands are entered with a single-letter abbreviation, which may be entered in uppercase or lowercase. The first command that you are likely to need is the Display, or Dump, command.

Displaying a Section of Memory

Entering D, with no address, will display eight lines of 16 two-place hexadecimal numbers, in two groups of eight separated by a hyphen. Each two-place digit represents a single byte of memory. At the right, any bytes that have byte values from 32 to 126 are represented by their ASCII characters. All other values are represented by periods. The display starts at the beginning of the file, if one was loaded, or at address 0100 (hex) in the first available memory segment.

You can specify the segment of memory that you want to display by following the D command with an address or a range. If you enter only a four-digit number, DEBUG will assume that the address is an offset in the default segment. To specify a segment, enter both the segment address and the offset, separated by a colon. You can specify how much memory to display in two ways: by following the address with an ending offset address, separated by a space, or by entering the starting address, a space, and the letter L, followed by a number representing the (hex) number of bytes to display. These forms are summarized in Table 3.4. Once you have displayed any segment of memory, the next 128 bytes are displayed each time you press D.

Other Ways to Look at Memory

There are two other ways to look at what is stored in memory, both more specialized than using the Dump command. One is using the Unassemble command. If you type U and an address, the contents of the segment of memory following that address will be displayed in the form of machine-language instructions. Be aware that what appears may not actually be instructions. DEBUG interprets strings (groups of ASCII characters) as the machine-language instructions represented by the binary values of the ASCII characters. You will use the Unassemble command to review the contents of the programs that you write in Chapter 6, where it will be explained in more detail.

Another way to look into memory is to examine the contents of the registers in your processor chip. Simply typing R will display the contents of all the registers. Typing R followed by the name of a register displays the contents of that register and allows you to enter new contents. You will use this technique in Chapter 6 as well.

Filling a Segment of Memory

Sometimes, in order to have a clear space in which to work, it is a good idea to fill a segment of memory with a known value. The Fill command is most often used to enter binary zeros or ASCII spaces (20 hex) into a working range to make sure that the area is cleared of extraneous data. To fill the current segment from offset 100 to offset 200 (hex) with binary zeros, type

F 100 200 0

COMMAND	PURPOSE
D	Displays the first 128 bytes of file or 128 bytes of the first available memory segment, beginning at offset 100 (decimal 256).
D 1000	Displays 128 bytes at offset 1000 (decimal 4096) from the default segment.
D 1F00:0000	Displays the first 128 bytes of memory segment 1F00 (decimal 7936).
D 1000 1D00	Displays memory from offset 1000 (decimal 4096) of the default segment to offset 1D00 (decimal 7424).
D 1000 L 1FF	Displays 1FF (511 decimal) bytes of memory beginning at offset 1000 (decimal 4096) of the current segment.

Table 3.4 ▲ *Syntax for Displaying Memory in DEBUG.*

As an example, Figures 3.2 and 3.3 show the same segment of memory before and after a fill operation.

Entering New Values

DEBUG has two versions of the Enter command. The syntax of the version used to enter a string of data into a series of addresses is

E *address data*

The address may be just the offset address if you want to use the current or default segment. You can enter data in either hexadecimal or ASCII format, and you may mix both in a single entry command, separated by spaces or commas. ASCII characters must be entered in quotation marks. For example,

E 100 "This is a string of characters." 0D 0A

enters the text "This is a string of characters." followed by a carriage return (Ctrl-M, which is ASCII 13 or hex 0D) and a line feed (Ctrl-J, which is ASCII 10 or hex 0A), the normal line-terminators in MS-DOS. These data will occupy the 33 bytes from hex address 100 to hex address 120 (decimal 256 to 288). You may leave out the leading zeros on the hex digits.

The syntax of the second version of the Enter command is

E *address*

```
A:\> DEBUG
-D 100 200
26C5:0100  00 EB C7 83 3E A1 4A 19-7D 01 C3 83 2E A1 4A 19   ....>.J.}.....J.
26C5:0110  E8 80 00 E8 57 00 EB 62-80 3E A4 4A 18 74 01 C3   ....W..b.>.J.t..
26C5:0120  83 06 A1 4A 19 E8 6B 00-E8 42 00 EB 4D 80 3E A3   ...J..k..B..M.>.
26C5:0130  4A 03 7F 01 C3 80 2E A3-4A 05 EB 3E A0 A3 4A 04   J.......J..>..J.
26C5:0140  05 3A 06 A4 4A 7E 01 C3-80 06 A3 4A 05 EB 2B 80   .:..J~.....J..+.
26C5:0150  3E A3 4A 00 75 01 C3 FE-0E A3 4A EB 1D A0 A3 4A   >.J.u.....J....J
26C5:0160  3A 06 A4 4A 7C 01 C3 FE-06 A3 4A EB 0D A0 A4 4A   :..J|.....J....J
26C5:0170  3A 06 A3 4A 7F 03 A2 A3-4A C3 A0 A3 4A B2 05 B4   :..J....J...J...
26C5:0180  00 F6 F2 8A D0 B0 0E F6-E4 8A E0 8A C2 05 01 02   ................
26C5:0190  E9 D0 7F E8 AC 7F BA 21-4A B4 1A E8 D8 7B C6 06   .......!J....{..
26C5:01A0  A5 4A 00 B4 11 8B 16 A1-4A 32 FF 80 FF 19 7D 2C   .J......J2....},
26C5:01B0  52 E8 33 00 5A 0A C0 75-23 C6 06 A5 4A FF 83 FA   R.3.Z..u#...J...
26C5:01C0  00 74 03 4A EB 12 52 8A-C7 E8 B1 FF BE 21 4A C6   .t.J..R.....!J.
26C5:01D0  04 00 E8 C9 7B 5A FE C7-B4 12 EB CF 0A FF 74 02   ....{Z........t.
26C5:01E0  FE CF 88 3E A4 4A C3 8B-16 1E 4A E9 88 7B 92 50   ...>.J...J..{.P
26C5:01F0  FE C0 FE C4 E8 6C 7F 58-92 C3 C3 89 36 64 4F E8   .....l.X....6dO.
26C5:0200  AF
-
```

Figure 3.2 ▲ *A Segment of Memory Displayed in DEBUG.*

```
-F 100 200 0
-D 100 200
26C5:0100  00 00 00 00 00 00 00 00-00 00 00 00 00 00 00 00   ................
26C5:0110  00 00 00 00 00 00 00 00-00 00 00 00 00 00 00 00   ................
26C5:0120  00 00 00 00 00 00 00 00-00 00 00 00 00 00 00 00   ................
26C5:0130  00 00 00 00 00 00 00 00-00 00 00 00 00 00 00 00   ................
26C5:0140  00 00 00 00 00 00 00 00-00 00 00 00 00 00 00 00   ................
26C5:0150  00 00 00 00 00 00 00 00-00 00 00 00 00 00 00 00   ................
26C5:0160  00 00 00 00 00 00 00 00-00 00 00 00 00 00 00 00   ................
26C5:0170  00 00 00 00 00 00 00 00-00 00 00 00 00 00 00 00   ................
26C5:0180  00 00 00 00 00 00 00 00-00 00 00 00 00 00 00 00   ................
26C5:0190  00 00 00 00 00 00 00 00-00 00 00 00 00 00 00 00   ................
26C5:01A0  00 00 00 00 00 00 00 00-00 00 00 00 00 00 00 00   ................
26C5:01B0  00 00 00 00 00 00 00 00-00 00 00 00 00 00 00 00   ................
26C5:01C0  00 00 00 00 00 00 00 00-00 00 00 00 00 00 00 00   ................
26C5:01D0  00 00 00 00 00 00 00 00-00 00 00 00 00 00 00 00   ................
26C5:01E0  00 00 00 00 00 00 00 00-00 00 00 00 00 00 00 00   ................
26C5:01F0  00 00 00 00 00 00 00 00-00 00 00 00 00 00 00 00   ................
26C5:0200  00                                                .
```

Figure 3.3 ▲ *The Same Segment of Memory Filled with Zeros.*

DEBUG will then display the current contents of the (one-byte) address and give you an entry line on which to make a change. Pressing the spacebar leaves the data unchanged. When you receive a patch from a software company, it is usually a series of entries to be made in this manner. To return to the prompt, press Return.

Searching for Data

When you want to revise a program or data file, you can use the Search command to find the appropriate points at which to make the changes.

To take an example, I have an accounting program that does not allow account names to be edited once they are entered. Recently, I opened a new account about which I wanted to record information immediately. Since I didn't yet know the name of the account, I entered the data under the name DUMMY. When I learned the correct name of the account, I loaded the account file in DEBUG rather than in the accounting program, searched for the string DUMMY, and entered the correct account name in its place. You will make use of this technique in modifying COMMAND.COM in Chapter 10 and in recovering a file from memory in Chapter 15.

The Search command takes the form

S *start-address* **L** *end-address list-of-data*

If the file is less than 64K, the form (using my account program example) would be

S 0 L FFFF "DUMMY"

The L tells DEBUG that the second number is the length to search rather than the ending address. FFFF is the hex representation of 65,535, or one less than 64K. If the search text is found, DEBUG displays every address at which it appears.

Hint: If DEBUG displays so many addresses that they scroll off the screen, you may want to start over and redirect the output to a file or your printer, so you can review each one. You could also press Ctrl-P to echo the output to the printer while it is being displayed on the screen.

You can use the Dump command with each address to see if the address contains the instance of the string that you want to modify, and then use the Enter command to change it.

Moving Segments of Memory

DEBUG's Move command moves the contents of one portion of memory to another address. This is sometimes necessary if you need to recover a file that got stranded in memory, a technique that we will examine in some depth in Chapter 15. To enter the command, you must generally enter a register name, the entire address (including both segment and offset addresses from which the data will be moved), the number of bytes to move, and the target address of the first byte in the range to be moved. For example,

M 2DF3:203D 1FF 100

moves the 511 (hex 1FF) bytes starting at address 2DF3:203D to the 511-byte range beginning at address 100.

Loading and Writing Files

You can load a file after DEBUG is already active. To do this, use the Name command, followed by the Load command:

N *FILENAME.EXT*
L

The Load command can also be used to read one or more sectors directly from disk into memory. We will learn more about this in Chapter 12, when we use the Load command to modify directory entries.

The Write command is used to write the file in memory back to disk. If you have made modifications to a file and you want to save them, you must write the file. You can simply press W, and DEBUG will respond with

Writing *NNNN* **bytes**

where *NNNN* is the length of the file. When you read disk sectors into memory and modify them, you write them by the same method. When you are actually creating a new file in DEBUG, as we'll do in Chapter 6, there are several additional steps that you must take, which will be explained in that chapter.

Advanced Commands

There are several advanced DEBUG commands that are of little use to average users, but are invaluable to programmers. These include the following commands:

A	Assembles machine language instructions
C	Compares a range of memory with another range
G	Executes the program in memory (Go)
H	Performs hexadecimal arithmetic
I	Inputs data from a port

O   Outputs data to a port

T   Traces a program step by step as it executes

P   Turns off tracing during interrupt or subroutine calls

A detailed review of these commands is beyond the scope of this book. For more information on these, consult your DOS manual.

The ANSI.SYS Device Driver

The ANSI.SYS device driver is a small file that can be loaded into your computer through the CONFIG.SYS file. It gives you access to a series of *escape sequences*—sequences of characters preceded by the escape character—that can assign the function of one keyboard key to another, place colors in various areas of your screen, and control the position of the cursor on your screen. With these capabilities, you have everything you need to create dramatic screen displays and custom menus for your system. Some software packages require that the ANSI.SYS device driver be loaded into your system before they will function properly. I mention it here only to let you know that it is one of the tools available to you with DOS. We will discuss it more fully in Chapter 9.

WORTHY
ADDITIONS TO
YOUR TOOLKIT

C H A P T E R

4

I N THE PREVIOUS CHAPTER, we looked at the tools MS-DOS provides for creating and editing files and for managing your system. But before you can take full control of your system, you need some additional tools. First, given the limitations of EDLIN, you need a word processor or text editor of some sort (which you probably already have). You also should have a macro-recording program, which will allow you to store text for instant recall with a single key, as well as to perform a great many functions automatically.

In addition, there are several other types of software that will simplify tasks considerably, for which DOS provides tools that are at best marginally adequate. Among them are

▲ Utilities to help you recover damaged or erased files (these programs usually include many other functions as well)

▲ Utilities that allow you to transfer data easily from one software package to another (many such utilities use a "cut-and-paste" technique that allows you to capture data directly from the screen and enter it into another program)

▲ Software that gives you access to DOS functions that may not be available from within the programs that you use

Often, utilities of these types are *RAM-resident*. This means that they stay in the computer's memory until you need them, at which time you can call them up with a simple combination of keystrokes, even while you are using another program. Moreover, many utility packages combine several of these functions.

In this chapter, we'll review some software that can perform these functions. While the list is by no means exhaustive, it will give you some clues as to what to look for.

TEXT EDITORS
FOR BATCH FILES AND SCREENS

One of the tools that you will need for creating batch files and display screens is a text editor or word processor. Any software that can create ASCII text files will do, but some packages offer better facilities for the purpose than others. The ideal software will

▲ Create ASCII text files without unwanted formatting characters

▲ Be able to use graphics characters

▲ Be able to do block-moves and block-copies

▲ Be able to search and replace text globally

▲ Allow you to insert control and escape characters

▲ Give you access to DOS

The first of these characteristics is essential. The second is necessary if you want to use the extended ASCII code's graphics characters in your displays. The third and fourth are largely a matter of convenience, but they are a great convenience. You need the fifth to include the occasional beep and to write the ANSI escape sequences needed to control the screen and keyboard. The final characteristic simplifies the task of testing your programs and displaying your screens.

SideKick and SuperKey

I have found the SideKick Notepad, especially when used in conjunction with SuperKey, to be ideal for creating the batch programs and display screens used in this book. It has all the essential and convenient characteristics and is also RAM-resident. Therefore, you can call it with a single keystroke combination and return to the DOS prompt quickly to test your files. Although the default size of a Notepad file is limited, you can increase it to 50,000 characters, which is more than enough for the longest files that you will encounter in this book. It also has a lightning-fast search-and-replace mode. However, this works very slowly unless you prevent it from updating the screen after each replacement. To do this, press F9 or F10 twice.

The SideKick Notepad does have several serious limitations. First, because the Alt key is used to call it from memory (in conjunction with the Ctrl key), when you hold down the Alt key for some period of time, the SideKick main menu will appear. This can make it difficult to enter graphics characters with the Alt-Shift keys.

Hint: You can overcome this limitation by redefining the keys that call SideKick. SuperKey can also help you to enter graphics characters. Included on the SuperKey program disk are a pair of macro files called GRAPH and GRAPH2. These files allow you to use the keys on the numeric keypad, in combination with the Ctrl and Alt keys, to enter specific graphics characters. In addition, you can assign other graphics characters to particular keys using SuperKey's Macro Edit function. You can no doubt achieve the same thing with any other macro editor.

Another one of SideKick's limitations is that it does not allow you to save a file under a different name. If you want to make several versions of the same file, you must copy the original to other files with different names using the COPY command at a DOS prompt, then edit the files individually, or mark the entire file as a block, then write the block to a file.

After this pair of RAM-resident programs, probably the next best choices are WordPerfect and Framework.

WordPerfect

WordPerfect is an extremely powerful word-processing program that has all the features you need. It has a mode for reading and writing ASCII text files, it allows you to insert all of the control characters from the keyboard (using Ctrl-[for Escape), and it not only permits you to use graphics, but has a built-in line-drawing mode, so you can easily create boxes and borders. Moreover, you can create formatted screens using its double-column mode and tabulation features, and then save the results as ASCII text files.

Hint: Save the screen as an ASCII text file as soon as the layout is correct; then add ANSI escape sequences or control characters as needed, and resave the file as an ASCII text file under a different name.

In addition, WordPerfect has a GOTO DOS command (the Shell key), so you can test your files and return immediately to editing. Word-Perfect also has a macro processor, but unfortunately, it will not transmit characters to the DOS prompt, so you can't use it to recycle the two or three DOS commands that you may need to test your files.

Framework II

Framework II is a powerful integrated software package, with word-processing, outlining, database, spreadsheet, graphics, and telecommunications capabilities. Its word processor is the easiest to learn and use that I have encountered, and it will create ASCII text files, although they will always have the extension .TXT. You can enter all graphics characters except 9 and 13 (the Tab and Return characters, respectively) using the Alt-Shift keys. There is a built-in programming language that allows you to write macros for almost any purpose. It will even record macros as you type them, so that you can assign the graphics characters to the keyboard.

 Hint: When creating a macro for vertical line characters, include a cursor-down *and* a cursor-left code after the character, so that you can draw your lines straight down the page.

Framework II gives you full access to DOS, and it will also save the output from your files in a window. This allows you to examine the results of a program at leisure, rather than gluing your eyes to the screen and watching the messages as they go by.

MS Word

Microsoft Word, like both WordPerfect and Framework's word processor, has all the capabilities you need. To create ASCII text files, before completing the Transfer Save command, select the Formatted setting from the menu, and press N for No.

MS Word gives you access to almost all the ASCII graphics characters: codes 1 through 6, 14 through 31, and 127 through 254. You can enter these characters by pressing only the Alt key and a key on the numeric keypad. You can enter the escape character as an ASCII 27. Finally, the Library Run function allows you to go to DOS, execute batch files, and return to MS Word with the EXIT command.

The IBM Professional Editor

If you prefer a line-oriented text editor to a word processor, the IBM Professional Editor is an excellent choice. Because it is line-oriented, you must press Return at the end of each line. However, you do still have access to the full screen. Although the Professional Editor does not do block operations in the same sense that a word processor does, it can move, copy, or delete a group of lines, and these functions are extremely rapid, as is the search-and-replace function.

As a text editor, it creates only ASCII text files, so you never have to worry about extraneous characters. The Professional Editor's screen display shows you exactly what will appear, which makes it easy to set up screens. It gives you access to ASCII codes 1 through 6, 11, 12, 14 through 31, and 127 through 254. The codes below 31 can be entered directly from the keyboard, using the Ctrl key and the associated letter. The Professional Editor also has a macro function, so you can assign graphics characters, files, or strings of characters to as many as 36 different keys.

Figures 4.1 and 4.2 show the macro-definition screen in the Professional Editor, with two different sets of macros installed. Figure 4.1 is set up to produce graphics characters for borders and line drawing. Although the arrangement of characters may seem arbitrary, it actually divides the keyboard into three separate graphics keypads. Keys Q through E, A through D, and Z through C produce double-line characters. Keys R through Y, F through H, and V through N produce single-line characters. The remainder of the keyboard produces characters that will connect a double-line border with a single-line separator. If you want to create a keyboard containing all the box and border characters that will work in any application, see Appendix G.

WordStar

WordStar is not in a class with the other programs mentioned, but I include it because it is quite popular. You can use it to create the types of

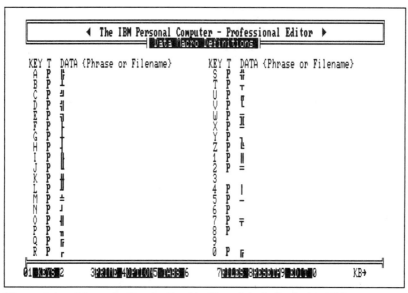

Figure 4.1 ▲ *Macros for Creating Graphics Keypads in the Professional Editor.*

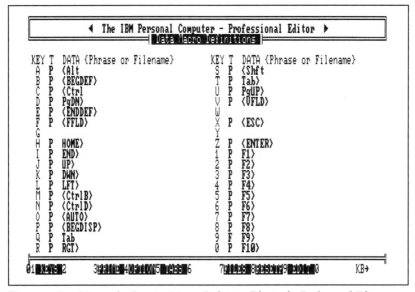

Figure 4.2 ▲ *Macros for Creating Macro-Definition Files in the Professional Editor.*

files we will need if you use it carefully and pay attention to its limitations. These limitations are different in WordStar 3.3 and WordStar 4.0, so we'll look at them separately.

With either program, you *must* use the non-document mode. You can enter control characters, including the Escape character, by pressing Ctrl-P followed by the control character. (To enter an Escape, press Ctrl-P [.)

Graphics are somewhat more problematic. You can enter graphics in WordStar 3.3 using the Alt key and the keypad, but they will not show up on the screen. Rather, the character with the ASCII value 128 less than the number you enter will be displayed.

WordStar 4.0 allows you to enter graphics characters using the Alt key, and also displays them. It even has a primitive line-drawing mode, using the Alt-function keys. You can also create macros and assign graphics characters to particular macro keys. However, there is a rather nasty catch. When WordStar 4.0 displays graphics characters on the screen, each character appears in the file preceded by an escape character and followed by a Ctrl-\. To create files without these extraneous characters you must first patch the ASCII printer driver, which normally replaces these characters with question marks. (Appendix F explains how and includes a patch file.)

Once you have patched the ASCII printer driver, you can create ASCII files. First, create the file in nondocument mode. Next, after you save the file, print it to disk under another file name, using the ASCII printer driver.

 Warning: Even in WordStar's nondocument mode, which is supposed to create ASCII text files, any time that you move or copy text from one point in a file to another, or use the Block command, the formatting characters are inserted at the ends of words.

 Hint: However, if you pass your programs through a filter such as WSFILTER or WSSTRIP, which are included in Chapter 7, you can use WordStar for batch files. But you still won't be able to use graphics.

The Norton Editor

The Norton Editor is a relatively simple full-screen editor that creates only ASCII files. It is relatively inexpensive and easy to learn, and has all the on-line help you need. It doesn't have such bells and whistles as a built-in macro recorder, but it will let you edit two files at once in separate windows and transfer text between windows. You can enter control characters (all except ASCII 0, 1, 10, 11, 13, and 26) by pressing Ctrl-P followed by the Ctrl-key combination you want. You can enter all the characters above 128 using the Alt-Shift method.

In the next section, we will discuss macro-recording programs. All the programs reviewed here allow you to create macro files in a text editor. You can assign the most commonly used commands to specific macro keys in the Professional Editor, as Figure 4.2 illustrates. This can be a great convenience because if you try to assign the spelled-out commands to specific keys using a macro-recording program, the program becomes terribly confused and refuses to recognize your macros.

MACRO RECORDERS

Once you have used a macro recorder, you will probably wonder how you ever did without one. At the very least, these programs allow you to assign a long series of keystrokes to a single key combination. This means that you can store words or blocks of text that you use frequently for instant recall and also record sequences of frequently used commands. Most macro recorders will also let you reassign keys on the keyboard, so you can make the cursor keys of your various programs behave similarly or assign the same commands to the same function keys in each program. The better ones give you a choice of recording a series of keystrokes as you enter them, editing your macros in a macro editor, or creating macro files in a text editor.

Although any of the popular macro-recorder programs will suffice, the files in this book were created with SuperKey. I chose this from among the programs discussed below because it is the easiest to learn, uses pull-down menus (which I happen to prefer), allows you to select a color scheme for each of its modules, and creates attractive display macros (used for help screens), some of which can be used as menus. If you choose a different program, you may be able to use the files in this book without altering them. If not, it is relatively simple to alter the files to conform to your program's requirements. Any text editor with a good global search-and-replace function can perform the task. If you're a clever programmer, you can probably write a BASIC program that will perform the conversions.

As a rule, macro-recording programs also offer quite a few additional features. All of those discussed here include

- ▲ A screen-protection feature that blanks the screen after a specified period of time

- ▲ A window to display a list of keys to which macros have been assigned, including titles which you assign to them

- ▲ A facility to display the actual contents of a macro

- ▲ Commands to control the way a macro is played back on the screen

- ▲ A key to allow you to skip a macro, so that you can use a defined key in its normal manner

- ▲ The ability to accept input within a macro and to specify the format of the input

- ▲ A built-in macro editor that you can use to alter macros that you have created without actually playing them back, or to create macros independent of any input into your foreground program

- ▲ The ability to edit your macro files with a text editor or word processor

- ▲ Menus or help screens that can be called as needed

- ▲ The ability to suspend the program temporarily or permanently, so that you can use software with which it is not compatible

In addition to these features, all but ProKey include a file-encryption facility (SmartKey's is in a separate program, which results in a considerable saving of memory); and all but Keyworks include some kind of program to create a complete new keyboard layout.

SuperKey

SuperKey, Borland International's macro program, includes the following features:

- ▲ A command stack, which lets you recall the last 30 or so DOS commands. This can be especially useful when creating batch programs. You can select a command from the command stack, press Return, and the command will be entered wherever you are currently working. You can open a file in your word processor, for example, or issue a COPY CON command, and then simply build a batch file from commands in the stack. You can also edit the commands in the command stack.

▲ Display macros, which are relatively easy to create. These will appear in your choice of colors on a color screen.

▲ Two types of file encryption

▲ A keyboard-lock feature, which lets you lock out unauthorized users. This can be used in conjunction with the screen-protection feature or separately.

▲ A cut-and-paste facility. This lets you transfer text from one application to another.

▲ Pull-down menus

The biggest drawback to SuperKey is that it uses up more operating memory than any of the other programs described here. If you have little memory to spare, SmartKey might be your best choice.

SmartKey

SmartKey requires the least memory and has the lowest price of the programs discussed here. Among the strongest features of the latest release (version 5.1) are

▲ An additional Shift key, called the SuperShift key. This allows you to define up to 504 separate macros—more than double the number available in any other program.

▲ A single command key, instead of a combination of two

▲ Access to DOS commands such as COPY, RENAME, TYPE, CHDIR, ERASE, and DIR, even if these commands are not available in the program you are currently using. (I have found this function to be a little bit unreliable, however.)

▲ A cut-and-paste feature

▲ Lotus-style menus across the top of the screen

▲ The ability to position the menu at the bottom, rather than the top, of the screen. This avoids conflict with programs such as 1-2-3, which display their own menus at the top of the screen.

▲ A separate, public domain program on the disk that creates a command stack. This allows you not only to recall commands, but to edit them, passing over existing characters with the cursor keys.

▲ A separate program that allows you to set up windows and create menus. These are true menus, unlike SuperKey's transparent display macros. However, this program is not as easy to learn as the display-macro function in SuperKey, and color is much harder to control.

ProKey

The current release of ProKey, 4.0, has two especially useful unique features. First, it can position its menu line anywhere on the screen. For example, you could position it just below the ruler line in WordStar. Second, you can define macros that are called by more than a single keystroke-combination. For example, you could have a macro that prints your name and address and call it by typing

    n&a

which is much easier to remember than, say Alt-N.

ProKey is by far the most expensive of the programs discussed here.

Keyworks

Keyworks includes all the features common to the programs described above, plus on-line help, DOS access, and relatively easy-to-design pop-up menus. An incorrectly written Keyworks macro, however, can bring your whole system crashing down.

MULTIPURPOSE UTILITY PACKAGES

What computer user has not, in a moment of distraction, erased a program that he or she thought was backed up, or mistyped a wild-card pattern and wiped out half a directory? It seems to be one of those unavoidable nightmares, and it always happens when you can least afford it. DOS offers you some help with such disasters, but not much. It's only moderately complicated to recover an erased file of one cluster or less. However, recovering larger files requires an intimate knowledge of the inner workings of the FAT. Fortunately, there are some fine programmers out there who have such knowledge and have made it available to you—for a price. The three utility packages discussed below all include a tool for recovering erased files as a major component. They also include facilities to recover from accidental formatting of a hard disk. These facilities are discussed in detail in Chapter 15.

These utility packages also include many other components. No computer user should be without an unerase program. However, your choice of a utility package will depend on the other components you need or want, how much you want to spend, and how you work. Note that *only* the specific releases of the programs discussed have all the features mentioned. These products have been competing for some time, and each company does its best to see that its latest release outclasses the competition in significant respects. In this battle, the users are the winners. For now we'll just get an overview of the features of these programs.

The Norton Utilities 4.0

The granddaddy of the file recovery programs is The Norton Utilities. At its core is a large program called NU. This program includes the principal unerase functions, a *byte editor*, and facilities that map disk usage and give you a technical description of your disk. In addition, the NU program lets you select items to work on, whether by file name, by sector, by cluster, or by groups of sectors or clusters. You can use the byte editor to edit any byte in any of these items. You can then write the results to disk, either in the same place, as a new file, or to a different disk.

One of the nicest features of NU is the way it treats directories. In addition to the usual directory information, it displays file attributes, starting cluster numbers, and the names of hidden and erased files. Moreover, it treats directories as files, so that you can select them from the *select file or subdirectory* menu. If you want a subdirectory of a subdirectory, you can select the parent directory, note its starting cluster, and then select the cluster. This becomes especially helpful if you want to modify information in directories, as discussed in Chapter 12.

The byte editor lets you display any file, sector, or cluster in a hexadecimal/text format similar to DEBUG's. (You can also display files in an all-text format or in a directory format.) Unlike DEBUG, however, NU allows you to move the cursor across either the hexadecimal or the ASCII display, changing data at will by entering the new information in place. Each change is highlighted on the screen. The editor includes an Undo command, so you can restore the data to its previous condition. In addition, when you finish, you have the option of writing the changes to disk, discarding the changes, or going back into the editor.

In addition to NU, The Norton Utilities 4.0 includes a set of external file and disk management programs, including the following:

▲ ASK allows input to batch files.

▲ BEEP sounds a tone of the pitch and duration you choose; it can also play back a series of tones recorded in a file.

▲ DS sorts directories by name, extension, time, date, or size, in ascending or descending order, including subdirectories if you wish. In its interactive mode you can also select file names and move them to wherever you want them in the directory.

▲ DT tests disks and files for bad sectors, marking them and moving the data from them at your request.

▲ FA displays or changes file attributes.

▲ FF finds files by name (including wild-card patterns) in any directory of a disk.

▲ FI allows you to attach a description of up to 32 characters to any file name.

▲ FS displays file sizes (useful when you want to find out if a group of files on a hard disk will fit on a floppy disk).

▲ LD lists directory names.

▲ LP formats text for printing.

▲ NCD, an advanced version of the CD command, allows you to change to any directory, no matter how deeply nested, if its name is unique. It even accepts partial and mistyped directory names. It also displays a diagram of your directory tree.

▲ QU provides a quick unerase facility.

▲ SA changes the screen colors (although the changes will be only temporary if you have installed colors in your prompt).

▲ SI reports on the hardware installed in your system and its operating speed.

▲ UD restores directories you have removed.

▲ VL adds volume labels to disks. This program will use upper- and lowercase characters as you enter them, but does not accept spaces as legitimate characters.

▲ WIPEDISK and WIPEFILE erase completely sensitive data from disks.

Every one of these programs has several switches, and there are others common to all of them. Thus, using these programs effectively would almost require you to keep a copy of the reference card in your hand at all times. However, the package also includes NI, the Norton Integrator, which lets you run all of these programs from a menu. The menu includes a complete description of all switches and runs interactively. Even so, you may find it helpful to set up a series of small batch files for the functions you use most often. You will see some examples of these in Chapter 5.

The Norton Utilities Advanced Edition

If this collection isn't enough for you, The Norton Utilities Advanced Edition includes several more goodies for half again as much money. There are two new external programs: FR, for recovering from the formatting of a hard disk; and SD, for unfragmenting files on any disk.

In addition, NU's editor includes several new facilities. Among them are a Partition Editor to look at or change partition data on a hard disk and a FAT Editor to edit the FAT or display it in a readable form (see Figure 2.6). In addition, the Directory Editor (shown in Figure 2.5) lets you alter directory entries simply by moving to a field with the Tab key and entering the new information. You can also select absolute sectors using the BIOS numbering scheme, rather than the DOS (logical) numbering scheme. (You need this capability to view the partition data.)

These added facilities are wonderful for snooping around in areas of your system normally hidden from you. However, they contain an inherent danger. Woe betide your data if you make changes to the partition information or the FAT without knowing what you are doing. Fortunately, the Advanced Edition includes a facility that will help you recover your data after trashing your FAT. The Advanced Edition of NU can be loaded in a *maintenance mode*, for working with a badly damaged disk. This mode bypasses the normal DOS organization of a disk so that you can recover data from a disk with a mangled FAT.

Mace Utilities 4.10

The central theme of Mace Utilities is data protection. At the heart of the utilities is a system to protect data from the dangers of being written to bad sectors or bad disks, or of unintentional disk reformatting. The package is broken into three units, each with its own disk and manual:

▲ RECOVERY, comparable to the operations of other recovery utilities described above

▲ Hot Rod, for improving system performance

▲ dbFIX, specifically designed to recover erased or damaged dBASE files

Every one of these programs can be run from a command line, and most require no parameters except a disk or directory to act on. However, the major functions are integrated in a menu, which includes some on-line help. The menu includes

▲ Diagnose Disk, which checks for bad sectors and other hardware errors, similar to The Norton Utilities' DT

▲ Remedy Disk, which finds bad sectors; recovers the data from them (if possible) and moves it to an unused part of the disk; and then marks the bad sectors in the FAT so they will not be used

▲ UnDELETE Files and Directories

▲ UnFORMAT Disk

▲ Sort Directory, which sorts by name, extension, date, time, or size, in ascending or descending order, including subdirectories, if you wish

▲ Squeeze Directory, which eliminates erased files from the directory in order to speed up operations

▲ UnFragment, which rewrites files that are scattered in pieces on the disk into contiguous chains

At this writing, the UnDELETE and UnFORMAT functions are probably the most sophisticated available. However, the competitors promise to catch up very soon.

The RECOVERY disk includes a pair of utilities that can be used to "soft-format" hard and floppy disks. As you may know, most versions of

DOS format a hard disk that has already been formatted simply by rewriting the FATs and the root directory. They do nothing to alter the data, although you lose access to it. If your version of DOS performs a read-write test when it formats your hard disk, it actually erases the data. If it does, you see a mess of

```
Writing sector NNNN
Reading sector NNNN
```

messages. If so, you probably want Mace Utilities, if only for its FORMAT-H program. The matching FORMAT-F program formats floppy disks in the same manner and is much faster than the DOS FORMAT command.

The Hot Rod disk, which includes the UnFragment utility and the utilities to sort and squeeze directories, also includes several speedup programs:

▲ VCACHE creates a cache buffer for data read from hard disks. Since most programs read from disks more often than they write to them, and read the same data repeatedly, a cache buffer can speed up disk-intensive software immensely. The VCACHE utility includes versions for conventional, AT extended, and expanded memory. Thus, you needn't tie up a great deal of your system's main memory if you have other memory available.

▲ VSCREEN rewrites a bit of the video BIOS to update the screen more quickly than usual in nongraphics applications.

▲ VKETTE speeds up access to floppy disks, reducing the time needed to format or copy disks or to copy files to and from disks.

▲ VKEYRATE speeds up the keyboard and/or the time elapsed before a key starts repeating.

PC Tools, R3.23

PC Tools aspires to be "the only utility package you'll ever need." It does come close to its goal. The core is a single, rather large program, which gives you a complete *DOS shell*, with access to all the DOS internal commands. You can also format and copy disks, search for text, and use extended directory utilities, even when other programs are running. You can even reorganize directory paths, rename directories, and move files from one directory to another with it. In addition, it includes a graphic directory-tree display, a very sophisticated disk-mapping function, and by far the simplest user interface and most attractive display. If you use a floppy disk system and can spare the memory to run PC Tools in resident mode, the DOS utilities alone can save you from countless headaches.

You can't select directories as files, so you must find them as clusters on disk in order to edit them. Moreover, the directory display does not include starting cluster numbers. However, it does allow you to display directories in either of two formats. The default is a two-column format without dates and times (although with an abbreviated attribute listing). The alternate format is full-width single columns with complete attribute data.

PC Tools has a byte editor rather like The Norton Utilities', but with fewer bells and whistles. As with The Norton Utilities, you can display files or disk sectors in either hexadecimal/ASCII or text format, and you can edit any byte in the former format.

There is also a screen on which you can alter any file's attributes, date, and time.

In addition to the main program there are several external programs:

▲ PCBACKUP and PCRESTOR form a hard-disk backup and restore package which matches the best in speed and efficiency. However, it is not as flexible as some of the backup software available.

▲ MIRROR and REBUILD protect a hard disk from inadvertent formatting.

▲ COMPRESS combines the Diagnose and Unfragment functions of Mace Utilities. It works on floppy as well as on hard disks. It will also install the format-protection file on the disk at your request.

As you can see from the above descriptions, the packages overlap but do not coincide. All of them do a good job of recovering erased files under most circumstances. All of them will protect your data from bad sectors and guard your hard disk against unintended formatting. (I've fortunately never had occasion to test the latter function on any of these programs and am unwilling to try them as an experiment.)

If you are especially interested in nosing around on your disks or want a group of varied utilities, The Norton Utilities package ($100) is the clear first choice. If you're a super-snoop, spring for the Advanced Edition ($150). If you want access to extended DOS functions while running other programs, PC Tools is the obvious choice. It's also an excellent choice for its backup utility and for its low price ($39.95). If you want maximum data protection, plus some facilities for turbocharging your system, or if you use a dBASE program, Mace Utilities ($99) is a must.

DOS ACCESS TOOLS

There are many programs that are not as well-behaved in their interaction with DOS as they should be. WordStar, for example, goes crazy if you try to use path names. Many other programs give you only limited access to DOS functions. For example, ThinkTank (one of my favorite programs) won't even give you a disk directory, let alone allow you to copy or rename a file. With such programs, it becomes very useful to have some kind of RAM-resident program that gives you access to the DOS functions that you need. Several of the programs already mentioned—SmartKey, Keyworks, and PC Tools—can provide these capabilities. PC Tools provides a great deal more, but it also uses a great deal of active memory.

HomeBase 2.5

Another program that provides DOS access is HomeBase. It's a desk-accessory program similar to SideKick, but with many additional features, some of which you may not need. HomeBase's DOS access is a virtually complete *DOS shell*—it not only gives you DOS functions, but a complete set of utilities, allowing you to display and edit files (in addition to editing with the text editor), make, change, and remove directories, and display several directories at once. However, it does not address file attributes.

As a complete package, HomeBase is quite well designed. You can access any module either from the main menu or from its own hot key. You select commands, each of which has a clear, single-line explanation, from a Lotus-style menu. In addition, the on-line help is actually quite helpful.

In addition, HomeBase is making a bid to become a full-fledged utilities package. Included with HomeBase are two other programs: Power Menu and Doctor DOS. The former is a system-menu program. While it does not offer the audit trails—complete records of who used what, when, for how long, whether they tried to use illegal passwords, and so on—provided by some more sophisticated menu programs, it does include a form of password protection. Moreover, it is extremely easy to set up and use. Doctor DOS includes two functions similar to Mace Utilities' VKEYRATE and VSCREEN. It also speeds up any calls that your software makes to DOS functions.

Both HomeBase and SideKick include the following features:

▲ A text editor

▲ A calculator with hexadecimal conversion and arithmetic capability

▲ A phone dialer

▲ A cut-and-paste facility

▲ A calendar with a built-in appointment recorder

▲ Programmers' tools such as an ASCII table

HomeBase also includes the following:

▲ A miniterminal program

▲ Multiple calendars

▲ A to-do list, organized so that old lists can be merged automatically into your current list and correlated to your appointment calendar

▲ A "Notebase" that allows both structured and free-form database record entries

▲ An on-screen clock that is updated every second

▲ An extremely flexible configuration system, so that you can set the program up to work with programs such as SmartKey or SuperKey

HomeBase's editor is not a full-ASCII text editor. Thus, you cannot use it to create the files in this book. In particular, it responds to ANSI escape sequences (explained in Chapter 9), rather than displaying them. Thus, not only are you unable to create and edit them, but you may also be unable to read files that contain them.

Although the entire set of programs takes up 180K, you can configure HomeBase to place part of its code on disk. If you do, you can have it use about 30K less memory than SideKick.

On the negative side, it does not interact well with other RAM-resident programs. I've experienced some very unfortunate lockups while using it. For example, when I tried to use HomeBase's cut-and-paste facility to add data to a notebase, things got hopelessly strange. Screens appeared and disappeared, menus turned into unreadable gibberish, and files seemed to fade into the ether. The technical support people at Amber Systems were unable to help me with this one. However, I was able to finish the job using SuperKey's cut-and-paste facility and had no further problems.

If you experience similar problems while using Homebase, the company's technical support staff is generally quite responsive and can help you with configuration if they are familiar with the other programs you are using. This is very important, because the configuration instructions in the manual virtually require a programmer's knowledge. However, once you are up and running, the on-line help is usually sufficient.

PolyWindows DeskPlus

PolyWindows DeskPlus is yet another desk-accessory program, but one with some unique advantages. First, it allows you access to a wide variety of applications, including the following:

▲ Memo pads

▲ Card files

▲ Appointment calendars (which are very much like SideKick's)

▲ Four types of calculators (including a decimal/hex/octal/binary converter)

▲ An ASCII table

▲ A phone dialer

▲ A cut-and-paste facility, called The Grabber

▲ Alarm clocks (although without a visible clock display)

▲ A small macro processor, with both some great advantages and some severe limitations

▲ Some form of the DOS DIR, RENAME, TYPE, MKDIR, CHDIR, ERASE, and FORMAT commands, and a report on how much disk space is left on any disk

You can even buy additional applications, such as a RAM-resident telecommunications terminal, an archiving facility, and an encryption tool, which you can install on the program's pull-down menus.

The big advantage, however, is that you can conserve memory by installing only those tools you actually need for any given application. You configure and include the various tools by means of command-line arguments, one for each tool. If you want to specify the size, shape, or color of the windows, the syntax can be quite complex. There is a separate program to make such changes permanent, but it, too, requires the same complex syntax. Once installed, however, DeskPlus is quite easy to use.

The macro processor, called PolyKeys, can hold up to 60 key definitions in a file. You create these definitions in a special definition window. You do not have the alternative of creating them "on the fly" or in a text editor. You can load more than one macro-definition file, and keep one active within DeskPlus and another within your application. PolyKeys lacks the advanced features of the macro-recording programs described earlier. It cannot accept input in the middle of a macro, delay playback, or create self-starting or display macros. The macros are strictly text. However, this package is fully compatible with ProKey version 4.0, which will give you access to a full-featured macro processor. Unfortunately, it locks up when you use it with SuperKey.

DeskPlus's memo pad does not permit the entry of escape or control characters or graphics, so it is not suitable for creating the files in this book. However, as a straight text editor, it is certainly adequate. It can load, merge, and copy files, and you can install several different memo pads on the menu under different names to give you access to files of different sizes. Its cursor-control functions differ in significant ways from those of DOS and most word processors, and I was not entirely successful in reprogramming them by means of PolyKey.

CUT-AND-PASTE TOOLS

Many programs provide some kind of file-translation utility among their arsenal of ancillary programs. 1-2-3 and Symphony, for example, include a TRANSLATE utility that will translate a number of spreadsheet and database file formats to Lotus format, and vice versa. WordPerfect has a CONVERT utility that will convert files to and from WordPerfect, WordStar, MultiMate, and Navy and Spreadsheet DIF formats. dBASE programs will convert their files to comma-delimited ASCII text files. Framework has utilities to translate from WordStar, DIF, and Lotus file formats, among others. There are also several programs that perform particular translations from one type of file to another.

However, it's awfully nice to be able, say, when working on a spreadsheet, to capture the contents of a block of cells directly from the screen and then paste them directly into a word-processing document. SuperKey, SmartKey, Keyworks, HomeBase, and SideKick all have some sort of a cut-and-paste facility to let you do just that.

SuperKey's cut-and-paste facility lets you grab a rectangular portion of the screen, assign it to a key, and then play it back as a macro. This is especially convenient if you want to cut several portions of the screen and paste them elsewhere. When you invoke it, a cursor appears in the home position. You move it to the upper left corner of the portion you want to cut and press B (for begin). A highlight appears, which you stretch with the cursor keys. When the entire area you want to cut is highlighted, you press Return. To paste the text into another application, you just press the key combination to which you have assigned the text.

SideKick's cut-and-paste function is part of its Notepad. When the Notepad is open, you press F4. At this point, you work the same way as you do with SuperKey, except the starting key is F7 and the ending key is F8. You then press the Copy Block command keys to transfer the information into the Notepad. You can save the text to a file, if you wish.

If you want to paste the text into another application, first mark it as a block in the Notepad. Then press Ctrl-K E and assign the text to a key. You can play it back as though it were a macro, either all at once or a line at a time. You cannot, however, paste the block into another document in the Notepad.

The Grabber is far less convenient to use than many other cut-and-paste utilities. The procedure for marking text to be moved is cumbersome. However, if your working situation is such that DeskPlus meets your needs better than the alternatives, The Grabber is adequate.

 Hint: You can use a cut-and-paste function in conjunction with the COPY CON command to edit files created by the COPY CON command. First, use the TYPE command to display the file on the screen, then issue the COPY CON command again. You can cut the various lines or groups of lines from the screen display using a cut function, then use the paste function to enter them into the new version of the file. If you paste only one line at a time, you can edit it before you paste the following line.

Ready!

Of the programs that allow you to transfer text between applications, Ready! deserves special mention. Ready! is a RAM-resident outline processor. It has some desk-accessory features, including a phone dialer, and you can use it to keep your address list, calendar, or any other reference material immediately available by assigning it to a function key. But its strength, in addition to its outline format, is its Setups menu. This menu allows you to install up to ten *setups,* (the file formats of different programs) from a list of 33 included with the package. If the one that you need is not included, you can create your own.

You can read any Ready! outline into Ready! with a few keystrokes. If the text that you want to use is not in Ready!'s format, you can import it as an ASCII text file. Then, when you want to send it to another program, you select the appropriate setup, switch to the receiving program, and press a three-key combination. If you have chosen the correct setup, the text will maintain its outline structure in the receiving program. This can be extremely useful for such tasks as

▲ Designing the left-hand column of a spreadsheet by moving entries around freely until you have the desired format

▲ Designing a database-entry form

▲ Keeping a database-entry form available so that, for example, you can take a customer order over the phone while working in your graphics or word-processing program, then add the information to your database as soon as you load it

If you are the kind of person who likes to work with an outline structure rather than the word-processor-like notepad, you may find Ready! a considerably more congenial tool than other desk-accessory programs.

A FINAL NOTE ON
RAM-RESIDENT SOFTWARE

Most of the programs described in this chapter (except for the word processors) are RAM-resident. While this sort of program is usually a great advantage, there are some dangers to using RAM-resident software, especially if you are using more than one such package. The problems you could encounter include the following:

▲ Some programs take over the keyboard completely and don't allow you access to a background program.

▲ Loading RAM-resident programs in the wrong order can cause your computer to freeze or to behave rather bizarrely.

▲ RAM-resident programs can take up quite a bit of memory that would otherwise be available for your foreground program.

Below are some general suggestions that may help you to avoid problems with RAM-resident packages.

Read the manual carefully—before buying the package, if possible—to make sure that the software you are interested in is compatible with the programs that you want to use with it. Check carefully to see when you need to load the package—some insist on being last, and you cannot use more than one such package. You should also check to see whether the keys required to call up a background program are compatible with your programs' keys, and if they can be assigned to different keys. If one program assigns special functions to the Esc key, for example, and another requires the Ctrl-Esc combination for special uses, using both programs may lock up your system tighter than the vault at Fort Knox.

Hint: The order in which the programs are loaded affects the keystrokes that can be passed. Each program in memory checks the keys that have been struck before passing their meaning on to the previously loaded program. Therefore, you can sometimes overcome a problem such as the Esc key lockup by loading the programs in a different order. Don't be afraid to experiment, but be sure that no vital files are open when you do.

Plan your use of RAM-resident software to conform to the way you work. You also want to see if it can be configured to suit your style of working. SideKick, for example, has configurations that omit some of its components, so you could use just the calculator with a spreadsheet, accounting program, or DEBUG. If you use programs such as ThinkTank, which give you no access to DOS whatsoever, a program that includes DOS utilities is considerably preferable to one that does not. With a program such as WordPerfect, on the other hand, neither DOS utilities nor windowing is very helpful because that program includes both.

It is not always a good idea to load all your RAM-resident utilities in your startup procedure. They may require more memory than you can spare, or they may not be needed with the foreground program that you plan to use. For example, some programs have built-in macro recorders, so you may not want a macro processor in the background when you use them (although there is a distinct advantage to being able to use the same procedures to record your macros regardless of the foreground program). Other programs provide windowing, so you may not need something like SideKick or HomeBase with them.

If you work from floppy disks, you can place copies of the packages that you want to use on your startup disk, in configurations compatible with your foreground program. If you also use a RAM disk, you can copy the help files or other facilities that do not remain resident in memory to the RAM disk, so that you can remove your startup disk without losing access to them. If the program insists that you start it from the drive where the help files reside in order to gain access to these files, copy the program to the RAM disk, then delete it after startup. In Chapters 8, 13, and 14, I'll show you some sample AUTOEXEC.BAT files that can help you deal with these situations.

INTRODUCTION
TO BATCH FILE
PROGRAMMING

A BATCH FILE IS, in essence, a series of commands that DOS executes
sequentially. The term is a holdover from mainframe computers. A
series of jobs would be entered into the mainframe via decks of punched
cards and run in sequence with no user interaction. All the operator
had to do was load the appropriate decks of cards, mount the data tapes,
and start the process moving.

The batch files that you can create using DOS can be somewhat more
complex than these noninteractive instructions. The command processor includes a handful of commands that make up a very limited
programming language. These commands permit

▲ Looping

▲ Conditional branching (although not true IF-THEN-ELSE
logic, as the DOS manual insists)   ·

▲ Processing of parameters entered on the command line

▲ Termination of a batch program before it is finished

▲ Prompting and pausing for user confirmation

▲ Passing of command-line parameters to temporary variables

They do not permit structured programming. They also do not allow
interactive user input. However, in the next chapter you will learn how
to get around this limitation.

This chapter introduces the batch file commands and the uses to which you can put them. Specific applications are explained in detail in later chapters.

WHEN TO USE BATCH FILES

Any time you find yourself performing the same series of operations more than twice, you can probably save yourself some time by creating a batch file. Any command recognized by DOS, including DOS internal and external commands and any .COM, .EXE, or .BAT file, can be executed in a batch program.

For example, suppose that you routinely place the DOS programs FORMAT.COM, CHKDSK.COM, and DISKCOPY.COM on your disks when you format them. You could type in the following series of commands, entering each after the previous one had finished executing:

```
FORMAT B:/S
COPY FORMAT.COM B:
COPY CHKDSK.COM B:
COPY DISKCOPY.COM B:
```

But it would be much simpler to create a batch file called, say, NEWFLPY.BAT, containing these commands. Then, all you have to do to execute them is type

```
NEWFLPY
```

on the command line.

You can use batch files to automate your startup procedures, to ensure that you back up your working files, to redirect output, or to give simpler names to commands that you use often. In Chapter 8, you'll be introduced to the AUTOEXEC file, which automates startup procedures, and in Chapters 14 and 15, we'll look at specialized AUTOEXEC and automatic backup files for use with RAM disks and hard disks. In Chapter 10, you'll learn some ways to create and enhance DOS commands using batch files.

HOW BATCH FILES WORK

When you run a batch file, DOS reads the disk twice for each command: first to see what the next command will be and then again to execute it. Unless you issue a BREAK (with Ctrl-C or Ctrl-Break, depending on your hardware), DOS will continue to execute the batch file until it reaches the last statement in it.

If at some point you have to switch disks, say, to load a program's over-lay files, DOS will still look for the end-of-file marker in the batch file and prompt you with

Insert disk with batch file
and press any key when ready

You can avoid this interruption by copying the batch file onto the disk on which the program execution continues. If the disk is in the same drive as the one from which the batch file was started, DOS won't know the difference and will continue until it reaches the end or you press the BREAK key. As soon as the current DOS operation is con-cluded (which does not necessarily mean as soon as the command has finished executing—it means any time DOS is invoked, such as when accessing the disk or sending characters from one device to another), and the BREAK is recognized, DOS displays the message

Terminate batch job (Y/N)?

If you press Y, execution will be halted. If you press N, it will continue. If you press any other key, the message will be displayed again. (Some versions of DOS require you to press Return after you respond to this message.)

DISPLAYING TEXT ON THE SCREEN

Normally, when a batch file is executing, the DOS prompt reappears after each command in the file, and the next command is displayed at the prompt. If you executed our example NEWFLPY.BAT file to format a disk, your screen would look exactly as though you had typed in the commands one at a time, as shown in Figure 5.1.

The ECHO Command

You can control the display of commands as they are executed with the batch command ECHO. If you start the batch file with the statement

ECHO OFF

```
A:\>NEWFLPY

A:\>FORMAT B:/S
Insert new diskette for drive B:
and strike ENTER when ready

Formatting...Format complete
System transferred


    362496 bytes total disk space
     62464 bytes used by system
    300032 bytes available on disk

Format another (Y/N)?N
A:\>COPY FORMAT.COM B:
        1 File(s) copied

A:\>COPY CHKDSK.COM B:
        1 File(s) copied

A:\>COPY DISKCOPY.COM B:
        1 File(s) copied

A:\>_
```

Figure 5.1 ▲ *Screen Display Generated by NEWFLPY.BAT.*

the statements in the file will not be displayed. However, DOS's responses to them, such as

1 File(s) copied

or

File not found

will be displayed. This can get to be a bit confusing, but there are ways you can control it. For instance, you could turn echoing off and on selectively at appropriate points, or direct output to the NUL device (see Chapter 7 for an explanation of redirection).

The ECHO command has three parameters:

ECHO OFF
ECHO ON
ECHO *message*

When you issue an ECHO ON statement, every command in the batch file will be displayed until the next ECHO OFF statement. If ECHO is off, you can follow the ECHO command with a message of up to 122 characters, and the message will be displayed without the preceding word *ECHO*. For example, if ECHO is off, the line

ECHO This is a message to the user

will result in the screen displaying

This is a message to the user

If ECHO is on, however, the resulting display would be

A> ECHO This is a message to the user
This is a message to the user

This fact has some interesting consequences. First, as you may have noticed, an ECHO OFF statement turns off the DOS prompt. You can type ECHO OFF at a DOS prompt, and the prompt will disappear. However, the cursor will still be active, and you will be able to enter commands as usual.

You will see in Chapter 6 how this technique can be used in conjunction with a macro processor to create a blank input screen. It is also noteworthy, however, that if you use a program that maintains a command stack (a record of commands that have already been issued) batch file commands that are executed while ECHO is off will not appear in the stack, but those executed while ECHO is on will be there.

DOS 3.3

In DOS 3.3, there is a new way to keep text from being displayed in a batch file. Precede any line that you do not want displayed with an @ symbol, and the text will not appear on the screen, just as if you had entered ECHO OFF. Indeed, you can even keep the ECHO OFF statement from appearing by entering it as

@ECHO OFF

This syntax will result in an error message in any other DOS release.

Adding Remarks

You can add comments, or remarks, to a batch file with the REM command. A REM statement is simply the word REM followed by any text that you want to insert. REM statements will be displayed only if ECHO is on.

The REM statement is the simplest way to display text in a batch file. You can have a batch file consisting of nothing but remarks, and they will be displayed on the screen in order. (Unfortunately, the word REM will also be displayed.) REMARKS.BAT, shown in Listing 5.1, is a perfectly acceptable batch file. This file displays each line at a DOS prompt, exactly as you see it in the file, when REMARKS is typed on the command line.

REM statements do have the disadvantage of slowing the file's execution. DOS has to read the disk for each statement in a batch file, even if it is a REM.

Another way to enter a remark into a batch file is to precede it by a colon. Statements preceded by a colon will not be displayed during execution whether ECHO is on or off. However, you can see them if you use the TYPE command to look at the contents of the file.

The PAUSE Command

The PAUSE command not only allows you to include a pause in the execution of a batch file, but also offers another way to display text. When ECHO is off, DOS displays the message

    Strike a key when ready ...

when the PAUSE command is executed. However, if ECHO is on, you can follow the PAUSE command with a message, and your message will be displayed along with the DOS message.

For example, you might use a statement such as

    PAUSE Insert data disk in drive B

Unfortunately, the word PAUSE will then be displayed along with the accompanying message. You might consider the following syntax more elegant:

    ECHO OFF
    :
    :
    ECHO Insert data disk in drive B
    PAUSE

```
1: REM This is a remark.
2: REM This is another remark.
3: REM A remark is a non-executable statement in a batch file.
4: REM If ECHO is off, you will see these lines when
5: REM you type REMARKS on the command line.
```

Listing 5.1 ▲ *REMARKS.BAT.*

You can also use the PAUSE command to give the user an opportunity to exit a batch program. You may find the following syntax useful:

```
ECHO OFF
.
.
.
ECHO Press Control-C to quit. Otherwise,
PAUSE
```

The TYPE Command

The problem with displaying text using REM and ECHO statements is that they execute so slowly. A couple of ECHO statements are fine for displaying a brief message, but if you want to give extensive instructions or display a help screen when incorrect parameters are issued, you can display the text considerably more quickly by creating an ASCII text file that contains the text. When you want to display the text, you can call it with the TYPE command within your batch file.

REPLACEABLE PARAMETERS

You can set up batch files so that parameters can be passed to the commands, rather than written into them directly. This is the simplest use of variables in the DOS batch language. There can be up to ten different *replaceable parameters* in a batch file, and an argument can be passed to each one on the command line.

A replaceable parameter is indicated by a single-digit number preceded by a percent sign, for example, %1. Suppose that you wanted to copy a series of files from one disk to another. You could set up a file such as MOVETHEM.BAT, shown in Listing 5.2. This file will copy up to nine files to the disk in drive B when you type

MOVETHEM *FILE1.EXT FILE2.EXT FILE3.EXT . . .*

```
1: COPY %1 B:
2: COPY %2 B:
3: COPY %3 B:
4: COPY %4 B:
5: COPY %5 B:
6: COPY %6 B:
7: COPY %7 B:
8: COPY %8 B:
9: COPY %9 B:
```

Listing 5.2 ▲ *MOVETHEM.BAT.*

where the italicized names are valid file names. You could even include a drive prefix, wild-card characters, or a directory path as part of the file name.

If there are fewer than nine command-line arguments, however, DOS will nonetheless dutifully cycle through every line in the program, displaying

```
A> COPY B:
B: File not found
```

for each line. You can use conditional tests and branches, which are discussed later in the chapter, to avoid this unnecessary repetition.

Notice that there are only nine parameters in MOVETHEM.BAT. The tenth, %0, is always the name of the batch file itself. You can use it to have a batch file call itself in its last line. This is one easy way to set up a repeating loop. You will see another use for the %0 parameter in the SK.BAT file presented in Chapter 15.

The replaceable parameters need not represent file names. They can be replaced by parts of file names or by internal DOS commands. For example, if you wanted to do something to all your files with a .BAK extension, you could create a batch file called DOIT.BAT, with the single line

```
%1 %2.BAK %3
```

You could then type

```
DOIT COPY THIS B:
```

to copy THIS.BAK to drive B, or type

```
DOIT DEL THIS
```

to delete THIS.BAK from the current drive. Not very useful, I admit, but you get the idea. We'll put replaceable parameters to better use in later chapters.

The replaceable parameter can also substitute for a directory path. For example, if your DOIT file contained the line

```
COPY \%1\CHAP%2.%3 B:
```

you could specify the directory on which the file was found, the chapter number, and the type of file. However, you would have to type these parameters as separate items on the command line. DOS would translate the command

```
DOIT BOOK 1 TXT
```

as

COPY \BOOK \CHAP1.TXT B:

The items that you place on the command line must replace exactly the variables that receive them. If you were to type the above command as

DOIT \BOOK \CHAP1.TXT

DOS would interpret the command as

COPY \\BOOK \CHAP1.TXT \CHAP. B:

which is full of syntax errors.

If you have groups of related files of different types that you like to back up regularly, you could create a sensibly designed file to do the job. BACKIT.BAT, which is shown in Listing 5.3, is an example of such a file. Then, when you type

BACKIT CHAPTER1

on the command line, your text, figure, and table files for Chapter 1 will all be copied to the disk in drive B, but your .BAK files will not.

Batch Files for Remembering Command Parameters

There are many situations in which you will want to use a set of command switches or parameters to accomplish a given task. You can do this by placing the command, with its parameters, in a batch file along with a replaceable parameter. Then you don't have to remember which set of switches you need every time you invoke the command. Following are three examples based on The Norton Utilities.

FI, in its default mode, truncates file descriptions while displaying complete directory entries. You may want it to list the complete description you have recorded for all the files in a directory, pausing when the screen is full. To produce this type of display, you could create the file INFO.BAT, containing the line

\NORTON\FI %1 /L /P

```
1: COPY %1.TXT B:
2: COPY %1.FIG B:
3: COPY %1.TBL B:
```

Listing 5.3 ▲ *BACKIT.BAT.*

The /L switch shows the long form of the description, shortening the directory listing to just the file name and extension. The /P switch tells the program to pause when the screen is full. The replaceable parameter %1 takes the name of the directory you want to display.

Similarly, you may want to print out the READ.ME files that come with many programs in a form that fits neatly into a five-by-seven-inch three-ring binder. The file PRINTDOC.BAT, shown below, will tell the LP program to do just that.

```
\NORTON\LP %1 /T3 /B15 /HEADER2
        /L3 /SET:\PRINTER\CONDENSD
```

In this command, \PRINTER\CONDENSD refers to a file on the \PRINTER directory, which contains the escape sequence needed to put your printer in condensed mode. The replaceable parameter %1 in this file is used to tell LP which file to print.

The SpeedDisk utility in The Norton Utilities Advanced Edition is another component you may want to invoke with a batch file. If you want the utility just to give you a report on which files are fragmented and how badly, rather than doing a complete disk reorganization, you can create the batch file ANALYZE.BAT, containing the following line:

```
\NORTON\SD %1\*.* /REPORT /S /P
```

This command line generates a report to the screen that includes all files in all subdirectories. The %1 tells DOS which drive to look on, and the /P, as before, tells the program to pause when the screen is full.

LOOPS AND LABELS

The DOS batch language allows you to construct two types of loops. The FOR loop executes a single command a finite number of times on the specified files. The file names can either be written into the code or passed to replaceable parameters in the loop from the command line. The second type of loop can execute any number of commands any number of times.

The FOR Loop

The syntax for the FOR loop command is

```
FOR %%VARIABLE IN (SET) DO COMMAND
```

where *SET* is any set of file names and *COMMAND* is any valid DOS command. The file names in the set may include wild-card characters. If wild cards are used, the loop will execute for each file matching the wild-card pattern before going on to the next item in the set.

The double percent sign before *VARIABLE* distinguishes a variable used internally in a batch file from a parameter to be replaced by a command-line argument. The variable is conventionally specified by a single letter, but it need not be. When the command is executed, each item in the set replaces the variable in turn.

You can enter a FOR loop directly on the command line, but then you cannot pass parameters to the variable (they would have to be specified in the set). The variable would then be preceded by only a single percent sign.

You could change the BACKIT.BAT file shown in Listing 5.3 to read

**FOR %%P IN (CHAPTER1.TXT CHAPTER1.FIG
CHAPTER1.TBL) DO COPY %%P B:**

This file will copy the specified files to drive B. If ECHO is off, DOS would display the screen shown in Figure 5.2. As you can see, DOS reinterprets the double percent sign as a single percent sign.

```
C:\>BACKIT

C:\>FOR %P IN (CHAPTER1.TXT CHAPTER1.FIG CHAPTER1.TBL) DO COPY %P B:

C:\>COPY CHAPTER1.TXT B:
        1 File(s) copied

C:\>COPY CHAPTER1.FIG B:
        1 File(s) copied

C:\>COPY CHAPTER1.TBL B:
        1 File(s) copied

C:\>
C:\>
C:\>_
```

Figure 5.2 ▲ *Screen Display from BACKIT.BAT, Version 2.*

We could just as well use replaceable parameters in the set.

FOR %%P IN (%1.TXT %1.FIG %1.TBL) DO COPY %%P B:

has the same effect as the original form of BACKIT.BAT. If this form is used, the parameter CHAPTER1 is passed to %1, which in turn passes it to %%P, as Figure 5.3 shows.

The SHIFT and GOTO Commands

If you need to execute more than one command on each of a group of files, or you want to use more than nine arguments with a command, you must construct a different type of loop. This loop requires three new elements: the SHIFT command, the GOTO command, and a label. The SHIFT command discards the first parameter on the command line after it has been acted upon and replaces it with the next one. After the program executes its commands on the first parameter, the second parameter becomes the first, the third becomes the second, and so on. Thus, with the SHIFT command, you can add as many arguments to your command line as you have room for (remembering that a command line may be up to 132 characters in length).

```
C:\>BACKIT CHAPTER1

C:\>FOR %P IN (CHAPTER1.TXT CHAPTER1.FIG CHAPTER1.TBL) DO COPY %P B:

C:\>COPY CHAPTER1.TXT B:
        1 File(s) copied

C:\>COPY CHAPTER1.FIG B:
        1 File(s) copied

C:\>COPY CHAPTER1.TBL B:
        1 File(s) copied

C:\>
C:\>_
```

Figure 5.3 ▲ *Screen Display from BACKIT.BAT, Version 3.*

After the SHIFT command is executed, you have to tell DOS to go through the loop a second time. The GOTO command tells DOS to continue execution at a specified point in the file, indicated by a *label*. A label is any combination of up to eight alphanumeric characters, preceded by a colon.

The general form of this type of loop is

```
:label
COMMAND1
.
.
.
COMMANDn
SHIFT
GOTO label
```

The command must include a replaceable parameter. Any number of commands may appear between the label and the SHIFT command.

As an example, let's rework MOVETHEM.BAT (Listing 5.2). Using this loop form, this program would read

```
:start
COPY %1 B:
SHIFT
GOTO start
```

Of course, you will have the same problem that you had with the original version, only worse. The original version ran through all nine commands, no matter how few parameters were given. This version will repeat an infinite number of times, repeating the

```
B:File not found
```

message each time it checks the command line and does not find more parameters.

CONDITIONAL TESTS AND BRANCHING

Now you know how to make a batch program execute a series of commands on a group of files. But what do you do when your program cycles forever, waiting for you to issue a BREAK? To prevent that, you must have your file test to see if there are additional parameters.

There are many other circumstances in which you might want your file to test for the existence or nonexistence of a condition. You may want different commands to be executed under different circumstances, or you may want a program to terminate if certain conditions exist. The DOS batch language provides the IF command for this purpose.

The IF Command

Although the batch language's IF command is extremely limited compared with the IF command in most other programming languages, it is sufficient for the task. The syntax for the command is

IF [NOT] *CONDITION COMMAND*

The IF command can directly execute only one other command. It is commonly used for branching to another part of a program, with the syntax

IF [NOT] *CONDITION* GOTO *label*

where *CONDITION* is the condition for which you want to test, and *label* is a label preceding the lines of code that you wish to execute.

There are four types of tests that the IF statement can perform: tests for the existence or nonexistence of a parameter, tests for the existence or nonexistence of a file, tests for equivalence, and a special test for a variable called ERRORLEVEL, which will be discussed in the next chapter. (As the syntax above shows, you can test for the nonexistence of the condition by placing the word NOT after the word IF.)

There is no true ELSE command to go along with IF. If you want to say "If this condition exists, do A, otherwise do B," for example, you must use statements of the form

IF *CONDITION* GOTO *labelA*
GOTO *labelB*

If you plan the structure of your programs in advance, you can sometimes avoid this form by placing the commands to be executed in the event of B immediately after your IF statement. However, you will need to use at least two more labels, unless you want the commands that are to be executed in the event of A to be executed as well. You might find it easier to conceptualize this if you think of the set of commands to be executed in either event as separate subroutines, each of which ends with a statement directing execution to the proper point. The form of this construction is

IF *CONDITION* **GOTO** label1
COMMAND1
.
.
.
GOTO continue
:label1
COMMAND2
.
.
.
:continue
COMMANDn

Testing for Equivalence

To test for equivalence, use the double equal sign. The syntax is

IF *STRING1* = = *STRING2 COMMAND*

This construction is virtually always used with a replaceable parameter. For example:

IF %1 = = end **GOTO** end

If ECHO is on when this statement is executed, and the condition is true, the screen will display this statement as

IF end = = end **GOTO** end

If it is not true—say, if the parameter encountered is TEXTFILE.TXT—the screen would display

IF TEXTFILE.TXT = = end **GOTO** end

and execution would not be transferred to the label :end.

 Warning: Since strings (consecutive groups of characters) are being compared, DOS will regard the two values as equivalent only if the case of each corresponding letter is equivalent, even though DOS commands may be entered without regard to case. Therefore, to be absolutely sure that the string for which you are testing has been entered, you must set up a series of statements of the form

```
IF %1 = = end   GOTO end
IF %1 = = END GOTO end
IF %1 = = End  GOTO end
IF %1 = = ENd  GOTO end
IF %1 = = EnD  GOTO end
IF %1 = = enD  GOTO end
IF %1 = = eND  GOTO end
IF %1 = = eNd  GOTO end
```

If the string for which you are testing has more than three characters, you will need a correspondingly greater number of lines to test for all possible combinations of uppercase and lowercase characters. In actual practice, however, you can probably get away with just the first three forms. It may be safe to assume that the Caps Lock key is either on or off, and if it is off, a user might capitalize the first letter out of habit.

Sometimes you may find it quite useful to test for the absence of a parameter. In version 3 of BAKIT.BAT, for example, you might want to test for the null string (a string of zero length). When it is encountered, you want the program to stop looping.

To test for a null string, you must use quotation marks around the parameter. For example:

```
IF "%1" = = " " GOTO end
```

means if the next parameter (after the SHIFT command has been executed) is a parameter of zero length, stop executing the loop.

 Warning: You may place both the parameter and the test string in quotation marks at other times without generating an error condition, but it is not necessary. However, the form

```
IF %1 = = "" GOTO end
```

will not trap the absence of a parameter, because DOS will try to match the parameter with a pair of quotation marks.

Hint: There is another way to test for the absence of a parameter. You create a dummy string and add it to the replaceable parameter:

IF %1@ = = @ GOTO end

In this instance, the dummy string is the character @, but any character can be used. If no parameter is encountered, DOS interprets the command as

IF @ = = @ GOTO end

Of course, this statement is true, so execution is redirected to the :end label, and no error message ensues.

Testing for the Existence of a File

You may want to perform a certain operation only if a given file is present or absent. The command to test for the existence or nonexistence of a file is EXIST. The syntax is

IF [NOT] EXIST *FILENAME.EXT COMMAND*

For example, if you want to copy a file to a given disk only if a file of that name is not already present on the disk, you could use a statement of the form

IF NOT EXIST B:%1 COPY A:%1 B:

If you wanted the command to create a backup file on the destination disk if the original is present, you would have to use two parameters, one for the file name and the other for its extension:

IF EXIST B:%1.%2 COPY A:%1.%2 B:%1.BAK

However, because there is no ELSE command to take care of both conditions, you would have to use a branching command of the form:

```
IF EXIST B:%1.%2 GOTO backup
COPY A:%1.%2 B:
GOTO end
:backup
COPY A:%1.%2 B:%1.BAK
:end
```

Warning: In some version of DOS the EXIST command recognizes files only on the current directory of a disk; however, it can be used on any drive's current directory. In these versions, EXIST does not recognize path names; in fact, they confuse it. A statement of the form

```
IF EXIST C:\UTIL\PROFILE\TEXT.PRF command
```

will not find the file TEXT.PRF whether or not you are logged onto the \UTIL\PROFILE directory of drive C. To make this test work, you need two commands:

```
CD C:\UTIL\PROFILE
IF EXIST C:TEXT.PRF COMMAND
```

I have turned up some unaccountable errors on occasion, however, when checking for the existence of a file on a drive other than the current one. It is safest to use the form

```
C:
CD \UTIL\PROFILE
IF EXIST TEXT.PRF COMMAND
```

to log onto the drive in question before performing the test.

CHAINING BATCH FILES

You can always call a batch program from another batch program if the second program is the *last* command in the calling program. If you pass control to a second batch program at any point before the end, control is permanently passed to the second program. You can use this creatively as a means of branching. For example, suppose that you used two different configurations, one for most of your everyday software and a second for a copy-protected version of dBASE III PLUS, which is rather hostile to RAM-resident software. You might have a batch program like the one shown in Listing 5.4 test for the existence of the proper configuration. If the computer is configured for dBASE III PLUS, control will be passed to a batch file called DB3.BAT, which will execute the program. Otherwise, the correct configuration will be created, and the computer will reboot itself for dBASE III PLUS.

Here is how this program works.

1: If the program called CONFIG.DB3 does not exist, presumably it has already been renamed by this program in line 3. If this is true, the dBASE III PLUS configuration has already been loaded into the computer, and execution is directed to line 7, so dBASE III PLUS can be loaded.

2–3: The regular CONFIG.SYS file is held in reserve by being renamed, and CONFIG.DB3 is made into the active configuration by being renamed.

4–5: The AUTOEXEC file is held in reserve by the same method, and the DB3.BAT file is set up so that it executes automatically when the computer is rebooted with the new configuration.

6: A BASIC program, which will be introduced in Chapter 14, automatically reboots the computer.

8: Executes dBASE.

This setup would require a complementary program something like the one shown in Listing 5.5, which would return the computer to the normal configuration, reversing all the steps in the present file. The same technique can be used to configure your computer for Framework II, which uses the same copy-protection system.

```
1: IF NOT EXIST CONFIG.DB3 GOTO end
2: REN CONFIG.SYS CONFIG.REG
3: REN CONFIG.DB3 CONFIG.SYS
4: REN AUTOEXEC.BAT AUTOEXEC.REG
5: COPY DB3.BAT AUTOEXEC.BAT
6: BASICA AUTOBOOT
7: :end
8: DBASE
```

Listing 5.4 ▲ *DB3.BAT.*

```
1: REN CONFIG.SYS CONFIG.DB3
2: REN CONFIG.REG CONFIG.SYS
3: DEL AUTOEXEC.BAT
4: REN AUTOEXEC.REG AUTOEXEC.BAT
```

Listing 5.5 ▲ *NODB3.BAT.*

Hint: If ECHO is off in the calling program, it will remain off in the called program unless you explicitly turn it on with an ECHO ON statement.

USING BATCH FILES AS SUBROUTINES

There is actually a way to call a second batch program from within a batch program and have control returned to the calling program. It requires two additional commands: COMMAND and EXIT.

To call a second batch program, you must also load a second copy of COMMAND.COM and turn control over to that copy while the second program is executing. Unlike when you load the first copy of COMMAND.COM, any variables, paths, prompts, etc., that have been established remain in effect. The syntax is

COMMAND /C *BATCH*

The /C switch tells DOS that this is a secondary copy of the command processor, and *BATCH* is the name of the batch file that you want to run.

The second program ends with the command EXIT, which unloads the second command processor and returns control to the first one. If it does not end with the EXIT command, processing will terminate at the end of the second batch program, with the second command processor still active. (This is how BASIC and programs such as Framework and WordPerfect provide access to DOS while the program is running. The EXIT command is built into BASIC's SHELL command.)

 DOS 2.X

If you have DOS 2.X, which does not allow you to execute a program that is not on the current directory or the search path, you can use this technique to include various batch programs as subroutines in your main batch program. For example, suppose that you want to include commands to have your macro processor unload itself or to load a certain file. Suppose further that your macro processor and its files are neither on the search path nor the default directory. You could have a second batch program call the macro processor and pass a command to it, then return control to the first program. The calling program would contain a line such as

COMMAND /C KEY DB2 /ML

The command following COMMAND /C tells SuperKey to load the macro file for dBASE II. The command in its present form calls a batch file called KEY.BAT, which is shown in Listing 5.6.

Hint: Once you have loaded a secondary command processor with the COMMAND /C command, ECHO will be restored to its default state, which is on. Therefore, if you want ECHO to remain off, you must turn it off explicitly.

KEY.BAT makes the SuperKey directory the default directory, so that the command can be passed to the SuperKey program (called KEY.COM). The name of the file, DB2, is passed to the first parameter, and the command to load the file, /ML, is passed to the second. The CD \ command makes the root directory the default directory, before returning control to the calling program.

Hint: If you call a program such as KEY.BAT on the command line, the EXIT command will have no effect unless a secondary command processor has been loaded. Therefore, it is safe practice to end any batch file that might be called by another batch program with the EXIT command.

DOS 3.X

In DOS 3.X, the EXIT command is not needed. When a batch file loads a secondary command processor to execute a batch file, control automatically returns to the calling program when the second batch file is finished executing.

```
1:  ECHO OFF
2:  CD \SUPERKEY
3:  KEY %1 %2
4:  CD \
5:  EXIT
```

Listing 5.6 ▲ KEY.BAT.

DOS 3.3

DOS 3.3 contains a new command that obviates loading a secondary command processor. The CALL command, placed in a batch file, automatically executes another batch file, starting at the point you specify. The syntax is

CALL *FILENAME* [*PARAMETERS*]

This command will call the batch file *FILENAME*, execute it, and pass any parameters to it if the called file has replaceable parameters.

DOS 3.X

The technique of using batch files to temporarily change directories is, in principle, unnecessary in DOS 3.0 and above. While earlier versions cannot execute programs unless they are on the current directory or the search path, DOS 3.X can follow a path to execute a program. Therefore, to execute the SuperKey command example in DOS 3.X, all you have to do is use the command

\SUPERKEY\KEY DB2 /ML

in the calling program. However, SuperKey will not be able to find its help file unless it is loaded while logged onto the directory in which it resides. Therefore, in this instance, the batch file technique is preferable.

ADDING POWER
TO THE
BATCH LANGUAGE

CHAPTER

6

▲　▲　▲

C HAPTER 5 SUMMARIZED just about everything you need to know to
use the DOS batch language in its intended manner. In this chapter, we
are going to expand the language so that it can do more. We will overcome the language's principal limitation by creating ways to make a
batch program accept user input while executing.

We will use two different methods for adding input functions to the
language. First, we will write two short machine-language programs to
accept different kinds of input. Don't panic! You don't have to know
anything about machine language to enter these programs. I'll give you
a method of creating them via a simple ASCII text file and tell you how
to debug them if they don't work. Second, we will see how to use
macros with batch files. We will create a self-executing macro that acts
as a batch file and another macro that passes some parameters to a batch
file while it is executing.

DEBUG is the tool we'll use to enter the machine-language programs. If you *are* a machine-language programmer, you may prefer to use
the original source code, which appears in Appendix C. These source-
code listings are fully annotated, so you can see how the programs work
step by step.

USING DEBUG AS AN ASSEMBLER

DEBUG has two functions that we did not discuss in Chapter 4. These functions, Assemble and Unassemble, allow you to write and examine machine-language programs. When you use DEBUG as an assembler, you invoke the Assemble command by entering A and then enter a series of machine-language instructions. If you make a mistake, you can enter U to examine the results with the Unassemble command and then make the necessary changes to specific lines.

As we discussed, the addresses displayed in DEBUG are in two parts: a 64K segment address and an offset, or number of bytes from the start of that segment. The segment is displayed to the left of the colon, the offset to the right. Since the segment depends on what's in your system at the moment, the program listings here will show only the offset address.

The two programs we will enter are called YN.COM and CHOOSE-.COM. The former appends

(Y/N)?

to the end of a message in a batch file and accepts yes or no input. The latter, somewhat more complicated program lets you specify a series of keys to be pressed to select choices from a menu.

(**Note:** A public domain program called ASK.COM works almost identically to YN.COM. It is included with SmartKey versions 5.1 and above. A program of the same name, included with The Norton Utilities 4.0 and the Advanced Edition, can substitute for both YN.COM and CHOOSE.COM. So can another program called CHOOSE.COM, which is listed in the magazine *Compute!* 65 [October 1985]. If you already have access to one of these programs, you need not enter the programs listed here, except for the experience.)

Entering the Programs in DEBUG

The machine-language instructions that comprise YN.COM appear in Listing 6.1. The entire program is 69 bytes long. The file YN.DEB is a *script file* that we will use as input for DEBUG. (For an explanation of this procedure, see the section on *redirected input* in Chapter 7.) Note that it includes both the code for YN.COM and the instructions to DEBUG for assembling the program.

To begin, type in this text in an editor that creates ASCII text files. Be sure that your text is typed exactly as it appears in the listing.

(You may use the space bar instead of the Tab key to enter a space after the first instruction on each line. Tabs are conventionally used to make the instructions easy to read.) An error could lock up your computer. Be sure to end each line with a carriage return, including the last line. Don't forget the blank line that appears five lines from the end.

Next, make sure that DEBUG and YN.DEB are on your current directory. Type

DEBUG < YN.DEB

This command will feed the necessary instructions to DEBUG, which, if all goes well, should create YN.COM for you automatically.

```
N YN.COM
A 100
MOV     BX,0081
ADD     BL,[0080]
MOV     BYTE PTR [BX],24
MOV     DX,0082
CALL    013F
MOV     DX,0134
CALL    013F
MOV     AH,07
INT     21
AND     AL,DF
CMP     AL,59
MOV     CL,01
JZ      0128
CMP     AL,4E
MOV     CL,00
JNZ     0116
MOV     DX,013C
CALL    013F
XCHG    AL,CL
MOV     AH,4C
INT     21
AND     [BX+SI],CH
POP     CX
DAS
DEC     SI
SUB     [BX],DI
AND     AL,0D
OR      AH,[SI]
MOV     AH,09
INT     21
RET

RBX
0
RCX
45
W
Q
```

Listing 6.1 ▲ *YN.DEB.*

Notice that the first line uses DEBUG's Name command to tell DEBUG which program is being assembled. The next line

A   100

tells DEBUG to begin assembling the instructions at byte 100 hex. The first 256 (100 hex) bytes are reserved for the *program segment prefix*, which the operating system creates automatically in order to communicate with the program. The lines after the blank line are also instructions to DEBUG, which we'll examine shortly.

Next, type in the code shown in Listing 6.2, observing the same precautions. This is the code and assembly instructions for CHOOSE-.COM. To create CHOOSE.COM from CHOOSE.DEB, type

DEBUG < CHOOSE.DEB

Again, DEBUG should create the file for you automatically.

THE ERRORLEVEL COMMAND

Both the YN and CHOOSE programs use an obscure command which we have not yet explored—ERRORLEVEL. Before we test the programs, we should see how the command works.

A program can assign a value to a variable within DOS called ERRORLEVEL. A batch program can then test for this value and take different actions depending on the result. Normally, the programs that use ERRORLEVEL are BACKUP, RESTORE, KEYB, FORMAT, GRAFTABL, and REPLACE.

Both YN and CHOOSE assign a value to ERRORLEVEL depending on the user's response and take the action prescribed in the batch program. The value need not have anything to do with an error condition. YN assigns a value of 1 to an uppercase or lowercase Y response and a value of 0 to an uppercase or lowercase N response. Any other input is rejected.

When a program tests for values of ERRORLEVEL, it must test for the highest possible value first, and then for each succeeding value. There is no equivalent to "greater-than-or-equal-to," so the program must test for each value separately. This forces you to construct a clumsy equivalent of a CASE structure (a feature of some structured programming languages) or of BASIC's ON . . . GOSUB or ON . . . GOTO command.

```
N CHOOSE.COM
A 100
CMP     BYTE PTR [0080],00
JZ      013E
DEC     BYTE PTR [0080]
MOV     BX,0082
XOR     CX,CX
MOV     CL,[0080]
AND     BYTE PTR [BX],DF
INC     BX
DEC     CX
LOOP    0114
CLD
MOV     AX,DS
MOV     ES,AX
MOV     DI,0082
XOR     CX,CX
MOV     CL,[0080]
MOV     AH,07
INT     21
AND     AL,DF
CMP     AL,41
JB      0120
CMP     AL,5A
JA      0120
SCASB
JZ      013E
LOOP    0137
JMP     0120
DEC     CL
MOV     AL,CL
MOV     AH,4C
INT     21

RBX
0
RCX
46
W
Q
```

Listing 6.2 ▲ *CHOOSE.DEB.*

CHOOSE takes a series of arguments that must be alphabetic upper-case characters, entered with no intervening spaces. The syntax of the command is

CHOOSE *ABCDEF*

where the letters A through F represent the choices you are offering the user. Note that *any* letters may be used; they need not be in alphabetical order.

CHOOSE assigns a value of 0 to the last letter in the argument, and it increments the value by 1 for each previous letter. Thus, using the sample syntax, if F is chosen, ERRORLEVEL will have the value of 0; if E is chosen, it will have the value of 1; if D, 2; if C, 3; and so on. Arguments and responses may be in either uppercase or lowercase.

CHECKING YOUR WORK

Before you actually use these programs as commands in batch files, you should be sure that they work correctly. Below are a pair of simple batch files that will test them for you. If they do not work as they should, refer to the following section, which explains how to make corrections.

Testing YN.COM

To test YN.COM to see if it is entered correctly, type in the batch program in Listing 6.3, TESTYN.BAT. This gives an example of how YN is used in a program. It should display the message

Do you want to repeat this message (Y/N)?

followed by a blinking cursor. If you press an uppercase or lowercase Y, the message should be repeated. On the other hand, if you press an uppercase or lowercase N, the message

You do not want to repeat this message

should appear. If you press any other key, nothing should happen. If the results are not *exactly* as described, see the section on making corrections.

Testing CHOOSE.COM

To test CHOOSE.COM, type in TESTCHS.BAT, shown in Listing 6.4. When you invoke the program, the screen should display

For First choice press F
For Second choice press S
For Third choice press T

Pressing an uppercase or lowercase F should display the message

This is the first choice

and the program should then end. Similar messages should appear if you press S or T, but nothing should happen if you press any other keys.

If you want to use keys other than the alphabetic characters—numbers or function keys, for example—you can use the ANSI.SYS device driver to reassign specific alphabetic characters to the keys of your choice before you invoke CHOOSE, as explained in Chapter 9. You will still have to use the alphabetic characters on the line that invokes CHOOSE, however.

```
 1: ECHO OFF
 2: :start
 3: YN Do you want to repeat this message
 4: IF ERRORLEVEL 1 GOTO start
 5: ECHO You do not want to repeat this message
```

Listing 6.3 ▲ *TESTYN.BAT.*

```
 1: ECHO OFF
 2: ECHO For First choice press F
 3: ECHO For Second choice press S
 4: ECHO For Third choice press T
 5: CHOOSE TSF
 6: IF ERRORLEVEL 2 ECHO This is the third choice
 7: IF ERRORLEVEL 2 GOTO end
 8: IF ERRORLEVEL 1 ECHO this is the second choice
 9: IF NOT ERRORLEVEL 1 ECHO this is the first choice
10: :end
```

Listing 6.4 ▲ *TESTCHS.BAT.*

Test this program several times, as it ends after each choice. If every choice produces the expected result, your work is done, and you can skip the next section.

Making Corrections

If your programs have not behaved as expected, you can *disassemble* them. Enter the command

DEBUG YN.COM

and then enter the Unassemble command by pressing U. You will see 12 lines of disassembled code. Each line will begin with a two-part address, as usual in DEBUG. Following that is a number, which you can ignore. The last two columns should be the same as the text you typed in.

The easiest way to proceed is to press Ctrl-P or Ctrl-PrtSc, to copy the screen to your printer, and type

U 100 143

This will give you a listing of the addresses and code for the entire program, which you can compare to the listing in the book. For help with the addresses, refer to Figure 6.1. (You may safely ignore the segment address before the colon, which is replaced by XXXX in the figure.) Proofread the version from your printer against the one in this book.

```
XXXX:0100 BB8100       MOV    BX,0081
XXXX:0103 021E8000     ADD    BL,[0080]
XXXX:0107 C60724       MOV    BYTE PTR [BX],24
XXXX:010A BA8200       MOV    DX,0082
XXXX:010D E82F00       CALL   013F
XXXX:0110 BA3401       MOV    DX,0134
XXXX:0113 E82900       CALL   013F
XXXX:0116 B407         MOV    AH,07
XXXX:0118 CD21         INT    21
XXXX:011A 24DF         AND    AL,DF
XXXX:011C 3C59         CMP    AL,59
XXXX:011E B101         MOV    CL,01
XXXX:0120 7406         JZ     0128
XXXX:0122 3C4E         CMP    AL,4E
XXXX:0124 B100         MOV    CL,00
XXXX:0126 75EE         JNZ    0116
XXXX:0128 BA3C01       MOV    DX,013C
XXXX:012B E81100       CALL   013F
XXXX:012E 86C1         XCHG   AL,CL
XXXX:0130 B44C         MOV    AH,4C
XXXX:0132 CD21         INT    21
XXXX:0134 2028         AND    [BX+SI],CH
XXXX:0136 59           POP    CX
XXXX:0137 2F           DAS
XXXX:0138 4E           DEC    SI
XXXX:0139 293F         SUB    [BX],DI
XXXX:013B 240D         AND    AL,0D
XXXX:013D 0A24         OR     AH,[SI]
XXXX:013F B409         MOV    AH,09
XXXX:0141 CD21         INT    21
XXXX:0143 C3           RET
```

Figure 6.1 ▲ *Debugging YN.COM.*

If any of the code or addresses do not match those in the listing, you will have to make corrections. Do so by using the Assemble command. You need not reassemble the whole program. Just type A, followed by the address where the erroneous information appears, and enter the correct information.

The next available address will then appear, ready for you to enter code. If the address is the correct one, press Ctrl-C or Return. Repeat the procedure for any other erroneous lines. Finally, you will have to write the corrected file. To do so, you will recreate the instructions at the end of the listing. When you are at a hyphen prompt, type

RBX

You should see the lines

BX 0000
:

If you do, press Ctrl-C. Otherwise enter a zero after the colon and press Return. Next enter

RCX

You should see

CX 0045

If you don't see 45, enter 45 next to the colon (this is the number of bytes in the program, in hex), and press Return. Otherwise, just press Return. Enter

W

to invoke the Write command and write the file to disk. You should see the message

Writing 0045 bytes

When the disk activity stops and you are returned to the hyphen prompt, enter

Q

to quit DEBUG.

Use the same procedure to debug CHOOSE.COM (see Figure 6.2). However, when you examine the CX register (the RCX command), you should see 46, not 45. If not, enter 46. Otherwise just press Return. When the file is written, you should see the message

Writing 0046 bytes

CREATING TRUE STRING VARIABLES

There is a little-known DOS command called SET. One MS-DOS manual explains the command as follows:

> Sets one string value equivalent to another string for use in later programs. These strings are placed in the environment of the command processor where they can be accessed by an application program that you create.

Underlying that cryptic explanation is a small bundle of dynamite. The obvious use of the SET command is to reveal some of what is currently stored in what DOS regards as the *environment*. Ordinarily,

```
XXXX:0100 803E800000    CMP     BYTE PTR [0080],00
XXXX:0105 7437          JZ      013E
XXXX:0107 FE0E8000      DEC     BYTE PTR [0080]
XXXX:010B BB8200        MOV     BX,0082
XXXX:010E 31C9          XOR     CX,CX
XXXX:0110 8A0E8000      MOV     CL,[0080]
XXXX:0114 8027DF        AND     BYTE PTR [BX],DF
XXXX:0117 43            INC     BX
XXXX:0118 49            DEC     CX
XXXX:0119 E2F9          LOOP    0114
XXXX:011B FC            CLD
XXXX:011C 8CD8          MOV     AX,DS
XXXX:011E 8EC0          MOV     ES,AX
XXXX:0120 BF8200        MOV     DI,0082
XXXX:0123 31C9          XOR     CX,CX
XXXX:0125 8A0E8000      MOV     CL,[0080]
XXXX:0129 B407          MOV     AH,07
XXXX:012B CD21          INT     21
XXXX:012D 24DF          AND     AL,DF
XXXX:012F 3C41          CMP     AL,41
XXXX:0131 72ED          JB      0120
XXXX:0133 3C5A          CMP     AL,5A
XXXX:0135 77E9          JA      0120
XXXX:0137 AE            SCASB
XXXX:0138 7404          JZ      013E
XXXX:013A E2FB          LOOP    0137
XXXX:013C EBE2          JMP     0120
XXXX:013E FEC9          DEC     CL
XXXX:0140 88C8          MOV     AL,CL
XXXX:0142 B44C          MOV     AH,4C
XXXX:0144 CD21          INT     21
```

Figure 6.2 ▲ *Debugging CHOOSE.COM.*

the environment comprises any resident DOS programs (such as PRINT, MODE, SETUP, or CONFIG), plus the name and location of the command processor, and the path and prompt if you have established any. Typing SET at a DOS prompt will reveal the latter three pieces of information. For example, it might display

```
COMSPEC = C:\COMMAND.COM
PATH = C:\;C:\DOS;A:\
PROMPT = $p$g
```

For another use of the SET command, these "strings" that "are placed in the environment" can be the names of string variables to which you can assign values dynamically, in the course of a program. And the program that makes the assignments and uses the variables can be a batch program.

The syntax for the command is

SET *VARIABLE* = *VALUE*

where *VARIABLE* is a string (a series of characters) and *VALUE* is another string. Thereafter, when you refer to *VARIABLE* in a program, DOS will interpret it as the value you assigned to it. Let's say, for example, that you type

SET NAME = DAVID

at a DOS prompt. The next time you type SET at a DOS prompt, the resulting screen display would include, along with the command processor, prompt, and directory path information, the line

NAME = DAVID

Suppose that you then want to call the value assigned to NAME from the environment because it's a particular user's name, and you want a batch file to change to that user's directory. You must refer to the variable name that is stored in the environment with the special syntax

%NAME%

In this example, the relevant line in a batch file would be

CD \\%NAME%

If ECHO were off, you would see

CD \\DAVID

when this line was executed.

You can also test for a given value of an environment variable by using an IF statement. However, the value you have assigned to the variable must then be preceded by a single percent sign, as if it were a replaceable parameter:

IF NOT %NAME% = = %DAVID CD \\BARBARA

With ECHO off and DAVID assigned to the variable NAME, this line would appear on the screen as

IF NOT DAVID = = DAVID CD \\BARBARA

In other words, if the variable NAME does not hold the value DAVID, the current directory should be set to BARBARA.

The environment grows in 128-byte increments, until you load one of the DOS programs that stays resident, such as GRAPHICS. Once you have loaded such a program, the environment will grow only to the end of the next 128-byte boundary. Therefore, it is a good idea to remove any environment variables after you no longer need them.

To do so, enter the variable name and the equal sign, with no value:

```
SET NAME =
```

So far, everything you have done with the SET command in a batch file could be done more easily with a simple replaceable parameter. Instead of taking the extra step of assigning a value to a variable with the SET command and then checking for it with this Byzantine syntax, you could just as well have the batch file contain the line

```
CD \%1
```

or

```
IF NOT %1@ = = DAVID@ CD \BARBARA
```

and set up your batch file to expect a parameter such as DAVID on the command line.

Saving Values for Later Use

If this were all there is to the SET command, I wouldn't devote this much space to it. However, one of the truly useful things that you can do with the SET command is to store values that would otherwise be thrown away and use them later. Let's take a brief look at a batch program that will be discussed at greater length in Chapter 10. CFILES.BAT, which appears in Listing 6.5, copies a group of unrelated files from one drive or directory to another.

If you always copy your files to a given directory, you could log onto the source directory and accomplish this with a batch file that contains the simple loop:

```
:start
IF "%1" = = " " GOTO end
COPY %1 B:
GOTO start
:end
```

You could even copy files from different directories by including a complete path specification as part of the parameter. However, you can build in even more flexibility by using the SET command.

CFILES.BAT takes advantage of the fact that the SHIFT command throws away each parameter after it is used. The syntax to invoke it is

CFILES *source destination FILE1.EXT FILE2.EXT. . .FILEN.EXT*

```
 1: ECHO OFF
 2: SET SRC=%1
 3: SET DEST=%2
 4: SHIFT
 5: SHIFT
 6: :start
 7: IF %1@==@ GOTO end
 8: COPY %SRC%\%1 %DEST%
 9: SHIFT
10: GOTO start
11: :end
12: SET SRC=
13: SET DEST=
```

Listing 6.5 ▲ *CFILES.BAT.*

Here is a line-by-line explanation of the relevant parts of the program.

2–3:   Assigns the source to the variable SRC and the destination to DEST. Both can be any valid drive or path specification.

4–5:   Executes two SHIFT commands to get to the third parameter on the command line.

6–11:   This is the loop described above, with a significant difference: each time the loop is executed, the proper source and destination directory names are called from the environment, while the file name is passed to the parameter %1.

12–13:   Removes the variables from the environment.

Modifying Variables in the Environment

Once you have used the SET command to place strings in the environment, you can later modify them. The easiest change to make is substituting one value for another. You accomplish this the same way you established the original value.

For example, you can use the SET command to establish what programmers call a *flag* to indicate whether a certain event has occurred or not. Let's assume that you use an EGA display card with an appropriate monitor and a RAM-resident program called EGAPRMOV.COM to alter the palette of colors displayed on your screen. This program in turn uses one of several programs called COSETNN.COM to establish particular palettes. (Don't look for these at your local software emporium; they were published in *PC Magazine*, 5, no. 15.) You want to call

EGAPRMOV only once, because it is loaded again every time you call it. You might include the command

SET EGA = false

in your AUTOEXEC.BAT file. Then, to load your EGA manager, you use the batch file shown in Listing 6.6.

The flag is tested in line 2 of this file. If the value of EGA, as established by the AUTOEXEC file, is not true, the complete file is executed. However, the value of this variable is changed to true by line 4 of this file. Therefore, the next time you run EGA.BAT to change the colors, line 2 will redirect execution past the call to EGAPRMOV, which is just what you want to happen.

DOS 3.X

If you use DOS 3.X, and you somehow run EGA.BAT before the EGA variable is placed in the environment, line 2 will generate a

Syntax error

message. This does no harm, but if you don't like it, you can fix it. In DOS 3.X, line 2 is interpreted as

IF = = true

The same line in DOS 2.X is interpreted as

IF EGA% = = true

which is a valid statement. To eliminate the error message, change line 2 to read

IF %EGA%@ = = %true@ GOTO continue

If you have not yet assigned a value to EGA, this line will be interpreted as

IF @ = = true@

which is a valid statement, although false. If you *have* assigned a value to EGA, the line will be interpreted as

IF true@ = = true@

You can also add to strings that are already in the environment. Let's say you want to keep track of which RAM-resident programs you have already loaded. This might remind you not to load a program that

```
1: ECHO OFF
2: IF %EGA%==%true GOTO continue
3: EGAPRMOV
4: SET EGA=true
5: :continue
6: COSET%1
```

Listing 6.6 ▲ *EGA.BAT.*

should be loaded first after a program that should be loaded last. If you load each of your resident programs using a batch file, you can easily do this. Each of these batch files should have

> SET TSR = %TSR%%0;

as its last line. This command will substitute the current value of the variable TSR for %TSR%. The first time this SET command is issued, of course, the value of %TSR% will be null, because you haven't yet placed the variable TSR in the environment.

Let's say the first RAM-resident program you load is SuperKey. You load it with a file called KEY.BAT, which ends with this line. When you run KEY.BAT your environment will include the variable

> TSR = KEY;

If you then call Ready! with a file called READY.BAT, the SET command in that file will substitute

> KEY;

for %TSR% and add the %0 parameter—the name of the batch file— to it. The next time you type SET, you will see, among other things

> TSR = KEY;READY;

You could use this technique to keep a running record of files you have opened, people who have used your computer, software packages you have used, or anything else. Of course, this information will disappear when you reboot the computer. In Chapter 13 you'll see some other applications for this technique.

Complex Conditional Tests

The WSRAM.BAT program, shown in Listing 6.7, demonstrates an even more powerful use of the SET command. You may have noticed that the batch language does not include any form of AND or OR.

```
 1: ECHO OFF
 2: IF %2@==@ GOTO lparam
 3: SET SRCDIR=%1
 4: SET FILE=%2
 5: GOTO continue
 6: :lparam
 7: IF %1@==@ GOTO noparam
 8: YN Is %1 a file
 9: IF ERRORLEVEL 1 GOTO file
10: SET SRCDIR=%1
11: SET FILE=NOFILE
12: GOTO continue
13: :file
14: SET FILE=%1
15: SET SRCDIR=WORDSTAR
16: GOTO continue
17: :noparam
18: SET SRCDIR=WORDSTAR
19: SET FILE=NOFILE
20: :continue
21: COPY C:\WORDSTAR\WS*.OVR D:>NUL
22: CD \%SRCDIR%
23: IF EXIST %FILE% COPY %FILE% D:
24: D:
25: CD C:\WORDSTAR
26: IF %FILE%==%NOFILE GOTO nofile
27: C:WSR %FILE%
28: COPY %FILE% C:\%SRCDIR%
29: GOTO finish
30: :nofile
31: C:WSR
32: :finish
33: C:
34: SET SRCDIR=
35: SET FILE=
```

Listing 6.7 ▲ *WSRAM.BAT.*

With a combination of YN, ERRORLEVEL, and SET, however, you can overcome this deficiency.

The purpose of the program is to allow you to edit a file on a RAM disk in WordStar 3.3. The file may be located in any directory on a hard disk. This program is necessary because WordStar has several quirks. First, although you can configure WordStar 3.3 so that it will find its overlay files on any drive you specify, as a rule, it can find them only if they are in the current directory of that drive. Second, WordStar can be made to open a specified file automatically if invoked with the syntax

WS *FILENAME.EXT*

The WSRAM.BAT program is designed to overcome the first quirk and to take advantage of the second. In addition, it checks the command line for two different types of parameters and takes appropriate action.

(Granted, there are easier ways to accomplish the same thing—I'll even show you one before the end of this chapter—but this complex exercise will demonstrate all the power lurking in the SET command.)

The syntax for executing this program is

WSRAM *PATH FILENAME.EXT*

The complexity is created by the fact that neither of the parameters is required, and different actions must be taken if both are given, if none are given, or if either one is given.

Although the language militates against the practice, I have created a series of modules, each of which is self-contained. Different modules will be executed depending on the conditions encountered.

Here is an overview of the program.

1–2: Turns off screen echoing; checks to see if a second parameter is present.

3–5: Statements to be executed if two parameters are given.

6–12: **:1param** module. This module is to be executed if there is no second parameter. Within this module is a conditional test using the YN program. If the single parameter is a path name, the rest of this module is to be executed. Otherwise, execution is directed to the **:file** module.

13–16: **:file** module. This module is to be executed if the first parameter is a file name.

17–19: **:noparam** module. This module is to be executed if there are no parameters on the command line.

20–29: **:continue** module. This module sets up the necessary housekeeping and contains another conditional test. Two different forms are given for invoking WordStar, depending on whether or not a file is to be opened. If not, execution is directed to the **:nofile** module.

30–31: **:nofile** module. This module contains the invocation for loading WordStar without opening a file.

32–35: **:finish** module. This module performs the cleanup work after leaving WordStar. (In Chapter 15, we'll add some additional code to make this program automatically back up the newly created or edited files to the proper directory of the hard disk.)

The flowchart in Figure 6.3 gives a graphic representation of the relationship between the modules in the program.

Now let's go over the details of the program, so you can understand what the SET, YN, and ERRORLEVEL commands are doing. The program makes the following assumptions:

1. The hard disk contains a directory called \WORDSTAR.

2. This directory includes WordStar's overlay files and a version of WordStar called WSR.COM.

3. WSR.COM has been configured to find the overlays on drive D.

4. Drive D is a RAM disk.

You will note that the program uses two environment variables: SRCDIR, for the source directory, and FILE, for the name of the file to be copied to the RAM disk and opened. The first test occurs in line 2. If both the source directory and the file name are specified on the command line, each is assigned to the appropriate variable name. The various tests are not needed, and execution skips over all the intervening modules, resuming at the **:continue** module.

So far, we have only checked for the existence of a second parameter. We have yet to determine whether there is a first parameter. If the test in line 2 finds no parameter, execution is directed to the **:1param** module, which tests for a single parameter in line 7. If none is found, execution continues at the **:noparam** module.

If there is a parameter, the program needs to know whether it is a file or a path name. This is asked of the user directly, by way of the YN command in line 8. If the parameter is a directory, its name is assigned to SRCDIR on line 10, and the value NOFILE is assigned to FILE on line 11. Later, the program will check to see if this value has been assigned, so that appropriate action can be taken if no file name has been given.

If the parameter is a file rather than a path name, line 9 directs execution to the **:file** module. In this module, the name of the file is assigned to the variable FILE. If you have not entered a path name as one of the parameters, \WORDSTAR is used as the default directory and assigned to SRCDIR.

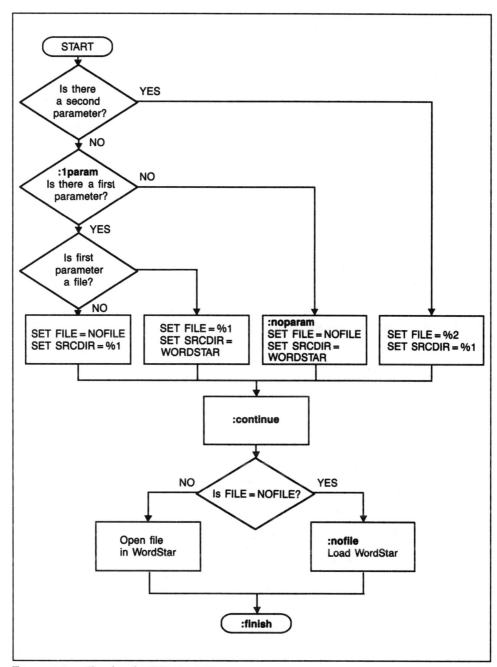

Figure 6.3 ▲ *Flowchart for WSRAM.BAT.*

Finally, if no parameters are given, the NOFILE flag is set, and the default directory is assigned in the **:noparam** module.

The real work of the program is contained in the **:continue** module. Here is a line-by-line explanation of this module.

21:     Copies the WordStar overlay files to the RAM disk.

22:     Makes the directory on the command line the current directory. If no directory is given, \WORDSTAR becomes the current directory.

23:     Checks the directory to see if the specified file already exists. If it does, it is copied to the RAM disk. If not, it will be created on the RAM disk.

24:     Makes drive D the current drive.

25:     Checks the FILE variable to see if a file name has been specified. If not, execution is directed to the **:nofile** module.

26:     Makes \WORDSTAR the current directory on drive C. (**Note:** If the \WORDSTAR directory is on the search path, this line should be omitted.)

DOS 3.X

Since DOS 3.X allows you to execute a program on a directory other than the current one (earlier versions do not), users of DOS 3.X should omit line 26 and change line 27 to read

    C:\WORDSTAR\WSR %FILE%

and line 31 to read

    C:\WORDSTAR\WSR %FILE%

27:     Invokes WordStar from drive C, and tells it to open the specified file if it exists or to create it if it does not.

28:     Backs up the new file to the directory specified on the command line, or to the \WORDSTAR directory if no directory was specified.

29:     Skips over the **:nofile** module.

The **:nofile** module, which follows, simply invokes WordStar from the hard disk. Its directory was already made current in line 26, unless the \WORDSTAR directory is on the search path or DOS 3.X is being used. Since no file name has been given, the only way to back up the new file automatically would be with a ✳.✳ command. However, this command would also back up the WordStar overlays, which you probably don't want to happen. Therefore, this module does not include automatic backup. In Chapter 10, I'll show you how to modify WSRAM.BAT so that it will back up any files except the overlays.

ADDING POWER THROUGH MACROS

You can do most of what the WSRAM.BAT program does with a great deal less work by using a simple self-executing macro. Although, as a rule, macro processors do not allow you to create and name variables, they do allow you to create a macro that assigns a series of keystrokes to a specific key. That key can then be invoked during the execution of the macro that created it. This is almost the same as assigning a value to a variable.

Let's take a slightly different situation to demonstrate this technique, and we'll solve a rather annoying problem at the same time. As you probably know, you can set up an AUTOEXEC.BAT file to take care of all the housekeeping you normally perform before beginning work in your application program. You can set the date and time, or read the battery clock if you have one; load your macro processor and/or your desk-accessory program; and create a RAM disk and copy the necessary files to it—all before beginning your work. The file will execute with no user intervention, unless you have included a DATE, TIME, or PAUSE command.

However, many programs will, if given a file name in their command line invocation, open the named file immediately upon beginning execution. This technique will work for any such program.

We'll assume the following conditions:

1. You have a system with two floppy disk drives and a RAM disk, but no hard disk.

2. You want to run WordStar (or some other application) on the RAM disk.

3. You also want your application to open a file on the RAM disk.

4. You don't always start your day using the same file.

Now there's a catch here. There is no point at which you can pass a parameter to the AUTOEXEC.BAT file. And you don't want to include the name of the file that you will use in a command in the AUTOEXEC.BAT file because you don't always use the same one. What you need is some way of telling DOS which file should be copied to the RAM disk. Even now, SuperKey is rushing to the rescue.

A Self-Executing Macro

Instead of including the command to invoke the program and open the file, the AUTOEXEC.BAT file shown in Listing 6.8 takes you up to that point and then transfers control to SuperKey, which will execute the command for you. Lines 1 through 3 of the program take care of the housekeeping and set up the RAM disk. Lines 4 through 6 place Word-Star on the RAM disk and make the RAM disk the default disk. Finally, SuperKey (which is assumed to be on drive A, along with its macro files) is invoked and told to load the macro file LOADFILE. (The /ML at the end of the command means *macro load*. Other macro processors may use a command such as /R for *read* or other syntax. Consult your manual.)

The LOADFILE macro appears in Listing 6.9. The <AUTO> in the first line of this macro means *automatic*, or self-executing. The entire macro is arbitrarily assigned to the CTR key on the keypad; you can assign it to another key if you prefer. As soon as it is loaded, the macro turns screen echoing off, which in this case has the effect of suppressing the DOS prompt (it can be distracting). Next, the macro displays the message

What file do you want to load?

Note that a new key definition begins immediately thereafter. Whatever is typed in response to this message is assigned to the Shift-F1 key. (This is not as arbitrary as the first key assignment. In Chapter 14, I'll show you a macro that can make use of the definition to back up the file to a floppy disk automatically.)

After the user types a response and presses Return, the macro issues an Escape character, so that the line, which is not a proper DOS command, will not be executed. Next, the macro executes the <ENTER> command (which has the same effect as pressing the Return key) to get another invisible DOS prompt. This prompt displays the message

What drive is it on?

```
 1: DATE
 2: TIME
 3: RAMDRIVE 320K
 4: COPY WS.COM C:
 5: COPY WS*.OVR C:
 6: COPY START.BAT C:
 7: C:
 8: A:KEY LOADFILE /ML
```

Listing 6.8 ▲ *AUTOEXEC.BAT File for Starting WordStar on a RAM Disk.*

```
 1: <BEGDEF><CtrlCTR><AUTO>
 2: ECHO OFF<ENTER>
 3: What file do you want to load? <BEGDEF><ShftF1>
 4: <ENDDEF>
 5: <ESC><ENTER>
 6: What drive is it on? <BEGDEF><ShftF2><ENDDEF>
 7: <ESC><ENTER>
 8: ECHO ON<ENTER>
 9: COPY <ShftF2><ShftF1> C:<ENTER>
10: <CMD>OW+<CMD>C:WS <ShftF1><ENTER>
11: <ENDDEF>
```

Listing 6.9 ▲ *LOADFILE.MAC.*

and the response is assigned to Shift-F2, again arbitrarily. Now, here's
where the program really does its work. Let's say you typed

    MYFILE

in response to the first message, and

    B:

in response to the second. Screen echoing is then turned back on, so
that the normal DOS commands will be displayed at a prompt. The following line enters the characters

    COPY

and executes the macros assigned to Shift-F2 and Shift-F1. Since these
macros are the responses you typed, the command line reads:

    COPY B:MYFILE C:

This is a perfectly valid DOS command, and DOS duly executes it. The
following line issues the macro processor's Disk Wait command, so that
the next command won't be issued until the copying is completed.

When it is, another valid command appears on the command line:

C:WS MYFILE

This command invokes WordStar and opens the specified file on the RAM disk. As this macro is executing, the screen looks like Figure 6.4.

Using a Macro as a Batch File

You can also use a macro processor to create and execute a batch file for you. One of the annoying things about complex batch files is that it's easy to forget the exact syntax required. CFILES.BAT (Listing 6.5), for example, requires you to enter the source and destination directories before you enter any file names. To make your work easier, you could create the same file as a macro and have it prompt you for input, as shown in Listing 6.10. You might include it in a file of macros to be loaded whenever you leave an application and return to DOS. (A sample of such a file appears in Chapter 17).

This listing is actually two macros, one of which is called by the other, creating a loop. The first one *must* appear before the second in the macro file, or it will not be executed properly. The file creates three key definitions "on the fly:" it assigns the source directory to Ctrl-1, the

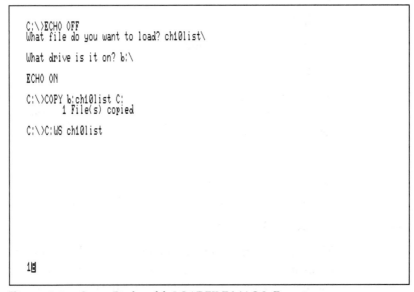

```
C:\>ECHO OFF
What file do you want to load? ch10list\

What drive is it on? b:\

ECHO ON

C:\>COPY b:ch10list C:
        1 File(s) copied

C:\>C:WS ch10list




1▓
```

Figure 6.4 ▲ *Screen Display while LOADFILE.MAC Is Executing.*

target directory to Alt-1, and the file name to Ctrl-2.

The primary macro, which is assigned to Alt-F5, begins in line 9. When you press that key combination, the screen clears and displays

What are the source drive and directory?

If you want the current directory of the current drive, just specify either one. If you want the root directory, however, you should *not* end the entry with a backslash, e.g.,

B:

When a source is entered, its directory is displayed by line 13, and the prompt

What are the destination drive and directory?

appears. The macro waits for input before proceeding. When the second prompt has been answered, the macro assigned to Ctrl-F5 is called, which displays the prompt

File to copy?

When this prompt has been answered, the COPY command is issued and executed, and the message

To copy more files press Ctrl-F5

is displayed. If the user presses that key, the macro displays the

File to copy?

```
 1: <BEGDEF><CtrlF5>ECHO OFF<ENTER>
 2: File to copy? <BEGDEF><Ctrl2><ENDDEF>
 3: <Esc><ENTER>
 4: COPY <Ctrl1>\<Ctrl2> <Alt1><ENTER>
 5: To copy more files press Ctrl-F5
 6: <Esc><ENTER>
 7: ECHO ON<ENTER>
 8: <ENDDEF>
 9: <BEGDEF><AltF5>ECHO OFF<ENTER>
10: CLS<ENTER>
11: What are the source drive and directory? <BEGDEF><Ctrl1><ENDDEF>
12: <Esc><ENTER>
13: DIR <Ctrl1> /W<ENTER>
14: What are the destination drive and directory? <BEGDEF><Alt1><ENDDEF>
15: <Esc><ENTER>
16: <CtrlF5>
17: <ENDDEF>
```

Listing 6.10 ▲ *Using a Macro as a Batch File.*

prompt again. The first prompt won't be shown again because the macro that assigns the source and target directories is invoked by Alt-F5, not Ctrl-F5. These assignments will not change until you press Alt-F5 again and enter new responses. The resulting screen display will look something like Figure 6.5.

Tips on Debugging Macro Files

If you create your macro files in a text editor, rather than "on the fly" or in the macro editor, you may find that some of them are not behaving as you expected. If you have a large macro file, you may have some trouble finding the errors. The most common error is the omission of a delimiter character around a key name (a < or >, or a [or], depending on the program that you are using). About equally common is a missing <BEGDEF> or <ENDDEF> statement. One way you can locate the error is to look in the window that displays the names of the keys to which macros have been assigned. If some that you know you have assigned are missing, and you know the order in which your macros are listed, you can narrow down the location of the error. The last one

```
What are the source drive and directory? b:\

DIR b: /W

 Volume in drive B has no label
 Directory of  B:\

NEWPT1   DB     NEWPT1   SAV    CH5LIST          CH5LST   CHS    CH5LST   YN
FORMATS  MAC    CH5             CH6              CH6HEADS        CH6LIST  TMP
CFILES   MAC    LOADFILE MAC    CH6FIGS          CH6LIST
        14 File(s)   149504 bytes free
What are the destination drive and directory? c:\unfiled\

ECHO OFF
File to copy? newpt1.db\

COPY b:\newpt1.db c:\unfiled
        1 File(s) copied
To copy more files press Ctrl-F5\

ECHO ON

C:\>_
```

Figure 6.5 ▲ *Screen Display from CFILES.MAC.*

before the missing key probably does not have an <ENDDEF> (or you spelled it <ENDEF>), or else the first missing key may not have a <BEGDEF>.

REDIRECTION, PIPES, AND FILTERS

CHAPTER

7

ONE OF THE FEATURES that gives DOS so much power is its ability to redirect input and output. Under normal circumstances, your computer looks for input from the keyboard (also referred to as the *standard input device*) and displays the results on the screen (the *standard output device*). This combination of keyboard and screen is called the *console* (which is what CON refers to in the COPY CON command). However, you can also send output to other devices, or to a file.

You are no doubt already familiar with redirecting output to a printer by using its device name as if it were a file name.

COPY *FILENAME.EXT* **PRN**

copies the file *FILENAME.EXT* to the printer. Similarly,

COPY *FILENAME.EXT* **COM1:**

will send the file to whatever device is attached to your first serial port. There is, however, another way to accomplish the same thing—one which gives you a great deal of control over the ultimate result. This technique is called *redirection*.

Redirection not only allows you to send data along a path other than the standard one, but also, through the use of pipes and filters, to make changes to the data on the way. In later chapters, you will learn many practical applications for redirecting data and using pipes and filters.

REDIRECTING INPUT AND OUTPUT

There are three symbols used to redirect input and output:

- ▲ > directs the output of a command to the destination specified after the symbol.

- ▲ < directs input into a command from the source specified after the symbol.

- ▲ >> directs output to the end of an existing file, or to a new file if the specified file does not exist.

Hint: You can include or omit the spaces around the redirection symbols without affecting the way they work.

Redirecting Output

The simplest use of redirection is to send output to a destination other than the screen. If the file in the COPY command examples shown at the beginning of this chapter were a text file, the commands

TYPE *FILENAME.EXT* >PRN

and

TYPE *FILENAME.EXT* >COM1:

would have the same effects as those commands. However, output redirection is useful is some circumstances where the COPY command will not work. For example, you cannot get a printed listing of a disk directory by typing

COPY DIR PRN

This command would result in a

File not found

message because there is no DIR file, and if you created one, DOS wouldn't find it. However, the command

DIR >PRN

will work just fine.

Redirection is very useful with batch file commands. For example, if the code to set your printer to condensed print is Esc-C, you could create a batch file that contained the single command

ECHO ^[C >PRN

Then all you would have to do in order to set your printer to condensed mode would be to enter the name of the file.

It is sometimes quite helpful to direct the output of a command to a file or the printer. Some programs that are not part of DOS generate a number of messages as they execute. You could let such a program run unattended and still be aware of any errors that may have occurred by redirecting the output to a file or to the printer. (DOS error messages are not redirected.)

DOS 3.X

There are other reasons to direct output to a file. You might want a complete record of all the files on your hard disk, for example. In DOS 3.X,

TREE /F

would display this information on your screen, but it might go by too fast for you to examine it. Moreover, on a large disk with a great many files, this command could take quite a long time to execute. If you entered the command as

TREE /F >HARDDISK.DIR

the information would appear in the file HARDDISK.DIR. You could load this file into your word processor, delete all the blank lines, and read it at leisure.

Similarly, if you back up your hard disk in increments, you may want to direct the output of the BACKUP command to your printer. Then you could run the BACKUP program unattended and have a printed list of all the files that had been backed up.

DOS 2.X

In DOS 2.X, the TREE command with the /F (for *files*) switch will not display the names of files in a root directory. However, you can accomplish the same thing with the command

CHKDSK /V >HARDDISK.DIR

The CHKDSK command with the /V (for *verbose*) switch will give you a considerably more compact listing of the files. Each file will be preceded by its path name, instead of grouped below several empty lines.

The >> operator is also used to direct output to a file. If the file does not already exist, it functions the same as the > operator. However, if the file does exist, this operator will *append* the output of the command to the file. If you have DOS 2.X, you could use the >> operator to create a small batch file that would emulate the TREE /F command of DOS 3.X. Such a file appears in Listing 7.1. Line 3 of this program creates the file HARD-DISK.DIR and copies the listing of the root directory to it. Line 4 appends the listing created by the TREE /F command to the existing file, so that it contains the names of all the files on your disk.

Similarly, you could create a catalog of all your floppy disks by placing a catalog disk in drive B, logging onto drive A, and then issuing the command

DIR >> B:DISKCAT

If you want to automate the process, log onto drive B and copy the batch file shown in Listing 7.2 onto your catalog disk. This program will beep and prompt you when it is time to switch disks. At the pause, press Ctrl-C or Ctrl- Break to stop the catalog program.

Redirecting Input

The principle of redirecting input is the same as that of redirecting output, except that redirected input *must* come from a file (wouldn't it be nice if you could reinsert text into a damaged file by redirecting input from the printer?). You can redirect input from a file to any DOS command that requires input. Most often, however, redirected input is used with the DOS filters described later in this chapter.

Redirecting input does have its uses. You saw an example of this in Chapter 6, when we created YN.COM and CHOOSE.COM. Here is another. Suppose, that you wanted to make a whole series of copies of a single floppy disk. You want to ensure the integrity of the copies, so you create the following batch file:

```
DISKCOPY A: B:
DISKCOMP A: B:
%0
```

This simple program will do the job. However, both the DISKCOPY and DISKCOMP commands prompt you for a keystroke twice. You thus have to press keys on four separate occasions to make each copy. DUPE.BAT, shown in Listing 7.3, streamlines the process. It takes its input from a text file called FLOPPIES, and copies the disk in drive A to a diskette in drive B. For this program to work, DUPE.BAT, FLOPPIES, and both the DISKCOPY and DISKCOMP programs must be on a drive other than A or B, and on the search path.

The file FLOPPIES contains

.N

```
1: ECHO OFF
2: CD\
3: DIR > HARDDISK.DIR
4: TREE /F >> HARDDISK.DIR
```

Listing 7.1 ▲ *ALLFILES.BAT.*

```
1: ECHO OFF
2: DIR A: >> DISKCAT
3: ECHO ^GInsert next disk for cataloguing in drive A.
4: PAUSE
5: %0
```

Listing 7.2 ▲ *DISKCAT.BAT.*

```
1: DISKCOPY A: B:<FLOPPIES
2: DISKCOMP A: B:<FLOPPIES
3: PAUSE ^GInsert a blank disk in drive B:
4: %0
```

Listing 7.3 ▲ *DUPE.BAT.*

without a carriage return. The file serves as input to both the DISKCOPY and DISKCOMP commands. The redirected input keeps the DISKCOPY command from waiting for you to press a key. Therefore, before you invoke the program by typing DUPE, you must have your source and destination disks in drives A and B, respectively.

Here is what happens as soon as you enter the command:

1:        Invokes the DISKCOPY command, and tells it to take its input from the FLOPPIES file. When DISKCOPY displays the message

       Strike a key when ready . . .

       it accepts the period from the file as a keystroke and proceeds immediately to copy the disk in drive A. When DISKCOPY displays the message

       Copy another (Y/N)?

       the N in the file is read, and understood as a keystroke.

2:        Invokes DISKCOMP, to ensure the integrity of the copy. Again, the FLOPPIES file is used to direct input to the command, so you don't have to press a key.

3–4:   Since ECHO has not been turned off, the PAUSE command can display a message, as well as wait for a keystroke. The message includes a Ctrl-G, which sounds a beep. This gives you a chance to switch disks in the destination drive before the program calls itself in line 4.

With this program, you can copy and compare floppy disks with only a single keystroke, instead of four, and you are warned with a beep when your intervention is needed.

Warning: You cannot use input redirection to supply command-line arguments to a command, and you also cannot redirect input into a batch program. Moreover, whenever you use input redirection, you risk locking up your computer or losing data if your input file is not constructed exactly as it should be, because you lose access to your keyboard.

PIPES

The redirection techniques we have discussed can be used to make the output of one program the input to another. For example, if you have a program called PROG1 that produces the data needed by a second program called PROG2, you could have the first program send the data to a file, and then redirect that file as input to the second program. The commands

> **PROG1 >PROG.DAT**
> **PROG2 <PROG.DAT**

will send the output from PROG1 to PROG.DAT, and the information in PROG.DAT will be used as input to PROG2. But you could use a *pipe* instead to accomplish the same thing with a single command.

You create a pipe by placing the name of each program through which the data will be passed on a command line, separating the names of the programs with a vertical bar (¦). Thus, the command

> **PROG1 ¦ PROG2**

does the same thing as the two previous commands, without creating an intermediate file, because DOS creates the intermediate file for you.

You can place as many programs in a pipeline as necessary. Often, the programs that are used in a pipeline are filters, which are discussed in the next section.

THE DOS FILTERS

A *filter* is a program that takes input from another program and changes it in some way. DOS includes three external programs that act as filters: MORE.COM, SORT.EXE, and FIND.EXE. These filters can be used in a pipeline to accomplish tasks for which highly complex pieces of software have been written. Since these are external DOS programs, they must be on the default directory or the search path if you want to use them.

MORE

Perhaps the easiest of the filters to understand is MORE. Its effect is the same as the /P switch to the DIR command, but it can be used with any ASCII text file. Thus, you can display any file a screen at a time by typing

> **MORE <*FILENAME.EXT***

After each screenful of data appears, the message

> ---More---

or

> **Strike a key when ready**

appears at the bottom of the screen (the message depends on which version of MS-DOS you are using).

In a pipeline, the syntax

> **TYPE** *FILENAME.EXT* ¦ **MORE**

is identical in effect to the previous example. Similarly,

> **DIR** ¦ **MORE**

is the same as DIR /P. However,

> **MORE <DIR**

will result in a

> **File not found**

message because DOS will look for a file named DIR to use as input to the MORE filter.

SORT

The SORT filter sorts the information in a text file or in a directory. It can sort on any column you specify. It is most useful if the file that you want to sort is a series of fixed-length records.

To display a directory sorted by file name, type

> **DIR** ¦ **SORT**

The command

> **DIR >SORT**

would not work for this purpose. It would result in the unsorted text of the directory being redirected to a file called SORT.

To sort on a column other than the first one, use the /+ switch, followed by the number of the column on which to sort (the first screen column, or, in a file, the first column after a carriage return, is 1, not 0). Thus, to sort a directory by file name extension, rather than by file name, type

> **DIR** ¦ **SORT /+10**

This will sort the directory by the tenth column, which is the first column of the extension.

SORT also can sort in reverse order. The /R switch reverses the normal ASCII sorting order. It can be used in conjunction with the /+ switch. For example:

DIR ¦ SORT / + 10/R

will give you a directory display sorted by extension in reverse alphabetical order.

FIND

The FIND filter is used to find particular examples of text in a file. The syntax is

FIND *"searchtext" FILE1.EXT FILE2.EXT . . . FILEn.EXT*

where "*searchtext*" is the pattern of characters that you want to find, enclosed in quotation marks. You can include as many files as necessary in the list of files to be searched, but you cannot use wild cards.

The case of the search text must be specified exactly. Uppercase characters will not be found if you specify the text in lowercase characters, and vice versa.

You can search for a quotation mark by preceding it with another quotation mark. Thus, if you want to find

"*I didn't like him,*" *said Ferdinand.*

the syntax would be

FIND ""I didn't like him,"" said Ferdinand." THISFILE.TXT

After the program runs, it will display the name of the file or files searched, followed by a copy of each line containing the specified text, as illustrated in Figure 7.1. Of course, you can use redirection to send the output of the FIND command to a file or a printer.

Hint: You may notice that not all lines where listings are mentioned in the previous two chapters appear in Figure 7.1. This is the result of the WordStar control codes, which change the final characters of words to the ASCII character with a value of 128 more than the character that you typed. You can display the additional lines by first passing the file through a filter that will strip the high-order bits from the file, so that no character has an ASCII value higher than 127. The program WSSTRIP, presented later in this chapter, does exactly that.

The FIND command has three switches:

▲ The /N switch precedes the actual display of the line with a number representing the number of lines from the beginning of the file to the current line, as shown in Figure 7.2.

▲ The /C switch displays only a count of the number of times the search pattern was found in each file.

▲ The /V switch displays only those lines *not* containing the search string. (You'll see a use for this in the program shown in Listing 7.5.)

A Directory of Subdirectories   A simple, short file will display a list of all the subdirectories on the specified drive. SUBS.BAT, shown in Listing 7.4, filters the specified directory through the FIND filter to display only

```
B>FIND "Listing" CH5 CH6

---------- CH5
Insert Listing 5.2
BListing 5.2: MOVETHEM.BAT.B
is shown in Listing 5.3. Then, when you type
Insert Listing 5.3
BListing 5.3: BACKIT.BAT.B

---------- CH6
Insert Listing 6.3
BListing 6.3: Characters for Creating YN.COM by the Entry Method.B
Insert Listing 6.4
Insert Listing 6.7
BListing 6.7: CFILES.BAT.B
Insert Listing 6.8
BListing 6.8: RAMWS.BAT.B
Insert Listing 6.9
macro appears in Listing 6.18.
Insert Listing 6.18
BListing 6.18: LOADFILE.MAC.B
Insert Listing 6.11
BListing 6.11: A Batch File in a Macro.B

B>_
```

Figure 7.1 ▲ *Output from the FIND Command.*

those entries that are subdirectory names. Since subdirectories are indicated in a directory listing by the tag

<DIR>

and the less-than symbol does not appear elsewhere in a directory listing, all we need to do is find that character. The syntax is

SUBS *DRIVE*

where *DRIVE* is the drive specifier, including the colon.

Hint: The Norton Utilities includes a program called LD, or LISTDIR, which does the same thing as this batch file. Similarly, when you ask PC Tools for a directory, it first displays a tree diagram showing all the directories on the specified disk.

```
B>FIND /N "Listing" CH5 CH6

---------- CH5
[295]Insert Listing 5.2
[296]ðListing 5.2: MOVETHEM.BAT.ð
[358]is shown in Listing 5.3. Then½ whef yoJ type
[365]Insert Listing 5.3
[366]ðListing 5.3: BACKIT.BAT.ð

---------- CH6
[909]Insert Listing 6.3
[910]ðListing 6.3: Characters for Creating YN.COM by the Entry Method.ð
[912]Insert Listing 6.4
[1158]Insert Listing 6.7
[1159]ðListing 6.7: CFILES.BAT.ð
[1221]Insert Listing 6.8
[1222]ðListing 6.8: RAMWS.BAT.ð
[1403]Insert Listing 6.9
[1414]macro appears in Listing 6.10.
[1416]Insert Listing 6.10
[1417]ðListing 6.10: LOADFILE.MAC.ð
[1491]Insert Listing 6.11
[1492]ðListing 6.11: A Batch File in a Macro.ð

B>_
```

Figure 7.2 ▲ *Output from the FIND Command with the /N Switch.*

```
1: ECHO OFF
2: ECHO Subdirectories in %1 directory:
3: DIR %1 |FIND "<"
```

Listing 7.4 ▲ *SUBS.BAT.*

Seeing Everything Except Subdirectories   NOSUB.BAT displays a list of all entries except subdirectories on the specified drive. It uses the /V switch to tell FIND to display everything *except* the entries with less-than symbols. This program appears in Listing 7.5.

Finding Information in the Environment   Since the FIND filter always displays a complete line, you can use it to examine variables in the environment. Let's expand on the technique described in Chapter 6 for keeping track of the RAM-resident programs you have loaded. You might want to view this information without all the extraneous data the SET command displays. You could use the simple batch file, TSR.BAT, shown in Listing 7.6, to view just the value of the TSR variable. When you execute this program, the screen would display a line such as

```
TSR = KEY;WTH;HB;
```

If there were no such string in the environment, the program would display nothing on the screen except the ECHO OFF command.

MORE COMPLEX PIPES

There is no reason you can't pass a file through several filters, or through the same filter more than once. This technique can be very useful for narrowing down a search to a few specific instances. For example, suppose you have a phone directory on disk, in the form of an ASCII file of fixed-length records. Each record includes a last name,

```
1: ECHO OFF
2: ECHO Files in %1 directory:
3: DIR %1 |FIND /V "<"
```

Listing 7.5 ▲ *NOSUB.BAT.*

```
1: ECHO OFF
2: SET|FIND "TSR"
```

Listing 7.6 ▲ *TSR.BAT.*

first name, address, occupation, and phone number. You recently talked with a salesman named Jones from somewhere in Chicago, and now you want to place an order. But you deal with several salesmen, clients, and engineers named Jones, and some of them are from Chicago. So you enter the command

> FIND "Jones" PHONE.DIR ¦ FIND "Sales" ¦ FIND "Chicago"

This command will first find all the lines in the PHONE.DIR file that contain the name Jones. This information will be passed through the FIND filter a second time to find all the listings that include the word "Sales." Finally, the remaining entries will be passed through the filter a third time, so that the output includes only those salesmen named Jones who are based in Chicago. The result might look something like Figure 7.3. You could easily sort the records in alphabetical order and send the result to a printer by adding

> ¦ SORT>PRN

to the end of the pipeline. In Chapter 10, we will look at several batch files that use equally complex pipes to copy selected groups of files and to sort directories by very specific criteria.

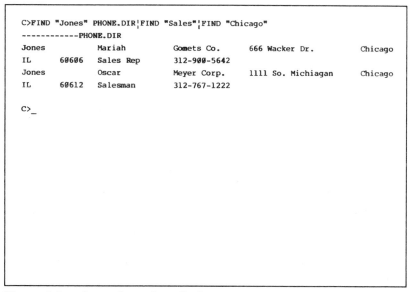

```
C>FIND "Jones" PHONE.DIR¦FIND "Sales"¦FIND "Chicago"
------------PHONE.DIR
Jones          Mariah        Gomets Co.       666 Wacker Dr.        Chicago
IL     60606   Sales Rep     312-900-5642
Jones          Oscar         Meyer Corp.      1111 So. Michiagan    Chicago
IL     60612   Salesman      312-767-1222

C>_
```

Figure 7.3 ● *Output from a Long Pipeline.*

CREATING AND USING YOUR OWN FILTERS

In addition to the filters supplied with DOS, you can create your own to serve other purposes. The examples in this section are BASIC programs.

Converting Lowercase Characters to Uppercase

UPSHIFT.BAS, shown in Listing 7.7, changes all lowercase letters and graphics characters to the uppercase equivalents of the low-order ASCII values. This program is designed to be compiled with a compiler such as the IBM BASIC Compiler or Microsoft's QuickBASIC Compiler. If you create UPSHIFT.BAS with the BASIC editor, you must save it with the syntax

    SAVE "UPSHIFT.BAS", A

so that it will be saved as an ASCII text file. To compile the program using either the IBM or Microsoft compiler, you must use the parameters

    /O/V;

after the name of the file to be compiled. The result will be a .EXE program that can have a file redirected to it as input or that can be used in a pipeline. Thus, for example,

    UPSHIFT < TEXTFILE

will display the file TEXTFILE on the screen entirely in uppercase characters.

Warning: The filters in both UPSHIFT and WSSTRIP.BAS will work *only* if you compile them. A command of the form

    TYPE TEXTFILE.WS ¦ BASICA WSSTRIP > TEXTFILE.ASC

simply will not work.

Here is a brief explanation of UPSHIFT.

10: Sets text and border colors to yellow (you can safely omit this line).

```
10  COLOR 14,0,6
100 KEY 15, CHR$(&H4)+CHR$(&H2E):ON KEY(15) GOSUB 200:KEY(15) ON
110 A$=INPUT$(1):A=ASC(A$)
120 IF A=26 GOTO 200
130 IF A>127 THEN A=A-128
140 IF A>96 THEN A=A-32
150 PRINT CHR$(A);
160 GOTO 110
200 END
```

Listing 7.7 ▲ *UPSHIFT.BAS.*

100: Enables trapping of Ctrl-C from the keyboard, so you can break out of the program.

110: Gets a single character from the input file; finds the character's ASCII value.

120: Checks for Ctrl-Z (end-of-file mark); ends the program if it is found.

130: Checks for graphics characters; converts them to standard ASCII.

140: Checks for normal lowercase characters; converts them to uppercase (see the ASCII table in Appendix H to see why this works).

150: Prints the converted character (on the screen if output is not redirected elsewhere).

160: Returns to line 110 to get the next character from the file.

You can also use this program from the keyboard by typing UPSHIFT at a DOS prompt. However, you will have to press Return after pressing Ctrl-C to exit the program, and no cursor appears on the screen while you are using the program.

Converting a WordStar File to ASCII

WSSTRIP.BAS, shown in Listing 7.8, changes a WordStar file to an ASCII file, deleting all the control codes (and, incidentally, any graphics characters that are not WordStar formatting codes) and fixing the ends of lines so that the lines break where the margins appear in WordStar. It must be compiled in the same way as UPSHIFT.

```
10 COLOR 11,0,3
100 KEY 15,CHR$(&H4)+CHR$(&H2E):ON KEY(15) GOSUB 300:KEY(15) ON
110 A$=INPUT$(1):A=ASC(A$)
120 IF A=26 GOTO 300
130 IF A=31 THEN GOSUB 200                    'fix soft hyphen
140 IF A>127 THEN A=A-128                      'strip high-order bit
150 A$=CHR$(A):IF A<32 THEN A$=""             'strip control characters
160 B$=B$+A$:IF A=13 THEN PRINT B$:B$=""      'print when carriage retur
170 GOTO 110
200 A$=INPUT$(1):A=ASC(A$):IF A<>141 THEN 210 ELSE B$=B$+"-"
210 RETURN
300 END
```

Listing 7.8 ▲ *WSSTRIP.BAS.*

For example, the command

WSSTRIP<TESTFILE.WS>TEXTFILE.ASC

will read the file TEXTFILE.WS, send it through WSSTRIP, and create
the ASCII file TEXTFILE.ASC on the default directory.

WSSTRIP is similar to UPSHIFT, but it is slightly more sophisticated
because it must check for more conditions and perform a few more complex conversions. Also, rather than printing one character at a time, it
concatenates a string of converted characters and does not print this
string (B$) until a carriage return is encountered (line 160). The pro-
gram also fixes soft hyphens, so that they are deleted if they appear anywhere other than at the end of a line or turned into hard hyphens if they
are at the end of a line (lines 200 through 210). Control characters are
stripped out (line 150), but dot commands are not affected.

A Substitute for a WordStar Filter

If you don't have a compiler and need something to convert WordStar
files to ASCII, the program WSFILTER.BAS, shown in Listing 7.9,
will serve the purpose. To run it, you must first load BASICA. This program performs the same conversions as WSSTRIP.EXE. However,
instead of using DOS pipelines, it prompts you for the destination of the
modified file: the screen, another file, or a printer. In addition, it can
modify your file so that lines shorter or longer than 80 characters are
adjusted to an 80-column width. Figure 7.4 shows the input menu for
this program.

If you use a monochrome monitor, but still want to take advantage of the
inverse video and highlighting included in WSFILTER, you must make a
few changes. First, leave out the COLOR statement in line 100. Next in

```
10 '    WSFILTER.BAS  -- strips WordStar formatting characters and control
        characters from file; outputs to screen, printer, or file
100 COLOR 15,3,3: CLS: KEY OFF
110 PRINT: PRINT " Input file name";: COLOR 4: INPUT FILE$: COLOR 15
120 '
130 ' output destination menu
140 PRINT: PRINT " Output to: "
150 LOCATE  6,8: COLOR 11,4: PRINT " S ";: COLOR 4,3: PRINT "creen"
160 LOCATE  8,8: COLOR 11,4: PRINT " P ";: COLOR 4,3: PRINT "rinter"
170 LOCATE 10,8: COLOR 11,4: PRINT " F ";: COLOR 4,3: PRINT "ile"
180 LOCATE 12,3: COLOR 15: PRINT "YOUR CHOICE ==> ";
190    DEST$ = INKEY$: IF DEST$ = "" GOTO 190
200    COLOR 4: PRINT DEST$: COLOR 15
210    IF DEST$ = "f" OR DEST$ = "F" GOTO 260
220    IF DEST$ = "s" OR DEST$ = "S" THEN OUTP$ = "CON": GOTO 290
230    IF DEST$ = "p" OR DEST$ = "P" THEN OUTP$ = "LPT1": GOTO 290
240 DEST$ = "": GOTO 180
250 '
260 PRINT: PRINT " Output file name";: COLOR 4: INPUT OUTP$: COLOR 15
270 IF FILE$ = OUTP$ THEN PRINT: COLOR 4:
        INPUT " Overwrite existing file (Y/N)"; SAFE$: COLOR 15: ELSE GOTO 290
280 IF LEFT$(SAFE$,1) <> "y" AND LEFT$(SAFE$,1) <> "Y" GOTO 260
290 PRINT: PRINT " Adjust for 80 columns (Y/N)";: COLOR 4: INPUT COL$: COLOR 15
300 Y = CSRLIN + 2
310 IF LEFT$(COL$,1) = "y" OR LEFT$(COL$,1) = "Y" THEN COL$ = "Y"
320 '
330 OPEN FILE$ FOR INPUT AS #1
340 OPEN OUTP$ FOR OUTPUT AS #2
350 IF DEST$ = "s" OR DEST$ = "S" THEN CLS
360 IF DEST$ = "f" OR DEST$ = "F" THEN LOCATE Y,27: COLOR 11,4:
        PRINT " WORKING...PLEASE WAIT "
370 '
380 ' input from file
390 WHILE NOT EOF(1)
400    A$ = INPUT$(1,#1): A = ASC(A$)
410    IF A = 141 AND COL$ = "Y" THEN GOSUB 600   'strip soft carriage return
420    IF A = 31 AND COL$ <> "Y" THEN GOSUB 700   'fix soft hyphen
430    IF A > 127 THEN A = A - 128                'strip high-order bit
440    A$ = CHR$(A): IF A < 32 THEN A$ = ""       'strip control characters
450    B$ = B$ + A$: IF A = 13 THEN PRINT #2, B$: B$ = "" 'print if CR
460    IF LEN(B$) >= 79 AND COL$ = "Y" THEN GOSUB 800: 'adjust to 80 columns
470 WEND: CLOSE
480 '
490 'termination routine
500 IF DEST$ <> "s" AND DEST$ <> "S" THEN LOCATE Y,18 ELSE LOCATE 2,18
510 COLOR 15: PRINT "Conversion complete...convert another (Y/N)";
520 INPUT AGAIN$: COLOR 15,3: PRINT AGAIN$
530 IF LEFT$(AGAIN$,1) = "n" OR LEFT$(AGAIN$,1) = "N" THEN END ELSE 110
590 '
599 ' Subroutine to strip soft carriage return
600    A$ = INPUT$(1,#1): A = ASC(A$): IF A = 160 THEN 600 'strip soft CRs
610    A$ = INPUT$(1,#1): A = ASC(A$)
620 RETURN
690 '
699 ' Subroutine to replace terminal soft hyphens with hard hyphens
700    A$ = INPUT$(1,#1): A = ASC(A$): IF A <> 141 THEN 710 ELSE B$ = B$ + "-"
710 RETURN
790 '
799 ' Subroutine to adjust lines to 80 columns and wrap words
800    FOR I = LEN(B$) TO 1 STEP -1
810      IF MID$(B$,I,1) <> " " THEN 840
820      C$ = LEFT$(B$,I): PRINT #2, C$: C$ = " "
830      B$ = RIGHT$(B$,79-I): I = 0
840    NEXT I
850 RETURN
```

Listing 7.9 ▲ *WSFILTER.BAS.*

```
Input file name? ch7list
Output to:
      Screen
      Printer
      File
YOUR CHOICE ==> f
Output file name? ch7list.asc
Adjust for 80 columns (Y/N)? n


            WORKING...PLEASE WAIT
```

Figure 7.4 ▲ *Menu Screen from WSFILTER.BAS.*

lines 150, 160, 170, 260, 270, 360, and 520, change a 3 or 11 in a COLOR statement to 0, and change any 4 in a COLOR statement to 7.

If your version of BASIC recognizes path names, you can include them as part of the source or destination file names. You also can include drive specifiers. If you choose output to a file, and give the same file name for the original and converted versions of the file, the program will prompt you for confirmation before proceeding.

If you choose the 80-column format, the program will adjust your lines so that words will not be broken at the end of a line. Instead, words that would extend the line beyond 80 columns will be moved to the following line.

CONFIGURING YOUR SYSTEM

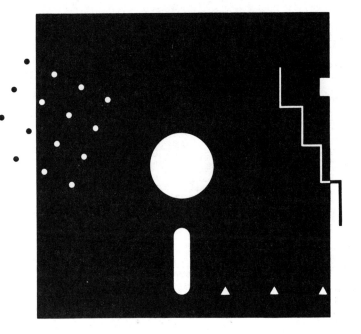

8

▲   ▲   ▲

THIS CHAPTER INTRODUCES two DOS files that give you a great deal of control over the way your computer behaves: the CONFIG.SYS file and the AUTOEXEC.BAT file. These files give DOS a series of instructions to perform automatically whenever you start up your computer.

The CONFIG.SYS file sets up your system. It controls various configuration features, particularly some aspects of the way memory is apportioned, and loads special files called device drivers, among its other functions.

The AUTOEXEC.BAT file is a batch file that allows you to automate routine tasks before beginning your actual work. It is also useful for customizing your hardware.

In this chapter, we will go over the basics of both of these files. In later chapters, beginning in the next one, you will learn specific applications for them.

THE CONFIG.SYS FILE

CONFIG.SYS is a special file designed to load certain information into your system even before COMMAND.COM takes over. It allows you to control the way memory is used, to tell your computer some important facts about your hardware, and to install the driver programs for various peripheral devices.

The CONFIG.SYS file must be on the root directory of the disk from which you boot DOS. It's simplest to keep any files that it loads on this directory as well. However, you can tell DOS where they are located by preceding their names with drive and path specifiers. You can create or modify CONFIG.SYS files with any text editor or word processor that can be used for batch files.

Setting the Number of Buffers

DOS establishes a number of buffers in RAM. These buffers hold data that have been read from a disk. On most PCs, the default number of buffers is two; on ATs and compatible computers, the default is three. You can change the number of buffers in your system by using the BUFFERS command in the CONFIG.SYS file. The syntax for this command is

BUFFERS = *NN*

where *NN* is the number of buffers.

Each buffer you add to the system uses 528 bytes of memory. The more buffers you use, the larger the amount of data read from a disk at one time. Most sources suggest that the ideal number of buffers is somewhere between 10 and 20. However, the ideal number depends on what's in your system and the kind of work you do. First, you must consider how much memory you can spare. If you have a limited amount of memory and use large application programs, you will probably want to have a small number of buffers. If you have disk-intensive software, you may need a large number. If you use a hard disk, a large number is preferable.

Using a large number of buffers can give your system the following advantages:

▲ Database applications that use random-access files can read records considerably more quickly.

▲ Disk-intensive software can run for longer periods of time without having to access the disks.

▲ If you use a hard disk with tree-structured directories, a long, complex path can be searched very quickly.

▲ Hard-disk backup programs function considerably more efficiently with a large number of buffers.

A large number of buffers also creates the following disadvantages:

▲ With too many buffers, it may take DOS longer to search through the buffers than to read a disk sector, especially if your file is on a hard or RAM disk.

▲ Too many buffers may reduce the efficiency of your application, so that overlay files have to be read more frequently. With a large application such as Symphony or Framework, too many buffers may severely limit the memory space available for data.

▲ A program such as Framework II, which gives you the option of setting the size of its own buffer for its overlay file, will not have enough memory for an expanded overlay buffer if there are too many DOS buffers.

The ideal number of buffers for your own work can be determined only by trial and error. If your application program runs more slowly than it should, try increasing or decreasing the number of buffers, and see what happens. You may even need a different number of buffers (which necessitates a different CONFIG.SYS file) for different applications.

Setting the Number of Files

The FILES command in the CONFIG.SYS file tells DOS how many files can be open at the same time. DOS reserves an area of memory to keep track of each open file; just as with buffers, the more files you allow to be open, the more memory you use. The minimum (and default) setting is 8, and the maximum is 255. The syntax for setting the maximum number of open files is

FILES = *NN*

where *NN* is the number of files DOS can handle at one time.

You may think you do not need many files open, but consider these facts:

▲ An application program that has overlay files must have at least two files open—one for the main program and one for the overlay. In addition, it no doubt uses data files. Even some simple programs automatically make backup copies of the file you are working on, and this increases the number of open files.

▲ If you install device drivers or RAM-resident software, each of these files must be open at some time.

The manuals that come with application programs sometimes tell you that you need a certain number of files in the FILES command. Database applications, particularly relational databases, often require as many as 20 files in the FILES statement to function properly.

The BREAK Command

The BREAK command in the CONFIG.SYS file has the same effect as the DOS BREAK command. However, the syntax is different. The default setting for both is off. When BREAK is off, DOS checks to see if Ctrl-Break or Ctrl-C is pressed only during input from the keyboard, output to the screen, output to the printer, and output to the serial port. However, if you place the command

BREAK = ON

in the CONFIG.SYS file, you can exit from many programs while they are executing, even if they perform few input or output operations. This is advantageous when, for example, you are recalculating a spreadsheet formula containing an infinite loop, and you want to make it stop.

On the other hand, some programs use Ctrl-C as a command of their own. Both WordStar and ThinkTank, for example, use Ctrl-C to scroll down one screen. If BREAK is on and you issue more Ctrl-Cs than your program is ready to absorb, you may find yourself unceremoniously dumped back into the operating system, with your file left hanging in memory.

There is no single rule as to whether it is better to have BREAK on or off. It depends on the nature of your software. In any case, you can change the setting by typing

BREAK ON

or

BREAK OFF

at a DOS prompt.

The Number of Drives in Your System

 DOS 3.X

DOS 3.X has an additional command that allows you to specify the number of disk drives in your system. Normally, the system defaults to

five drives, A through E. However, if you use the JOIN or SUBST commands (explained in Chapter 14), or if you are connected to a local-area network, you may need to create fictitious drives that are actually directories. If so, you must tell DOS that there are drives beyond E. The syntax for doing so is

LASTDRIVE = X

where X is the drive specifier, minus the colon. As far as I can tell, it costs you nothing to set the last drive as Z, but it probably doesn't gain you anything either.

Installing Device Drivers

The CONFIG.SYS file can also be used to install *device drivers*, which are short programs that tell DOS how to handle input and output from various peripheral devices. If you own an IBM computer, you will find an extensive technical explanation of them in the *DOS Technical Reference*, complete with assembly-language source code for writing a RAM-disk driver. (Some other manufacturers include this material in their DOS manual.) If you do not program in assembly language, you need not bother with this information. What you need to know is the types of devices that can be installed through the CONFIG.SYS file and the effect of installing them in this manner.

There are many devices whose drivers can be installed through the CONFIG.SYS file. They include RAM disks, expanded memory, mice, clock/calendar devices, print spoolers, and some types of memory-resident software. In addition, there is the ANSI.SYS device driver included with DOS, which we will discuss briefly here and explain in detail in the next chapter.

The syntax for installing device drivers is

DEVICE = FILENAME.EXT

where *FILENAME.EXT* is the name of the driver. Device drivers generally have the extension .SYS or .BIN (although some are .COM files).

In some cases, you can gain further control over your system by specifying parameters after the driver name in the DEVICE command. Most RAM-disk drivers, for example, allow you to choose the size of the disk, root directory, and disk sectors, and the number of sectors per cluster. We'll look at the advantages of the various RAM-disk configurations in Chapter 13.

The device-driver files installed through the CONFIG.SYS file must be on your startup disk if you use a dual-floppy system. If you use a hard disk, and the files are not on your root directory, you must include a complete path to the location of the driver as part of the device name. For reasons that will be explained in Chapter 14, it is a useful practice to keep nothing in the root directory of a hard disk except your various startup files (including device drivers) and your subdirectories.

Many multifunction boards, such as the AST Six-Pak and the Quadram Quadboard, and some expanded memory boards come with a collection of software, that includes a clock driver, a RAM-disk driver, and a print spooler. Some products also include a disk-cache system (which is more or less equivalent to the DOS buffers, except that it makes DOS look first in the buffers that contain the data you use most often). Consult the disk directory and the manual that came with the product to find out what items are available to you and how to install them.

Some types of drivers *must* be installed via the CONFIG.SYS file. Most RAM-disk drivers are of this type, and some MS-DOS computers that are not 100 percent IBM-compatible require you to install a hard-disk driver through the CONFIG.SYS file. Other types of drivers give you a choice of loading the device through the CONFIG.SYS file, or directly at a DOS prompt or through an AUTOEXEC.BAT file. In these cases, you may want to use the direct option because it gives you the choice of loading the driver or not, depending on your current needs, and may save memory. Some clock drivers, for example, can be either loaded as drivers through the CONFIG.SYS file or invoked as programs at a DOS prompt. If you have this choice, you are better off reading the clock from DOS, since all you need to do is pass the information from the clock to the DOS internal clock (which is normally set by the DATE and TIME commands).

Sometimes the choice of how to install drivers will depend on the combination of software that you want to use. For example, if you use ProKey and HomeBase, you have to install a pair of HomeBase drivers in the CONFIG.SYS file so that they are loaded before ProKey, and then send parameters to them after ProKey is invoked. In other circumstances, HomeBase can be installed through the AUTOEXEC.BAT file.

Talking to Your Disk Drives

DOS 3.2,3.3

The types of disk drives a computer can address are set largely in the hardware. When 720K drives were introduced, they were incompatible with older disk drive controllers. Therefore, some means had to be created whereby you could fit your computer with external drives retroactively. The solution is a file called DRIVER.SYS, introduced in DOS 3.2. You add the driver to the CONFIG.SYS file with a command in the form

DEVICE = DRIVER.SYS /D:*N* [/T:*NN*] [/ S:*NN*] [/H:*NN*][/N] [/F:*N*][/C]

where /D:*N* specifies the physical drive number. Floppy drive A is 0, and each successive physical drive has the next number, as in the Load command in DEBUG. Hard drives are numbered starting with 128, or 80H (hex). Whether you use a decimal or hexadecimal number depends on the version of DOS you use.

The switches that follow the drive designation are initially set to the default values for a 720K disk. They can also be used to install any other type of external drive.

- ▲ /T:*NN* specifies the number of tracks per side (the default is 80).
- ▲ /S:*NN* specifies the number of sectors per track (the default is 9).
- ▲ /H:*N* specifies the number of heads (the default is 2).
- ▲ /N indicates a nonremovable (hard disk) drive.

There are two additional switches. The first, /F:*N*, specifies the drive type (F, for some reason, stands for *form factor*). For some types of drives, IBM and Microsoft use different values to designate the same drive, as shown in Table 8.1. For an external disk drive that has a drive-type value, you need only specify the drive type with the /F switch. You do not need to specify the number of heads, number of tracks, and number of sectors. You must, however, specify these dimensions for hard disk drives. For a drive that does not have a drive-type value, use 2 if you have PC-DOS and 7 if you have MS-DOS.

DEVICE TYPE	PC-DOS VALUE	MS-DOS VALUE
2S2D floppy disk	0	0
1.2MB disk	1	1
720K microfloppy	2	2
8" single density	—	3
8" double density	—	4
Hard disk	—	5
Tape drive	—	6
1.44MB microfloppy	7	—
Other	2	7

Table 8.1 ▲ *Drive Type Values for DRIVER.SYS.*

The second additional switch, /C, allows you to install two logical drives on a single physical drive. This can be extremely useful if you have two or more floppy disk drives of different types.

As you probably know, in a single-drive system you can copy disks or copy files from one disk to another with a command such as

DISKCOPY A: B:

or

COPY A:*FILENAME.EXT* B:

When your computer's memory contains as much of the data to be copied as it can hold, you see the message

Insert disk for drive B:
Strike a key when ready. . .

You take the source disk out of drive A and insert the target disk in the same drive. Thus, logical drives A and B occupy the same physical drive.

However, if you have, say, an AT with a 1.2MB disk drive and a second drive of another type, you can't copy from one 1.2MB disk to another without help. The DRIVER.SYS command gives you the help you need. If you make the last line in your CONFIG.SYS file

DEVICE = DRIVER.SYS /D:0 /F:1 /C

your 1.2MB drive A will now also have a second drive specifier. It will be the next letter after the last drive installed in your system (including RAM disks installed through CONFIG.SYS). If you have a hard disk and a RAM disk in addition to your dual-floppy drives, the second drive specifier will be drive E. You can then copy a high-density disk with the command

DISKCOPY A: E:

You'll have to switch the source and destination disks in the drive several times, but at least you'll be able to do the job.

The ANSI.SYS Device Driver   The ANSI.SYS device driver is an extended screen and keyboard driver. It appears as a separate file on the DOS system disk in all versions of DOS since 2.0. This driver allows you to position the cursor on the screen while working in DOS, to set colors for various areas, to display messages at particular points on the screen, and to reassign keys on the keyboard. Some programs, such as SuperKey, require that ANSI.SYS be loaded. To load it, include the line

DEVICE = ANSI.SYS

in your CONFIG.SYS file.

If your computer is made by IBM, you may wonder why you have never heard of the ANSI.SYS file. Its documentation is contained in a separate volume called the *DOS Technical Reference*, rather than in the PC-DOS manual.

In Chapter 9, you will learn how to use ANSI.SYS to customize your screen and keyboard.

 Warning: Device drivers make use of DOS's "terminate-and-stay-resident" feature. This means that they are RAM-resident, just like packages such as HomeBase or SmartKey. Although device drivers occupy a special segment of memory set aside for them, you can still have problems if they are not loaded properly. Some must be loaded first, and others insist on being last, while most don't care when they are loaded.

The worst thing that can happen if drivers are loaded in the wrong order or with the wrong parameters is that your computer will lock up. More likely, the installed device won't function or will function incorrectly. You may have to revise your CONFIG.SYS file several times before your setup works properly. If you have any problems, try removing one driver at a time from the CONFIG.SYS file. Reboot your computer after each change. Eventually, you will discover which driver is causing the trouble.

Controlling the Size of the Environment

DOS 3.2, 3.3

If you use the SET command frequently, or if you use a long, complex prompt or PATH statement, you will sooner or later be confronted with the message

Out of environment space

This means that the environment space does not have enough room for all the data (and DOS resident programs) that you want to store in it. DOS versions 3.2 and 3.3 have enhancements to the COMMAND and SHELL commands that let you remedy this situation. (We'll look at the enhancements to the SHELL command later in this section.) A command of the form

COMMAND /E:*NNNN*

loads a secondary command processor and sets the size of the environment. The number following the /E switch must be a multiple of 16 between 160 and 32768. Thus, you can set aside up to 32K of memory for the environment. This can give you quite a bit of room for storing variables with the SET command. I use a long path and prompt, and have found 960 bytes sufficient.

DOS 3.1

The SHELL command has been available since DOS 2.0. However, in earlier releases it was of interest principally to programmers. Its purpose was to load a command processor other than COMMAND.COM, one appropriate to the particular application. However, you can use an undocumented feature of the SHELL command to set the size of the environment space on startup, without loading a secondary command processor. To do so, include a line of the following form in the

CONFIG.SYS file:

SHELL = COMMAND.COM [/P] /E:*NN*

where *NN* × 16 is the intended size for the environment in bytes. You must include the /P (for permanent) switch in the command if you want an AUTOEXEC file to be executed.

DOS 3.2, 3.3

The enhancement of the SHELL command is documented in PC-DOS versions 3.2 and 3.3, but not in the equivalent MS-DOS versions. However, for all of these DOS versions, the syntax is changed. If you use these later releases, the form of the command is

SHELL = COMMAND.COM [/P] /E:*NNNNN*

where *NNNNN* is the actual size of the environment in bytes. As with the environment switch in COMMAND, the environment may be anywhere from 160 to 32,768 bytes, in multiples of 16.

THE AUTOEXEC.BAT FILE

After DOS has followed all the instructions in the CONFIG.SYS file, it next looks for a file called AUTOEXEC.BAT. The only difference between the AUTOEXEC.BAT file and any other batch file is that it is executed automatically when you boot up. You can use this file for many purposes:

- ▲ To load background programs that are not loaded through the CONFIG.SYS file
- ▲ To place programs on your RAM disk
- ▲ To customize your screen colors and add a great deal of useful information to your prompt (with the help of the ANSI.SYS device driver)
- ▲ To establish a search path
- ▲ To place COMMAND.COM on your RAM disk in such a fashion that DOS will be able to find it there even if you switch disks in drive A

▲ To initialize serial ports for serial printers or telecommunications

▲ To back up your hard disk automatically

▲ To start your application program automatically

In general, you can, and should, use the AUTOEXEC.BAT file to take care of any housekeeping chores that you routinely perform before beginning work in your application.

What you include in the AUTOEXEC.BAT file depends on a number of factors: your hardware configuration, your style of working, and the character of your software. The contents of this file will probably be quite different if you use a hard disk, if you use a macro processor at all times rather than only with certain programs, if you use a RAM disk, or if you use a single application almost exclusively.

Essential AUTOEXEC.BAT Commands

Generally speaking, you should place an AUTOEXEC.BAT file on any disk that you use as a boot disk. The simplest AUTOEXEC file should contain at least the following:

```
ECHO OFF
DATE
TIME
PROMPT $p$g
```

The DATE and TIME Commands   Not surprisingly, the DATE and TIME commands allow you to set the date and time. Many programs keep track of file activity by the date and time stamps in the directory entries. This information also can help you to recognize which version of a file has most recently been updated. When DOS finds an AUTOEXEC file, it bypasses the normal date and time prompts. If you have a real-time (battery-operated) clock, and its driver is not loaded in the CONFIG.SYS file, substitute the command that invokes your clock driver for the DATE and TIME commands.

The PROMPT Command   If you ever use a subdirectory, you should include the PROMPT command in your AUTOEXEC file. The form illustrated above will display a prompt consisting of the drive specifier, the name of the current directory, and the > character. For example, it might look like this:

C:\LOTUS>

If you have more than one directory, it's a great convenience to know which one you're working in, so you don't enter commands that obviously cannot be executed from that directory.

There are many ways you can use the PROMPT command to customize your prompt, even without ANSI.SYS installed. For example, you could include your name, the time and date, or a welcoming message. We will look at these aspects of the PROMPT command in Chapter 9.

Invoking an Application If the disk is a boot disk for a particular application, or if you boot from a hard disk and routinely start with a particular application, the AUTOEXEC file should end with the command that invokes the application. If you want your application to load a particular file, you might use a command such as

KEY LOADFILE /ML

in place of the invocation command. This command invokes SuperKey and loads the LOADFILE macro shown in Listing 6.9, which you can modify to suit your application. Of course, this means that SuperKey and LOADFILE.MAC must be on your boot disk.

Configuring Your Hardware

If your hardware needs special configuration, or if you simply want to establish some preferences, you can use the MODE (or SETUP or CONFIG) command with the appropriate parameters in your AUTOEXEC file. To do so, the external program (MODE.COM or SETUP.COM or CONFIG.COM) must also be on your boot disk. Generally, when you invoke one of these programs, a portion of it remains in memory (the programming that makes this possible is what has led to the development of RAM-resident software packages).

For example, some printers can be set to 80 or 132 characters per line and six or eight lines per inch by means of the command

MODE LPT1: *length, lines*

If your printer is attached to your serial port, you need to tell the computer this and establish the communications parameters for the printer. For most serial printers, the appropriate commands are

```
MODE COM1:12,N,8,1,P
MODE LPT1: = COM1:
```

The first MODE command establishes the parameters of 1200 baud, no parity, 8 data bits, 1 stop bit. The P at the end tells the computer to keep trying to access the printer if it appears to be unavailable. The second MODE command tells the computer that your first printer is attached to COM1, the first serial port.

DOS 3.X

If you use DOS 3.X and want to set your printer's line length and spacing, as well as redirect printer output to the serial port, you should set the line length and spacing first. In this version of DOS, a statement of the form

```
MODE LPT1:
```

followed by any parameters other than a reassignment automatically assigns LPT1 to the first *parallel* port, even if it has previously been assigned to a serial port. In earlier versions of DOS, the only way to undo a reassignment is to reboot the computer.

You can use the MODE command to configure your serial port's communications parameters for a modem in the same way as you would for a serial printer. If you have a printer attached to the first serial port and a modem attached to a second, address the modem as COM2 rather than COM1.

DOS 3.X

In DOS 3.X, the colon after the reserved device names in these commands is optional.

If you use both monochrome and color monitors, or if you have a multifunction color and graphics board, you may want to use the MODE command to select the appropriate screen output for your application. To start the display on the monochrome screen, use the command

```
MODE MONO
```

To start the display on the color screen, in 80-column mode, use

MODE CO80

To start the display on the color screen, but in black-and-white mode, use

MODE BW80

If you want a 40-column display, substitute a 40 for the 80 in the above commands. For a combined color and graphics adaptor, you can use just the 40 or 80 with the MODE command to determine the number of columns your screen will display. MODE will also establish various graphics-display modes.

 Warning: If you have a multifunction graphics board, and you are not sure whether the internal switches are set for monochrome or color, you should include a MODE MONO command in the AUTOEXEC.BAT file to prevent your monochrome monitor from burning out.

If your screen display is off-center, you can use the MODE command to shift the display to the left or to the right. Append

,L

after the 40 or 80 to shift two spaces to the left, or

,R

to shift two spaces to the right. You can add

,T

following either of these parameters, and a test pattern of the digits 0 through 9 will appear across the top of the screen. DOS will then ask you

Do you see the rightmost 9? (Y/N)

or

Do you see the leftmost 0? (Y/N)

depending on whether you specified left or right. If you press N, the pattern will shift two spaces in the specified direction, and the question will appear again, so you can continue to adjust the display.

Setting a Search Path

If you do not set up a search path, DOS looks only in the current directory of the current drive for the necessary file when you give it a command to execute. Of course, you can execute a program on another drive by prefacing the file name with a drive specifier, and in DOS 3.X you can even execute a program on another directory by spelling out the complete path to the program. If the program is not in the location you indicate, DOS responds with the message

Bad command or filename

By using the PATH command, you can extend the range of DOS's search. The PATH command tells DOS which directories to search for the specified file. When a PATH command has been issued, you can execute a file in any of the directories specified in the path. You can include as many drives and directories as you want. The syntax is

PATH [*DRIVE*]*PATHNAME*;[*DRIVE*]*PATHNAME* . . .

To include the root directory, specify it with a backslash. The directories listed in the PATH command must be separated by semicolons.

Warning: The PATH command affects only executable files. If you want to use the COPY, RENAME, ERASE, or TYPE commands, you must still specify the entire path to the file if it is not in your current directory.

If you have a sophisticated system, you will find the PATH command very useful. For example, if you have two floppy disk drives and a RAM disk, you can save yourself quite a bit of time and trouble by including the command

PATH C:\\;A:\\;B:\\

in your AUTOEXEC.BAT file. If you have a hard disk system, the PATH command is actually indispensable. We'll look at it in greater detail when we discuss hard disk navigation in Chapter 14.

A Search Path for Nonexecutable Files

MS-DOS 3.2, DOS 3.3

With MS-DOS 3.2, a new external command, APPEND, was introduced to give DOS a path to search for nonexecutable files. IBM included this command in its network software, but did not add it to its version of DOS until release 3.3. The DOS version of the APPEND command is incompatible with the one included in the network software. Do not use it if your computer is on a network that uses the APPEND command.

There are two different syntax forms for the DOS 3.2 version of APPEND, while DOS 3.3 has added a third. They each function quite differently, so we'll look at all three of them.

The simplest syntax for the APPEND command is the same as that of the PATH command. However, the PATH command tells DOS to search the specified path for executable files (those with .BAT, .COM, or .EXE extensions) only. DOS will search only the current directory for other types of files. The APPEND command tells DOS to search the directories named in its argument for other types of files as well.

The APPEND command is almost essential if you have a hard disk and your software uses overlay files, printer drivers, or other nonexecutable files. If so, you probably won't be able to execute the program by using its full path name, because DOS will look only in the current directory for these files. Placing the directories for such software on the search path doesn't help much either, because the PATH command doesn't affect these ancillary files. This is where the APPEND command comes in.

For example, if you try to call an unprotected version of ThinkTank with the command

    \TANK\TANK

you will see the opening screen and then watch drive lights go on and off as the program frantically searches for its configuration file, TANKOPTS.DAT. After that, your computer will probably lock up. The same thing will happen if the \TANK directory is on the search path and you invoke ThinkTank with the command

    TANK

However, if you also include the \TANK directory in an APPEND statement, you can call ThinkTank from any directory on any drive.

The APPEND command works the same wonders for WordStar 3.3. Normally, unless the two overlay files are copied to every directory from which you intend to call WordStar, the program won't run. However, with WordStar's directory included in an APPEND statement you can use WordStar from any point in your system. (In Chapter 14 you'll see another way to make your computer find WordStar's overlays no matter what directory or drive is current.)

The standard syntax places a copy of the APPEND program in memory, as with MODE.COM. This takes up about 1.7K with DOS 3.2 and 3K with DOS 3.3.

The alternative syntax for the APPEND command uses the SET command to place the APPEND statement in the DOS environment space:

SET APPEND = [*DRIVE*]*PATHNAME*;[*DRIVE*]*PATHNAME*;...

The advantage of using this syntax is that you can see what directories are appended by using the SET command. You'll also learn a technique for extending the list of appended directories (and directories on the search path) on the fly in Chapter 13.

Warning: The method you use to establish a list of appended directories has some effect on the way APPEND works. Most programs work perfectly well with the SET syntax. However, some do not respond to it at all. SuperKey, for example, cannot find its help file when you use the SET syntax. Nor can it find KEY.COM when you want to change defaults and save the changes. RightWriter and CorrectStar cannot find their dictionary files when their directory is appended with the SET syntax. There may be other programs that respond in the same way. In addition, if you load a secondary command processor, any appended directories established by the SET command will become invisible.

There is nothing to stop you from using both versions of the command. You might use the standard syntax for those programs that don't respond to the SET syntax and the SET syntax for other directories. This will allow you to view the appended directory list in the environment for at least some of the directories.

You can delete all directories from the appended list with a single command. The syntax for this command depends on the syntax you used to set up the APPEND list. If you used the APPEND command by itself, you can eliminate the directories by typing

APPEND ;

If you set it up using the SET command, you can eliminate the directories by typing

SET APPEND =

Be aware that each syntax form deletes from the list only those directories placed there by the corresponding method. That is, if you have used both syntax forms for appending directories,

APPEND ;

deletes only those established by the APPEND command and

SET APPEND =

deletes only those established by the SET command.

DOS 3.3

DOS 3.3 has added two new switches to the APPEND command. To use them, you must issue two APPEND statements. The syntax is

APPEND */switch*
APPEND [*DRIVE*]*PATHNAME;*[*DRIVE*]*PATHNAME;*...

The first switch, /E, allows you to place the list of appended directories in the environment, just as the SET APPEND syntax does. I have found no advantage to this method of placing the list in the environment. The SET APPEND syntax works just as well, although it is no longer documented.

The /X switch extends the scope of the command greatly, although not always to your advantage. The /X switch makes any command that involves locating a file (such as DIR, COPY, RENAME, or ERASE) search appended directories for file names matching the one you specify. This extends the reach of your software as well. For example, a spreadsheet program can open a file that is not in your current directory but is in an appended directory. However, when you save the file, you will probably save it to the current directory. Thus, you will end up with two copies of the file, only one of which is updated.

It should be obvious that such a capability, while helpful, is also extremely dangerous. You could easily delete files on several directories at once, without even knowing you had done so. You could also overwrite different files of the same name on different directories.

In addition, the APPEND /X command is a bit quirky. DOS will not search all of the appended directories. For example, if you have files with the extension .TXT on several directories on the list, the effect of the command

   DIR *.TXT

depends on which directory is current. If your current directory has matching files, those on the current directory will be displayed. If not, DOS will search the appended directories, in the order of their appearance in the APPEND statement, until it finds a matching file. Once a directory has been found with a matching file, the search stops, and all matching file names on that directory will be displayed. This can be confusing at best, since the display will show the name of the current directory. You won't see all matching files on all the appended directories, and DOS won't even tell you which directory the matching files are on. Nonetheless, you can edit them if DOS can find them.

DOS 2.X

If you would like to have some or all of these capabilities, and you use DOS 2.X, you can purchase *path-extension* software. Several programs on the market duplicate the effects of the APPEND command. (It might be better to say that the APPEND command duplicates their effects, since they were all on the market before DOS 3.2.) Some of them have many other capabilities. Several path-extension programs are discussed in Chapter 15.

CUSTOMIZING YOUR SCREEN AND KEYBOARD

C H A P T E R

9

D OS GIVES YOU quite a few ways to control the appearance of your
screen display. You can set colors and other video attributes both
through BASIC programs and through the ANSI.SYS device driver,
which is the principal subject of this chapter. This driver, especially
when used in conjunction with the PROMPT command, gives you the
ability to control many aspects of the screen display that you might
have thought were established by the computer itself.

First, we'll take a look at the ways that BASIC handles color. Then
we'll explore the features of the ANSI.SYS device driver in detail,
along with the full range of possibilities afforded by the PROMPT command. In addition, you'll learn how to use the key-reassignment function included in ANSI.SYS.

ADDING COLORS WITH BASIC

If you have a color monitor and are bored with the same old black-and-
white screens, the easiest way to add color is with a BASIC program. A
single-line program can establish the text, background, and border colors.

Warning: Be aware that if you use the ANSI.SYS device driver, it will override any colors that you set up with BASIC except the border color. Even if you do not set up colors with ANSI.SYS, the text color will still be low-intensity white, and the background will be black—the default colors.

The syntax of BASIC's COLOR command is

COLOR *text, background, border*

where *text*, *background*, and *border* are the numeric codes for the desired colors, as listed in Table 9.1. Only the colors in the first column can be used for the background and border. The colors in the second column are high-intensity, or bright, renditions of the colors in the first column. To make the text blink, add 16 to its color code.

You don't have to include a color for each of these portions of the screen. For example, to create a cyan border on your screen but leave the text and background as they are (or set them up with ANSI.SYS), use the statement

COLOR ,,3

If you have a set of colors that you prefer for all your screens, a one-line program such as

10 COLOR 15,1,3: SYSTEM

will establish them. This program sets the text to high-intensity white, the background to blue, and the border to cyan. Give the program the

0	Black	8	Dark Gray
1	Blue	9	Light Blue
2	Green	10	Bright Green
3	Cyan	11	Bright Cyan
4	Red	12	Pink
5	Magenta	13	Bright Magenta
6	Brown or Gold	14	Yellow
7	White (Light Gray)	15	White

Table 9.1 ▲ *Color Codes in BASIC.*

name COLORS.BAS, and any time you type BASICA COLORS, these colors will be reestablished. You might have to run the program after exiting each application, as most applications leave the screen in its default state.

 Warning: If you use an EGA adapter and monitor, you may have trouble setting border colors. Borders on an EGA monitor usually turn out to be thin, high-intensity lines around the display area. What's worse, the border color spills over into the left half of the text area, obscuring the display.

A Color Menu

If you want to have a choice of colors, the program SETCOLOR.BAS, shown in Listing 9.1, will display a menu from which to choose colors. Figure 9.1 shows the menu screen. Each color name appears in its actual color (except for Black, which appears in yellow). The second column appears only after you have selected the background and border colors from the first column. When you have chosen all three colors, the screen clears, and the new screen shows your selected colors and the message

Are these colors OK (Y/N)?

in the text color. If you press N, the process is repeated, except that if one of the colors in the first column matches the background color that you originally selected, its name will appear in yellow on the menu.

You can refer to the discussion on entering graphics characters in the "How to Enter the Programs in This Book" section (at the beginning of the book) for hints on how to type in the menu border. Table H.4 in Appendix H provides a quick reference to the ASCII codes for the border characters.

Setting Monochrome Video Attributes with BASIC

If you use a monochrome monitor, any text color from 2 through 7 will appear on your screen as normal text, and any color from 8 through 15 will appear as highlighted text. A text color of 1 will display underlined text. The only color combinations that will give you inverse video are black text on a white background:

COLOR 0,7

and

COLOR 8,7

These COLOR statements produce the same effect.

Color numbers from 16 through 31 produce blinking text, as they do on color monitors.

```
100 CLS: KEY OFF: FO = 14: FL = 0: DIM COLR$(15): GOSUB 800
110 GOSUB 300
120 LOCATE CSRLIN + 3,1: REGION$ = "background": GOSUB 500
130 IF FL AND A$ = "" GOTO 140 ELSE BK = VAL(A$)
140 REGION$ = "border": GOSUB 500
150 IF FL AND A$ = "" GOTO 155 ELSE BO = VAL(A$)
155 X = CSRLIN + 1: GOSUB 600
160 FL = 1: COLOR FO, BK, BO
170 CLS: PRINT: PRINT: PRINT "    Are these colors OK (Y/N)?"
180 YN$ = INKEY$: IF YN$ = "" GOTO 180
190 IF YN$ = "n" OR YN$ = "N" GOTO 110
200 IF YN$ = "Y" OR YN$ = "y" THEN CLS: SYSTEM ELSE GOTO 180
297 '
298 '          ******   Display Menu   ******
299 '
300 CLS: IF FL THEN COLOR FO ELSE COLOR 14
310 PRINT: PRINT
320 PRINT "                    ┌──────────────────────────┐"
330 PRINT "                    │      AVAILABLE   COLORS      │"
340 FOR I = 0 TO 9
350 PRINT "                    ║                          ║": NEXT
355 IF FL THEN LOCATE 14, 26: PRINT "[RETURN]  =  no change"
360 PRINT "                    └──────────────────────────┘"
370 FOR I = 0 TO 7: LOCATE I + 6, 23: IF I = BK THEN COLOR 14 ELSE COLOR I
380 PRINT I; COLR$(I): NEXT
390 COLOR FO: RETURN
497 '
498 '     ******   Ask for Color Selection for Screen Regions   ******
499 '
500 PRINT: PRINT "    Choose "; REGION$; " color";: INPUT " — > ",A$
510 IF FL AND A$ = "" GOTO 530
520 IF A$ < "0" OR VAL(A$) > 7 GOTO 500
530 RETURN
597 '
598 '     ******   Display and Ask for Character Colors   ******
599 '
600 FOR I = 8 TO 9: COLOR I: LOCATE I - 2, 37: PRINT I; COLR$(I): NEXT
610 FOR I = 10 TO 15: COLOR I: LOCATE I - 2, 36: PRINT I; COLR$(I): NEXT
680 LOCATE X, 5: COLOR FO: INPUT "Choose character color — > ",A$
685 IF FL AND A$ = "" GOTO 710
690 IF A$ < "0" OR VAL(A$) > 15 GOTO 680
700 FO = VAL(A$)
710 RETURN
797 '
798 '     ******   Read in Colors   *******
799 '
800 FOR I = 0 TO 15: READ COLR$(I): NEXT: RETURN
810 DATA Black,Blue,Green,Cyan,Red,Magenta,Brown,Light Gray,Dark Gray
820 DATA Light Blue,Light Green,Bright Cyan,Pink,Brt Magenta,Yellow,White
```

Listing 9.1 ▲ *SETCOLOR.BAS.*

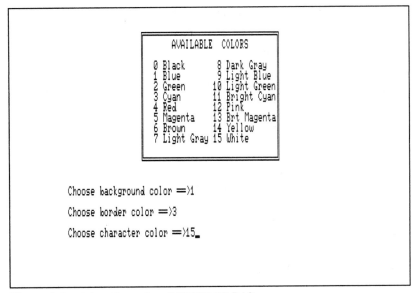

Figure 9.1 ▲ *Menu Screen from SETCOLOR.BAS.*

INTRODUCTION TO THE ANSI.SYS DEVICE DRIVER

The ANSI.SYS device driver has three basic functions:

▲ Positioning the cursor on the screen

▲ Controlling colors and other aspects of the graphics display on your screen

▲ Assigning special meanings to the keys on the keyboard, including swapping key positions and assigning string values to the keys

In conjunction with the PROMPT command, you can use the escape sequences recognized by ANSI.SYS to add a great deal of useful or merely entertaining information to your screen. The third function of ANSI.SYS gives you access to a mini-macroprocessor with severe limitations.

What Is an Escape Sequence?

An escape sequence recognized by ANSI.SYS usually has the following four elements:

1. The Escape character

2. A left bracket

3. A numeric parameter

4. A terminating code indicating the function of the sequence

For example, a sequence to set the cursor at the upper left corner of the screen takes the form

^[[1;1f

where *1;1* is the horizontal and vertical position of the cursor, and *f* is the code telling ANSI.SYS that this is the horizontal-and-vertical position sequence.

 Warning: If your editor or word processor displays the Escape character as ^ [, it's easy to miss the second left bracket. If you do, the sequence won't work properly. It's also important to use the correct case of the terminating code. If you enter a code that should be uppercase in lowercase, or vice versa, the actual character you entered will be displayed on the screen, along with the numeric parameter, and the sequence will not work.

Entering Escape Sequences

Escape sequences can be entered in three ways: through ECHO statements, through PROMPT statements, and as part of ASCII text files. Each has advantages:

▲ You can insert an escape sequence in an ECHO statement without disturbing your regular prompt. However, if you include such a statement in a batch file, it sometimes results in the subsequent line being skipped during execution. You can overcome this quirk by adding a blank line following an ECHO statement containing an escape sequence.

▲ In the PROMPT statement, the Escape character can be represented by the characters $e, so you don't have to do any fancy tricks to insert it. The disadvantage to using PROMPT statements is that if you want to temporarily change some aspect of your screen, you will have to reload your regular prompt (either by putting it at the end of the file that includes the altered PROMPT statement or by calling a batch file that contains nothing but your regular prompt).

▲ For displaying more than one line of text on the screen, a command of the form

   TYPE *TEXTFILE.ASC*

(even in a batch file) displays the desired text considerably more quickly than either of the other methods. Even if you want to enter a series of escape sequences other than text, the TYPE command is the fastest way to do so. We'll see examples of this technique in Chapters 10 and 17.

SETTING VIDEO ATTRIBUTES WITH ANSI.SYS

If you include an escape sequence for color in the PROMPT statement in your AUTOEXEC.BAT file, the colors you set will determine the screen's text and background colors whenever you are working in DOS or in any program that does not override these settings. The escape sequence for color is

   ^ [[*N*m

where *N* is a color or video-attribute code, as listed in Table 9.2. For ease of reference, the colors are listed in the same order as they appear in Table 9.1 (BASIC's color codes).

   Note that ANSI.SYS controls various video attributes separately. That is, different codes are used for foreground and background colors, and there are separate codes for the other video attributes. An additional code cancels all the previously set video attributes.

   If you want to set several video attributes—say text color, background

COLOR	FOREGROUND	BACKGROUND
Black	30	40
Blue	34	44
Green	32	42
Cyan	36	46
Red	31	41
Magenta	35	45
Yellow	33	43
White	37	47

VIDEO MODES	PARAMETERS
All attributes off	0
High-intensity text	1
Underlined text*	4
Blinking text	5
Inverse video	7
Concealed text	8

*Available in monochrome only.

Table 9.2 ▲ *ANSI Codes for Video Attributes.*

color, and high-intensity—you can include them all in a single escape sequence, separated by semicolons. For example:

```
^[[1;33;41m
```

will display bright yellow text on a red background.

To test the video-attribute codes, create the file ANSITEST.TXT, shown in Listing 9.2. The messages are self-explanatory. To see the effects, enter the command

```
TYPE ANSITEST.TXT
```

```
 1: ^[[1;34;44mThis should be light blue on blue, high inensity in monochrome.
 2: ^[[1;4;37mThis should be high intensity white, high intensity in monochrome
 3: ^[[5mThis should blink.
 4: ^[[0mAttributes off: this should be normal colors, not blinking.
 5: ^[[8mConcealed mode: this should be barely visible, if at all.
 6: ^[[40;30mBlack on black, still concealed:
 7:         this should be totally invisible.
 8: ^[[0mThis should make things normal again.
 9: ^[[4mThis should be underlined in monochrome, blue on black in color.
10: ^[[44mThis should be high intensity underlined in monochrome,
11:         bright blue in color.
12: ^[[0;7mThis should be black on white in color,
13:         inverse video in monochrome.
14: ^[[0mEverything should be back to normal once again.
```

Listing 9.2 ▲ *ANSITEST.TXT.*

Warning: Some RAM-resident programs take over the screen and impose their own colors. Both SideKick and SuperKey, for example, are set up so that when you clear the screen, the background will always be black, and any border color you may have established through BASIC will be erased. Your text color will still be active, however—so it had better not be black—and your background color will reappear as soon as enough text has been displayed for the text to start scrolling up from the bottom of the screen.

Hint: You can overcome this problem in part by using the escape sequence to clear the screen— ^ [[2J—instead of the CLS command. Also, unlike the CLS command, this escape sequence will not erase your border color when a RAM-resident program that takes over the screen is loaded. If you precede this escape sequence by one that establishes colors, the screen will clear to the specified background color, and the colors you establish will remain until you return to a DOS prompt. If your DOS prompt does not establish screen colors, these colors will be active until you change them. For example,

ECHO ^ [[0;30;45m ^ [[2J

will create a magenta screen with black text. If you don't include a color escape sequence, the colors set by your PROMPT statement will be restored.

SETTING THE VIDEO MODE WITH ANSI.SYS

If you do not have both monochrome and color boards in your system, you can use ANSI.SYS in place of the MODE (or CONFIG or SETUP) command to set the display mode. If you want to use ANSI.SYS for any of its other functions, and you don't need to address the serial ports with special configurations, this technique can save some memory because you don't have to load the resident portion of MODE.COM.

 Warning: If you have both monochrome and color boards, you must use MODE CO80 or MODE CO40 to initialize the color board and monitor before any of the following sequences will work.

The code for the video mode includes two special characters:

^ [[= Nh

where N is a numeric code for setting the video mode, as listed in Table 9.3. You must precede the code with an equal sign and follow it with a lowercase h. You can set graphics as well as text modes.

Controlling Word Wrap

The code 7 does not appear in Table 9.3 because it functions slightly differently from the others. Its prefix character is a question mark, rather than an equal sign.

VIDEO MODE	CODE	EQUIVALENT MODE COMMAND
40 × 25 black & white	0	MODE BW40
40 × 25 color	1	MODE CO40
80 × 25 black & white	2	MODE BW80
80 × 25 color	3	MODE CO80

Table 9.3 ▲ *ANSI Codes for Video Mode.*

The code

⌃[[?7h

sets the computer so that the TYPE command automatically wraps lines that are more than 80 characters long (this is the default condition.) However, the code

⌃[[?7l

sets it so that when lines are longer than 80 characters, every character after the seventy-ninth will be displayed successively in the eightieth column. The *l* is technically a terminating code for *resetting* the mode, but all the numeric parameters, except 7, work the same with either the *h* or *l* terminating code.

CONTROLLING THE CURSOR

ANSI.SYS also contains codes that move the cursor to any position on the screen. These codes work on the principle that the screen has 80 columns and 25 lines, and do not wrap if you enter a code that would appear to send the cursor beyond the screen's natural boundaries. For example, a code that would appear to move the cursor to a horizontal position of 90 will leave it in the last column of the current line, rather than sending it to column 10 of the following line. Similarly, a code to backspace 50 columns from the center of the screen will move the cursor only to column 1, and a vertical code of 27 will leave the cursor at the bottom of the screen, rather than placing it one line down from the top.

Table 9.4 summarizes the cursor-positioning codes. The numeric parameter is the number of rows or columns for the cursor to move.

Later in the chapter, you'll see how these codes work with specialized prompts. You could also use them in creating a cursor-driven menu.

ASSIGNING NEW VALUES TO KEYS

As noted, ANSI.SYS also contains a mini-macroprocessor. Although it contains no recording facilities, it does let you assign strings to various keys or to assign the function of one key to another. For example, you could use this feature before invoking the CHOOSE.COM program presented in Chapter 6 and offer the user choices to be selected with the function or number keys, rather than with alphabetic characters.

ESCAPE SEQUENCE	EFFECT
^ [[*row;column*H	Moves the cursor to the specified row and column; when no parameters are given, places the cursor in the home position.
^ [[*row;column*f	Has the same effect as the H terminating code.
^ [[*row*A	Moves the cursor up the specified number of rows.
^ [[*row*B	Moves the cursor down the specified number of rows .
^ [[*column*C	Moves the cursor forward the specified number of columns.
^ [[*column*D	Moves the cursor backward the specified number of columns.
^ [[s	Records the position of the cursor at the time the escape sequence is issued for later recall.
^ [[u	Restores the cursor to the position recorded by ^ [[s.
^ [[2J	Clears the screen, and places the cursor in the home position.
^ [[K	Erases text from the current cursor position to the end of the current line.

Table 9.4 ▲ *ANSI Escape Codes for Positioning the Cursor.*

The elements of the escape sequence for redefining a key are as follows:

- ▲ The Escape character
- ▲ A left bracket
- ▲ The ASCII code of the key to be redefined
- ▲ A semicolon
- ▲ The new value for the key (which may be expressed as characters in quotation marks or as the ASCII codes for the characters)

▲ The terminating code *p*

Thus, for example, to assign the lowercase *p* to the uppercase A, you would use the code

^ [[65;112p

because 65 is the ASCII code for the uppercase A and 112 is the one for the lowercase p.

Assigning Extended ASCII Codes to Keys

But what's the point of this type of key reassignment? Well, by using the *extended ASCII codes* shown in Table A.3, you can assign values to any of the keys that do *not* have normal ASCII codes, such as the function keys, the Ins and Del keys, and the keys on the numeric keypad. Not only that, you can assign separate values to Alt-function keys, Ctrl-function keys, and Shift-function keys as well. You can also use the extended ASCII codes to assign values to the combination of the Alt key and any key that has a normal ASCII code. To use the extended ASCII codes, preface the code in Table A.3 with a 0 and a semicolon. For example, to assign DIR plus a carriage return to the F10 key, use the code

^ [[0;68;"DIR";13p

(The 13 is the ASCII code for a carriage return.) Listing 9.3 shows how this technique can be used to create a simple menu.

Line 1 of this text file assigns the strings representing the names of the batch files that call the programs (or of the programs themselves, if they are on the search path) to the keys F1, F3, F5, and F7. Line 3 clears the screen and positions the cursor five lines down. The rest of the file displays messages on the screen.

```
1: ^[0;59;"LOTUS";13p ^[[0;61;"DBASE";13p ^[[0;63;"WS";13p ^[[0;65;"SK";13p
2:
3: ^[[2J^[[5;1H
4:
5:          Press F1 to load 1-2-3
6:          Press F3 to load dBASE II
7:          Press F5 to load WordStar
8:          Press F7 to load SideKick
```

Listing 9.3 ▲ *PROGMENU.*

Clearing Key Assignments

There's one catch to using these escape sequences for reassigning keys. Some programs take over the keyboard and will override your assignments, and others do not. If you reassigned DIR to the F10 key, you may find yourself entering DIR into a spreadsheet cell when you are trying to copy its contents to another cell, or whatever else the F10 key is supposed to do in that particular application. Therefore, unless you are sure that your program takes over the keyboard, you have to clear any assignments you may have made before you begin your application. To clear the assignment of a key, assign its original value to it. To clear the assignment of the A key, for example, use

^[[65;65p

To clear the assignment of the F10 key, use

^[[0;68;0;68p

Later in the chapter, I'll show you a shortcut to make this procedure less tedious. In the meantime, you might be contemplating ways to do the same thing with your macro processor, which can no doubt clear all key assignments with a single command (and is probably a better tool to use for the entire key-reassignment procedure).

In the PROGMENU file (Listing 9.3), you could just as well have assigned the strings to Alt-L, Alt-D, Alt-W, and Alt-S. Then the chance of the reasssigned keys conflicting with the keys that your program uses would be reduced. However, with the program in its present form, each of these programs would have to be called by a batch file whose first line was

ECHO ^[[0;59;0;59p ^[[0;61;0;61p ^[[0;63;0;63p ^[[0;65;0;65p

and this line should be followed by a blank line, just to be on the safe side.

CUSTOMIZING YOUR PROMPT

As we noted in Chapter 8, there are many ways to customize your prompt even without the ANSI.SYS driver installed. We'll look at these possibilities before we go on to consider what ANSI escape sequences can add.

Using Metastrings

The PROMPT command allows you to use something called (Lord help us!!) *metastrings* to insert various information into the prompt. A metastring is a character that stands for either another character or a function, preceded by a $ symbol. You can also include text in your prompt. The metastrings are listed in Table 9.5.

METASTRING	EFFECT
$t	Displays the current time.
$d	Displays the current date.
$p	Displays the current drive and path name.
$v	Displays the DOS version number.
$n	Displays the default drive specifier.
$h	Backspaces one character.
$e	Inserts an Escape character, which you can follow with an ANSI escape sequence.
$_	Inserts a carriage-return/line-feed pair.
$g	>
$l	<
$b	¦
$q	= (equal sign, not ASCII 205)

Table 9.5 ▲ *PROMPT Command Metastrings.*

Let's look at some examples. The PROMPT command by itself, unadorned with any arguments, displays your system's standard prompt, which is probably the drive specifier and a > character. You can also specify this prompt with

PROMPT ng

If you want to add a message on a line before the actual drive prompt, you can use the underscore character to create a two-line prompt. For example, the command

PROMPT Keep your sticky hands off my machine!$_$p$g

would display the message on the first line, followed by the current drive and directory on the second:

Keep your sticky hands off my machine!
C:\DOS>

If you have color, you could display such a prompt in several colors using the appropriate ANSI escape sequences. For example,

PROMPT $e[1;37;41mWhat do you want, Boss? $_$e[0;32;
43m pg$e[$1;33;46m

would display the message

What do you want, Boss?

in high-intensity white on a red background, followed on the next line by the drive and directory specifier, one space indented (that's what the space after *43m* does) in green on a gold background. Any other text on the screen would be displayed in high-intensity yellow on a cyan background.

Warning: Although these long prompts may wrap in your word processor, be sure that your word processor does not insert a hard carriage return between the first and second lines. If it does, the second line of the prompt will be interpreted as a separate command by DOS. It will generate the message

Bad command or file name

and will not be included in the prompt.

A Customized Prompt

My own prompt is shown in Listing 9.4. We'll go over this code a step at a time because it's difficult to read. First, the video-attribute escape sequence *$e[1;37;41m* sets the color to high-intensity white on a red background. The sequence *$e[s* memorizes the cursor position. Next, the sequence *$e[1;61H* places the cursor at line 1, column 61. The *$t* displays the current time, and the six *$h* metastrings backspace over the seconds and hundredths of seconds. Next there is a space, followed by the date (*$d*). This places the time and date in the upper right corner of the screen, in white on red. The sequence *$e[u* restores the cursor to its former position. The *$p* displays the name of the current directory, followed by a double arrowhead, or French close-quote, which is ASCII 175 (I prefer this to the single > generally used by DOS). The *$e[44;33m* video-attribute escape sequence changes the screen color to blue and the character color to yellow. Finally, the cursor sequence *$e[1C* moves the cursor forward one position, so that there is a space between the red directory prompt and the cursor.

If you have a program such as HomeBase, which constantly updates a clock in the upper right corner of the screen, you might want to omit the time from such a prompt. You could add enough spaces to color the line all the way to the edge of the screen, setting the cursor location at $e[1;50H, or wherever you need to to make room for the clock display after the date.

Displaying System Information

You can use the PROMPT command to display useful system information. Listing 9.5, for example, creates a prompt that displays the date at the upper left corner of the screen, the current path at the upper center, and the DOS version number at the upper right, all in inverse video, or in black on white on a color monitor. The Ctrl-P creates an arrowhead character. Be sure to enter a Ctrl-P, not a caret and a P. An Alt-205 inserts the double horizontal bars. The spaces in the listing display inverse-video stripes that extend one space beyond the information on either side to make the text easier to read. The actual command-line prompt is displayed at the lower left. A screen using this prompt is shown in Figure 9.2.

Saving and Restoring Prompts, Paths, and Other Default Settings

You may need to run a program that requires you to change your regular search path, or you may want to use a prompt other than your usual one for a special purpose. For these reasons, it's often helpful to have a way

```
PROMPT $e[1;37;41m $e[s$e[1;61H$t$h$h$h$h$h $d$e[u$p >> $e[44;33m$e[1C
```

Listing 9.4 ▲ *A Personal Prompt.*

```
    1: ECHO OFF
    2: PROMPT $e[1;1H$e[7m Date =^P $d $e[1;30H Directory =^P $p
$e[1;58H $v $e[0m$e[25;1HCOMMAND  =^P
```

Listing 9.5 ▲ *LINEPRMT.BAT.*

```
┌──────────────────────────────────────────────────────────────────┐
│  ▐Date ═▶ Wed  7-01-1987▌    ▐Directory ═▶ E:\▌      ▐MS-DOS Version 3.20▌  │
│  Volume in drive E is FAST FILES                                   │
│  Directory of  E:\                                                 │
│                                                                    │
│  BIGTEAM  BAT    295   6-30-87   9:06a                              │
│  FNC      BAT    175   6-22-87   9:44a                              │
│  FWC      BAT    124   6-16-87   2:59p                              │
│  FWH      BAT     66   5-14-87   9:35a                              │
│  TEAM     BAT    227   6-30-87   9:05a                              │
│  HOMEBASE BAT    363   6-10-87  12:08p                              │
│  OLDEGA   BAT     49   6-05-87   1:37p                              │
│  HDBKUP   BAT    864   7-01-87  11:23a                              │
│  QDC      BAT     63   2-27-87   9:40a                              │
│  S        BAT   3145   6-02-87  10:04a                              │
│  SPARE    BAT    281   6-01-87   9:08a                              │
│  PROCEED  BAT    511   7-01-87  11:08a                              │
│  TH       BAT    244   6-30-87   9:07a                              │
│  TTSETUP  BAT    443   2-26-87   9:04a                              │
│  WSSETUP  BAT    465   3-05-87   9:39a                              │
│  CAROUSEL BAT     71   6-30-87   9:05a                              │
│  KILLKEY  BAT    138   7-01-87   9:12a                              │
│  WINDOWS  BAT    146   6-30-87   9:08a                              │
│       18 File(s)        7168 bytes free                            │
│                                                                    │
│  COMMAND  ═▶_                                                       │
│                                                                    │
│              Power Users Guide to MS DOS fig9-2                     │
└──────────────────────────────────────────────────────────────────┘
```

Figure 9.2 ▲ *A Screen with the Prompt Created by LINEPRMT.BAT.*

of restoring your system's default settings. One way to do so is with a batch file such as SYSRESET.BAT, shown in Listing 9.6. Here is a line-by-line description of its effects.

1: Turns off screen echo.

2: Turns on concealed mode, which automatically sets the background color to black and changes the text color to black. A second escape sequence homes the cursor.

3: Reestablishes my standard path.

4: Reestablishes my list of appended directories, an APPEND statement in the environment.

5: Reestablishes my standard prompt.

6: Reestablishes 80 × 25 color mode using the appropriate ANSI escape sequence.

7: Calls the batch file that runs the BASIC program to set the border to my preferred color.

8: Turns off the video attributes that have previously been set, so that those established by the PROMPT command can take over; a second ANSI escape sequence homes the cursor again, without clearing the screen, so that the border is not erased.

```
1:  ECHO OFF
2:  ECHO ^[[8;30m ^[[H
3:  PATH C:\DOS;C:\BATCH;C:\UTIL\SUPERKEY;C:\UTIL;C:\WORDSTAR;C:\
4:  APPEND C:\BATCH;C:\UTIL\SUPERKEY;C:\UTIL;C:\WORDSTAR;C:\DICT
5:  PROMPT $e[1;37;41m $e[s$e[1;61H$t$h$h$h$h$h $d$e[u$p » $e[44;33m$e[1C
6:  ECHO ^[[=3h
7:  COMMAND /C BORDER
8:  ECHO ^[[0m^[[H
```

Listing 9.6 ▲ *SYSRESET.BAT.*

A FUNCTION KEY MENU

To demonstrate the full power of ANSI.SYS, we'll now create a DOS-enhancement program using ANSI escape sequences both to assign frequently used commands to the function keys and to display a menu screen to go with the key assignments. We'll also look at a quick method of clearing key assignments.

Assigning the Keys

DOSMENU, shown in Listing 9.7, is in two parts. The first part assigns many commonly used DOS commands and parts of commands to function keys F5 through F10 and to all of the Alt-function key combinations. The second part displays a menu, which is illustrated in Figure 9.3. To activate this menu, type

TYPE DOSMENU

Lines 1 through 6 of DOSMENU assign strings to keys F5 through F10. Lines 7 through 16 assign strings to the Alt-function keys.

Some of the strings terminate in a carriage return, and some do not. The carriage return appears in the menu as an arrowhead pointing to the left, which is displayed by the Ctrl-Q character. The commands that require arguments, such as COPY and TYPE, are not terminated with a carriage return, so that you can enter the arguments on the command line. For the F7 through F9 keys, the drive designators are terminated by carriage returns, but those for the Alt-F7 through Alt-F9 keys are not. This allows you to construct a command such as

COPY A: ★ . ★ C:

by typing Alt-F5 Alt-F7 Alt-F2 F9. Since the string assigned to F9

```
   1: ^[[0;63;"CLS";13p
   2: ^[[0;64;"CHKDSK "p
   3: ^[[0;65;"A:";13p
   4: ^[[0;66;"B:";13p
   5: ^[[0;67;"C:";13p
   6: ^[[0;68;"DIR /P";13p
   7: ^[[0;104;"DEL "p
   8: ^[[0;105;"*.* "p
   9: ^[[0;106;"CD \"p
  10: ^[[0;107;"REN "p
  11: ^[[0;108;"COPY "p
  12: ^[[0;109;"TYPE "p
  13: ^[[0;110;"A:"p
  14: ^[[0;111;"B:"p
  15: ^[[0;112;"C:"p
  16: ^[[0;113;"DIR "p
  17:
  18: ^[[2J^[[2B^[[0;36;44m
  19:        ┌─────────────────────────────^Q^[[31;47m DOS FUNCTION KEYS ^P^[[36;44m
  ═══════════╗
  20:        ║
  21:        ║^[[1;31m F1^[[0;36;44m 3 Copy one character      3^[[1;31m
F2 ^[[0;36;44m 3 Copy to character       :
  22:        ║^[[1;31m F3^[[0;36;44m 3 Copy last command       3^[[1;31m
F4 ^[[0;36;44m 3 Skip to character       :
  23:        ║^[[1;31m F5^[[0;36;44m 3 Clear screen            3^[[1;31m
F6 ^[[0;36;44m 3 CHecK DiSK (drive)      :
  24:        ║^[[1;31m F7^[[0;36;44m 3 A:^Q                    3^[[1;31m
F8 ^[[0;36;44m 3 B:^Q                    :
  25:        ║[1;31m F9^[[0;36;44m 3 C:^Q                     3^[[1;31m
F10^[[0;36;44m 3 DIRectory with pages    :
  26:        ║
  27:        ║^[[1;37m AF1^[[0;36;44m3 ERASE (filename)        3^[[1;37m
AF2 ^[[0;36;44m3 *.*                     :
  28:        ║^[[1;37m AF3^[[0;36;44m3 CD \                    3^[[1;37m
AF4 ^[[0;36;44m3 RENAME [old] [new]      :
  29:        ║^[[1;37m AF5^[[0;36;44m3 COPY [from] {d:}[to]    3^[[1;37m
AF6 ^[[0;36;44m3 FORMAT disk in B:       :
  30:        ║^[[1;37m AF7^[[0;36;44m3 A:                      3^[[1;37m
AF8 ^[[0;36;44m3 B:                      :
  31:        ║^[[1;37m AF9^[[0;36;44m3 C:                      3^[[1;37m
AF10^[[0;36;44m3 DIR                     :
  32:        ╚
```

Listing 9.7 ▲ *DOSMENU.*

terminates with a carriage return, you don't have to press Return to execute the command.

The Menu

The menu is displayed by lines 19 through 32. Consult Table H.4 for the ASCII values of the graphics characters used. You may find it easiest to type in the menu so that it matches the screen display shown in Figure 9.3, and then add the escape sequences. Each line is indented nine spaces. Although the lines wrap in the listing, be sure that you do not

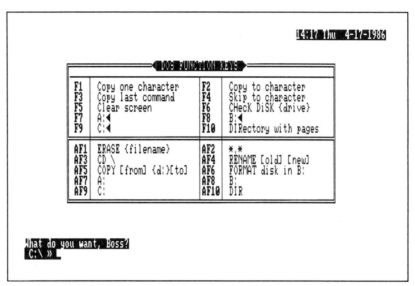

Figure 9.3 ▲ *The Key Assignment Menu Screen.*

break them with a carriage return. Each numbered line is a single logical line, and the carriage return should come only before the next numbered line. Otherwise, parts of each line will appear on the following screen line, and the display will be a mess.

The escape sequences on line 18 clear the screen, place the cursor two lines from the top, and set the screen colors to a blue background with a cyan foreground. The other escape sequences in the menu display are for color. The key names of the function keys appear in light red, and those of the Alt-function keys are in high-intensity white. The borders and the text, except for the title at the top, are all in cyan. The title is in red on white. The triangular ends to the title stripe are created by Ctrl-Q and Ctrl-P, respectively.

Changes for Monochrome Screens   If you are using a monochrome screen, the only *necessary* changes are the substitution of

^ [[7m

for the first escape sequence in line 19 and

^ [[0m

for the second. This will make the title appear in inverse video. Without this change, it will be in normal text on a monochrome screen, or, if you have a monochrome screen running from a graphics board (such as in a Compaq), the title will be invisible.

You can save yourself some typing, however, if you replace the sequences in lines 21 through 31 that begin with ^ *[[1* with a simple ^ *[[1m*, and those that begin with ^ *[[0* with ^ *[[0m*. This will display the key names in high intensity and the rest of the screen in normal intensity (which is how they will appear in monochrome in any case).

Redisplaying the Menu   The menu will stay on the screen until you have issued enough commands to make it scroll off the top or enter the CLS command. If you want to see the menu again, you could simply type

   TYPE DOSMENU

a second time to redisplay it, but you would then repeat the whole program, which isn't necessary. There are two ways to deal with this. The simpler method is to make a second copy of the menu display (lines 18 through 32) and assign to a little-used key an additional command to display the menu. For example, you could call the second copy DOS.MNU and assign it to Shift-Tab by adding the line

   ^ [[0;15;"TYPE DOS.MNU";13p

after line 16.

   The procedure for the more complex method I will merely suggest, leaving the details to your imagination and your late-night hours. First, consider the fact that there are escape sequences to save the cursor position, restore the cursor position, and erase to the end of the line. Thus, careful use of these escape sequences will set up the screen so that after each command is executed, the cursor returns to the same position on the screen as it previously occupied, with a blank command line.

Clearing the Key Assignments

I promised you a simple method of clearing the key assignments, and here it is. Listing 9.8, CLRKEYS.ALL, reassigns all the function keys to their original definitions and tells you what it's doing as it proceeds. Type in this file, and then type the command

   TYPE CLRKEYS.ALL

and your computer should never know that anything had been changed in the first place. If you don't need such a complete clearing, you might make separate files for each type of key (for example, CLRKEYS.NRM, CLRKEYS.SHF, CLRKEYS.CTL, and CLRKEYS.ALT).

```
 1: Clearing  Function Keys
 2:
 3: ^[[0;59;0;59p ^[[0;60;0;60p ^[[0;61;0;61p ^[[0;62;0;62p ^[[0;63;0;63p
 4: ^[[0;64;0;64p ^[[0;65;0;65p ^[[0;66;0;66p ^[[0;67;0;67p ^[[0;68;0;68p
 5:
 6: Clearing Shifted Function Keys
 7:
 8: ^[[0;84;0;84p ^[[0;85;0;85p ^[[0;86;0;86p ^[[0;87;0;87p ^[[0;88;0;88p
 9: ^[[0;89;0;89p ^[[0;90;0;90p ^[[0;91;0;91p ^[[0;92;0;92p ^[[0;93;0;93p
10:
11: Clearing Ctrl-Function Keys
12:
13: ^[[0;94;0;94p ^[[0;95;0;95p ^[[0;96;0;96p ^[[0;97;0;97p ^[[0;98;0;98p
14: ^[[0;99;0;99p ^[[0;100;0;100p ^[[0;101;0;101p ^[[0;102;0;102p
15: ^[[0;103;0;103p
16:
17: Clearing Alt-Function Keys
19:
20: ^[[0;104;0;104p ^[[0;105;0;105p ^[[0;106;0;106p ^[[0;107;0;107p
21: ^[[0;108;0;108p ^[[0;109;0;109p ^[[0;110;0;110p ^[[0;111;0;111p
22: ^[[0;112;0;112p ^[[0;113;0;113p
```

Listing 9.8 ▲ *CLRKEYS.ALL.*

Warning: I have used this file successfully on a PC-AT and on several MS-DOS machines from other manufacturers with absolutely no trouble. However, on plain vanilla IBM PCs, I have had the computer lock up completely during the fourth set of assignment clearings, no matter in which order they appear. You can get around this problem by creating four separate files and calling them separately from the command line. Calling all four from a batch file creates the same lockup as using the complete file. Apparently, speedy though it is, the IBM PC needs some time to digest the information, and too much of this diet makes it balk.

OTHER POSSIBILITIES

As you can see, there is a great deal of power to be gained through the combination of the PROMPT command and the ANSI escape sequences. Although a macro processor offers considerably more flexibility for redefining keys, there is really no other way to gain as much control over your screen display as you do using the ANSI escape sequences.

You could devise a batch program that would let you select foreground and background colors the same way that SETCOLOR.BAS (Listing 9.1) does. It would probably have to be driven by command-line parameters, but it would allow you to change colors at will, and those colors would remain in effect any time you worked at the operating-system level.

SOFTWARE SOLUTIONS: COLOR

There are simpler ways to change colors than using either BASIC or ANSI escape sequences. The Norton Utilities includes a short program called SA.COM (Screen Attributes), which accepts English commands such as

SA BRIGHT GREEN ON YELLOW

However, if you include ANSI escape sequences for color in your prompt, those colors will return as soon as you issue a DOS command.

Several public-domain programs can set your colors for you, among them SETCOLOR.COM and KOLOR.COM. Such programs generally require some obscure numeric parameters. However, they will override colors set with ANSI.SYS, and will probably override some of the colors in your application programs as well. On the other hand, most of these programs allow you to change colors at will, just by invoking the program with new parameters.

CREATING AND ENHANCING DOS COMMANDS

C H A P T E R

10

▲ ▲ ▲

I N THIS CHAPTER, we'll use two techniques for altering the command
structure of DOS: through batch files and through the DOS command processor. First, we'll develop a library of batch files to alter or streamline existing commands. Next, we'll create some new commands using batch files.
Finally, we'll look at the DOS command processor itself and consider ways
it might be altered for special purposes.

PROTECTING YOUR HARD DISK FROM ACCIDENTAL FORMATTING

 DOS 3.X

Some versions of DOS won't let you format your hard disk by accident.
PC-DOS 3.X is kind enough to check to see what kind of disk you have
asked to format. If it is a hard disk, you'll see the message

**WARNING, ALL DATA ON NON-REMOVABLE
DISK DRIVE C: WILL BE LOST!
Proceed with Format (Y/N)?**

MS-DOS late releases

Some late releases of MS-DOS have a separate HDFMT command for formatting the hard disk, and they will not format a hard disk when the FORMAT command is issued.

DOS 2.X

However, if you have a hard disk, use DOS 2.X, and keep the DOS files on it, you stand an excellent chance of completely wiping out the information on your hard disk. All you have to do is type

FORMAT

with no drive specifier while logged onto the hard disk, and DOS will blithely erase multimegabytes of information without so much as a by-your-leave. To prevent such a disaster, take two steps:

1. Rename FORMAT.COM (in this example, we'll rename it to NEWDISK.COM).

2. Type in FORMAT.BAT, the batch file displayed in Listing 10.1, and save it to the same disk and directory as your DOS files.

The syntax for this revised format command is

FORMAT A

or

FORMAT B

```
 1: ECHO OFF
 2: IF "%1"=="" GOTO warning
 3: IF "%1"=="/s" GOTO warning
 4: IF "%1"=="/S" GOTO warning
 5: IF "%1"=="/v" GOTO warning
 6: IF "%1"=="/V" GOTO warning
 7: IF "%1"=="c" GOTO warning2
 8: IF "%1"=="C" GOTO warning2
 9: NEWDISK %1: %2 %3
10: GOTO end
11: :warning
12: ECHO                    ^GYou must specify the drive letter!
13: GOTO end
14: :warning2
15: ECHO                    Type NEWDISK C: to format the hard disk.
16: :end
```

Listing 10.1 ▲ *FORMAT.BAT*

You need not type the colon. In fact, a colon will generate an error message. Leave the colon out of line 9 if you want to use the standard syntax. Here is a line-by-line explanation of the FORMAT.BAT file.

1:	Turns screen echoing off.
2:	Checks to see whether any parameters are specified; redirects execution to the warning message if not.
3–6:	Checks to see whether the parameter is a drive letter. If not, redirects execution to the warning message.
7–8:	Checks to see whether the hard disk is specified, and issues the second warning message if it is. It is assumed that drive C is a hard disk. If another designation is used for your hard disk, enter a different letter between the quotes on these two lines. If you have more than one hard disk, enter similar lines for each hard-disk specifier.
9–10:	Issues the new version of the FORMAT command, and accepts parameters.
11–14:	Issues warning messages. Ctrl-G (^ G) issues a beep.

MAKING A SYSTEM DISK

The BOOTDISK.BAT file, shown in Listing 10.2, can be used to make a bootable system disk with a single command. If the syntax used is incorrect, a help message is displayed. This version is for two floppy disk drives, and it assumes that the DOS disk will be in drive A. If you have a hard disk, change the drive A specifier in lines 3, 4, and 5 to C. If your DOS's

```
 1: ECHO OFF
 2: IF NOT "%1"=="" GOTO help
 3: NEWDISK B: /S/V
 4: COPY COMMAND.COM B:
 5: CHKDSK B:
 6: GOTO end
 7: :help
 8: ECHO          This command creates a bootable system diskette on drive B.
 9: ECHO          The syntax of the command is BOOTDISK with no parameters.
10: ECHO            Any data currently on the diskette will be erased.
11: :end
```

Listing 10.2 ▲ *BOOTDISK.BAT.*

version of FORMAT with the /S switch transfers COMMAND.COM to the destination disk automatically, omit line 4. Line 5 issues the CHKDSK command just for an extra margin of safety.

Enhancing BOOTDISK

If you have a macro processor such as SuperKey, you might want to add the line

KEY BOOTDISK /ML

to your batch program between lines 2 and 3 and create the macro BOOTDISK.MAC, with the following text:

```
<BEGDEF><AltN><AUTO> <CMD>OW+ <CMD>n
<ENTER>
<ENDDEF>
```

This macro, which is arbitrarily assigned to the Alt-N key, will automatically send a single character to the NEWDISK (formerly FORMAT) program when the prompt

Insert new diskette for drive B:
and strike any key when ready

appears. It will then wait for disk activity to stop (that's what <CMD>OW+<CMD> does), and automatically answer N when FORMAT asks you if you want to format another disk, so the CHKDSK program can proceed without intervention.

   If you want to set up the program so that it repeats automatically, you can add the label

:start

at the beginning, and append

YN Do you want to make another system diskette
IF ERRORLEVEL 1 GOTO :start

If you have not typed in the YN program from Chapter 4, you can substitute lines containing an appropriate ECHO statement and a PAUSE for these lines.

STREAMLINING DISK CHECKING

The CHKDSK command is notoriously hard to remember. Is there an E in it or an I? You can streamline it by typing in CHECK.BAT, which appears in Listing 10.3. The syntax is simply

CHECK A

where A is the drive specifier (again, the colon is not permitted). Since you will not rename CHKDSK.COM, the standard syntax can be used as well. This file includes the /F switch, which automatically writes corrections to disk. Some versions of DOS will ask your permission before writing corrections, even if the /F switch is specified. If yours does not, and you prefer to take other steps (perhaps using some kind of file-recovery software) do not include this switch in the file.

```
1: ECHO OFF
2: CHKDSK %1: /F
```

Listing 10.3 ▲ *CHECK.BAT.*

REVERSING THE EFFECT OF WILD CARDS

Have you ever wished you could look at a directory and see everything *except* some specified files? For example, you might use a word processor or spreadsheet that requires a large number of ancillary files, such as printer drivers and configuration files, and all you really want to see is your data files.

Directories Showing "All But . . ."

DIRSKIP.BAT, shown in Listing 10.4, will allow you to see all but the files that you specify. It simply uses the FIND filter (which must be on your default drive or on your search path) to eliminate the unwanted entries before displaying the rest. To issue the command, type DIRSKIP, followed by the pattern of characters that you do not want included. For example,

DIRSKIP BAS

will show all files except those with BAS in their file names. There is a catch, though: you must type in the character pattern in uppercase letters.

```
1: ECHO OFF
2: DIR |FIND /V "%1"
```

Listing 10.4 ▲ *DIRSKIP.BAT.*

Copying Files "All But . . ."

Suppose that you want to back up only some types of files from one disk or directory to another. You might, for example, want to back up a group of programs to one disk and text files explaining them to another disk (as I've been doing as I write this chapter). The two programs that follow, used together, will make this possible. The CSKIP.BAT file, shown in Listing 10.5, scans the directory for the files that you want and writes the list of desired files to a temporary file. CSKIP.BAS, shown in Listing 10.6, is a BASIC program that writes a second batch file to do the actual work. After that, control is returned to the first batch file, and the three intermediate files are erased. For these programs to work, BASICA and the FIND filter program must be on your default directory or the search path.

How CSKIP.BAT Works   The syntax for CSKIP is

CSKIP *SOURCE STRING STRING STRING . . .*

where *source* is the source drive and directory. You must enter the directory from which the files are to be copied, even if it is your current directory, because the program checks the first parameter you type and saves it, passing it to the DIR command later. The patterns of characters to be searched for, represented by *STRING*, must be entered in uppercase characters because the FIND filter does not regard uppercase

```
 1: ECHO OFF
 2: IF NOT %1@==@ GOTO start
 3: ECHO  ^GEnter source drive and directory, followed by the pattern
 4: ECHO  of file name characters to be skipped in uppercase letters.
 5: GOTO end
 6: :start
 7: SET SRC=%1
 8: ECHO %1 >TEMP1.DAT
 9: SHIFT
10: DIR %SRC% |FIND /V "e" |FIND /V "<" >TEMP1.DIR
11: :repeat
12: COPY TEMP1.DIR TEMP2.DIR >NUL
13: FIND /V "%1" TEMP2.DIR > TEMP1.DIR
14: SHIFT
15: IF NOT %1@==@ GOTO repeat
16: BASICA CSKIP
17: COMMAND /C TEMP2
18: ERASE TEMP?.*
19: SET SRC=
20: :end
```

Listing 10.5 ▲ *CSKIP.BAT.*

and lowercase characters as equivalent. For example,

CSKIP C:\NEWDIR BAT COM EXE

would search the directory NEWDIR on drive C and copy all files except those whose names contain the combinations of characters BAT, COM, and EXE. This does not mean that only those with these extensions would not be copied, however. A file named BATCH.BAS or one named COMMAND.TMP would be skipped over in the copying process as well because their names include the specified strings. You cannot match extensions, since the period does not appear in the directory listings.

Here is a line-by-line explanation of how the CSKIP.BAT program works.

1:	Turns screen echoing off.
2:	Checks for a parameter. It does not check to see if the parameter is correct; it only checks to see if one exists.
3–5:	Displays a message if no parameter was entered, and aborts the program.
6–9:	Assigns the name of the source directory to the variable SRC with the SET command, which stores it in the DOS environment space, as well as in a file that can be read by

```
10  '      CSKIP.BAS    Used with CSKIP.BAT to selectively copy files
100 CLS: KEY OFF: SCREEN 0: WIDTH 80
110 OPEN "TEMP1.DAT FOR INPUT AS #1: INPUT #1, SOURCE$: CLOSE #1
120 INPUT "Target drive and directory ==> "; TARGET$
130 ON ERROR GOTO 300: MKDIR TARGET$: ON ERROR GOTO 0
140 OPEN "TEMP1.DIR" FOR INPUT AS #1
150 OPEN "TEMP2.BAT" FOR OUTPUT AS #2
160 PRINT #2, "ECHO OFF": PRINT #2,"VERIFY ON"
170 LINE INPUT #1, FILE$
180    IF EOF(1) GOTO 280
190    IF MID$(FILE$,20,2)=" 0" GOTO 270            'Skip zero-length files
200    X=0:FOR I=1 TO 9                         'Eliminate file name spaces
210      IF MID$(FILE$,I,1)=" " THEN X=I-1:I=10
220    NEXT I
230    FILE$=LEFT$(FILE$,X) + "." + MID$(FILE$,10,3) 'Add file name extension
240 IF LEFT$(FILE$,1)="." GOTO 270
250 PRINT #2, "COPY "; SOURCE$; FILE$; " "; TARGET$; ">NUL"
260 PRINT #2,"ECHO Copying "; FILE$
270 GOTO 170
280 PRINT #2, "EXIT"
290 CLOSE: SYSTEM
300 RESUME NEXT
```

Listing 10.6 ▲ *CSKIP.BAS.*

the BASIC program. This parameter is then passed over, so that it is not among the strings to be searched for.

10:     First passes the directory name stored in the environment variable SRC to the DIR command. Next, passes the directory to the FIND filter to eliminate all lines with a lowercase e. This includes all the lines that are not directory entries:

> Volume in drive X ....
> Directory of X:\
> *NNNNN* bytes free

The result is sent to a temporary file called TEMP1.DIR. This name is used so that it can be erased by the same command that erases all the other temporary files.

11–15: Forms a loop. First, TEMP1.DIR is copied to TEMP2.DIR. Output of the COPY command is directed to the bit bucket to avoid messages that might be confusing. TEMP2.DIR is searched for the first parameter given. All entries that don't match are discarded, and the result is written to TEMP1.DIR. This is a new version of TEMP1.DIR that replaces the old one. In line 13, the next parameter is shifted to the first position, so that it becomes equal to "%1". Line 14 then checks to see if another parameter exists. If so, execution is directed back to line 10. Each version of TEMP1.DIR is a version of TEMP2.DIR with one more file-name pattern deleted.

16:     Calls BASICA and tells it to execute CSKIP.BAS.

17:     Loads a second copy of COMMAND.COM (necessary when you want to call a second batch file and return control to the calling program), and executes TEMP2.BAT, the program created by CSKIP.BAS.

18:     Deletes the temporary files TEMP1.DIR, TEMP2.DIR, TEMP1.DAT, and TEMP2.BAT. It is for this reason that the secondary command processor had to be loaded in line 16. The only other place a command to delete TEMP2.BAT could be entered would be in TEMP2.BAT itself, and a file cannot delete itself while it is executing.

18–19: Removes the variable assigned to SRC from the environment, and the program ends.

How CSKIP.BAS Works CSKIP.BAS is the program called by CSKIP.BAT. It begins by asking you for the destination drive and target directory. If the target directory is the current directory on the destination disk, you need only enter the drive specifier. You must include the colon. If the directory does not exist, the program will create it.

Here is a line-by-line explanation of the CSKIP.BAS program.

100: Sets up the screen.

110: Opens the file created by CSKIP.BAT that contains the name of the source directory and assigns it to the variable SOURCE$.

120: Asks for the destination drive and target directory, assigning them to the variable TARGET$.

130: Attempts to create the target directory. If the target directory already exists, BASIC reports an error. If an error is reported, execution is directed to line 300, which says to continue as if there were no error.

Warning: If your version of BASIC does not recognize path commands, this line will generate a syntax error, which will also be trapped. You should instead create the target directory from DOS before invoking CSKIP.BAT and omit this line.

140–150: Opens the file, and creates the second batch program, TEMP2.BAT.

160: Begins writing to the batch file with the commands to turn off screen echoing and turn on the VERIFY command, which assures that copies are exact duplicates of the original.

170: Begins the main processing loop. One line from TEMP1.DIR is read and assigned to the variable FILE$.

180:   Checks for the end-of-file marker of TEMP1.DIR, which is file #1.

190:   Checks the last two columns of the file-size entry to see if they contain a space followed by a 0, denoting an empty file. Since the pipe in CSKIP.BAT will create several temporary files that will be empty by the time CSKIP.BAS begins executing, there will definitely be empty files in the directory.

200–220: Goes through the file name one character at a time to find the first space. Since directory entries display file names in exactly 12 spaces (eight for the name, followed by a space and the extension, if any), and since DOS will not recognize file names with spaces in them if they are typed on the command line, the file name must be reduced to its significant characters, without the spaces.

230:   Appends a period after the last significant character in the file name, and then appends the extension. File names with no extension will appear with a period followed by three spaces, but this presents no problem for DOS.

240:   The FIND filter always creates a header for its output, followed by two blank lines. There will be such a combination of lines in TEMP1.DIR for each pass through the filter. When line 230 reconstructs the file names, they will have a period for the header, followed by the two blank lines. Line 240 simply assures that these nonexistent file names are not written to the batch file.

 Warning: This line is absolutely vital because DOS interprets a single period as equivalent to the current subdirectory. If your current directory is not a root directory, the syntax

```
COPY .
```

is functionally the same as

```
COPY *.*
```

Without this line, the blank lines after the headers would turn into file names consisting of a single period, and every file on the current directory would be copied as many times as there are blank lines before the selected files are copied, totally defeating the purpose of the program.

250: For each file name, writes an entry to the batch file with the COPY command, the source drive and directory, the file name, a space, and the destination drive and target directory. Output of the COPY command is directed to the bit bucket, so that you don't have to be bothered with the message

1 File(s) copied

after each file is written.

260: Places a command in the batch file to tell you which file is being copied at any given moment, so you can abort the process if necessary.

270: Returns to the beginning of the processing loop to get the next file name from TEMP1.DIR.

280: Adds the EXIT command to the temporary batch file to return control to CSKIP.BAT, so that it can erase all the temporary files.

290: Closes the files, and returns control to DOS, at which point CSKIP.BAT continues.

300: Traps the error condition caused by an existing target directory.

SENDING A DIRECTORY TO THE PRINTER

A simple file will automatically redirect your directories to the printer. The normal syntax for this redirection is

DIR > PRN

However, the PDIR.BAT file, which appears in Listing 10.7, will let you type a shorter command with a bit less fuss. All you have to type is

PDIR *N*

where *N* is the letter designating the drive of the directory.

```
1: ECHO OFF
2: DIR %1: > PRN:
```

Listing 10.7 ▲ *PDIR.BAT.*

If you are sure that you won't forget to turn the printer on, omit lines 2 and 3.

PRINTING OUT MULTIPLE FILES

PRINTOUT.BAT, shown in Listing 10.8, will allow you to send any number of files to your printer with a single command. Just type

PRINTOUT *FILE1.EXT FILE2.EXT . . . FILEN.EXT*

If the files are on different drives or directories, you can specify the paths as part of the file names.

After each file is printed, the character Ctrl-L is echoed to the printer in line 4. This character sends a form feed to the printer, so that each file starts on a new page.

Warning: If you use wild cards in the file names that are arguments to the PRINTOUT command, the form feed will be issued only after each group of files represented by the wild-card pattern is printed, not after each file. Execution does not proceed to line 5 until all the files specified by whatever is currently replacing %1 have been sent to the printer.

If your files are long, however, you can save yourself some time by using the PRINT command or a print spooler. Like many of these short programs, PRINTOUT sets up a loop with the SHIFT command, cycling through each argument in turn. The first line of the loop checks

```
1: ECHO OFF
2: :start
3: IF "%1"=="" GOTO end
4: COPY %1 PRN
5: ECHO ^L >PRN
6: SHIFT
7: GOTO start
8: :end
```

Listing 10.8 ▲ *PRINTOUT.BAT.*

for the existence of an argument that has not been used before cycling through the loop again. If no argument is found, the program ends. It would have been possible to end the program with

IF NOT "%1" == "" GOTO :start

and omit the test just after the :start label, but for some reason, this ending line will be echoed on the screen the last time through the loop. This is no disaster, but it is somewhat less elegant than having the program execute with no extraneous messages.

VIEWING THE CONTENTS OF MULTIPLE FILES

LOOK.BAT, shown in Listing 10.9, displays a series of files on the screen. It uses the same basic logic as the PRINTOUT.BAT file. However, in place of the COPY command, we will use each file as input to the MORE filter, so that your files will be displayed a page at a time. In place of the form feed in line 5 of PRINTOUT.BAT, we will use the PAUSE command, so that the next file will be displayed only when you are ready to see it. The syntax is simply

LOOK *FILENAME.EXT FILENAME.EXT* . . .

Although you cannot use wild cards in the file names, you can display files from various drives and directories by including the drive prefixes and paths.

```
1: ECHO OFF
2: :start
3: IF "%1"=="" GOTO end
4: MORE <%1
5: PAUSE
6: SHIFT
7: GOTO start
8: :end
```

Listing 10.9 ▲ *LOOK.BAT.*

COPYING A GROUP OF UNRELATED FILES

CFILES.BAT, shown in Listing 10.10, allows you to enter the names of several files to be copied on a single command line. It will accept wild-card characters for file names and as many file names as you can fit on a single command line (up to 128 characters). The syntax is

   CFILES *SOURCE DESTINATION FILENAME.EXT*
     FILENAME.EXT . . .

where *SOURCE* is the source drive and/or path and *DESTINATION* is the drive and/or path to which you want the files to be copied. You must specify both the source and destination, or you will get an error message from DOS.

Notice the syntax of the replaceable parameters. %SRC% is separated from %1 by a backslash. This means that, if the source is a subdirectory on the currently logged drive, it must be preceded by a backslash. To demonstrate why, consider the following examples. First, let's suppose that you have entered the command

   CFILES C: B: WS∗.∗ ∗.TXT

This would be perfectly acceptable because DOS would translate the parameters in line 8 as

   COPY C:\WS∗.∗ B:

and

   COPY C:\ ∗.TXT B:

The backslash after the drive specifier indicates the root directory, which is presumably what you wanted. If, however, you are logged to drive C in a directory called WORDSTAR, and you entered the command as

   CFILES WORDSTAR B: WS∗.∗ ∗.TXT

```
 1: ECHO OFF
 2: SET SRC=%1
 3: SET DEST=%2
 4: SHIFT
 5: SHIFT
 6: :start
 7: IF "%1"=="" GOTO end
 8: COPY %SRC%\%1 %DEST%
 9: SHIFT
10: GOTO start
11: :end
12: SET SRC=
13: SET DEST=
```

Listing 10.10 ▲ *CFILES.BAT.*

the first translation DOS would make in line 8 would be

COPY WORDSTAR\WS∗.∗ B:

which would work only if WORDSTAR is one directory level below the current directory. On the other hand,

CFILES \WORDSTAR WS∗.∗ ∗.TXT

would be perfectly acceptable. Including a source drive other than the current one or a directory on such a drive would also work.

As in CSKIP, the SET command is used to remember the source directory; it is also used here to remember the target directory, so that both can be entered as parameters for the COPY command. Because this program uses the SHIFT command, each file name or file-name pattern is acted on in turn. When there are no more parameters, the program removes the environment variables and ends.

SAVING FILES THAT HAVE NOT BEEN BACKED UP

SAVE.BAT, shown in Listing 10.11, follows essentially the same logic as CFILES.BAT, with one exception. It copies files only if they do not already exist on the target directory. It uses the EXIST command in line 8 to check whether a file by the same name is present before copying the file. The syntax is identical to that of CFILES, except that the command is SAVE.

```
 1: ECHO OFF
 2: SET SRC=%1
 3: SET %DEST%=%2
 4: SHIFT
 5: SHIFT
 6: :start
 7: IF %1!==! GOTO end
 8: IF NOT EXIST %DEST%\%1 COPY %SRC%\%1 %DEST%
 9: SHIFT
10: GOTO start
11: :end
12: SET SRC=
13: SET DEST=
```

Listing 10.11 ▲ *SAVE.BAT.*

MOVING FILES FROM ONE DISK OR DIRECTORY TO ANOTHER

The MOVE.BAT program, shown in Listing 10.12, moves a file from one directory to another. Like SAVE.BAT, it first checks, in line 9, to see if the file exists on the target directory. If so, it beeps to check to see if you want to proceed. After copying a file (in line 15), it erases that file from the source directory (in line 16). As an added precaution, the VERIFY command is included to ensure that the copy is accurate before erasing the source file. The syntax, like that of all the other programs in this group, is

MOVE *SOURCE DESTINATION FILE1.EXT*
FILE2.EXT . . .FILEN.EXT

```
 1: ECHO OFF
 2: VERIFY ON
 3: SET SRC=%1
 4: SET DEST=%2
 5: SHIFT
 6: SHIFT
 7: :start
 8: IF %1$==$ GOTO end
 9: IF NOT EXIST %DEST%\%1 GOTO ok
10: YN ^G%1 already exists in %DEST%. Proceed anyway
11: IF ERRORLEVEL 1 GOTO ok
12: SHIFT
13: GOTO start
14: :ok
15: COPY %SRC%\%1 %DEST%
16: ERASE %SRC%\%1
17: SHIFT
18: GOTO start
19: :end
20: SET SRC=
21: SET DEST=
```

Listing 10.12 ▲ *MOVE.BAT.*

In Chapter 11, we will create a menu-driven BASIC program that will encompass all of the functions of the CSKIP, CFILES, SAVE, and MOVE programs.

VIEWING DIRECTORIES IN SORTED ORDER

You can make use of DOS's filters to view directories in just about any form that you choose. We'll look at techniques for sorting directories in various forms and for piping them to files. By the end of this section, we'll have developed a batch file that provides menu-driven choices of sorted directories, complete with a help screen. You will not, however, be able to rewrite disk directories on disk in sorted order. That requires a much higher level of programming expertise than this book assumes. If you are interested in writing such directories, you can use the utility software described in Chapter 5.

The Basic Technique

The basic technique for sorting directories is to make use of the DOS SORT filter. The SORT command will sort on any column that you specify. Thus, for example, you could issue the command line

DIR B: ¦SORT / + 10

to display the directory sorted by extension, that is, by the tenth character in a directory entry (eight columns are reserved for the file name, followed by one for a space). However, it's hard to remember the syntax for such a command, so we'll streamline it by putting the options into a batch file, which you can invoke with a simple command-line argument.

DIRS.BAT, Version 1

We will create two different versions of DIRS.BAT, using two different strategies. The first version, shown in Listing 10.13, requires a specific syntax, and it will display a help screen if parameters are missing. It is constructed using only DOS commands. The second version uses the CHOOSE program from Chapter 6 and employs a different strategy in handling replaceable parameters, so that the DIRS command can be used with no arguments. If you don't mind including arguments, you can use the first version's strategy in the second version and rewrite the menu accordingly.

Both versions will display the directory sorted by file name, extension, size, time of creation, or date of creation. If you choose to sort by date, the dates will not be sorted by year, since 1-01-86 is earlier in the ASCII collating sequence than 3-01-81. For this program to work, the DOS SORT and FIND filters must be on the default directory or the search path.

The syntax required to invoke version 1 is

DIRS *SORTKEY DRIVE [PATH]*

where *sortkey* is the first letter of the item on which you want to sort, *drive* is the letter representing the drive (without the colon), and *path* is the path name. For example,

DIRS E B TEXT

will sort the subdirectory TEXT on drive B by extension. You must enter a drive. However, if a path is not entered, the default is assumed. If you want to specify a longer path, you must, as usual, separate the levels with backslashes:

DIRS E B TEXT\LETTERS\LETTERS.OLD

Here is a line-by-line description of version 1 of the DIRS.BAT program.

```
 1: ECHO OFF
 2: IF "%1"=="" GOTO help
 3: IF "%2"=="" GOTO help
 4: GOTO header
 5: :select
 6: IF "%1"=="N" GOTO name
 7: IF "%1"=="n" GOTO name
 8: IF "%1"=="E" GOTO ext
 9: IF "%1"=="e" GOTO ext
10: IF "%1"=="S" GOTO size
11: IF "%1"=="s" GOTO size
12: IF "%1"=="D" GOTO date
13: IF "%1"=="d" GOTO date
14: IF "%1"=="T" GOTO time
15: IF "%1"=="t" GOTO time
16: GOTO help
17: :name
18: DIR %2:\%3 |SORT |FIND /V "e" |FIND /V "."
19: GOTO end
20: :ext
21: DIR %2:\%3 |SORT/+10 |FIND /V "e" |FIND /V "."
22: GOTO end
23: :size
24: DIR %2:\%3 |SORT/+14 /R |FIND /V "e" |FIND /V "."
25: GOTO end
26: :date
27: DIR %2:\%3 |SORT/+23 |FIND /V "e" |FIND /V "."
28: GOTO end
29: :time
30: DIR %2:\%3 |SORT/+33 |FIND /V "e" |FIND /V "."
31: GOTO end
32: :header
33: CLS
34: VOL %2:
35: ECHO  Directory of %2:\%3
36: GOTO select
37: :help
38: CLS
39: TYPE DIRS.HLP
40: :end
```

Listing 10.13 ▲ *DIRS.BAT.*

1:   Turns off echoing.

2–3:   Checks for the absence of parameters; if none are present, it causes the help file to be displayed on the screen (see Listings 10.15, 10.16, and 10.17 for plain, highlighted, and color versions of these help screens, respectively).

4:   Redirects execution to the :header subroutine.

5–15:   Intercepts the first parameter, and directs execution to the appropriate part of the program, indicated by the label in each line. Uppercase and lowercase characters are checked for separately.

16:   Displays the help file if the parameters given are unacceptable.

17–19:   Sorts by name, redirects execution to end.

20–22:   Sorts by extension, redirects execution to end.

23–25:   Sorts by size in reverse order, redirects execution to end.

26–28:   Sorts by date, redirects execution to end.

29–31:   Sorts by time, redirects execution to end.

32–36:   :header subroutine. Clears the screen, and displays the volume label and directory name, as is normal for a directory display. These lines would appear in irregular places in the display if they were not filtered out in lines 17–31. After the header is printed, execution is returned to line 5, where the first parameter is checked and execution is directed to the proper point.

38–39:   Calls the help file.

Notice the syntax for the replaceable parameters. Because the drive and path are specified as

%2:\%3

the presence of the colon or backslash would result in an invalid drive specification or directory path. For example, entering

B:\TEXT

as the second argument would result in %2:\%3 being replaced by

B::\\TEXT

However, this syntax allows us to separate the drive from the path, so that the drive specifier can be passed to the VOL command in the :header module at line 32. The alternative strategy is to use a single value as the replaceable parameter for the entire drive and path specifier. DOS will accept this value, but the VOL command will not accept it if a path is entered. You will see how this works in version 2 of DIRS.BAT.

Hint: If your directories tend to include more than 20 entries, add

| MORE

to the ends of the pipelines in lines 18, 21, 24, 27, and 30.

The Help Screen

Listings 10.14, 10.15, and 10.16 display three different versions of the help screen for DIRS.BAT. This screen is displayed by the TYPE command when no sort parameter is entered. Listing 10.15 includes bold and inverse video for monochrome monitors, and Listing 10.16 includes color. To use either of these versions of the help screen, you must have the ANSI.SYS device driver loaded in your CONFIG.SYS file. Figure 10.1 illustrates the screen displayed by Listing 10.16. If you don't like the colors, you can change them by substituting different ANSI escape codes (see Appendix B for a full list of these codes).

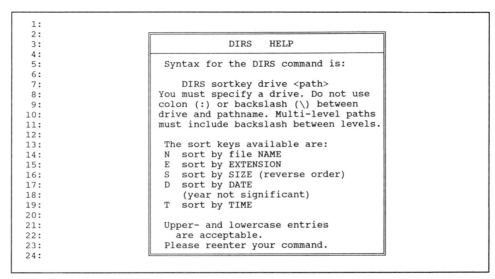

```
 1:
 2:
 3:                        DIRS    HELP
 4:
 5:           Syntax for the DIRS command is:
 6:
 7:               DIRS sortkey drive <path>
 8:           You must specify a drive. Do not use
 9:           colon (:) or backslash (\) between
10:           drive and pathname. Multi-level paths
11:           must include backslash between levels.
12:
13:           The sort keys available are:
14:           N   sort by file NAME
15:           E   sort by EXTENSION
16:           S   sort by SIZE (reverse order)
17:           D   sort by DATE
18:               (year not significant)
19:           T   sort by TIME
20:
21:           Upper- and lowercase entries
22:              are acceptable.
23:           Please reenter your command.
24:
```

Listing 10.14 ▲ *DIRS.HLP.*

I created these files using SideKick's Notepad and SuperKey's GRAPH and GRAPH2 macro files. However, you can type them in any

```
 1: ^[[0m
 2:
 3:                    ^[[1m DIRS    HELP^[[0m              ‖
 4:
 5:          Syntax for the ^[[1mDIRS^[[0m command is:     ‖
 6:
 7:              ^[[7mDIRS sortkey drive <path>  ^[[0m     ‖
 8:          You must specify a drive. Do not use
 9:          colon (:) or backslash (\) between
10:          drive and pathname. Multi-level paths
11:          must include backslash between levels.
12:
13:          The sort keys available are:
14:          ^[[7m N ^[[0m sort by file ^[[1mNAME^[[0m
15:          ^[[7m E ^[[0m sort by ^[[1mEXTENSION^[[0m
16:          ^[[7m S ^[[0m sort by ^[[1mSIZE^[[0m (reverse order)
17:          ^[[7m D ^[[0m sort by ^[[1mDATE^[[0m
18:              (year not significant)       ‖
19:          ^[[7m T ^[[0m sort by ^[[1mTIME^[[0m
20:
21:          Upper- and lowercase entries
22:            are acceptable.
23:          Please reenter your command.
24:
```

Listing 10.15 ▲ *DIRS.HLP with Escape Codes for Bold and Inverse Video.*

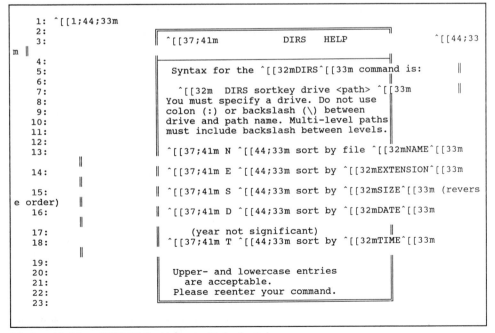

```
 1: ^[[1;44;33m
 2:
 3:    ^[[37;41m              DIRS    HELP              ^[[44;33
m ‖
 4:
 5:        Syntax for the ^[[32mDIRS^[[33m command is:      ‖
 6:
 7:            ^[[32m  DIRS sortkey drive <path> ^[[33m       ‖
 8:        You must specify a drive. Do not use
 9:        colon (:) or backslash (\) between
10:        drive and path name. Multi-level paths
11:        must include backslash between levels.
12:
13:    ‖   ^[[37;41m N ^[[44;33m sort by file ^[[32mNAME^[[33m
         ‖
14: ‖  ^[[37;41m E ^[[44;33m sort by ^[[32mEXTENSION^[[33m
         ‖
15: ‖  ^[[37;41m S ^[[44;33m sort by ^[[32mSIZE^[[33m (revers
e order)  ‖
16: ‖  ^[[37;41m D ^[[44;33m sort by ^[[32mDATE^[[33m
         ‖
17:            (year not significant)       ‖
18: ‖  ^[[37;41m T ^[[44;33m sort by ^[[32mTIME^[[33m
19:
20:        Upper- and lowercase entries
21:          are acceptable.
22:        Please reenter your command.
23:
```

Listing 10.16 ▲ *DIRS.HLP with Escape Codes for Color.*

text editor or word processor that accepts graphics characters. The SuperKey macro files redefine the keys on the numeric keypad as line and border characters, which can be entered when the keypad keys are used in combination with the Ctrl and Alt keys. If you do not have these facilities available to you, you can enter the border characters by using the method described in the section on how to enter the programs (at the beginning of the book).

There are 17 spaces before the first vertical border, and the horizontal lines are 39 characters in length between the borders.

DIRS.BAT, Version 2

The second version of DIRS.BAT, shown in Listing 10.17, uses the CHOOSE program. In this version, only %1 is used as a replaceable parameter. Thus, to get a sorted view of the default directory, you can simply type

DIRS

Here is a line-by-line description of version 2 of DIRS.BAT.

1:        Turns off screen echoing.

2–3:   Clears the screen and displays the menu.

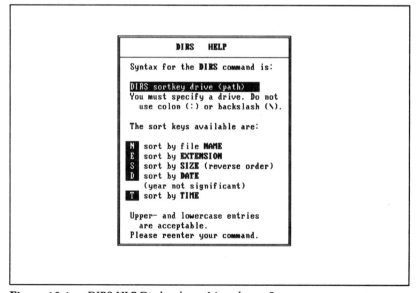

Figure 10.1 ▲ *DIRS.HLP Displayed on a Monochrome Screen.*

4: Invokes the CHOOSE program with the arguments N, E, S, D, and T, representing name, extension, size, date, and time. (Remember, the arguments for CHOOSE must be entered in uppercase letters.)

5, 27–30: Checks the command line to see whether a parameter was entered. If so, a header is displayed, telling which directory is to be displayed. Because only a single parameter is accepted, there is no way to separate the drive from the path if a path is entered. Since the VOL command will not accept an argument in the form

D:\PATH

the command is not invoked, as it was in version 1.

6–11: Uses the ERRORLEVEL statement to check the responses to the CHOOSE command, and directs execution to the appropriate routine. Note that T

```
 1: ECHO OFF
 2: CLS
 3: TYPE DIRS.MNU
 4: CHOOSE NESDT
 5: IF NOT %1@==@ GOTO header
 6: :select
 7: IF ERRORLEVEL 4 GOTO name
 8: IF ERRORLEVEL 3 GOTO ext
 9: IF ERRORLEVEL 2 GOTO size
10: IF ERRORLEVEL 1 GOTO date
11: GOTO time
12: :name
13: DIR %1 |SORT |FIND /V "e" |FIND /V "."
14: GOTO end
15: :ext
16: DIR %1 |SORT/+10 |FIND /V "e" |FIND /V "."
17: GOTO end
18: :size
19: DIR %1 |SORT/+14 /R |FIND /V "e" |FIND /V "."
20: GOTO end
21: :date
22: DIR %1 |SORT/+23 |FIND /V "e" |FIND /V "."
23: GOTO end
24: :time
25: DIR %1 |SORT/+33 |FIND /V "e" |FIND /V "."
26: GOTO end
27: :header
28: CLS
29: ECHO  Directory of %1
30: GOTO select
31: :end
```

Listing 10.17 ▲ *DIRS.BAT, Version 2.*

generates an error level of 0; however, since it is the only remaining value, it need not be tested explicitly.

12–26:   Routines to display the sorted directory. They are identical to those in version 1.

If you want to display a volume label as in version 1, you must alter this program as follows:

1. In place of the replaceable parameter %1, use %1:\%2.

2. Add the command

   VOL %1

   after line 28.

3. Change line 5 to read

   IF "%1" == "" GOTO :help

4. Add a line following line 5, reading

   GOTO :header

5. Add an appropriate help message, displaying the proper syntax, which will then be

   DIRS *DRIVE [PATH]*

   with no colon after the drive specifier and no backslash before the path.

The menu for this program is displayed in Listing 10.18. I have included only a text version. You may add the escape sequences if you wish. There are 17 spaces before the first character on each line, and the horizontal borders are 36 characters long. The arrowhead after "Your choice" is a Ctrl-P.

Hint: In order for the cursor to appear after the arrowhead, you *must* enter a Ctrl-Z (end-of-file) immediately after the Ctrl-P. If you enter a carriage return, the cursor will appear on the next line.

```
 1:
 2:                    ┌─────────────────────────────────────┐
 3:                    │            DIRS    MENU              │
 4:                    │  The directory for the drive and     │
 5:                    │  directory you specified will be      │
 6:                    │  displayed in sorted order. If you    │
 7:                    │  did not specify a drive or path,     │
 8:                    │  the default will be displayed.       │
 9:                    │                                       │
10:                    │  The sort keys available are:         │
11:                    │                                       │
12:                    │  N   sort by file NAME                │
13:                    │  E   sort by EXTENSION                │
14:                    │  S   sort by SIZE (reverse order)     │
15:                    │  D   sort by DATE                     │
16:                    │      (year not significant)           │
17:                    │  T   sort by TIME                     │
18:                    │                                       │
19:                    │  Upper- and lowercase entries         │
20:                    │                                       │
21:                    └─────────────────────────────────────┘
22:       Your choice ══^P
```

Listing 10.18 ▲ *DIRS.MNU.*

REWRITING THE COMMAND PROCESSOR

Up to now, we've been customizing DOS by using batch files. These files create new commands that do a bit more than the standard commands. Now you'll learn how to alter commands by rewriting COMMAND.COM itself.

Why would you want to rewrite the command processor? There may be several reasons. You might want to rewrite the display that appears as a sign-on message (this is legal as long as you leave the copyright notices intact). More significantly, you may have some public-domain programs or other utility software that improve on COMMAND.COM's internal commands. There are some programs, for example, that display files on the screen, filtering out characters that may disrupt the display, unlike the TYPE command. Other programs may display more useful directory listings than the one created by the DIR command. If you want to invoke these programs by using DOS's internal command names such as TYPE and DIR, you must rewrite the command processor, because DOS always looks at the command processor first to see whether a command on the command line is an internal one. Thus, a program with a name such as DIR.EXE or TYPE.COM will never be executed unless the internal DIR and TYPE commands have been removed.

Another reason for rewriting the command processor is to disable specific commands for security. If your computer is used by many individuals, you may want to eliminate the ERASE and RENAME commands to prevent accidental loss of data, for example.

To make any of these changes to COMMAND.COM, use DEBUG to access the code, edit the code as desired, and write the new version to disk under another name.

First, copy COMMAND.COM to another file named COMMAND.TMP. Next, issue the command

DEBUG COMMAND.TMP

Then look in the CX register to see how long the file is. Type

RCX

and make note of the number that appears. Then press Return.

Next, you will search for the text to be altered. You will use the Length (L) parameter to tell DEBUG to search the entire file. For example, to search the entire file for the ERASE command, type

S 0 L *NNNN* **"ERASE"**

where *NNNN* is the number you found in the CX register. When the address appears, ask for a display. Your screen will look something like Figure 10.2.

Next, replace the command with spaces, using the ENTER command. You can enter either hex 20s or actual character spaces. The latter is easier. Since, in this example, ERASE appears at address 4D19, the command would be

E 4D19 "   "

or

E 4D19 20 20 20 20 20

```
C:\> debug command.tmp
-s 0 l ffff "ERASE"
347F:4D29
-d 4d00
347F:4D00  4C 45 56 45 4C 85 08 05-45 58 49 53 54 18 08 00   LEVEL...EXIST...
347F:4D10  03 44 49 52 03 91 0C 06-52 45 4E 41 4D 45 01 C0   .DIR....RENAME..
347F:4D20  0F 03 52 45 4E 01 C0 0F-05 45 52 41 53 45 01 68   ..REN....ERASE.h
347F:4D30  0F 03 44 45 4C 01 68 0F-04 54 59 50 45 01 38 10   ..DEL.h..TYPE.8.
347F:4D40  03 52 45 4D 02 04 01 04-43 4F 50 59 03 61 26 05   .REM....COPY.a&.
347F:4D50  50 41 55 53 45 02 5B 0F-04 44 41 54 45 02 C9 1D   PAUSE.[..DATE...
347F:4D60  04 54 49 4D 45 00 CC 1E-03 56 45 52 00 2E 11 03   .TIME....VER....
347F:4D70  56 4F 4C 01 D8 10 02 43-44 01 DB 15 05 43 48 44   VOL....CD....CHD
```

Figure 10.2 ▲ *A Portion of COMMAND.COM Displayed in DEBUG.*

Now when DOS checks COMMAND.COM for an ERASE command, it will not find one. (Don't forget to replace DEL with three spaces at address 4D32, or there won't be much point to this undertaking.)

When you have made all your changes, write the altered file to disk. The command is a single W. After that, issue the Quit command (Q).

If you keep careful track of which version is on which disk, you could simply call all your command processors COMMAND.COM and boot from the disk that contains a given version only when you want to use that version. Otherwise, you will have to give each version an appropriate name—something like NODEL.COM for a version without a DEL or ERASE command, for example. Use the SET COMSPEC= command in your AUTOEXEC.BAT file to tell DOS to use this altered command processor. You can, of course, restore the missing or altered commands by rebooting with the original version of COMMAND.COM.

If you want to substitute an external program for the command that you have eliminated, you must change the name of the program to that of the deleted command and make sure that it is on the search path when you are working. For example, perhaps you want to use Computer Thaumaturgy's EDIR program, which lists file attributes along with the other information normally shown in a directory, or PC magazines DDIR program, which displays the directory in two columns. To do so, eliminate the DIR command from the command processor, and rename the program you will use to DIR with the appropriate extension.

 Warning: If you plan to use batch files, such as CFILES.BAT, that use the commands you want to replace (in this instance COPY), you *must not* disable the commands called by the batch files, or the batch files will not work.

Creating a Somewhat Protected System

You could use the technique of rewriting the command processor, together with a series of batch files, to create a degree of password protection for a multi-user hard disk system. First, make a version of COMMAND.COM with the DIR, DEL, ERASE, RENAME, MKDIR, and MD commands disabled. Make a second version with the MKDIR, MD, CD, and CHDIR commands disabled. Boot up with the first version, and use the file shown in Listing 10.19 as your AUTOEXEC.BAT file.

This file will create a screen that displays nothing but the prompt

> **Type your first name and Social Security Number:**
> **###-##-####**

The cursor will be at the beginning of the second line, which serves as an edit mask. This line allows up to eight spaces for a name, followed by a template for a social security number. The root directory will contain a series of batch files with the names of the authorized persons. Each one includes a test for that person's social security number. A sample of such a batch file appears in Listing 10.20.

If an incorrect number is entered, a message is displayed, and the AUTOEXEC file is rerun. If the number is correct, the person's authorized directory becomes the current directory, and the program he or she uses is loaded. When the user exits from the program, the computer automatically reboots, reloading the original command processor. This effectively prevents access to other directories, even though somebody could easily break the system by placing a normal DOS disk in the floppy disk drive and rebooting.

As a challenge to yourself, you might want to try to devise a way to use the SET command to place the authorized social security number in the environment and use it to restrict access to specific files.

```
 1: ECHO OFF
 2: PROMPT $e[fType your first name and Social Security Number: $_
###-##-####$e[19D
 3: CLS
 4: SET COMSPEC=C:\COMMAND.COM
```

Listing 10.19 ▲ *An AUTOEXEC.BAT File for Checking Passwords.*

```
 1: ECHO OFF
 2: IF NOT "%1"=="555-00-2468" GOTO noaccess
 3: CD\NANCY
 4: SET COMSPEC=C:\NANCY\NOPATH.COM
 5: CLS
 6: ECHO ^[[f        :moves cursor to home position
 7: PROMPT Welcome to the System!$_$p$g
 8: :you could put the name of the program she uses here
 8: BASICA AUTOBOOT
10: :noaccess
11: ECHO Your Social Security Number is not valid
12: AUTOEXEC
```

Listing 10.20 ▲ *A Batch File to Permit Authorized Access.*

ADVANCED FILE MANAGEMENT

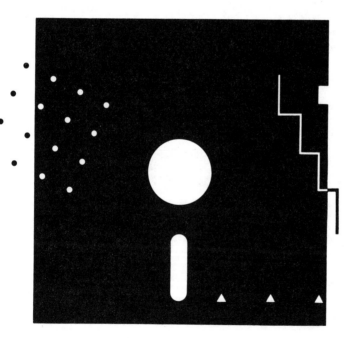

11

THE PREVIOUS CHAPTERS have covered most of what you need to know to manage disk files successfully. This chapter supplies the remaining details. It explains some advanced features of the COPY command that are not widely understood and how the order in which you copy files can make a significant difference in the speed at which they load and execute.

We'll look at some tricks that will help you obtain the best organization of your files on disk. You'll also learn how to combine and separate files. The last part of the chapter presents a BASIC program that functions as an all-purpose file-management utility.

THE ARRANGEMENT OF FILES ON A DISK

When DOS searches for a file, it always searches from the beginning of the directory until it finds the starting cluster specified in the FAT. Therefore, the order in which your files appear on a directory has some effect on the speed with which DOS accesses them. Here are some ways that you can make your file arrangement more efficient:

▲ If there are some files that you always use on startup, make sure that they are the first files on the disk.

▲ If your program uses overlay files extensively, have them appear next on the disk.

▲ If you have batch files that use the TYPE command to display text on the screen, place each text file next to the batch file that calls it on the disk. This way, the drive head doesn't have to jump all over the disk looking for the text file before returning to the batch file.

You can control the order in which the files appear by copying them to a new disk, one at a time, in the desired order. Another advantage of this technique is that it ensures that your files are laid out in consecutive clusters. As we discussed in Chapter 2, when a file is written to disk, DOS begins writing in the first available cluster and continues writing to the consecutive clusters in order, unless they are already part of another file. If so, the occupied clusters are skipped, and the file is written to the next available group of clusters.

When files are updated frequently, you may end up with a disk full of fragmented files. You can find out if this is true in either of two ways. The command

    CHKDSK [*DRIVE*] *.*

will report the name of each file containing noncontiguous blocks and the number of noncontiguous blocks it contains.

Alternatively, any of the file-recovery programs described in Chapter 4 will display a file-by-file map of the disk that will give you a visual picture of the layout of each file. Copying the files one at a time to a new disk, or even copying them with *.*, will organize each file into contiguous clusters, so that it loads as quickly as possible.

Hint: For this reason, the COPY *.* command is better than the DISKCOPY command for backing up floppy disks. You could also make a batch file of COPY commands to make backups of startup disks with the files in the proper order.

Of course, if you are working with a hard disk, this technique isn't much help, because you probably don't have a medium large enough to copy all the files to. What's worse, because a hard disk contains so many files, fragmentation of the files will degrade performance considerably.

Normally, all you can do is perform a complete backup as described in Chapter 14, reformat your hard disk, and restore all the files to it. However, there are several utilities that can unfragment files directly. See the section on "Improving Efficiency" in Chapter 14 for details.

USING THE COPY COMMAND TO CONCATENATE FILES

There are times when it is useful to combine several files into one larger file. You may want to combine files for the following reasons:

▲ To combine a set of standard subroutines with a main program.

▲ To store a group of related files in a single file for archival purposes.

▲ To combine files to perform a global search-and-replace operation for a given item in a group of files. This way, you would only have to perform the operation once.

Most word processing programs will let you append one file to another one in memory, but when you have many files to combine, this procedure can be quite tedious. A little-known feature of the COPY command allows you to combine files in one stroke. The syntax

COPY ∗.BAT BAT.TXT

will copy all your .BAT files into a single file called BAT.TXT, leaving the originals undisturbed.

The files will be combined in the order in which their names appear in the directory, unless you specify each file by name. To specify the files to copy by name, use the concatenation operator, which is a plus sign. The command

COPY *FILE1.EXT* + *FILE2.EXT* + *FILE3.EXT* NEWFILE.EXT

will combine the first three files into the file NEWFILE.EXT.

You can, as the first example indicates, use wild-card characters in the names of the files to be concatenated. However, if the target file name (the file name separated by a space from the files to be concatenated) is among those represented by the wild-card pattern, that file will be destroyed by the time COPY wants to write to it.

If you do not specify a target file, all the files will be combined under the *first* file name in the list. The original version of the first file will be gone, but its contents will appear as the first part of the combined file.

You can use the concatenation feature of the COPY command to combine files with the same name but different extensions. Consider the command

COPY *.TXT + *.FIG + *.TBL *.OUT

It will not, as you might expect, combine any and all files with the extensions .TXT, .FIG, and .TBL into a single file, because of the wild-card character in the target file name. Rather, each group of files with the *same* name will be combined in a single file with a matching name and the extension .OUT. Thus, for example, if your directory contains the files

CHAPTER1.FIG

CHAPTER1.TBL

CHAPTER1.TXT

CHAPTER2.FIG

CHAPTER2.TBL

CHAPTER2.TXT

EXTRA.FIG

NEW.FIG

NEW.TBL

CHAPTER3.TXT

only two files would be created: CHAPTER1.OUT and CHAPTER-2.OUT. The former would combine all files with the name CHAPTER1, and the latter would combine all files with the name CHAPTER2. The remaining four files would not be concatenated, because there aren't three matching file names with the appropriate extensions.

In addition, you can add a switch to any of the file names in the list to tell DOS whether or not to append an end-of-file mark (Ctrl-Z) to that portion of the combined file. The /A switch (for ASCII) appends a Ctrl-Z, while the /B switch (for binary) prevents the Ctrl-Z from being appended.

Getting Rid of Extra End-of-File Marks

So here you are, ready to perform a global search-and-replace operation in all your batch files in one fell swoop. You load your text editor and the file, and lo and behold, only the first of your files appears. A quick check of the directory shows you that TEMP.BAT is long enough to contain all of your batch files. So where are the rest?

Chances are that this quick check will also reveal that some of the batch files that you know are only two or three lines long take up 128 or 256 bytes in the directory. This is because some word processors append enough Ctrl-Zs to the end of a nondocument file to fill out the file length to the nearest 128 bytes. The concatenating COPY command removed the last Ctrl-Z in each of the combined files before the last file, but it didn't know about the others. (In some word processors, they will show up on the screen as nulls— ^ @—rather than Ctrl-Zs, but they still function as end-of-file marks.) The text editor stopped at the first end-of-file mark.

To get rid of the extra Ctrl-Zs, load the file in DEBUG with the command

DEBUG TEMP.BAT

Next, find the file's length as explained in Chapter 10, and search for all the Ctrl-Zs (hex 1A) with the command

S 0 L *NNNN* 1A

You will probably want to redirect the output of this command to your printer so that you can see the results. Finally, enter a space (hex 20) in each of the locations occupied by a Ctrl-Z except the last one. You will then be able to read the entire combined file in your word processor.

To separate the files again, you will have to mark each one as a block and write it to the correctly named file.

SHARING FILES AMONG APPLICATIONS

The two ways of sharing files among applications that we've already discussed—using cut-and-paste utilities and using utility programs that translate files from one program's format to another—are sufficient for most purposes. Most programs accept input in the form of ASCII characters entered from the keyboard, no matter how they store the results. Cutting text from a database or spreadsheet and pasting it into a word processor is probably the easiest way to create a table, and many pro-grams allow you to paste tabular data from another application into your spreadsheet or database. But the form of the data to be pasted may be a stumbling block.

Let's take an example. Suppose that you have some tabular information in an accounting program and you want to paste it into a Framework II spreadsheet. In this program, each time a space in an ASCII text file is encountered, the next item is placed in the following column, and each time a carriage return is encountered, a new row is begun. However, your source has some blank columns and formats dates as

   3 Aug88

when the day of the month is only one digit long, but as

   30Aug88

when it's two digits long. In this case, you must edit some of the source information before you import it, or you will have quite a mess on your hands.

This transfer may require using an intermediate file format. There are three common formats that you can use:

▲ The ASCII text file format

▲ The comma-delimited format

▲ The DIF format

If your source program creates ASCII text files, you can edit them in a word processor before importing them to the spreadsheet, adding dummy values to the empty cells and globally searching and replacing the unwanted spaces with something else.

The *comma-delimited* format places quotation marks around each item of data (each field in a database or each column in a spreadsheet, for example) and inserts a comma between each of the items. Many spread-sheet and database programs that would stumble over a simple ASCII text file can read a comma-delimited file. You can create one in a word processor by selectively replacing the spaces with

   ","

and manually adding the beginning and ending quotation marks to each line. This way, you could leave the spaces in the date format, and they would be included as part of the data to appear in a single column.

The *DIF* format is a special type of ASCII file that includes information about the proper row and column location of each item of data. Many programs that cannot read either ASCII text files or comma-delimited files can read DIF files. An explanation of the internal structure of the DIF file format is beyond the scope of this book. For a full discussion, see *Mastering VisiCalc* by Douglas Hergert (SYBEX, 1983). For further information about ways to transfer data among programs, consult *Data Sharing with 1-2-3 and Symphony* by Dick Andersen (SYBEX, 1985). In addition to the programs mentioned in the title, this book discusses importing and exporting data from dBASE II and III, Framework, and programs that use the DIF format.

AN AUTOMATIC FILE MANAGER

It is only appropriate that a chapter about advanced file management include an advanced file-management system. The program presented here is a rather lengthy BASIC program that combines the functions of the CFILES, CSKIP, MOVE, and SAVE programs from Chapter 10 in one complete menu-driven system. It also allows you to selectively erase files and to make backup copies of files that exist on both the source and target directories. We saw an example of a batch program with this function in Chapter 5.

The complete program appears in Listing 11.1. I won't go into great detail about the way the various lines of code work, but I will explain the structure of the program and the function of its various routines.

 Warning: This program uses the SHELL command and path-related commands extensively. Therefore, it will work *only* with BASIC 3.0 or those updated versions of BASIC that include these commands. It would be extremely difficult to modify the program so that these commands are unneccessary. Also, COMMAND.COM, SORT.EXE, and your version of BASIC must be on the search path for this program to execute properly.

In this program, instead of inserting the graphics characters with the Alt-Shift technique, as in other programs in this book, I have set up

```
10 '******************** YOUR FILE MANAGER ****************************
20 '     by Jonathan Kamin, (c) 1986, 1987, Jonathan Kamin and Sybex, Inc.
30 '                    File Name: FILEMGR.BAS
40 '
100 DIM INCLUDE$(160)
110 KEY OFF: SCREEN 0: WIDTH 80
120 COLOR 14,1,3: CLS: FLAG = 0: FL2 = 0: GOSUB 5000 'draw box
130 LOCATE 1,31: COLOR 14,4: PRINT CHR$(201);
140 FOR I=1 TO 19: PRINT CHR$(205);: NEXT I: PRINT CHR$(187)
150 LOCATE 2,31: PRINT CHR$(185);: COLOR 15: PRINT " YOUR FILE MANAGER ";
160 COLOR 14: PRINT CHR$(204)
170 LOCATE 3,31: PRINT CHR$(200);: FOR I=1 TO 19: PRINT CHR$(205);:
        NEXT I: PRINT CHR$(188)
180 LOCATE 5,8: COLOR 15,4
190 PRINT " C ";: COLOR ,1: PRINT"opy all specified files"
200 LOCATE 7,8: COLOR ,4
210 PRINT " E ";: COLOR ,1: PRINT"rase all specified files"
220 LOCATE 9,8: COLOR ,4
230 PRINT " S ";: COLOR ,1:
        PRINT"ave all specified files not on target directory"
240 LOCATE 11,8: COLOR ,4
250 PRINT " M ";: COLOR ,1: PRINT"ove all specified files to target directory"
260 LOCATE 13,8: COLOR ,4
270 PRINT " B ";: COLOR ,1:
        PRINT"ackup copy of specified files to target directory"
280 LOCATE 15,20: COLOR ,4: PRINT " H ";: COLOR ,1: PRINT"elp"
290 LOCATE 15,45: COLOR ,4: PRINT " Q ";: COLOR ,1: PRINT"uit"
300 LOCATE 19,8: COLOR 14: PRINT "Choose by first letter MMM> ";
310 TASK$ = INPUT$(1):J = 0
320 IF TASK$ = "c" OR TASK$ = "C" THEN TASK$ = "COPY ": J = 1
330 IF TASK$ = "e" OR TASK$ = "E" THEN TASK$ = "ERASE ": J = 2
340 IF TASK$ = "s" OR TASK$ = "S" THEN TASK$ = "SAVE ": J = 3
350 IF TASK$ = "m" OR TASK$ = "M" THEN TASK$ = "MOVE ": J = 4
360 IF TASK$ = "b" OR TASK$ = "B" THEN TASK$ = "BACKUP ":J = 5
370 IF TASK$ = "h" OR TASK$ = "H" THEN GOSUB 6000: GOTO 120
380 IF TASK$ = "q" OR TASK$ = "Q" THEN GOTO 20000
390 IF J = 0 GOTO 310
400 COLOR 15,4: PRINT " "; TASK$: COLOR ,1
410 PRINT: PRINT TAB(3); "Include .BAK files (Y/N)? ";
420 BAK$ = INKEY$: IF BAK$ = "" THEN 420
430 IF BAK$ <> "y" AND BAK$ <> "Y" AND BAK$ <> "n" AND BAK$ <> "N" GOTO 420
        ELSE PRINT BAK$
440 PRINT: PRINT TAB(3); "Today's files only (Y/N)? ";
450 D$ = INKEY$: IF D$ = "" GOTO 450
460 IF D$= "n" OR D$ = "N" GOTO 480 ELSE IF D$ <> "y" AND D$ <> "Y" GOTO 450
470 DT$ = LEFT$(DATE$,6) + RIGHT$(DATE$,2)
480 IF LEFT$(DT$,1) = "0" THEN DT$ = " " + RIGHT$(DT$,7)
490 GOSUB 1000: GOSUB 2000
500 ON J GOSUB 3000, 3100, 3200, 3300, 3400
510 IF J = 1 THEN SHELL "FILEMGR.BAT >NUL" :GOTO 580
520 IF J = 2 GOTO 560
530 TEMP$ = "COPY FILEMGR.BAT " + TARGET$: IF FL2 = 2 THEN TEMP$ = TEMP$ + "\":
        SHELL TEMP$
540 A$ = SOURCE$ + "\FILEMGR.BAT": KILL A$
550 IF J <>4 GOTO 570: IF FLAG = 1 THEN SHELL SDRIVE$ ELSE CHDIR SOURCE$
560 IF FLAG = 1 THEN SHELL TDRIVE$ ELSE IF FL2 <> 2 THEN CHDIR TARGET$
        ELSE CHDIR ROOT$
570 SHELL "FILEMGR.BAT >NUL"
580 GOSUB 4000
```

Listing 11.1 ▲ *FILEMGR.BAS.*

```
590 IF FL2 = 1 THEN A$ = ROOT$ + "TEMP.DIR" ELSE A$ = SOURCE$ + "\TEMP.DIR":
       KILL A$:
600 IF FL2 = 2 THEN A$ = ROOT$ + "FILEMGR.BAT"
       ELSE A$ = TARGET$ + "\FILEMGR.BAT":    KILL A$
610 GOTO 120
997 '
998 ' *******   SELECT DIRECTORIES, INITIALIZE FILES   *********
999 '
1000 COLOR 0,2,6: CLS: LOCATE 5,29: COLOR ,6: PRINT CHR$(201);
1010 FOR I = 1 TO 20: PRINT CHR$(205);: NEXT I: PRINT CHR$(187)
1020 LOCATE 6,29: PRINT CHR$(186); " SELECT DIRECTORIES "; CHR$(186)
1030 LOCATE 7,29: PRINT CHR$(200);: FOR I = 1 TO 20: PRINT CHR$(205);: NEXT I
1040 PRINT CHR$(188): COLOR 15,2: LOCATE 8,9.
1050 PRINT "When entering a path name, you must precede it with a backslash."
1055 PRINT TAB(9); "Enter the root directory as a single backslash."
1060 LOCATE 11,3: COLOR 0: PRINT "Source drive (enter letter only) MM> ";
1070 SDRIVE$ = INKEY$: IF SDRIVE$ = "" OR SDRIVE$ = CHR$(13) GOTO 1070
1080 SDRIVE$ = SDRIVE$ + ":": PRINT SDRIVE$
1090 ON ERROR GOTO 10000: SHELL SDRIVE$
1100 LOCATE 12,3: INPUT "Source path (RETURN for default) MM> ", SPATH$
1110 SOURCE$ = SDRIVE$ + SPATH$: IF SPATH$ = "" GOTO 1130
1120 CHDIR SOURCE$: IF SPATH$ = "\" THEN FL2 = 1: ROOT$ = SOURCE$
1130 ON ERROR GOTO 0
1140 SHELL "DIR|SORT>TEMP.DIR": IF J = 2 GOTO 1340
1150 ON ERROR GOTO 10100: LOCATE 14,3
1160 PRINT "Target drive (enter letter only) MM> ";
1170 TDRIVE$ = INKEY$: IF TDRIVE$ = "" OR TDRIVE$ = CHR$(13) GOTO 1170
1180 TDRIVE$ = TDRIVE$ + ":": PRINT TDRIVE$
1190 TEMP$ = "VOL " + TDRIVE$ + ">NUL":SHELL TEMP$
1200 ON ERROR GOTO 0: LOCATE 15,3
1210 INPUT "Destination path (RETURN for default) MM> ", DPATH$
1220 TARGET$ = TDRIVE$ + DPATH$: IF DPATH$ = "\" THEN FL2 = 2: ROOT$ = TARGET$:
       GOTO 1300
1230 IF DPATH$ = "" GOTO 1340
1240 PRINT:
       PRINT "Do you want to create this directory on the target disk (Y/N)?"
1250 YN$ = INKEY$: IF YN$ = "" THEN 1250
1260 IF YN$ = "n" OR YN$ = "N" THEN 1290 ELSE IF YN$<>"y" AND YN$<>"Y" THEN 1250
1270 ON ERROR GOTO 10100
1280 MKDIR TARGET$
1285 ' temp$ = "MKDIR" + target$: SHELL TEMP$
1290 ON ERROR GOTO 0
1300 IF SDRIVE$ <> TDRIVE$ THEN CHDIR TARGET$: FLAG = 1
1305 ' temp$ = "CHDIR" + target$: SHELL TEMP$
1310 IF FL2 = 0 GOTO 1340
1320    IF SPATH$ = "\" THEN SOURCE$ = SDRIVE$
1330    IF DPATH$ = "\" THEN TARGET$ = TDRIVE$
1340 OPEN "TEMP.DIR" FOR INPUT AS #1
1350 OPEN "FILEMGR.BAT" FOR OUTPUT AS #2
1360 PRINT #2, "ECHO OFF": PRINT #2,"VERIFY ON"
1370 '       skip lines without file names
1380 FOR I = 0 TO 3:LINE INPUT #1, FILE$:NEXT I
1390 RETURN
1997 '
1998 '           ******* FILE SELECTION ROUTINE *******
1999 '
2000 COLOR ,0,3: CLS: LOCATE 25,21: COLOR 15,4
2010 PRINT " SELECT FILES, PRESS ";: COLOR 0,7: PRINT " Q ";
2020 COLOR 15,4: PRINT " WHEN DONE "
2025 'LOCATE 23,1:COLOR ,0: PRINT SPACE$(160)'eliminate stripe from IBM screen
2030 LOCATE 3,1: COLOR 7,0: COUNT = 0
2040 LINE INPUT #1, FILE$
```

Listing 11.1 ▲ *FILEMGR.BAS (continued).*

```
2050    IF EOF(1) GOTO 2250
2060    IF (D$ = "y" OR D$ = "Y") AND MID$(FILE$,24,8) <> DT$ GOTO 2240
2070    IF LEFT$(FILE$,1) = " " OR MID$(FILE$,20,2) = " 0" GOTO 2240
2080    IF INSTR(FILE$,"<") OR INSTR(FILE$,".") GOTO 2240
2090    IF BAK$ = "n" OR BAK$ = "N" THEN IF MID$(FILE$,10,3) = "BAK" GOTO 2240
2100 '        eliminate spaces from file name
2110    X = 0: FOR I = 1 TO 9
2120       IF MID$(FILE$,I,1) = " " THEN X = I - 1:I = 10
2130    NEXT I
2140    FILE$ = LEFT$(FILE$,X) + "." + MID$(FILE$,10,3)
2160    IF FILE$ = "TEMP.DIR" OR FILE$ = "FILEMGR.BAT" GOTO 2240
2170    PRINT FILE$; TAB(20); TASK$; " (Y/N/Q)? ";
2180    A$ = INKEY$:IF A$ = "" THEN 2180
2190       IF A$ = "n" OR A$ = "N" THEN COLOR 28: PRINT "N": COLOR 7: GOTO 2240
2200       IF A$ = "y" OR A$ = "Y" THEN COLOR 26: PRINT "Y": COLOR 7: GOTO 2230
2210       IF A$ = "q" OR A$ = "Q" THEN 2250
2220    GOTO 2180
2230    COUNT = COUNT + 1: INCLUDE$(COUNT) = FILE$
2240 GOTO 2040
2250 CLOSE #1
2260 LOCATE 25,20: COLOR 15,4: PRINT "              Everything OK (Y/N)?              ":
        COLOR 7,0: BEEP
2265 'LOCATE 24,1:COLOR ,0: PRINT SPACES$(80)'eliminate stripe from IBM screen
2270 YN$ = INKEY$: IF YN$ = "" THEN 2270
2290 IF YN$ <> "n" and YN$ <>"N" goto 2270
2300 CLOSE: IF not FLAG THEN SHELL sDRIVE$ ELSE CHDIR source$
2310 gosub 1340: GOTO 2000
2280 IF YN$ = "y" or YN$ = "Y" GOTO 2320
2320 RETURN
2997 '
2998 '            **** COPY ****
2999 '
3000 FOR I = 1 TO COUNT
3010    PRINT #2, TASK$; SOURCE$; "\"; INCLUDE$(I); " "; TARGET$; "\";
 ·              INCLUDE$(I)
3020 NEXT I: CLOSE #2: RETURN
3097 '
3098 '            **** ERASE ****
3099 ,
3100 CLOSE #2 .
3110 FOR I = 1 TO COUNT
3120 KILL INCLUDE$(I)
3130 NEXT I: RETURN
3197 '
3198 '            **** SAVE ****
3199 '
3200 FOR. I = 1 TO COUNT
3210    PRINT #2, "IF NOT EXIST "; TDRIVE$; INCLUDE$(I); " COPY ";
3220'   PRINT #2, SOURCE$; "\"; INCLUDE$(I); " "; TARGET$; "\"; INCLUDE$(I)
3230 NEXT I: CLOSE #2: RETURN
3297 '
3298 '            **** MOVE ****
3299 '
3300 FOR I = 1 TO COUNT
3310    PRINT #2, " COPY " SOURCE$; "\"; INCLUDE$(I); " "; TARGET$; "\";
        INCLUDE$(I)
3320    PRINT #2, "IF  EXIST "; TDRIVE$; INCLUDE$(I);
3330    PRINT #2, " ERASE "; SOURCE$; "\"; INCLUDE$(I)
3340 NEXT I: CLOSE #2 :RETURN
```

Listing 11.1 ▲ *FILEMGR.BAS (continued).*

```
3397 '
3398 '        ****  BACKUP  ****
3399 '
3400 FOR I = 1 TO COUNT
3410   PRINT #2, "IF EXIST "; TDRIVE$; INCLUDE$(I); " COPY ";
3420   PRINT #2, SOURCE$; "\";  INCLUDE$(I); " "; TARGET$; "\";
3430   PRINT #2, LEFT$(INCLUDE$(I),(LEN(INCLUDE$(I))-3)); "BAC"
3440   PRINT #2, "IF NOT EXIST "; TDRIVE$; INCLUDE$ (I); " COPY ";
3450   PRINT #2, SOURCE$; "\" INCLUDE$(I); " "; TARGET$; "\"; INCLUDE$(I)
3460 NEXT I: CLOSE #2: RETURN
3997 '
3998 '       **************  DISPLAY RESULTS  ***************
3999 '
4000 CLS: LOCATE 3,1
4010 IF FL2 = 1 THEN SOURCE$ = ROOT$
4020 IF J = 1 OR J = 5 GOTO 4050
4025 IF FLAG = 1 THEN SHELL SDRIVE$ ELSE CHDIR SOURCE$
4030 PRINT "Directory of "; SOURCE$: FILES SDRIVE$: PRINT
4040 IF J = 2 GOTO 4080
4050 IF FL2 = 2 THEN TARGET$ = ROOT$
4060 IF FLAG = 1 THEN SHELL TDRIVE$ ELSE CHDIR TARGET$
4070 PRINT: PRINT "Directory of "; TARGET$ :FILES TDRIVE$
4080 LOCATE 25,26: COLOR 15,4: PRINT " Press any key to continue "
4085 'LOCATE 23,1:COLOR ,0: PRINT SPACE$(160)'eliminate stripe from IBM screen
4090 A$ = INKEY$:IF A$ = "" GOTO 4090
4100 RETURN
4997 '
4998 '            **********  DRAW BOX  **************
4999 '
5000 COLOR 14,1:PRINT:PRINT TAB(3); CHR$(201);
5010 FOR I = 1 TO 73: PRINT CHR$(205); :NEXT I:PRINT CHR$(187)
5020 FOR I = 1 TO 14: PRINT TAB(3); CHR$(186); TAB(77); CHR$(186):NEXT I
5030 PRINT TAB(3); CHR$(200);
5040 FOR I = 1 TO 73: PRINT CHR$(205); :NEXT I: PRINT CHR$(188)
5050 RETURN
5997 '
5998 '            *******  HELP SCREEN  *******
5999 '
6000 COLOR 15,3,1: CLS: LOCATE 3,6
6010 PRINT "Each of this program's functions allows you to perform operations"
6020 PRINT "   on files that you select from a directory of your choice.": PRINT
6030 PRINT: PRINT TAB(6);: COLOR 15,4: PRINT " COPY ";: COLOR 0,3
6040 PRINT " copies the selected files from the directory that you choose to "
6050 PRINT "   the target directory that you specify."
6060 PRINT: PRINT TAB(6);: COLOR 15,4: PRINT " ERASE ";: COLOR 0,3
6070 PRINT " erases the selected files from the directory that you specify."
6080 PRINT: PRINT TAB(6);: COLOR 15,4: PRINT " SAVE ";: COLOR 0,3
6090 PRINT " copies the selected files to the target directory only if"
6100 PRINT "   they do not already exist on the target directory."
6110 PRINT: PRINT TAB(6);: COLOR 15,4: PRINT " MOVE ";: COLOR 0,3
6120 PRINT " copies the selected files to the target directory, erasing"
6220 PRINT "   them from the source directory after they have been successfully"
6230 PRINT "   copied."
6240 PRINT: PRINT TAB(6);: COLOR 15,4: PRINT " BACKUP ";: COLOR 0,3
6250 PRINT " checks first to see whether the selected files exist on"
6260 PRINT "   the target directory. If not, they are copied to the target"
6270 PRINT "   directory.  If so, they are copied to the target directory with"
6280 PRINT "   their extension changed to .BAC."
6290 LOCATE 25,6:COLOR 15,4:PRINT " Press ";: COLOR 0,7: PRINT " M ";
6300 COLOR 15,4:
        PRINT " to return to Menu; any other key for more information. "
```

Listing 11.1 ▲ *FILEMGR.BAS (continued).*

```
6305 'LOCATE 24,1:COLOR ,3: PRINT SPACE$(80)'eliminate stripe from IBM screen
6310 A$ = INKEY$: IF A$ = "" THEN 6310
6320 IF A$ = "M" OR A$ = "m" GOTO 6460
6330 COLOR 0,3: CLS: LOCATE 3,6
6340 PRINT "The program will check to see whether the directories that you"
6350 PRINT "  select exist on the selected drive, and give you a chance to "
6360 PRINT "  reenter them if they do not. While the program cannot check for"
6370 PRINT "  invalid drives, DOS will do so, and display a message. If you see"
6380 PRINT: PRINT TAB(10);: COLOR 15: PRINT "Invalid drive specification"
6390 COLOR 0: PRINT: PRINT "    or"
6400 PRINT TAB(10);: COLOR 15: PRINT "Not ready error reading drive"
6410 COLOR 0: PRINT :PRINT "   you have probably specified an invalid drive. ";
6420 PRINT "Press ";: COLOR 15,4: PRINT " CTRL-BREAK ";: COLOR 0,3
6430 PRINT "   and start over."
6440 LOCATE 25,26: COLOR 15,4: PRINT " Press any key to continue "
6445 'LOCATE 24,1:COLOR ,3: PRINT SPACE$(80)'eliminate stripe from IBM screen
6450 A$ = INKEY$:IF A$ = "" GOTO 6450
6460 RETURN
9997 '
9998 '         ********* ERROR TRAPPING ROUTINES *********
9999 '
10000 COLOR 15,4: LOCATE 25,22: BEEP
10010 PRINT " Cannot find path; please reenter. "
10020 LOCATE 10,1: COLOR ,2: PRINT SPACE$(240): GOTO 1060
10030 '
10100 LOCATE 25,10: BEEP: COLOR 15,4
10110 PRINT " Cannot create desired directory. You must select another. "
10120 LOCATE 13,1: COLOR 0,2:PRINT SPACE$(240): GOTO 1150
20000 CLOSE: END: SYSTEM
```

Listing 11.1 ▲ *FILEMGR.BAS (continued).*

the code so that they are entered by their ASCII values using the CHR$ function. The statements that accomplish this are in lines 120 through 170, 1000 through 1040, and subroutine 5000. These codes are easier to enter, although they execute more slowly. The only lines that contain graphics characters to be entered with the Alt-Shift technique are 300, 1060, 1100, 1160, and 1210, where ASCII 205s are used to draw the shaft of the arrow. You can substitute equal signs if you like.

The program creates a batch file with the appropriate commands for the function you select and the files you choose to include. It creates a temporary directory file (TEMP.DIR) from which to read the necessary information. You may find some of the code familiar from CSKIP.BAS, which was presented in Chapter 10.

The Main Menu

Figure 11.1 shows the main menu, which is created in lines 110 through 480 and subroutine 5000 (which draws the frame). As you can see, you have the options of copying, erasing, saving, moving, or backing up files. Each is selected by pressing its first letter. In addition, H calls a help screen, and Q exits the program.

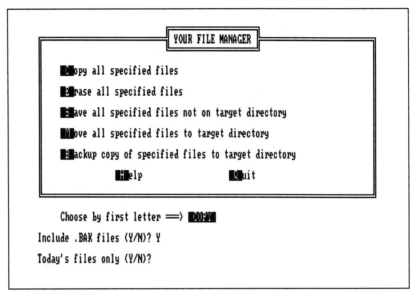

Figure 11.1 ▲ *The File Manager Main Menu.*

The Copy option is the standard DOS COPY function. The Move and Save options function just as they do in the batch programs presented in Chapter 10. The Erase option uses the BASIC KILL command instead of the DOS ERASE command in order to avoid going from BASIC to DOS when it isn't necessary. The Backup option creates a file on the target directory with the extension .BAC if the file exists on both the source and target directories. The .BAC extension is used to avoid overwriting .BAK files that may be on the target directory. You also can choose to exclude .BAK files from consideration, as well as exclude any files with a date earlier than the current one.

Selecting Directories

The next screen, shown in Figure 11.2, allows you to select directories (subroutine 1000). You can specify the source and target drive and directory. An error-trapping routine in lines 10000 through 10020 will warn you if you enter a source directory that does not exist and send you back to enter another. If you enter a target directory other than the default, you are asked whether you want to create it. Another error trap, at lines 10100 through 10120, will warn you if DOS cannot create the directory and allow you to change your response.

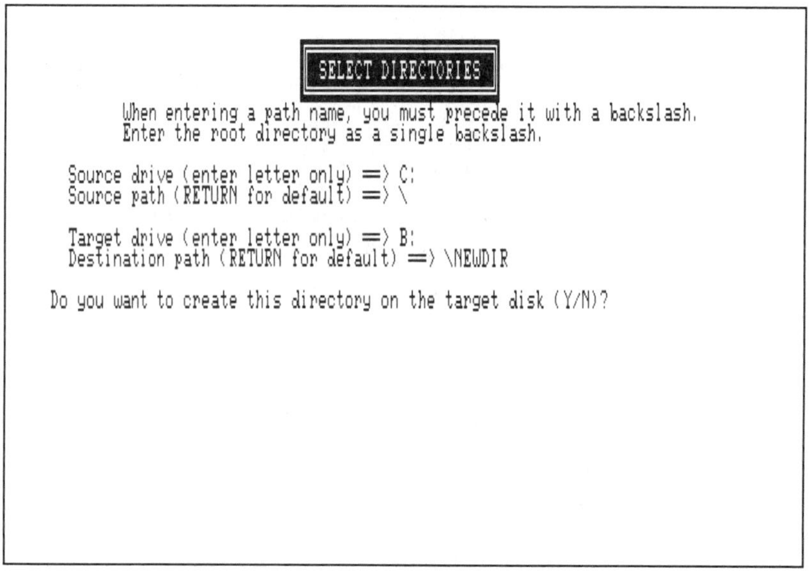

```
          ┌─────────────────────┐
          │  SELECT DIRECTORIES │
          └─────────────────────┘
        When entering a path name, you must precede it with a backslash.
        Enter the root directory as a single backslash.

      Source drive (enter letter only) ==> C:
      Source path (RETURN for default) ==> \

      Target drive (enter letter only) ==> B:
      Destination path (RETURN for default) ==> \NEWDIR

   Do you want to create this directory on the target disk (Y/N)?
```

Figure 11.2 ▲ *The Directory-Selection Screen.*

One error that the program cannot trap is the entry of a drive that does not exist. However, DOS will trap this error and display the message

Invalid drive specification

or

Not ready error reading drive *n*
Abort, Retry, Ignore?

If you see this message, press Ctrl-Break and start over.

Selecting Files

Subroutine 2000 creates the temporary directory, in sorted order, and displays the file names one by one. You are asked if you want to include the displayed file in the current operation. If you press N, a flashing red N appears next to the file name; if you press Y, a flashing green Y appears.

If you have included all the files that you want to work with before the directory listing ends, or if you see that you have made a mistake, press Q. The message

Everything OK (Y/N)?

will be displayed at the bottom of the screen, and the computer will beep. If you press N, the file-selection routine will start over from the beginning. If you press Y, execution will proceed to one of the subroutines beginning at line 3000. Figure 11.3 shows a sample file-selection screen.

```
AUTOBKUP.BAS     COPY   (Y/N/Q)? Y
AUTOBOOT.BAS     COPY   (Y/N/Q)? Y
BASIC.BAT        COPY   (Y/N/Q)? N
BKGBORDR.BAS     COPY   (Y/N/Q)? N
BOOT.HLP         COPY   (Y/N/Q)? N
BOOTABLE.BAT     COPY   (Y/N/Q)? N
BORDER.BAT       COPY   (Y/N/Q)? Y
COLRFILE.BAS     COPY   (Y/N/Q)? Y
CPA.BAT          COPY   (Y/N/Q)? N
CYAN.BAS         COPY   (Y/N/Q)? N
EDLIN.BAT        COPY   (Y/N/Q)? N
ELF.BAT          COPY   (Y/N/Q)? Y
FILECOPY.BAS     COPY   (Y/N/Q)? Y
FILEMGR.BAS      COPY   (Y/N/Q)? Y
FILEMGR.NEW      COPY   (Y/N/Q)? N
FILEMONO.BAS     COPY   (Y/N/Q)? Y
FW.BAT           COPY   (Y/N/Q)? N
MYDOS.MAC        COPY   (Y/N/Q)? Y
MYDOS.NEW        COPY   (Y/N/Q)? N
NANCY.BAT        COPY   (Y/N/Q)? N
QBASIC.BAT       COPY   (Y/N/Q)? Y
RAMED.BAT        COPY   (Y/N/Q)? Y
RAMSIZE.BAT      COPY   (Y/N/Q)? Y
RAMTANK.BAT      COPY   (Y/N/Q)?
                 SELECT FILES, PRESS  Q  WHEN DONE
```

Figure 11.3 ▲ *The File-Selection Screen.*

Executing the Options

There are five separate routines beginning at line 3000, one for each of the program's functions. The correct routine is selected by the assignment of a value to the variable J (for JOB) in lines 310 through 360, which is used to select the routine in line 500. The selected routine creates the file FILEMGR.BAT, containing the correct commands for the task.

In lines 530 through 560, control is temporarily handed over to DOS by the SHELL command, so that the batch file can be executed. When the batch file is finished, subroutine 4000 displays an abbreviated listing of the source and/or target directory, as appropriate, so you can check your work. When you press a key, the temporary files are deleted, and the program starts over. Subroutine 6000 contains the help screen, which can be called only from the main menu.

Hint: Some versions of Microsoft BASIC allow you to display a message on the last line of the screen if the display of key values is turned off (as it is by the KEY OFF statement in line 110). In these versions of BASIC, the message will occupy only the bottom line of the screen, and it will stay there without scrolling until the screen is cleared. In other versions, the display is not as precise. For example, the color assigned to the statement on the bottom line spills over into the two preceding lines in some versions of BASIC. If this bothers you, you can either eliminate the COLOR statement from those lines that include the statement LOCATE 25,*N*, or remove the apostrophe at the beginning of lines 2025, 2265, 4085, 6305, and 6445. This will make these lines into executable statements. Their effect is to "paint" the offending lines in the proper background color, but they also make the screen display jump.

Adapting FILEMGR.BAS for Monochrome

The FILEMGR.BAS program makes extensive use of color. You can modify it for monochrome screens by loading it into a text editor or word processor and performing the following global search-and-replace operations:

▲ Change COLOR 0, to COLOR 7,

▲ Change COLOR 7,7 to COLOR 7,0

▲ Change COLOR 15,4 to COLOR 0,7

▲ Change COLOR ,4 to COLOR 0,7

Tips on Debugging FILEMGR.BAS

FILEMGR.BAS is unfortunately not crashproof, because it makes use of some very unorthodox interactions between BASIC and DOS. There is also always the possibility that you made some typing errors while entering the program. Before you use it on a valuable set of files or an irreplaceable disk, try it out with some dummy files and a dummy directory to make sure that everything behaves as it should.

One way to see exactly what the batch file created by the BASIC program is doing is to make the following changes:

▲ Eliminate >NUL from lines 510 and 570.

▲ Eliminate the statement PRINT #2, "ECHO OFF": from line 1360.

▲ Place an apostrophe after the first colon in line 590.

With these changes, every line of the batch file, and DOS's responses, will be displayed on the screen as the file is executing. You can then see whether the syntax of the lines in the batch file is correct. The third change prevents the temporary files from being erased automatically, so you can check their contents after the program has finished executing.

Finally, if you consistently get errors at lines 1280 or 1300, follow the line numbers of these lines with an apostrophe (which makes the statement a nonexecuting remark) and remove the apostrophes at the beginnings of lines 1285 and 1305.

Advanced File-Management Commands

DOS 3.2 includes two new file-management commands that virtually obviate the FILEMGR program: XCOPY (extended copy) and REPLACE. In both commands, either the source or the target drive and/or directory must be specified, depending on which one is current. If neither is current, both most be specified. Wild-card characters can be used in the file names to work with multiple files.

The basic syntax of the command is

REPLACE [*SOURCE*]*FILENAME.EXT* [*TARGET*] [*/switch*]

A source file name *must* be specified. A target file name may or may not be specified. For example,

REPLACE C:\DOS*.COM A:\UTIL

will copy any files on the \DOS directory of drive C to the \UTIL directory of drive A.

With no switches, REPLACE does the opposite of the BACKUP command in the FILEMGR program. It copies only those files that already exist on the target directory, overwriting the old ones. It does not copy any files that are not on the target directory.

The command

REPLACE [*SOURCE*]*FILENAME.EXT* [*TARGET*] /A

is the same as the SAVE command in the FILEMGR program. This command copies files from the source drive and/or directory to the target drive and/or directory only if they do *not* already exist on the target.

The command

REPLACE [*SOURCE*]*FILENAME.EXT* [*TARGET*] /S

searches all subdirectories of the target for matching file names, replacing them wherever they are. This can be useful if you are updating a software package on a hard disk. Of course, /A and /S cannot be used together.

 Warning: Be careful, however, that your source doesn't have file names that might exist on more than one directory of the target drive. This command searches the directories on the target in their logical order—that is, in the order in which their names appear in their parent directory. If your source contains a file named READ.ME, you could easily replace a file of the same name in another directory.

You can also have the REPLACE command ask you for permission before each replacement by adding the /P switch, or wait for you to swap disks in the target drive with the /W switch. The /W switch is vital if you need to take the disk containing the REPLACE command out of the drive before copying. The /P switch allows you to copy files selectively.

XCOPY also helps you copy files selectively. Its syntax is more like that of the BACKUP command than that of the COPY command. However, it makes usable copies, not encrypted ones. Moreover, it is much faster than the COPY command, because it reads as many files as memory can hold before writing. COPY writes each file before reading the next.

The basic syntax for XCOPY is

XCOPY [*SOURCE*][*FILENAME.EXT*] [*TARGET*][*FILENAME.EXT*]
[*/switch*]

As with REPLACE, you must specify either a source or a target, or both if neither is current. If you do not specify a source file name, all files on the source meeting the characteristics specified by the switches will be copied. You may also specify a target file name if you want to change the names of the files as you copy them.

With no switches, XCOPY is the same as COPY. The /P and /W switches have the same effect as those for the REPLACE command. In addition, XCOPY has the following switches:

▲ /A copies only files with the archive bit set, but does not clear the archive bit of either copy.

▲ /M, like the /M switch for the BACKUP command, copies only those files whose archive bit is set and clears the archive bit of the source copy.

▲ /D:*mm-dd-yy* copies only files created on or after the specified date (use the date format selected with the SELECT command).

▲ /E creates subdirectories on the target disk to match those on the source. However, if the other switches you specify result in there being no files to copy from that directory, the matching subdirectory on the target disk will be empty.

▲ /S, like the /S switch for the BACKUP command, copies files from the subdirectories of the specified source drive or directory, as well as the source directory. It does not create equivalent subdirectories on the target, however, unless the /E switch is also used.

▲ /V, like the /V switch for the COPY command, turns on the VERIFY option during the copying process.

In Chapters 13 and 14, you'll see the XCOPY and REPLACE commands put to use.

FILE-MANAGEMENT UTILITIES

If you like FILEMGR, but find that it doesn't go far enough, you may be interested in a file-management utility. These programs are usually referred to as *DOS shells*, because they can be used as an overlay to the operating system. They give you a great deal more information than any prompt could supply and are designed to be kept in memory as a starting point for running your software. Some even include the tools to build a menu system for an entire hard disk.

For the sophisticated user such as yourself, however, their main use is in managing files. They generally include

▲ A menu of file-management commands, to move, copy, locate, delete, and rename files, individually or in groups

▲ A diagrammatic representation of your directory tree

▲ An expanded directory display, including the ability to sort file names by several criteria and show file attributes

▲ The ability to mark files—individually or by wild-card patterns—for inclusion in the action of a command (you can generally also untag files that you want to exclude from a wild-card group)

▲ The ability to print directories, files, and your tree diagram

With an arsenal such as this, it becomes much easier for you to keep your files organized and get rid of duplicate copies you don't need. HomeBase and PC Tools, which we've already glanced at, include some features of a file manager. Other file managers include QDOS II, XTree, DirecTree, 1Dir Plus, KeepTrack Plus, and the Norton Commander. My personal favorite is QDOS II, because it's easy to use and has useful on-line help. However, every one of them has some features that you might find essential. When they start getting into system menus, however, they tend to become unneccessarily complex.

A D V A N C E D
D I R E C T O R Y
M A N A G E M E N T

12

I N THIS CHAPTER, you'll learn how to manipulate disk directory entries. We'll look at the way the directory information is encoded on disk and explore ways to alter that information. Finally, we'll review some software packages that make directory manipulation much easier.

THE STRUCTURE OF A DIRECTORY ENTRY

Each directory entry contains certain specific information. The directory display format

    COMMAND   COM   25307   3-17-87   12:00p

indicates that somewhere in those sectors of the disk devoted to the directory is the information needed to display the name of each file and its extension, its size in bytes, and the date and time of its creation or most recent modification. The directory sectors also contain information about each entry's type—file, subdirectory, or volume label—as well as other data that are not listed when you display a directory. Because it is in the form of a complex set of binary codes, rather than a simple ASCII text file, all this information is stored in only 32 bytes.

First, we'll look at the way a directory entry is actually coded on disk. Figure 12.1, based on an illustration in *The MS-DOS Handbook* by Richard Allen King (2d edition, SYBEX, 1986), shows the structure of a single directory entry. We'll go over the items in an entry one by one. Note that the bytes are numbered beginning at 0, not 1.

The File Name and Extension

The file name and its extension occupy the first 11 bytes, from byte 0 through byte 10. The file name appears entirely in uppercase characters. There is neither a space (which is supplied by the operating system when a directory entry is listed on the screen) nor a period (which is expected by the system when a file is requested) between the file name and its extension.

The Attribute Byte

Byte 11 is the *attribute byte,* a single byte that contains a great deal of information regarding the nature of each file. The attribute byte takes

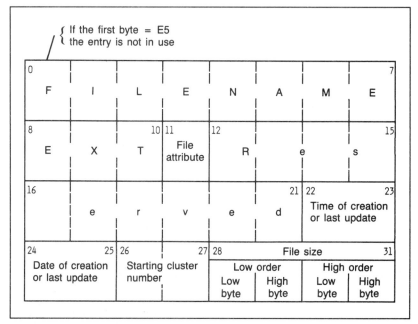

Figure 12.1 ▲ *The Structure of a Directory Entry.*

on a different value depending on the file's characteristics, or attributes. The attributes a file may have and their bit values are summarized in Table 12.1.

For each attribute, the value of the relevant bit is changed from 0 to 1. If the file has more than one of the possible attributes, the bit values for each one are added. Thus, a read-only, hidden system file such as IBM-BIO.COM, with its archive bit set, will have the hex value of

$$1 + 2 + 4 + 20 = 27$$

We'll look at how you can change the setting of the attribute byte later in the chapter.

Read/Write Files   If no bits are set in the attribute byte (its value is 0), the file is a normal, read/write file, such as a data file created by virtually any program. Most program files are also of this type, since they can be modified and erased.

Read-Only Files   If the first bit is set, the file is a read-only file. If no other bits are set, the file will be listed when you display a directory. However, you cannot change or erase it. Since it is a terrible nuisance not to be able to rearrange the files on a disk and group them in a convenient manner, the majority of programs, including most commercial software, are read/write files.

BIT	DECIMAL VALUE	HEX VALUE	ATTRIBUTE
0	0	00	Normal read/write files
1	1	01	Read-only files
2	2	02	Hidden files
3	4	04	System files
4	8	08	Volume labels for root directories
5	16	10	Subdirectory names
6	32	20	The archive bit
7	64	40	Empty

Table 12.1 ▲ *Bit Values and File Types Recorded in the Attribute Byte.*

DOS 3.0, 3.1

DOS 3.0 and 3.1 include an external ATTRIB command that allows you to change the first bit of the attribute byte, making a read/write file into a read-only file, and vice versa.

To make a file read-only, thus preventing it from being altered or erased, enter

ATTRIB +R *FILENAME.EXT*

To make a read-only file into a read/write file, enter

ATTRIB −R *FILENAME.EXT*

Hidden Files   Hidden files do not show up in a directory listing. Therefore, they are not copied when you issue a

COPY *.*

command, nor are they erased by an

ERASE *.*

command. The only way that you can copy hidden files is to use the DISKCOPY command. To erase them, you must use the FORMAT command. Thus, when you erase all the files from a system disk, it will still contain the hidden system files. All you need to do to make the disk bootable again is copy COMMAND.COM onto it.

Many copy-protected software packages either include hidden files on the distribution disk or create hidden files on the installed floppy disk or the root directory of a hard disk. This means that you cannot free the space occupied by the hidden files, which can be a colossal nuisance if you have deleted a package from a hard disk without following its "uninstall" procedures, or if you want to reuse the working disk for another purpose.

System Files   A system file is, by definition, any file that has its bit set for this attribute. It is a read-only file, and therefore cannot be written to or erased.

Volume Labels   Only the volume label for the root directory has the volume-label attribute set. The system regards the volume label as a hidden file of 0 length, as it takes up no data space.

Subdirectory Names   Subdirectory names take the same form as file names—eight characters with a three-character extension. There is no way to force them to take the same form as a root-directory volume label. The actual subdirectories are files on the disk, and can, with some effort, be read just like any other file. The form of the entries in subdirectories is the same as those in root directories.

The Archive Bit   The archive bit is used by the hard disk BACKUP program. Whenever a file is created or modified, this bit is set to on. When the BACKUP program copies the program to a backup medium, it resets this bit to off. Thus, if you back up your hard disk in increments—backing up only files that were modified since the previous backup operation—the BACKUP program knows which files need to be copied.

Several other programs that back up hard disks also work with this bit, and some software packages can change this bit for you directly. This can come in handy if, for example, you want to back up your hard disk in increments, but don't want to include the .BAK files.

DOS 3.2, 3.3

With DOS 3.2 the ATTRIB command has been enhanced to address the archive bit as well as the read-only bit. To set the archive bit, enter

ATTRIB + A *FILENAME.EXT*

To clear it, enter

ATTRIB − A *FILENAME.EXT*

The Reserved Area

Bytes 12 through 21 are reserved for mysterious, unspecified purposes. They are normally filled with zeros. Placing any other value in these bytes may make the directory unusable.

Time and Date

The time and date are stored in a rather arcane format taking two bytes each. Time is recorded to the nearest two seconds, although directory entries display only hours and minutes. Later in the chapter, I'll show you ways to change the date and time in a directory entry.

Starting Cluster Number

The starting cluster number tells the operating system where the file begins on a disk. When the operating system looks for a file, it first finds this number in the directory entry, then reads the equivalent reference in the FAT. The rest of the file's clusters are read from the FAT. It is vital to be able to read this information (which is not normally displayed in a directory) if you wish to alter a file or subdirectory entry.

File Size

Bytes 28 through 31 are reserved for displaying the size of the file in bytes. Again, this is not a simple numeric representation. You might think of it as a four-byte word. As each byte fills up, the value spills over into the next byte. Table 12.2 shows the structure of this number. The four bytes are arranged in order from *least significant* to *most significant*. The lowest numeric values appear in the least significant byte, and each succeeding byte takes on progressively higher values.

Here is how the file-size representation works:

1. Byte 28, like any byte, can take values up to 255, or hex FF. If the file is less than 256 bytes in length, this byte will show its length, and the other four bytes will have a value of 0.

2. When a file grows from 255 to 256 bytes, byte 28 takes the value of 1, and byte 29 has the value of 0. To find the value of this byte, multiply its *decimal* equivalent by 256. Thus, a value of FF in byte 29 denotes a file of 255 × 256 = 65,280 bytes. Files up to 65,535 (65,280 + 255) bytes, or one byte short of 64K, can be recorded in the first two bytes alone.

3. Byte 30 takes the spillover from byte 29. As soon as a file reaches 64K, or 65,536 bytes, the value of byte 30 increments to 1. For each additional 64K in the file, byte 30 is incremented by 1.

BYTE	DECIMAL	HEX
28	× 1	× 1
29	× 256	× 100
30	× 65,536	× 1,000
31	× 16,777,216	× 10,000

Table 12.2 ▲ *The File-Size Bytes in a Directory Entry.*

Thus, a file of exactly 64K would be represented in bytes 28 through 31 as

00 00 01 00

To determine the value of the number in byte 30, multiply it by 65,536. The maximum value for this byte is thus 255 × 65,536 = 16,711,680 bytes, or 16,320K. Files up to 16,777,215 bytes, or one byte short of 16,384K (or 16.384MB), will use only these three bytes in the directory entry.

4. For all practical purposes, byte 31 will never be used. If you have a 60MB hard disk and create immense spreadsheets or databases that still won't fit in memory, it's conceivable that you might find some number larger than 0 in this byte. If you do, you are probably keeping too much information in one file for it to be processed efficiently. Just for the record, the maximum value of the number in this byte is 255 × 16,777,216 = 1,278,190,080 bytes = 1,248,232K, or 1,248MB.

MANIPULATING DIRECTORY ENTRIES

Before you can manipulate directory entries, you have to be able to access the directory sectors of your disk. The root directory of any type of disk begins in the first disk sector after the FAT. Consult Table 2.3 for the exact starting sector of your type of disk's directory. Next, you have to read the directory into the computer's memory in the appropriate form. For now, we'll see how to do this using DEBUG. Later, we'll review three commercially available programs that make the job considerably easier.

! **Hint:** The calculator and ASCII-table features of RAM-resident desk-accessory programs are extremely helpful when using DEBUG. If you don't have such a program, use the ASCII table in Appendix H to convert from decimal to hex and back. All ASCII codes up to 255 (decimal) are listed with both values; for higher numbers, such as those in the high-order bytes of the file-size record, you can convert to decimal and do simple arithmetic.

With a DOS disk in the drive (which will not be necessary if DOS is on your hard disk), load DEBUG with no parameters or file names. Then issue the Dump command to display a stretch of memory by entering a D. You should see all zeros on the hex side of the DEBUG screen and nothing but periods on the ASCII side. If you see random data in about every eighth byte, that's all right, too. There are often some random data in the computer when you boot it up or left over from previous programs.

Next, you have to read the directory into that sector of memory. To do so, use the Load command. This takes the form

L *address drive-number starting-sector number-of-sectors*

where *address* is the starting point of the stretch of memory that you are going to use (usually 100), *drive-number* is 0 for A and increases by 1 for each drive letter, and *starting-sector* for the directory on a floppy disk is 5 (the directory is sectors 5 through 11). For *number-of-sectors,* you can read in as many sectors as you want, up to 128 (hex 80). The number of sectors must be entered in hex. There's no need to read more sectors than there are directory entries, and a single sector will hold 16 entries, so make this number proportional to the size of the directory. Figure 12.2 shows a directory sector displayed in DEBUG. Since each display line in DEBUG is 16 bytes long, and a directory entry is 32 bytes, each entry begins on the left margin and takes two lines.

To make changes to any entry, use the Enter command. The syntax is

E *address hexdata*

or

E *address "character data"*

When calculating the address, remember that there are 16 characters, numbered 0 through F, on each line of a DEBUG display. The

```
-l 100 1 5 6
-d 100
30FF:0100  49 42 4D 42 49 4F 20 20-43 4F 4D 27 00 00 00 00   IBMBIO  COM'....
30FF:0110  00 00 00 00 00 00 60 6D-67 0A 02 00 5C 25 00 00   ......'mg...\%..
30FF:0120  49 42 4D 44 4F 53 20 20-43 4F 4D 27 00 00 00 00   IBMDOS  COM'....
30FF:0130  00 00 00 00 00 00 60 6D-67 0A 0C 00 70 6C 00 00   ......'mg...pl..
30FF:0140  41 4E 53 49 20 20 20 20-53 59 53 20 00 00 00 00   ANSI    SYS ....
30FF:0150  00 00 00 00 00 00 60 6D-67 0A 28 00 73 06 00 00   ......'mg.(.s..
30FF:0160  41 53 53 49 47 4E 20 20-43 4F 4D 20 00 00 00 00   ASSIGN  COM ....
30FF:0170  00 00 00 00 00 00 60 6D-67 0A 2A 00 E5 05 00 00   ......'mg.*.....
-d
30FF:0180  41 54 54 52 49 42 20 20-45 58 45 20 00 00 00 00   ATTRIB  EXE ....
30FF:0190  00 00 00 00 00 00 60 6D-67 0A 2C 00 F3 3A 00 00   ......'mg.,..:..
30FF:01A0  42 41 43 4B 55 50 20 20-43 4F 4D 20 00 00 00 00   BACKUP  COM ....
30FF:01B0  00 00 00 00 00 00 60 6D-67 0A 3B 00 C9 15 00 00   ......'mg.;.....
30FF:01C0  42 41 53 49 43 20 20 20-43 4F 4D 20 00 00 00 00   BASIC   COM ....
30FF:01D0  00 00 00 00 00 00 60 6D-67 0A 41 00 80 45 00 00   ......'mg.A..E..
30FF:01E0  42 41 53 49 43 41 20 20-43 4F 4D 20 00 00 00 00   BASICA  COM ....
30FF:01F0  00 00 00 00 00 00 60 6D-67 0A 53 00 80 6B 00 00   ......'mg.S..k..
-d
30FF:0200  43 48 4B 44 53 4B 20 20-43 4F 4D 20 00 00 00 00   CHKDSK  COM ....
30FF:0210  00 00 00 00 00 00 60 6D-67 0A 6E 00 DB 24 00 00   ......'mg.n..$..
30FF:0220  43 4F 4D 4D 41 4E 44 20-43 4F 4D 20 00 00 00 00   COMMAND COM ....
30FF:0230  00 00 00 00 00 00 60 6D-67 0A 78 00 AA 5A 00 00   ......'mg.x..Z..
30FF:0240  43 4F 4D 50 20 20 20 20-43 4F 4D 20 00 00 00 00   COMP    COM ....
30FF:0250  00 00 00 00 00 00 60 6D-67 0A 8F 00 50 0E 00 00   ......'mg...P...
30FF:0260  44 49 53 4B 43 4F 4D 50-43 4F 4D 20 00 00 00 00   DISKCOMPCOM ....
30FF:0270  00 00 00 00 00 00 60 6D-67 0A 93 00 E9 0F 00 00   ......'mg.......
-d
30FF:0280  44 49 53 4B 43 4F 50 59-43 4F 4D 20 00 00 00 00   DISKCOPYCOM ....
30FF:0290  00 00 00 00 00 00 60 6D-67 0A 97 00 E9 10 00 00   ......'mg.......
30FF:02A0  45 44 4C 49 4E 20 20 20-43 4F 4D 20 00 00 00 00   EDLIN   COM ....
30FF:02B0  00 00 00 00 00 00 60 6D-67 0A 9C 00 5D 1C 00 00   ......'mg...]...
30FF:02C0  46 44 49 53 4B 20 20 20-43 4F 4D 20 00 00 00 00   FDISK   COM ....
30FF:02D0  00 00 00 00 00 00 60 6D-67 0A A4 00 ED 1F 00 00   ......'mg.......
30FF:02E0  46 49 4E 44 20 20 20 20-45 58 45 20 00 00 00 00   FIND    EXE ....
30FF:02F0  00 00 00 00 00 00 60 6D-67 0A AC 00 03 19 00 00   ......'mg.......
```

Figure 12.2 ▲ *A Directory Sector Displayed in DEBUG.*

starting address for the bytes you want to change should be counted from the leftmost data column as column 0, and it should be added to the hex number *after* the colon in the column at the left margin. You can enter either hex values or ASCII characters. You can even mix them in a single entry, provided the ASCII characters are in quotation marks and the hex values are not.

When you have finished making changes, you must write the data back to the disk. Issue the Write command with the same parameters as you used for the Load command. For example, if you issued the command

L100 1 5 7

you will now enter

W100 1 5 7

Any changes you have made will be written at this time.

 Warning: Manipulating directory data entails certain risks. An erroneous entry can do serious damage. You should never enter anything in the reserved area, change the file size, or change the starting cluster number. Other practices to avoid are mentioned throughout this section.

Changing File Names

You can use the technique of loading the data directly from the disk sectors into DEBUG, entering new values, and writing the data back to disk to change file names. Of course, for most files, you can use the RENAME command, which is considerably simpler.

Suppose, however, that you have created a BASIC program whose name includes a space (which some BASICs allow). Then you find that you cannot open the file or enter its name at a DOS prompt because DOS regards the space as a separator between parameters. You also can't erase it for the same reason. This is where the direct-to-disk technique comes in handy.

 Hint: There is an easier method, however. Say the file is named

REC NUM.BAS

You could rename it with a wild card by issuing a command such as

RENAME REC?NUM.BAS RECNUM.BAS

or use the command

ERASE REC?NUM.BAS

to erase it.

You can also use the direct-to-disk technique to change file names so that they include lowercase letters or other illegal characters. However, using illegal characters is generally a very bad idea. Trying to load such a file from DOS will result in a

File not found

message, and you can only rename or delete it by using wild-card characters, as described in the hint above.

Creating and Changing Volume Labels

In versions of DOS before 3.0, there is no way to create a volume label on a disk once it has been formatted or to change one that has already been created. If your version does not permit these operations, you can use the direct-to-disk technique to add or change volume labels. If there is an unused directory entry, you can place the information in that space. If not, you can replace the name of an erased file.

Moreover, you can safely include uppercase and lowercase characters in a volume label, along with spaces and periods, without causing trouble. DOS doesn't do anything with this information except display it.

Suppose that you want to name a volume New Data #1. First, load the directory sectors into memory as described above. Then use the Dump command until you find an empty directory entry, such as the one shown in Figure 12.3, or an erased directory entry. (An erased entry is one that has the hex value E5 as its first character, or, in the utility programs described at the end of the chapter, a ç on the text side of the screen.) Enter the volume label at the address of the entry, set the attribute byte to 8, fill the rest of the entry with zeros (if they aren't already there), and write the sector back to disk. You should also enter a date and time, as described below; otherwise, some very peculiar data will appear when you use the CHKDSK command. Bytes 26 through 31 (the starting cluster and file length) *must* be set to 0.

If your entry were at the location shown in Figure 12.3, the command to enter the new data, including a date and time stamp, would be

```
E E00 "New Data #1" 8 0 0 0 0 0 0 0 0 0 0 0 60 21 10 0 0 0 0 0 0
```

or

```
E E00 "New Data #1"
F E0C E16 0
E E17 60 21 10
F E1A E1F 0
```

Your new entry will be dated January 1, 1988, and have a time stamp of 12:00 p.m. To see the result, type

```
D E00
```

```
30FF:0E00  00 F6 F6 F6 F6 F6 F6 F6-F6 F6 F6 F6 F6 F6 F6 F6   ................
30FF:0E10  F6 F6 F6 F6 F6 F6 F6 F6-F6 F6 F6 F6 F6 F6 F6 F6   ................
```

Figure 12.3 ▲ *An Empty Directory Entry Displayed in DEBUG.*

The display should look like Figure 12.4. Then issue the Write command, and your volume label is entered.

Changing Directory Names

You can use essentially the same technique—writing directly to disk—to rename subdirectories. Load the directory sectors as described, and keep pressing D until the directory name you want to change appears on the screen. Next, enter the string values you want to replace, in quotation marks, just as described above for volume labels. There is no need to change any of the rest of the entry. In fact, it is best not to, unless you know what you are doing.

Changing Entries in a Subdirectory

The method of changing entries in a subdirectory is the same as that for changing entries in a root directory, except that there is one additional step. First, you must load the root directory in DEBUG and find the name of the subdirectory. Next, look at bytes 26 and 27 of the entry, as shown in Figure 12.1, to find the subdirectory's starting cluster number. The addresses of clusters numbered up to 255 (hex FF) are stored in byte 26. To find the value of byte 27, multiply its *decimal* equivalent by 256. If an address uses both bytes, add the decimal value of byte 26 to the calculated value of byte 27, and convert the resulting value to hex.

When you know the disk sector address of the cluster, *do not write the subdirectory back to disk*—it's best not to write directly to disk any more than absolutely necessary, since it's a risky business. Next, fill your work area with zeros, and load at least the first cluster of the sector into memory. You can then work with file names, dates, times, and subdirectory names just as though they were in the root directory.

Changing Directory Dates

Bytes 24 and 25 are the date field, which consists of two 2-digit hex numbers. The first one controls the day and the month, and the second

```
30FF:0E00   4E 65 77 20 44 61 73 61-23 31 08 00 00 00 00 00   New.Data.#1.....
30FF:0E10   00 00 00 00 00 00 00 60-21 10 00 00 00 00 00 00   .......'!.......
```

Figure 12.4 ▲ *The Same Memory Area After Entering a Volume Label.*

controls the month and the year. The actual values are stored bit-by-bit, rather than byte-by-byte. For an explanation of the binary representation, see *The MS-DOS Handbook* by Richard Allen King (2d edition, SYBEX, 1986). However, you do not need to understand the format in which this information is stored to be able to alter it. If you follow my instructions carefully, you can make the directory display any date just by manipulating the four hex digits in this field.

Let's begin by looking at the assumptions that govern the recording of dates in this field. First, each month has 32 days, from 0 through 31. The system is programmed to skip nonexistent days automatically, but you can include them. It's possible to date a file June 0 or February 31, for example. Second, the theoretical starting date is January 1, 1980, which is represented in hex digits as 21:00. A 20:00 in this field will give you January 0, 1980, and any lower number will eliminate the date from the directory display.

Setting the Month To advance the month by 1 without changing the day or the year, increase the leftmost of the four digits (the leftmost digit of byte 24) by 2 (hex).

When you get to E (the second highest digit), add 1 to the value of byte 25 and repeat the cycle of values for the leftmost digit, beginning with 2 again. In Table 12.3, the first two columns represent the values in bytes 24 and 25, and the third column shows how the month will be displayed in a directory.

Setting the Day As mentioned, the month changes as you increase the value of the first digit by 2. The intervening digits (3, 5, 7, 9, B, D, and F), together with the second digit of byte 24, determine the day of the month. Days are numbered consecutively from 0 to 15 (hex 0 to F) in the second digit of byte 24. When 15 (hex F) is reached, you must increase the *first* digit by 1 to increase the day to 16. Thus, January uses all the values from 21 to 3F. January 1 is represented by hex 21, January 2 by hex 22, January 15 by hex 2F, January 16 by hex 31, and hex 3F is January 31. The next number higher, 40, is February 0. Table 12.4 shows the values to enter for each day of the month.

Setting the Year The second digit in byte 25 represents the year. Increasing the value of the two-digit hex number by 2 increases the year by 1.

HEX VALUE		
BYTE 24 ★	BYTE 25 ★ ★	MONTH
2N	N X	Jan
4N	N X	Feb
6N	N X	Mar
8N	N X	Apr
AN	N X	May
CN	N X	Jun
EN	N X	Jul
0N	N X+1	Aug
2N	N X+1	Sep
4N	N X+1	Oct
6N	N X+1	Nov
8N	N X+1	Dec

★ N represents any number (varies depending on the month and year currently displayed).

★ ★ X represents any day of the month currently displayed. Adding 1 to the value of X increases the number of the month by 7.

Table 12.3 ▲ *Values to Enter in Bytes 24 and 25 to Display a Given Month.*
(The intervening values affect the month, as described above.) The starting year for the system is 1980, which is represented by 00 in byte 25. Thus, for example, the following values of byte 25 correspond to the year represented:

Byte 25	Year
00	1980
02	1981
04	1982
...	
0E	1987

HEX VALUE BYTE 24 ★	HEX VALUE BYTE 25 ★ ★	DAY OF MONTH	HEX VALUE BYTE 24 ★	HEX VALUE BYTE 25 ★ ★	DAY OF MONTH
X 0	NN	00	X+1 0	NN	16
X 1	NN	01	X+1 1	NN	17
X 2	NN	02	X+1 2	NN	18
X 3	NN	03	X+1 3	NN	19
X 4	NN	04	X+1 4	NN	20
X 5	NN	05	X+1 5	NN	21
X 6	NN	06	X+1 6	NN	22
X 7	NN	07	X+1 7	NN	23
X 8	NN	08	X+1 8	NN	24
X 9	NN	09	X+1 9	NN	25
X A	NN	10	X+1 A	NN	26
X B	NN	11	X+1 B	NN	27
X C	NN	12	X+1 C	NN	28
X D	NN	13	X+1 D	NN	29
X E	NN	14	X+1 E	NN	30
X F	NN	15	X+1 F	NN	31

★ X represents any number depending on the month currently displayed. Incrementing X by 1 increments the date by 16.

★ ★ N represents any number (varies depending on the month and year currently displayed).

Table 12.4 ▲ *Hex Values for Days of the Month.*

10	1988
...	
20	1996
...	
30	2004

Each increment of the left digit of the hex number increases the year by 8, while each increment by 2 of the right digit increases the year by 1. The years will continue into the twenty-first century, as Figure 12.5 shows. The first part of the listing in this figure is a regular DOS directory listing, while the second is produced by another program. As you can see, the date of creation of DEBUG has been altered in both versions.

Placing unreasonably high values in byte 25 will produce bizarre results, such as a four-digit listing of the year in the directory display.

Changing Directory Times

The time display is controlled by bytes 22 and 23. The procedure for manipulating the time of creation or modification displayed in a directory is similar to that for changing the date, but the numbers are much trickier.

Times are recorded in two-second intervals, but they are displayed only to the nearest minute. Thus, you could make many changes to the values in these bytes that will have no effect on the display. We will only explore how to change the actual display.

Part of the difficulty in manipulating the time field is that minutes are split across the two hex numbers, just as months are. To completely eliminate the time display in the directory entry, set all four digits of the time field to 0.

Hours are controlled by byte 23. Each increment of the rightmost digit of this byte by 8 increases the hour by 1, as Table 12.5 illustrates. The intervening values of 1 through 7 and 9 through F increment the minutes by 8, as shown below:

Byte 23	Time
01	12:08 a.m.
02	12:16 a.m.
...	
06	12:48 a.m.
08	1:00 a.m.
09	1:08 a.m.
...	
0E	1:48 a.m.
10	2:00 a.m.

```
RAMWS      BAT      384    1-28-86   8:45a
CH12             31232    1-28-86   4:18p
CH12TABL          2048    1-28-86   4:19p
DEBUG      COM    15552    3-07-66   1:43p


C:RAMWS      BAT       384   28 Jan 1986   8:45 am
C:CH12             31232   28 Jan 1986   4:18 pm
C:CH12TABL          2048   28 Jan 1986   4:19 pm
C:DEBUG      COM    15552    7 Mar 2066   1:43 pm
```

Figure 12.5 ▲ *Two Forms of a Directory Listing Showing an Altered Date.*

Byte 23	Hour	Byte 23	Hour	Byte 23	Hour	Byte 23	Hour
00	no time	30	6:00 a.m.	60	12:00 p.m.	90	6:00 p.m.
08	1:00 a.m.	38	7:00 a.m.	68	1:00 p.m.	98	7:00 p.m.
10	2:00 a.m.	40	8:00 a.m.	70	2:00 p.m.	A0	8:00 p.m.
18	3:00 a.m.	48	9:00 a.m.	78	3:00 p.m.	A8	9:00 p.m.
20	4:00 a.m.	50	10:00 a.m.	80	4:00 p.m.	B0	10:00 p.m.
28	5:00 a.m.	58	11:00 a.m.	88	5:00 p.m.	B8	11:00 p.m.

Table 12.5 ▲ *Byte Values for the Hours Display.*

The values 7 and F control the seconds, and changing them does not affect the displayed time.

The intervening minutes are displayed by incrementing the leftmost of the four hex digits by 2. When you reach the end of the series, increment the rightmost digit by 1.

Bytes 22 and 23	Time
00 01	12:08 a.m.
20 01	12:09 a.m.
40 01	12:10 a.m.
60 01	12:11 a.m.
80 01	12:12 a.m.
A0 01	12:13 a.m.
C0 01	12:14 a.m.

E0 01	12:15 a.m.
00 02	12:16 a.m.
20 02	12:17 a.m.

 Hint: You cannot create a directory time of 12:00 a.m. using the procedures just described. If you follow the logic, no time will appear in the directory entry. However, you can set a time of 12:00 a.m. by entering the values OE OO in bytes 22 and 23.

Another Method of Altering the Date and Time

Several little-known options to the COPY command provide another way to alter the date and time. When using COPY to concatenate files, you can add the parameter /A to indicate ASCII text files, which inserts a Ctrl-Z at the end of the file. On the other hand, you can use the /B parameter, for binary files, which does not add a Ctrl-Z. However, even if you are concatenating ASCII text files, you can use the /B parameter and concatenate that file to a null file.

For example, if DEBUG is in the default drive, the command

```
COPY /B DEBUG.COM + ,,
```

will simply stamp the current date and time on it. You can alter the time that is stamped by using the DATE and TIME commands to reset the system time before performing this operation.

Working with the Attribute Byte

You may want to alter the value in the attribute byte (byte 11) for various reasons:

- ▲ To make a read-only file into a read/write file so that you can erase it
- ▲ To make a hidden file visible so that you can copy it
- ▲ To clear the archive bit on a .BAK file so that it will not be included when you are backing up a hard disk in increments
- ▲ To make a master file into a read-only file on a multiuser system
- ▲ To enter a volume label on an already formatted disk

You can combine any number of attributes by adding their hex values. (Here's another point at which a RAM-resident converting calculator comes in handy.) Refer to Table 12.1 for the hex values of each attribute. If you are uncomfortable with hex arithmetic, you can add or subtract the numbers in decimal and refer to the ASCII table in Appendix H for the appropriate hex equivalent of the result. For example, let's say that you want to make the DOS system files into visible files, but don't want them to be tampered with, so you will change them from read-only, hidden system files to read-only system files. The attribute byte value for a file of the latter type is

$$1 + 2 + 4 = 7 \text{ (hex)}$$

To remove the hidden attribute, you would subtract 2 and enter the value 05 into the attribute byte. The file will then show up on the directory, but it will still be a read-only file and function as a system file. To make it erasable, remove the read-only and system attributes by subtracting 5, making the value of the attribute byte 0.

Warning: You should never attempt to combine incompatible attributes in the attribute byte, such as entering a hex 30 to combine the attributes of volume label and subdirectory name, or try to change the attribute of a subdirectory name. These types of changes can make your directory permanently unreadable.

SOFTWARE SOLUTIONS

Several commercially available utility packages can simplify writing directory entries directly to disk. Probably the easiest to use is the NU program in The Norton Utilities Advanced Edition. Among its facilities are a screen that lets you select subdirectories as though they were files, and a Directory Editor. You saw a screen from the Directory Editor in Figure 2.5. With the Directory Editor, you can use the Tab key to move the cursor to any field displayed and type a new value. This is, of course, risky, since you can inadvertently change a starting cluster number and lose a file. However, changes appear in a contrasting color, and you always have a chance to escape before writing the changes to disk.

The Norton Utilities 4.0 and PC Tools each have a byte editor, with which you can make changes to any byte. You can select files to work with or choose disk sectors.

The Norton Utilities is preferable if you want to alter data in subdirectories because of two features. First, it displays the starting cluster number of each file, including subdirectories. Second, it lets you select clusters as well as sectors. Thus, you don't have to do the nasty arithmetic explained in Chapter 2 to find a particular subdirectory on disk.

PC Tools' byte editor is as effective and easy to use as The Norton Utilities'. However, PC Tools doesn't give you cluster information. To find a subdirectory on a hard disk, your best bet is to use the Find command on the Disk Services menu to locate a file name that you know is in the directory you want. Otherwise, you may have to scroll through the entire disk before you find what you are looking for. (This can be a bit of a pain on a large hard disk, but is a minor problem on a floppy disk.) The price, however, may be a deciding factor.

Two other packages that can perform some of these tasks are Mace Utilities and Computer Thaumaturgy's DOS Utilities. Let's compare these and a few other utilities, to see how well they perform the tasks we've attempted to complete using native DOS tools.

File, Directory, and Volume Names

PC Tools and the main program (NU) in both editions of The Norton Utilities allow you to alter names in a directory by writing directly to the directory sectors. Thus, you can use them to alter file, directory, and volume names. In The Norton Utilities Advanced Edition, you can use the Directory Editor for this purpose. A number of other utilities are also available that rename volumes and directories without forcing you to write to directory sectors.

The hex-display screen, which is similar to the DEBUG screen, allows you to move across the data with the cursor, making changes as you go. You can make changes in either the text or the hex column. You can then switch to the directory-display format and see the results of any changes you have made. Thus, for example, you can see whether you have set the date and time as you intended without first writing the information to disk.

Figure 12.6 and 12.7 show a directory sector displayed on The Norton Utilities 4.0's byte editor and on its directory-display screen, respectively.

```
Sector 5 in root directory in hex format      Cursor at offset 511, hex 1FF
444F5342 4F4F4B50 52475308 00000000 00000000 00004370 DOSBOOKPRGS▓.........Cp
860B0000 00000000 3235364B 52414D20 42415400 00000000 å∂......256KRAM BAT...
00000000 0000047C 7E0B2200 04020000 3338344B 52414D20 .....◆¦˜∂''.◆▐..384KRAM
42415400 00000000 00000000 0000387C 7E0B2300 FE010000 BAT.........8¦˜∂#.▪▓..
3634304B 52414D20 42415400 00000000 00000000 0000997B 640KRAM BAT..........ö{
7E0B2400 F6010000 4155544F 424B5550 42415300 00000000 ˜∂$.÷▓..AUTOBKUPBAS...
00000000 00005C7A 840B0700 1A010000 52414D57 534E4F20 ......\zä∂◆.÷▓..RAMWSNO
4A455420 00000000 00000000 00009353 280C7500 B9010000 JET .........öS(♀u.╢▓..
42415349 43202020 42415400 00000000 00009958 BASIC    BAT..........öX
7D0B0B00 25000000 424B4742 4F524452 42415320 00000000 }∂∂.%..BKGBORDRBAS ....
00000000 00003C4A 850B1E00 74040000 424F4F54 20202020 ......<Jà∂▲.t◆..BOOT
484C5000 00000000 00000000 00004745 4B0B0C00 80020000 HLP..........GEK∂♀.Ç▐..
424F4F54 41424C45 42415400 00000000 00000000 000077A4 BOOTABLEBAT..........wñ
6D0B2100 89000000 424F5244 45522020 42415420 00000000 m∂!.ë...BORDER  BAT ....
00000000 00007749 850B2D00 0C000000 52414D57 53504B20 ......wIà∂-.♀...RAMWSPK
554E5020 00000000 00000000 00002D49 980B7E00 80010000 UNP ........-Iì∂˜.Ç▐..
4D59444F 53202020 4D414320 00000000 00000000 0000316C MYDOS    MAC .......11
4E0C8400 060D0000 57535345 54202020 42415420 00000000 N♀ä.◆Ƒ..WSSET    BAT ...
00000000 00005C4F 4A0C8700 04030000 4A455542 41434B20 ......\0J♀ç.◆♥..JETBACK
20202010 00000000 00000000 0000C251 300C3200 00000000 ▶.........┬Q0♀2.....
52454750 524F4D50 42415420 00000000 00000000 00008B63 REGPROMPBAT ..........ïc
4E0C8B00 73000000        Press Enter for help         N♀ï.s...
```

Figure 12.6 • *Directory Sector Display in The Norton Utilities.*

```
Sector 5 in root directory shown in directory format

Filename Ext    Size    Date       Time  Cluster Attributes

DOSBOOKPRGS             Fri Dec  6 85  2:02 pm          Volume-Label
256KRAM  BAT     516 Sat Nov 30 85  3:32 pm      34
384KRAM  BAT     510 Sat Nov 30 85  3:33 pm      35
640KRAM  BAT     502 Sat Nov 30 85  3:28 pm      36
AUTOBKUP BAS     282 Wed Dec  4 85  3:18 pm       7
RAMWSNO  JET     441 Wed Jan  8 86 10:28 am     117 Archive
BASIC    BAT      37 Fri Nov 29 85 11:04 am      11
BKGBORDR BAS   1,140 Thu Dec  5 85  9:17 am      30 Archive
BOOT     HLP     640 Fri Oct 11 85  8:42 am      12
BOOTABLE BAT     137 Wed Nov 13 85  8:35 am      33
BORDER   BAT      12 Thu Dec  5 85  9:11 am      45 Archive
RAMWSPK  UNP     384 Tue Dec 24 85  9:58 am     126 Archive
MYDOS    MAC   3,334 Fri Feb 14 86  1:33 pm     132 Archive
WSSET    BAT     772 Mon Feb 10 86  9:58 am     135 Archive
JETBACK              Thu Jan 16 86 10:14 am      50 Directory
REGPROMP BAT     115 Fri Feb 14 86 12:28 pm     139 Archive

               Press Enter for help
```

Figure 12.7 ▲ *A Directory Display in The Norton Utilities.*

In addition to these utilities, The Norton Utilities includes an external program called VL for changing volume labels. It's a bit persnickety as to which nonalphanumeric characters it will accept, but it does let you enter volume labels in upper- and lowercase letters.

PC Tools   With PC Tools, you can use the disk view/edit (byte editor) mode in the same manner as The Norton Utilities' byte editor, overwriting bytes in either the hex or the text column. (As with The Norton Utilities, there is also a text-only display mode, in which you cannot edit.) However, you must switch to the File Services menu and look at the directory in the Directory Service screen to see the results. For comparison, the same directory shown in Figures 12.6 and 12.7 is shown in PC Tools' byte editor and directory display in Figures 12.8 and 12.9.

For adding or changing volume labels, PC Tools has a Rename command on the Disk Services menu.

Computer Thaumaturgy's DOS Utilities   Computer Thaumaturgy's DOS Utilities are a series of short programs that can be used as if they were DOS commands. They reflect a different design philosophy from Norton's external programs. The external programs in The Norton Utilities all have numerous switches that make them very flexible; however, the resulting syntax is hard to remember. CT's utilities, on the other hand, have simple, mnemonic names. To change a volume name, you simply enter

VOLNAME [*DRIVE*]*LABEL*

```
PC Tools - Disk View/Edit Service

Path=A:\
                  Relative sector being displayed is: 0000005

Displacement ──────────── Hex codes ──────────────    ASCII value
0000(0000)   44 4F 53 42 4F 4F 4B 50 52 47 53 00 00 00 00 00    DOSBOOKPRGS▓
0016(0010)   00 00 00 00 00 00 43 70 86 0B 00 00 00 00 00 00       Cpàð
0032(0020)   32 35 36 4B 52 41 4D 20 42 41 54 00 00 00 00 00    256KRAM BAT
0048(0030)   00 00 00 00 00 00 04 7C 7E 0B 22 00 04 02 00 00      ♦¦˜ð" ♦☻
0064(0040)   33 38 34 4B 52 41 4D 20 42 41 54 00 00 00 00 00    384KRAM BAT
0080(0050)   00 00 00 00 00 00 38 7C 7E 0B 23 00 FE 01 00 00       8¦˜ð# ■☺
0096(0060)   36 34 30 4B 52 41 4D 20 42 41 54 00 00 00 00 00    640KRAM BAT
0112(0070)   00 00 00 00 00 00 99 7B 7E 0B 24 00 F6 01 00 00      ŏ{˜ð$ ÷☺
0128(0080)   41 55 54 4F 42 4B 55 50 42 41 53 00 00 00 00 00    AUTOBKUPBAS
0144(0090)   00 00 00 00 00 00 5C 7A 84 0B 87 00 1A 01 00 00      \zäð‡ →☺
0160(00A0)   52 41 4D 57 53 4E 4F 20 4A 45 54 20 00 00 00 00    RAMWSNO JET
0176(00B0)   00 00 00 00 00 00 93 53 28 0C 75 00 B9 01 00 00      ôS(♀u ╢☺
0192(00C0)   42 41 53 49 43 20 20 20 42 41 54 00 00 00 00 00    BASIC   BAT
0208(00D0)   00 00 00 00 00 00 99 58 7D 0B 0B 00 25 00 00 00      ŏX}ðð %
0224(00E0)   42 4B 47 42 4F 52 44 52 42 41 53 20 00 00 00 00    BKGBORDRBAS
0240(00F0)   00 00 00 00 00 00 3C 4A 85 0B 1E 00 74 04 00 00      <Jàð▲ t♦

Home=beg of file/disk   End=end of file/disk
ESC=Exit  PgDn=forward  PgUp=back  F2=chg sector num  F3=edit
```

Figure 12.8 ▲ *A Directory Sector Display in PC Tools.*

Similarly, to rename a directory, you first make sure that the directory to be renamed is not current and then enter

RENDIR [*DRIVE*]*PATHNAME NEWNAME*

Other Utilities Peter Norton's DOS shell/menu program, called The Norton Commander, has a Rename command that works equally well on files and subdirectories. In addition, there are several public-domain utilities, called DIRNAME, RENDIR, and VOLNAME, which accomplish the same tasks.

Dates and Times

Many programs let you alter dates and times directly, rather than altering hexadecimal bytes.

PC Tools The simplest tool for changing the times and dates displayed in a directory is PC Tools. You select Attribute to get to the File Status Service screen, shown in Figure 12.10. On this screen, you can simply type over the old date and time to enter the ones you want. Then press U to update the directory and Esc to return to the menu. Selecting 12:00 a.m., however, results in no time appearing in the directory display.

```
PC Tools - Directory Service                      Volume Label=DOSBOOKPRGS

Path=B:\*.*
    Name     Ext    Size #Clu    Date      Time   Attributes
    256KRAM  BAT    516     1 11/30/85   3:32p  Normal
    384KRAM  BAT    510     1 11/30/85   3:33p  Normal
    640KRAM  BAT    502     1 11/30/85   3:28p  Normal
    AUTOBKUP BAS    282     1 12/04/85   3:18p  Normal
    RAMWSNO  JET    441     1  1/08/86  10:28a  Normal,Archive
    BASIC    BAT     37     1 11/29/85  11:04a  Normal
    BKGBORDR BAS   1140     2 12/05/85   9:17a  Normal,Archive
    BOOT     HLP    640     1 10/11/85   8:42a  Normal
    BOOTABLE BAT    137     1 11/13/85   8:35p  Normal
    BORDER   BAT     12     1 12/05/85   9:11a  Normal,Archive
    RAMWSPK  UMP    384     1 12/24/85   9:09a  Normal,Archive
    MYDOS    MAC   3334     4  2/14/86   1:33p  Normal,Archive
    WSSET    BAT    772     1  2/10/86   9:58a  Normal,Archive
    REGPROMP BAT    115     1  2/14/86  12:28p  Normal,Archive
    COLRFILE BAS   2036     2 11/11/85   3:57p  Normal
    CPA      BAT     53     1 12/05/85   8:59a  Normal,Archive
    SEL7     BAS   5240     6  3/22/86  10:54a  Normal,Archive
      49 entries listed totaling      124099 bytes.    89088 bytes available.
↑↓=Scroll  PgUp=Page Up  PgDn=Page Down  Home=Top  End=Bottom  ESC=Exit
F1=Print directory list  F2=Add a sub-directory to this directory
F7=Directory Sorting  F8=Directory List Argument  F10=Directory Selection
```

Figure 12.9 ▲ *A Directory Display in PC Tools.*

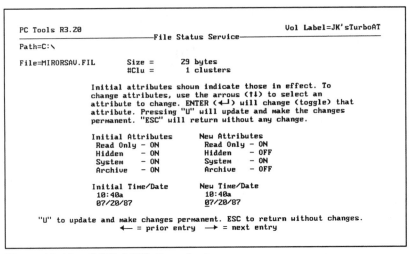

Figure 12.10 ▲ *PC Tools' File Status Service.*

The Norton Utilities   The Directory Editor in The Norton Utilities Advanced Edition also lets you type over directory dates and times. The day, month, year, hour, and minute are each regarded as a separate field. If you want to change several dates and times at once—say, if you are releasing a software package and want all modules to show the time that the code was officially frozen—this may be even easier than the equivalent operation in PC Tools.

The regular edition of The Norton Utilities is considerably less helpful. All you can do is use the byte editor to enter values based on the principles explained earlier in this chapter. (You can do the same in PC Tools.) Of course, it's still a lot easier than doing the same thing in DEBUG, where you have to count bytes from the left margin and use the Enter command.

Other Software   A public-domain program called FDATE lets you change dates and times from a command line. Enter

    FDATE *FILENAME.EXT* /mm-dd-yy

to change a date or

    FDATE *FILENAME.EXT* /hh:mm

in 24-hour format to change a time.

File Attributes

As you know, the DOS ATTRIB command can address the archive and read-only bits of the attribute byte, but not the others. However, there are many occasions when you may want to alter a file's attributes. Fortunately, numerous programs let you work with all of the file attributes. Therefore, it is only as a last resort that you have to load a directory sector in DEBUG and alter an attribute by entering a new value for byte 11 of a directory entry.

The Norton Utilities   Both editions of The Norton Utilities include an external program called FA for addressing file attributes. It's one of the ones with infuriating syntax, but it works. Entering FA with no switches or parameters displays the attributes of every file on the current directory. Entering

> **FA** *FILENAME.EXT*

shows the attributes of the named files. To change attributes, you must enter

> **FA** *FILENAME.EXT* /*switch*

The attribute switches include

- ▲ /A, for files with the archive bit set
- ▲ /R, for read-only files
- ▲ /SYS, for system files
- ▲ /HID, for hidden files

Adding one of these switches will display only the names of those files whose attributes match those of the switch you have entered. To change the attribute, add a + to set or a − to clear, as in the ATTRIB command.

In addition, there are five action switches:

- ▲ /CLEAR clears all attributes, making the file a normal file.
- ▲ /P is a pause switch, acting like the MORE filter.
- ▲ /S extends the scope of the command to subdirectories.

▲ /T results in a display of only the total number of files and total number of bytes affected by the attribute in question, without a display of file names.

▲ /U results in a display of only those files whose attribute byte does not have a value of 0 (that is, of files with an unusual attribute).

In contrast, the Advanced Edition's Directory Editor, shown in Figure 2.5, lets you move the highlight to an attribute field and toggle the attribute on or off with the space bar.

PC Tools   PC Tools lets you change file attributes on the File Status Service screen shown in Figure 12.10. You move the highlight to an attribute with the cursor keys and toggle it on or off by pressing Return. Press U to update the directory and Esc to return to the menu.

PC Tools' normal directory display includes the symbols R, H, S, and A for the read-only, hidden, system, and archive attributes, respectively. The expanded directory display, shown in Figure 12.9, spells out the attributes fully.

Computer Thaumaturgy's DOS Utilities   Computer Thaumaturgy's DOS Utilities include a number of simple commands for viewing or changing file attributes. To change attributes, use the commands listed below followed by the name of the file whose attribute you want to change.

▲ SETARC sets the archive bit.

▲ CLRARC clears the archive bit.

▲ HIDESYS sets the hidden and system attributes.

▲ UNHIDE reveals a hidden file.

▲ READWRIT makes a read-only file into a read/write file.

▲ READONLY makes a read/write file into a read-only file.

Computer Thaumaturgy also includes two utilities that allow you to view attributes—EDIR and DMAP. Both display directories with subdirectories marked by DIR, read-only files by RO, and archive files by ARC. With the /H and /S switches, they can display and indicate hidden and system files, respectively. DMAP will also display all subdirectories of the current directory.

Shell Programs   Virtually all shell programs include some method of displaying file attributes in at least one style of directory display. Most of them also include a method for changing attributes. Often, you can make a change globally on a set of files that you select. One unfortunate exception is HomeBase's DOS facility, which does not address the attribute byte at all and cannot list hidden or system files.

Public-Domain Software   Several programs named ATTR and several others named CHMOD (after a UNIX command) will display and/or change file attributes. There is no way to tell from the name which of several versions you might be looking at if you come across one. However, they don't work like each other, so there is no point in discussing them. The command most likely to be flaky is the one to unhide hidden files. Since hidden files are invisible to DOS, they may be invisible to these attribute-changing programs as well.

Sorting Directories

As noted in Chapter 11, the order in which files appear in a directory affects the speed at which your work gets done. Having your directories sorted also makes it easier to find specific files. That's why we wrote the DIRS programs in Chapter 10.

Many programs will display file names sorted in an order of your choice. You can usually choose to sort by name, extension, size, date, or time, in ascending or descending order. Some public-domain programs do nothing other than display directories in a sorted order.

DOS shells all include options to display file names in sorted order. Some also include an option to display them unsorted, as they appear on the disk.

Writing sorted directories is another matter, however. Only the big utility packages—The Norton Utilities, Mace Utilities, and PC Tools—let you write sorted directories. The Norton Utilities' DS (Directory Sort) external program lets you sort by a primary and a secondary criterion, in ascending or descending order, by entering switches on a command line. Mace Utilities will sort all directories on a disk by a given criterion when you choose its Sort/Squeeze option. PC Tools lets you choose a sort order from the File Services menu and offers you the option of writing the sorted directory to disk. All of them routinely place subdirectory names ahead of file names in a sorted directory.

You may not want to sort all your directories by the same criterion. If a directory contains both software and data files, for example, you may prefer to sort by extension, to separate the programs from the data. However, if you have a directory of nothing but correspondence, it may be more useful to sort in reverse order by date, so you can see your most recent letters first.

An additional advantage of writing sorted directories is that the names of erased files will automatically be moved to the end of the directory. This shortens the time it takes DOS to find a file, because it doesn't have to skip over erased directory entries during its search.

Only one program allows you to choose the precise arrangement of your file names in a directory, regardless of any sorting order. That program is The Norton Utilities' external program DS, in both current releases. (Oddly enough, a program to write sorted directories in an order of your choice has been available on the lowly Commodore 64 for years!) When you enter the DS command with no parameters (other than a path name), you are shown a list of all the files in the specified directory. You may then choose a basic sorting order from a menu, or tag file names and move them to any point in the listing. You can even place subdirectory names last. When the order is to your liking, you can then write the sorted directory to disk.

This has several great advantages over other programs. Not only can you group related files, but you can also arrange them for maximum efficiency. You can place your CONFIG.SYS and AUTOEXEC.BAT files first, for example, to speed up your startup procedures. Or you can place all your overlay files first, which will let DOS find them more quickly when you are running the application that uses them. Little tricks like this can make your work go faster and more smoothly, unless you get so hung up in the process of setting up your directories that you forget to get on with your work.

You can use some indirect methods to get a DOS shell to sort a directory on disk. The trick is to first choose a sorting order, then tag the files that you want in the directory, and finally copy the files to a new floppy disk. On a hard disk, you would have to copy the files to a new directory and then delete the old one. Among the programs that can sort directories using this method are QDOS II, XTree, KeepTrackPlus, and the Norton Commander.

MANAGING AND USING RAM DISKS

13

THE MOST OBVIOUS BENEFITS of a RAM disk are that it gives you another place to put files and that it can't be taken out of the machine. The greatest bonus, however, is its speed. Disk input and output is probably the slowest aspect of computer operations. Everything else in the computer (except for printer operations) takes place at the speed of light. A RAM disk is thus up to 5,000 percent faster than a floppy disk.

On the other hand, a RAM disk has the drawback of being *volatile*— it's gone once you turn off the computer. And if you don't back up files from your RAM disk, they are gone with it. (However, as we'll see soon, there is one way to have a nonvolatile RAM disk.)

In this chapter, we'll look at several types of RAM disks and ways to maximize their utility while minimizing the risks. Most of the examples will be based on the assumption that you have two floppy disk drives and no hard disk. Therefore, unless otherwise stated, the RAM disk is assumed to be drive C. If you do have a hard disk, the section at the end of this chapter describes how to use it with a RAM disk. Moreover, most of the examples presented here can be adapted for use with hard-disk systems.

SO WHERE DO I GET ONE?

If you have DOS 3.X, you already have a RAM disk. If you use PC-DOS, it's in a file called VDISK.SYS. If you use MS-DOS, it will be called either VDISK.SYS or RAMDRIVE.SYS, depending on which version of MS-DOS you have.

If you have IBM's *DOS Technical Reference* and an assembler, you can have a RAM disk with DOS 2.0 as well. The code described as a "Sample Device Driver" in Chapter 2 of the *Technical Reference* is the code for VDISK.SYS. (Some MS-DOS manuals also include this code.) You can type in and assemble this code to create the driver.

You create the RAM disk by including a line in your CONFIG.SYS file to load the device driver. Later in the chapter, I'll explain these drivers in detail.

If you have an add-on memory board, it probably came with a disk of assorted software utilities, among which is a RAM-disk driver. But not all RAM-disk drivers are created equal. Depending on the software, some have considerably greater utility than others. Some are limited in that they offer only a fixed-size disk, and others do not allow you to specify the sector or directory size.

If you have a fully populated motherboard (512 or 640K), and you use DOS 2.X, probably the most inexpensive way to acquire a RAM disk is to order the QuadMaster III software from Quadram. This package, which includes a device driver called RAMDRIVE.SYS, costs only $10. Install the driver through your CONFIG.SYS file, followed by the size (in kilobytes) of the disk you want. For example, you would enter

```
DEVICE = RAMDRIVE.SYS 128
```

for a RAM disk of 128K.

Two add-on packages are worthy of special mention: the JRAM Combo Disk software, from Tall Tree Systems, and the X2C Expanded Memory Board, from ABM Computer Systems.

The JRAM Combo Disk

Even if you already have all the memory you need and a RAM-disk driver as well, you should consider using the JRAM Combo Disk. It includes JDRIVE, one of several RAM-disk drivers that will protect a RAM disk after a warm boot. Most such drivers are supplied with memory-expansion boards, and this one is no exception. However, the

Combo Disk is also available separately and does not require a JRAM board to operate.

Installing the RAM disk with JDRIVE actually requires two files. The first, JBOOT.BIN, establishes the amount of memory allocated to DOS, with the remainder (rounded to a multiple of 64K) set aside for a RAM disk. The second, JDRIVE.BIN, allows you to configure the RAM disk for a given sector size, number of sectors per cluster, and number of directory entries. It also allows you to specify many other options, such as whether or not the RAM disk should be restored automatically after a warm boot. If you also have a JRAM memory board, JDRIVE can establish RAM disks at memory locations above 640K, even without an extended memory driver.

The JRAM Combo Disk also includes a very sophisticated (but difficult to use) print spooler and a program called JET, which copies files eight times faster than the DOS COPY command. We'll see how these utilities work in this and following chapters.

DOS 3.2, 3.3

If you use DOS 3.2 or later, you may not find JET especially useful. The XCOPY and REPLACE commands between them will do everything that JET does. Besides, they use the current directory on a disk as their default, rather than the root, which is much less confusing.

The X2C Expanded Memory Board

The second alternative, the X2C board, is considerably more expensive. However, if you want to add memory to your system, or you need expanded memory (above 640K), this piece of hardware deserves special consideration. It is the only way I know of that you can have *nonvolatile RAM*. This means that you can set up your RAM disks so that the files you place on them will remain there even if the power is shut off for long periods of time. (The secret is a separate power cable that keeps the board electrically active and also charges a battery that takes over when the power goes off for short periods.)

The X2C board's RAMDRIVE.SYS device driver doesn't give you as much flexibility as JDRIVE. The disks it creates have 512K sectors, and the number of directory entries is proportional to the size of the disk. However, an additional RAMDRIVE.COM program lets you create or remove up to four RAM disks on the fly, without rebooting your computer. Moreover, the option of having the files on your RAM disks remain there after the power goes off more than makes up for the decreased flexibility.

CONFIGURING YOUR RAM DISK

Most RAM disks are created by loading their device drivers through the CONFIG.SYS file. As a rule, most RAM-disk software will allow you to create as many RAM disks as you want, simply by loading the device driver once for each disk. You can configure each one differently if you wish.

RAM Disk Size

First, you must decide how large a RAM disk you need. This depends on the applications you use. With 1-2-3, which creates spreadsheets as large as available memory, you might want a small RAM disk of about 64K to store some of the most frequently used DOS files—CHKDSK, FORMAT, and DISKCOPY, for example—or the help file for SideKick. With WordStar, which can run in as little as 192K, you will probably want to make the RAM disk as large as you can. Since WordStar reads from its overlay files frequently, and it loads only a small part of the text file you are editing into memory, the amount of time you save by editing WordStar files on a RAM disk is enormous.

The ideal sector size, cluster size, and number of directory entries also depend on your application. The main points to remember are that an entire cluster is allocated for a file of even one byte and that a sector of 512 bytes can hold 16 directory entries. If you use the default settings for most RAM disks, about 11K will be allocated for the boot record, two copies of the FAT, and a 112-entry directory. If you plan to work with small files, you should set your sector size as small as possible. If you are working with a few very large files, the sector size is less critical, but you can add at least 3K to the usable size of your disk by limiting the size of your directory.

The number of sectors per cluster is as critical as the sector size, since the cluster is the actual allocation unit. If you establish a 128-byte sector size and eight sectors per cluster, each cluster will take up 1K, just as it would if you used settings of 512-byte sectors with two sectors per cluster. The tradeoff is that since an entire cluster is read into memory at a time, input/output is a bit slower with smaller clusters. With the speed of a RAM disk, however, the difference is negligible.

Drive Designation

When you establish a RAM disk, it normally takes on the next available drive designation. If you have two floppy disks, for example, the RAM disk will become drive C. If you have a hard disk designated as C, the RAM disk will be drive D.

The JRAM Combo Disk package includes a program to create a dummy disk. If you work with two computers, one with a hard disk and one without, you can use this driver to create a dummy disk designated drive C. Then you could use drive D as your RAM disk on both machines, which will make your work much easier, especially if you have hard-coded the drive designator into your batch files or configured your software to find certain files on drive D.

Configuring DOS's RAM Disk

VDISK.SYS (RAMDRIVE.SYS in most MS-DOS versions) is a RAM disk driver supplied with DOS 3.X. This driver allows you to specify the total size of the disk, the sector size, and the number of directory entries. In addition, it includes switches that let you place the disk in expanded memory or in AT extended memory, if you have it. These drivers will create a RAM disk of any size up to 64K less than your total memory. If you have an expanded memory board or AT extended memory, you can place the RAM disk in these using only about 1K of normal memory for the device driver. (*Expanded* memory refers to memory above 640K that conforms to a standard developed by the Lotus, Intel, and Microsoft Corporations and requires a special device driver. *Extended* memory is memory above 640K included in PC/ATs and compatibles that can be addressed directly by the microprocessor chip but not by DOS.)

To create a RAM disk with VDISK.SYS, add the following line to the CONFIG.SYS file:

DEVICE = VDISK.SYS [*size*] [*sector size*] [*root size*] [*/switch*]

For MS-DOS, substitute RAMDRIVE.SYS for VDISK.SYS. Of course, the driver must be on your startup disk, or else the DEVICE= statement must include the path to its location.

Since the defaults for these two drivers are slightly different, we'll look at them separately. Note that the DOS manuals say a lot of things that either are not true or don't make sense about these drivers, so we'll look at them very closely.

___

PC-DOS 3.X

VDISK.SYS   For VDISK.SYS, the default *size* is 64K, the minimum is 1K, and the maximum is the amount of conventional memory less 64K if the disk is in conventional memory. Within these limits, the disk can be any size, in 1K increments. You specify the size as a number of kilobytes.

VDISK has one switch, with an optional parameter. If you place an /E switch after the other parameters, VDISK will place your RAM disk in AT extended memory if you have it. If you place the disk in extended memory, the maximum size is the amount of extended memory you have. If you use the form /E:N, where *N* is a number from 1 to 8, you can determine how many sectors will be read into memory at once. (This is in some sense a cluster size; however, the number you specify does not affect the amount of storage space a file will occupy.) The default is 8. If you lose some data while reading from the RAM disk, reduce this number gradually until the problem disappears. The default *sector size* is 128 bytes, but 256 and 512 are also acceptable values. You can set up the root directory to hold from 4 to 512 entries. The default is 64.

According to the manual, the driver will adjust the root directory to allow the last directory sector to hold as many 32-byte entries as will fit in a sector. Thus, with a 512-byte sector, the minimum directory size should be 16 entries. However, you truly *can* specify as few as 4 entries, in which case you will not be able to place more than three files on the disk unless you create a subdirectory. (The fourth entry is a volume label.)

VDISK.SYS lets you add comments between the parameters explaining what the parameters mean. For example, you could create your RAM disk with an entry in the CONFIG.SYS file reading

```
DEVICE = VDISK.SYS of only 32 kbytes 128 it will hold just
    4 directory entries
```

However, you will only see these comments if you read your CONFIG.SYS file. As DOS loads the device driver, the screen will display

```
VDISK Version 3.30 virtual disk C:
Buffer size: 32 KB
```

Sector size: 128
Directory entries: 4

◦   MS-DOS 3.X

RAMDRIVE.SYS   RAMDRIVE.SYS has two switches, both of which allow you to determine where the disk will be placed. The /E switch puts the disk in an AT's extended memory. The /A switch places the disk on an expanded memory board. If you do not specify a switch, your disk will occupy a portion of conventional memory.

For RAMDRIVE.SYS, the default *size* is 64K, the minimum is 16K, and the maximum is the amount of conventional memory less 64K if the disk is in conventional memory. Within these limits, the disk can be any size, in 1K increments. You specify the size as a number of kilobytes.

The default *sector size* is 128 bytes, but 256, 512, and 1024 are also acceptable values. You can set up the root directory to hold from 2 to 1024 entries; the default is 64. Like VDISK, RAMDRIVE claims to adjust the directory size upward to the nearest sector boundary. However, it will actually let you create a root directory with room for only one file name and a volume label. You might want to create such a disk for a swap file used by a program such as Microsoft Windows or Home-Base. If so, you will also want to specify the largest sector size.

ORGANIZING YOUR STARTUP DISK

When you're using a RAM disk, you must organize your startup disk accordingly. First, the way that you construct your AUTOEXEC.BAT file will depend on how you plan to use your RAM disk. Second, you will want to give special consideration to the files that you place on your startup disk. Simple programs that can be loaded from one disk may end up requiring two, one to set up the system and one to actually run the program. (Yes, I know, this is one of the reasons so many people have gone to hard disks, but once you get the system set up, you can use the methods described in this chapter to make your work run much more smoothly.)

The AUTOEXEC.BAT File

There are four things to consider when constructing an AUTOEXEC file to be used with a RAM disk:

▲ Some RAM-disk drivers must be loaded from a DOS prompt, rather than through the CONFIG.SYS file.

▲ Because batch files execute slowly, you will want to transfer control to the RAM disk as quickly as possible.

▲ It would be extremely useful if COMMAND.COM were somewhere in your computer where it could not be removed—such as on a RAM disk, if you don't have a hard disk.

▲ You will probably want to have your AUTOEXEC file transfer some files to the RAM disk.

Most of the time it takes to execute a batch file is a consequence of the disk drive head moving back to the batch file to find the next command after executing each one. If you eliminate this physical motion by transferring the operations to a RAM disk, the time savings will be immense. The easiest way to transfer control to the RAM disk is to create an AUTOEXEC.BAT file consisting of the following five lines:

```
ECHO OFF
[MODE set video mode, if necessary]
COPY CONTINUE.BAT C:
C:
CONTINUE
```

This file simply copies a file, CONTINUE.BAT, to the RAM disk and transfers control to it. In CONTINUE.BAT, you will place all of the commands normally included in the AUTOEXEC file. This may require prefacing a number of them with a drive specifier, but it still saves time.

More generally, if you have batch files that you use frequently, such as some of those illustrated in Chapter 10, you can save time by putting them on your startup disk and having the AUTOEXEC file copy them to the RAM disk. The time you save running the FILEMGR program in Chapter 11 from a RAM disk is incredible.

Teaching Your Computer to Find DOS on the RAM Disk

Having COMMAND.COM on a RAM disk is especially helpful with programs such as Microsoft Chart, Reflex, Symphony, and 1-2-3, which both overwrite COMMAND.COM and require you to switch disks. Wouldn't it be nice to never see the message

Insert COMMAND.COM disk in drive A
Then press any key when ready

To set this up, you must first copy COMMAND.COM onto your RAM disk and then tell the computer where to look for it.

DOS 3.X

In DOS 3.0 and above, it's relatively simple to accomplish this. Include in your AUTOEXEC file the following lines:

COPY COMMAND.COM C:
SET COMSPEC = C:\COMMAND.COM

DOS 2.X

If you use DOS 2.X, this addition simply doesn't work. You can enter the SET COMSPEC command as described, and if you type SET at a DOS prompt, it will appear that your computer is really using the copy of COMMAND.COM on the RAM disk. However, you can still run into that pesky message. Instead, you can use an undocumented switch that will allow you to make the copy of COMMAND.COM on the RAM disk the default command processor. Start your AUTOEXEC file with the lines shown in Listing 13.1.

```
1: ECHO OFF
2: C:
3: [A:MODE set video mode if necessary]
4: IF EXIST COMMAND.COM GOTO continue
5: COPY A:COMMAND.COM C:>NUL
6: COPY A:AUTOEXEC.BAT C:>NUL
7: COMMAND C:\ /P
8: :continue
```

Listing 13.1 ▲ *Beginning Lines of an AUTOEXEC.BAT File to Run COMMAND.COM from a RAM Disk.*

Use this code exactly as listed. I've tried numerous variations on it, and none of them work. Here's an explanation of the lines.

1:      Turns off screen echoing.

2:      Makes the RAM disk the default drive.

3:      Whether you need this line depends on your equipment. If you have both monochrome and color boards, and/or the dip switches aren't set correctly for your hardware, this line is essential. Otherwise, skip it.

5–6:   Copies COMMAND.COM and the AUTOEXEC.BAT file to the RAM disk.

7:      This is the command, not documented in most versions of DOS 2.X, that tells the computer to find DOS on the RAM disk. It's a relative of

   COMMAND /C

in that it loads a second copy of the command processor. However, the C:\ tells DOS to load COMMAND.COM from the root directory of drive C, and the /P switch tells it to regard this as a *permanent* loading of the command processor. Unlike COMMAND /C, it wipes out any values that have been established in the environment, such as a path and prompt (or settings created with the MODE command; this is why it comes after the loading of MODE).

4:      It is only after these events have taken place that line 4 becomes relevant. When the second copy of COMMAND.COM is loaded with the /P switch, it automatically looks for an AUTOEXEC file on the default drive (which is now the RAM disk). Thus, the AUTOEXEC file, which was copied to the RAM disk in line 6, will begin executing all over again. Line 4 directs control to the label at line 8, so that the processes that occurred in lines 5 through 7 do not repeat infinitely, and the rest of the AUTOEXEC file can be executed.

Incidentally, it's not a bad idea to include the line

   ECHO ^ [[35[^ [[5;7m WORKING ^ [[0m

between lines 3 and 4, and at any other point where there's a great deal of disk activity that is not reflected in messages on the screen. This line displays the word WORKING, flashing in inverse video, centered on the screen. If you have color, you can replace code 7 with an appropriate color code, as will be shown later in the chapter.

SOME APPLICATION EXAMPLES

Once you have set up your RAM disk and have experimented a bit, you will no doubt be able to think of many ways to use it with your applications. If you have WordStar or ThinkTank, you will find the examples in this section extremely useful. If you use other software, you can apply the same principles to your own special requirements. And if you use a variety of programs, the general utility setup at the end of this section can make your other applications function more smoothly.

Running WordStar on a RAM Disk

Because it is so disk-intensive, both in its use of overlays and its handling of data files, WordStar is one of those applications for which RAM disks appear to have been invented. It has many other irritating quirks, but it is nonetheless the *lingua franca* of the computer-using world.

You can overcome some of WordStar's deficiencies with a desktop organizer and a macro processor. In this example, SideKick is loaded to add windowing, which allows you to look at a file in the Notepad while a different file is open in WordStar and to cut and paste between the two. A SuperKey macro file is used to overcome some of the vagaries of WordStar's keyboard layout and simplify many of its multikeystroke commands.

The following discussion is based on the limitations of WordStar 3.3 and DOS 2.1 on a floppy disk system. Later in the chapter, we'll modify the procedures presented here to take advantage of the improvements built into WordStar 4.0, DOS 3.2, and a hard disk system.

Once these batch files have run, you can actually use all three programs without ever having to access the floppy disks (unless you want to refer to SideKick's data files), so you will want to include some kind of automatic backup procedure. The macros described in this chapter make it easy to back up the current file to a floppy disk.

The Startup Disk   The startup disk includes the following files:

- ▲ The system files

- ▲ The CONFIG.SYS and AUTOEXEC.BAT files

- ▲ The device drivers loaded through the CONFIG.SYS file, including ANSI.SYS, the RAM-disk software, and the JSPOOL print spooler, which is part of the JRAM Combo Disk

- ▲ The JET fast copy program (again, from the JRAM Combo Disk)

- ▲ The two configuration files to operate the spooler, MAKEFILE.COM and SPOOLCOM.COM

- ▲ SuperKey, its help file, and its WordStar macro file

- ▲ SideKick, its help file, and its data files

Figure 13.1 illustrates the directory of this disk.

The print spooler, which is discussed in Chapter 16, sets up a very small spooler buffer in system memory. Through the use of the configuration

```
Volume in drive A is WS BOOTDISK
Directory of  A:\

COMMAND   COM    23210     3-07-85      1:43p
CONFIG    SYS      111     2-24-86     10:09a
AUTOEXEC  BAT      505     4-21-36      1:45p
ANSI      SYS     1651     3-07-85      1:43p
JBOOT     BIN     5568    11-08-85      7:02a
JDRIVE    BIN     2026    11-08-85      6:47a
JSPOOL    BIN     7015     1-17-85      6:38p
FILELIST  A         92     2-20-86     12:14a
FILELIST  B         39     2-20-86     12:02a
JET       COM     7680     9-01-85      7:34a
WSRAM     BAT      259     4-21-86      3:05p
KEY       COM    40960     2-24-86     10:41a
KEY       HLP    38400     6-26-85      5:44p
SK        COM    39515     4-21-86      2:38p
SK        HLP    53632     8-02-85     12:40p
WS        MAC    10194     4-21-86      3:01p
MODE      COM     5295     3-07-85      1:43p
PHONE     001     3048     4-16-86      3:27p
APPOINT   APP      920     4-16-86      9:12a
BORDER    EXE    21372    11-26-85     11:34a
CFILES    BAT      163     2-23-86      4:05p
LOOK      BAT      156     2-23-86      4:06p
FORMAT    COM     9398     3-07-85      1:43p
CHKDSK    COM     9435     3-07-85      1:43p
SETPRINT  BAT      782     2-19-86      9:47a
MAKEFILE  COM     4608    12-03-83     11:02p
SPOOLCOM  COM     1012     1-17-84      9:59p
       26 File(s)     81853 bytes free
```

Figure 13.1 ▲ *The Directory of the WordStar Startup Disk.*

files, a large spooler buffer can be created on the RAM disk. It is assumed that if you need a spooler, you can insert the startup disk and run the programs through WordStar's Run a Program command.

Notice that WordStar is not among the files on the startup disk, as there is not enough room. The three WordStar files are loaded from a separate disk, as we shall see shortly.

The AUTOEXEC File and JET   Eight of the first nine lines of the AUTOEXEC file, shown in Listing 13.2, are essentially the same as the starting code shown in Listing 13.1. Line 7 presents a new wrinkle. The JET program will copy any number of files to another disk. Although you can use it with the same syntax as the COPY command, it has many other options. Among them is the ability to copy all of the files in a *file list* with a single command. The AUTOEXEC file in Listing 13.2 uses JET with a file list called FILELIST.A, which is shown in Listing 13.3. It is a list of the programs to be copied from drive A to the RAM disk.

```
 1: ECHO OFF
 2: MODE CO80
 3: CLS
 4: ECHO ^[[35C^[[5;7m WORKING ^[[0m
 5: C:
 6: IF EXIST COMMAND.COM GOTO continue
 7: A:JET A: C: A:FILELIST.A /F/C >NUL
 8: COMMAND C:\ /P
 9: :continue
10: VERIFY ON
11: DATE
12: TIME
13: CLS
14: ECHO ^[35C^[[5;7m WORKING ^[[0m
15: PATH C:\;A:\;B:\
16: PROMPT ^[[41;37m $p / $e[s$e[1;61H$t$h$h$h$h$h$h $d$e[u$e[44;33m
17: C:
18: RAMWS
```

Listing 13.2 ▲ *AUTOEXEC.BAT File for Enhanced WordStar on a RAM Disk.*

```
 1: COMMAND  COM
 2: AUTOEXECBAT
 3: RAMWS    BAT
 4: KEY      COM
 5: KEY      HLP
 6: SK       COM
 7: SK       HLP
```

Listing 13.3 ▲ *FILELIST.A.*

The command

A:JET A: C: A:FILELIST.A /F/C >NUL

tells JET to copy from drive A to drive C all the files named in FILE-LIST.A, which is on drive A. The /F switch tells it to copy the files in the list (without which it would merely copy the file FILELIST.A), and the /C switch tells it to include COMMAND.COM. Because of the >NUL at the end of the line, no messages are displayed while this process takes place. As you can see from Listing 13.3, the files to be copied include COMMAND.COM, the AUTOEXEC file, and a second batch file, as well as SuperKey, SideKick, and their help files.

The syntax of a file list for JET is quite precise. You *must* list file names in exactly 11 characters, with no period or space between the file name and its extension.

Warning: When using JET in conjunction with a hard disk, be aware that in important ways, JET behaves contrary to DOS conventions. It always defaults to the *root*, rather than the current directory, so if you ask it to copy something from the current directory, you *must* include the full path specification. Moreover, if you ask it to copy something to a drive that isn't there, it will automatically copy the specified files to the root directory of the current disk, or worse, create a new directory that has a drive specifier as a name. You cannot access such a directory through DOS, and you will have to rename the directory using a utility program before you can copy or erase the files on it. We'll look at some of the advantages of using JET with a hard disk in Chapter 14.

The rest of the AUTOEXEC file is self-explanatory. The prompt in line 14, which was discussed in Chapter 9, displays the time and date at the upper-right corner of the screen.

RAMWS.BAT   At the end of the AUTOEXEC file, control is transferred to another batch file, RAMWS.BAT, which appears in Listing 13.4. This is an important file, so we'll go over it line by line.

1–2:   Invokes SuperKey and SideKick.

3–4:   Erases SideKick and the AUTOEXEC file, which are no longer needed, from the RAM disk. SuperKey, which will

```
 1: KEY
 2: SK
 3: DEL SK.COM
 4: DEL AUTOEXEC.BAT
 5: ECHO ^[[2J ^[[1;44;33m
 6: ECHO                    ^G Place WordStar disk in drive B:
 7: pause
 8: JET B: C: A:FILELIST.B/F>NUL
 9: ECHO          ^G Replace the disk in drive B: with your data disk.
10: PAUSE
11: KEY A:WS /ML
12: BORDER
```

Listing 13.4 ▲ *RAMWS.BAT.*

be invoked again by a command in this batch file, must remain present for the invocation to be effective; therefore it is not erased.

5: Uses ANSI escape sequences to clear the screen and reestablish the colors set up in the prompt.

6–7: At this point, it is time to copy WordStar to the RAM disk. A message tells the user, with a beep, to place the WordStar disk in drive B. Note that the disk in drive A is not yet replaced.

8: Invokes JET a second time. It loads the files listed in FILELIST.B, which is on the disk in drive A. As you can see from Listing 13.5, these are WordStar files on the disk in drive B. This disk is presumably a normal WordStar disk, containing whatever ancillary files you keep on such a disk—WINSTALL, WS.INS, and so on. Its only unusual feature is that WordStar must be configured, either through WINSTALL or through a software patch, to find its overlays on drive C rather than drive A.

9–10: Instructs the user to replace the WordStar disk, which is no longer needed.

11: Invokes SuperKey and tells it to load a WordStar macro file from drive A. This file begins with the LOADFILE macro shown in Listing 6.9. This macro asks for the file to be loaded, assigns its name to Shift-F1, copies it to the RAM disk, and starts WordStar with the specified file already open.

```
1: WS       COM
2: WSMSGS   OVR
3: WSOVLY1  OVR
```

Listing 13.5 ▲ *FILELIST.B.*

12: The border color is established by the program BOR-DER.EXE on the startup disk. This is a compiled version of a BASIC program that contains only a COLOR statement. It must be invoked after SideKick and SuperKey because both of these programs automatically clear the entire screen to black.

Automatic File Backup Within the WordStar macro file are several other macros that make saving the file virtually automatic. These macros are shown in Listing 13.6. The Alt-K macro, in line 4, simply assigns to a single key the familiar Ctrl-K S Ctrl-Q P sequence, which saves the file and restores the cursor to its former position. This backs up the file to the RAM disk, which is of no help if the power goes off. The real magic is in the other four macros.

The Ctrl-F2 macro, in lines 8 through 11, performs the automatic backup to drive B. First, it invokes the Alt-K macro, so that the file on the RAM disk is current. Then it issues the Ctrl-K O command, which is the form of the file-copy command that is used while a file is open. The drive B prefix is automatically entered at WordStar's prompt, and the macro assigned to Shift-F1, which is the file name, is played back. Finally, when WordStar displays the prompt

FILE B:*FILENAME.EXT* EXISTS – OVERWRITE (Y/N)?

a Y is automatically entered. If there is no copy of your file on drive B, this will enter a Y into it, but it's easy enough to delete this character. Thus, to back up your file to the floppy disk in drive B, all you have to do is press Ctrl-F2.

After you finish working on your initial file, you may want to go on to edit other files on the RAM disk. You need some means of backing up those files as well. This is accomplished by the Alt-D macro, in lines 1 through 3, and the Alt-N macro, in lines 5 through 7. Instead of loading a document file by entering just a D and a nondocument file by entering an N, you will now use the Alt key in conjunction with these keys. The

```
 1: <BEGDEF><AltD><TITLE>Document File<TITLE>d
 2: <BEGDEF><CtrlCTR><ENDDEF><ENTER>
 3: <ENDDEF>
 4: <BEGDEF><AltK><TITLE>Save & Kontinue<TITLE><CtrlK>s<CtrlQ>p<ENDDEF>
 5: <BEGDEF><AltN><TITLE>Non-Document File<TITLE>n
 6: <BEGDEF><CtrlCTR><ENDDEF><ENTER>
 7: <ENDDEF>
 8: <BEGDEF><CtrlF2><TITLE>Backup to drive B<TITLE><AltK>
 9: <CtrlK><CtrlO><CtrlCTR><ENTER>
10: B:<CtrlCTR><ENTER>
11: Y<ENDDEF>
12: <BEGDEF><AltF2><TITLE>Backup to drive A<TITLE><AltK>
13: <CtrlK><CtrlO><CtrlCTR><ENTER>
14: A:<CtrlCTR><ENTER>
15: Y<ENDDEF>
```

Listing 13.6 ▲ *Automatic Backup Macros for WordStar.*

macros assigned to Alt-D and Alt-N automatically assign the name of any new file you open to Shift-F1, so the automatic backup macro activated by Ctrl-F2 will work with it as well.

You might at this point want to use more than one data disk, since all your essential files are now on the RAM disk. The macro assigned to Alt-F2 takes care of this by performing the same automatic backup procedure, placing the backups on the disk in drive A. If you remember to press Ctrl-F2 or Alt-F2 every few minutes, you will lose no more than a few minutes' work even if the power goes out and your RAM-disk files evaporate.

Automatic Backup for ThinkTank

ThinkTank is one of those programs that gives you no access to DOS whatsoever, not even to view a directory or copy a file. Moreover, although the entire program is loaded into memory, ThinkTank creates extremely large disk files, which it accesses frequently. These characteristics of the program make it an ideal candidate for use with a RAM disk. They also suggest that you need some kind of system that you can use often to back up files to a floppy disk.

The program requires 320K to run effectively. If you use it with some background programs (I use it with SideKick and SuperKey), you will need even more memory. This means that you either use a very small RAM disk or find some place else to put the program. The following discussion assumes that an expanded memory board is in the computer—one that expands memory beyond 640K. Because other applications use most of the expanded memory, the RAM disk still has to be rather small. However, because ThinkTank's files are large, you have to make the best use of the limited amount of memory available.

The Startup Disk and the CONFIG.SYS File   ThinkTank's program code and and its ancillary files take more than 153K, and a great many startup files are required to set up this system. Therefore, two disks are required for startup. However, the disks are set up so that once the system has been configured, no further swapping is necessary. Figures 13.2 and 13.3 show the directories of the startup disk and the working disk, respectively. Listing 13.7 shows the CONFIG.SYS file, which explains

```
Volume in drive A is TTANK BOOT
Directory of  A:\

COMMAND   COM     23612    7-07-86   12:00p
CONFIG    SYS       110    7-20-87    1:18p
ANSI      SYS      1651    7-07-86   12:00p
EMM       SYS      7522    1-08-87    4:49p
RAMDRIVE  SYS      6680    8-01-86    5:59a
AUTOEXEC  BAT       493    7-20-87    1:27p
KEY       COM     40960    7-07-87    8:53a
KEY       HLP     38400    6-26-85    5:44p
SK        COM     39515    7-06-87    4:47p
SK        HLP     53632    8-02-85   12:40p
TANK      BAT       288    7-20-87    1:22p
TANKOPTS  DAT      4608    7-20-87   12:18p
GRAPHICS  EXE     13170    7-07-86   12:00p
MODE      EXE     13928    7-07-86   12:00p
        14 File(s)     65536 bytes free
```

Figure 13.2 ▲ *The Directory of the ThinkTank Startup Disk.*

```
Volume in drive A is TTank 2.4NP
Directory of  A:\

APPOINT   APP      1581    7-20-87   10:47a
AUTOEXEC  BAT       493    7-20-87    1:27p
COMMAND   COM     23612    7-07-89   12:00p
CONFIG    SYS       110    7-20-87    1:18p
KEY       HLP     38400    6-26-85    5:44p
PHONE     DIR      8575    7-06-87    4:46p
SK        HLP     53632    8-02-85   12:40p
TANK      EXE    140320    4-19-87   10:52a
TANK      BAT       288    7-20-87    1:22p
TANKOPTS  DAT      4608    7-20-87   12:18p
TTANK     MAC      1331    6-29-87    5:54p
YN        COM        70    2-07-86    5:33p
        12 File(s)     35840 bytes free
```

Figure 13.3 ▲ *The Directory of the ThinkTank Program Disk.*

what some of the files are for. Both disks have copies of the same CONFIG.SYS, AUTOEXEC.BAT, and TANK.BAT files, just for safety. Let's look at the CONFIG.SYS file first.

1: Loads the ANSI.SYS device driver.

2: Loads the Expanded Memory Manager for the memory board.

3: Sets up the RAM disk on the expanded memory board, with room for 16 directory entries and a sector size of 128. Since it will be used primarily to hold two files—the .DB and .SAV files used by ThinkTank—and since .DB files tend to be large, the directory is large enough to hold a few extra temporary files. As we'll see, at least three other files will be placed on the disk. The small sector size assures that each file takes up as little storage space as possible. (If the sectors were, say, 1024 bytes, and if the file extended one byte beyond a sector, an additional 1K of the RAM disk would be used.) On the other hand, the small cluster size makes reading from the RAM disk slower than it might be.

4: Establishes 16 DOS buffers. This helps overcome the slower access resulting from the small cluster size.

The AUTOEXEC.BAT File and the Auto-Load Macro   The rest of the files on this disk are used by the AUTOEXEC file, so now let's turn our attention to that file, which appears in Listing 13.8. It deserves a detailed explanation.

1–8: Sets up the RAM disk so that DOS will find COMMAND.COM there, assuming DOS 3.X is used. Users of earlier versions of DOS can substitute lines from Listing 13.1. The escape sequences in line 5 display the WORKING message in flashing red on a white background.

```
1: DEVICE=ANSI.SYS
2: DEVICE=EMM.SYS
3: DEVICE=RAMDRIVE.SYS 256 128 16
4: BUFFERS=16
```

Listing 13.7 ▲ *CONFIG.SYS File for Use with ThinkTank.*

9: Establishes a search path. Since only data files will be on drive B, drive B is not placed on the search path.

10: Clears the screen (^ [[2]), erasing the DATE and TIME information, and repeats the WORKING message.

11–13: Gives you the opportunity to set the date and time, and establishes a prompt.

14–15: Copies TANK.BAT (the automatic backup file) and SuperKey to the RAM disk. The latter is necessary because there is no room for SuperKey on the working disk, but the program has to be present in the computer in order for some of its commands to work.

16–18: Invokes SuperKey and SideKick. Since the search path includes drive A, changing the default drive to A is not strictly necessary. However, neither of these programs can find their help files unless they are invoked from the directory on which the help files reside. Because disks will be switched when this batch file has finished executing, the help files, as well as all of SideKick's data files, appear on the second disk, which will stay in drive A. The programs won't notice the switch.

```
 1: ECHO OFF
 2: CLS
 3: C:
 4: A:MODE CO80
 5: ECHO ^[[35C^[[0;5;47;31m WORKING ^[[0m
 6: COPY A:COMMAND.COM >NUL
 7: SET COMSPEC=C:\COMMAND.COM
 8: COPY A:AUTOEXEC.BAT >NUL
 9: PATH C:\;A:\
10: DATE
11: TIME
12: PROMPT ^[[41;37m $p ═══^P $e[s^[[1;61H$t$h$h$h$h$h$h $d$e[u$e[44m$e
13: COPY A:TANK.BAT >NUL
14: COPY A:KEY.COM  >NUL
15: A:
16: KEY
17: SK
19: C:
20: ECHO ^[[1;44;33m^[[2J^[21C^GPut ThinkTank Program Disk in drive A:
21: ECHO                        Put data disk in drive B:
22: PAUSE
23: KEY A:TTANK /ML
```

Listing 13.8 ▲ *AUTOEXEC.BAT File for ThinkTank.*

19: Returns control to drive C for faster execution.

20–22: Uses escape sequences to clear the working area of the screen (but not the border) and reestablish the colors (bright yellow on blue). At this point, it is time to switch to the second disk. Appropriate messages are displayed, accompanied by a beep.

23: Asks SuperKey to load the appropriate macro file from the second disk. This file begins with an auto-start macro similar to LOADFILE.MAC, presented in Listing 6.9. This file displays the message

What file do you want to load?

and records the answer as a key definition. The macro uses the key definition to copy the file from drive B to the RAM disk. It then issues the command TANK to invoke the automatic backup file, followed by the newly defined key, which enters the file name as a parameter. This invokes the TANK.BAT file, shown in Listing 13.9.

The Automatic Backup Batch File The TANK.BAT file is relatively simple. Lines 4, 7, and 8 are strictly cosmetic (they clear and color the screen and repeat the WORKING message). Line 3, which is where the main work of the program begins, accepts the file name assigned to a key in the auto-start macro as the parameter for %1 and invokes ThinkTank from drive A, opening the file on the RAM disk.

When the user exits ThinkTank, control is returned to this batch file, which first prompts the user, with a beep, to be sure that the proper data

```
 1: ECHO OFF
 2: :saveit
 3: A:TANK C:%1
 4: ECHO ^[[2J
 5: ECHO ^G                          Is data disk in Drive B:?
 6: PAUSE
 7: ECHO ^[[35C^[[0;5;47;31m WORKING ^[[0m
 8: ECHO ^[[1;33;44m
 9: COPY C:%1.* B:
10: YN ^G                            Want to continue
11: IF ERRORLEVEL 1 GOTO saveit
12: IF ERRORLEVEL 0 GOTO end
13: :end
```

Listing 13.9 ▲ *TANK.BAT.*

disk is in drive B (in case you replaced the disk with another one to import a text file into ThinkTank or to read something into SideKick). This being established, the file is copied to the floppy disk in line 9.

The rest of the program gives the user a chance to return to the same program and file. Using the YN program from Chapter 6, the file displays a prompt inquiring whether the user wants to continue. If so, control is directed to the label

:saveit

in line 2. Otherwise, the cycle ends after the file is backed up.

A General Utility Environment

Even if you don't have such special requirements, you can effectively use a RAM disk to set up a general utility environment for use with a variety of programs. Let's assume that you have 640K of system memory. Of this, 128K will be allocated to a RAM disk, as shown in Listing 13.10.

The first line of this file uses the VDISK.SYS device driver supplied with DOS 3.X to establish a RAM disk of 128K. This disk has a sector size of 512 (the default is 128) and a directory of 16 entries, or one sector, the minimum directory size for a RAM disk with sectors of 512 bytes. Each entry is 32 bytes, and the directory will be assigned in multiples of a sector. The rest of the file should be self-explanatory.

The AUTOEXEC.BAT file for this environment, which appears in Listing 13.11, has some significant differences from the others we have looked at, so we'll go over it carefully. Lines 1 and 2 are self-explanatory; we'll begin at line 3.

3–5: A message in line 3 explains the action of lines 4 and 5—any old .BAK files left over from editing either the AUTOEXEC or CONFIG.SYS files are deleted.

6: Establishes a UNIX-like prompt, of the form
      [A:\]

```
1: DEVICE=VDISK.SYS 128 512 16
2: DEVICE=ANSI.SYS
3: FILES=20
4: BUFFERS=16
5: BREAK=ON
```

Listing 13.10 ▲ *CONFIG.SYS File for a General Utility Environment.*

7:      A PATH command places the root directories of both floppy disk drives and the RAM disk on the search path.

8:      Tells DOS 3.X to look for COMMAND.COM on the RAM disk. It isn't there yet, but since it is not overwritten by this batch file during execution, it doesn't matter at this point. Users of earlier versions of DOS can substitute the commands from Listing 13.1.

9–10:   Displays a message and issues the SET command, so that the user can see the path, prompt, and default command processor that have been established.

11:     The ECHO statement, followed by a null, creates a blank line on the screen for clarity (this can be entered in EDLIN by typing Ctrl-V @).

12–15: Self-explanatory.

16:     Turns ECHO on, so that the names of the files being copied to the RAM disk are displayed as they are copied.

```
 1: ECHO OFF
 2: VERIFY ON
 3: ECHO Removing old CONFIG.BAK, AUTOEXEC.BAK from A:\
 4: DEL A:AUTOEXEC.BAK
 5: DEL A:CONFIG.BAK
 6: PROMPT [$p]
 7: PATH C:\;A:\;B:\
 8: SET COMSPEC=C:\COMMAND.COM
 9: ECHO System configuration . . .
10: SET
11: ECHO ^@
12: ECHO Logging onto RAM drive C:
13: C:
14: ECHO ^@
15: ECHO Setting up RAM disk . . .
16: ECHO ON
17: COPY A:AUTOEXEC.BAT
18: COPY A:CONFIG.SYS
19: COPY A:COMMAND.COM
20: COPY A:CHKDSK.COM
21: COPY A:FORMAT.COM
22: COPY A:EDLIN.COM
23: COPY A:HGC.COM
24: COPY A:SETPRINT.BAT
25: ECHO OFF
26: HGC DIAG
27: ECHO Hercules Monochrome Graphics Card configured for IBM monochrome
28: ECHO ^@
29: DATE
30: TIME
```

Listing 13.11 ▲ *AUTOEXEC.BAT File for a General Utility Environment.*

17–22: Copies the DOS utility files, along with AUTOEXEC.BAT and CONFIG.SYS, to the RAM disk. Since control has already been transferred to the RAM disk in line 13, once the AUTOEXEC file is on the RAM disk, it will execute from there, rather than from the floppy disk. Since the AUTOEXEC and CONFIG.SYS files are now on the RAM disk, they can be edited there using EDLIN, and the new versions copied back to drive A. This would normally obviate lines 3 through 5, which are included as an extra precaution.

23: Copies the driver for the Hercules Graphics Card to the RAM disk.

24: Places the file SETPRINT.BAT, which will be introduced in Chapter 16, on the RAM disk for easy access. This file allows the user to change the style of print on the printer.

25–27: Turns ECHO off, invokes the Hercules Graphics driver, and notes the established configuration on the screen. The rest of the file is self-explanatory.

A RAM disk configured in this or a similar manner provides an environment in which the most commonly used DOS external programs are always available in the computer, for use with any application program. With this setup, the user may safely switch disks in either drive and still be able to use these programs or configure the printer or the monitor. If you have some other utilities that you use frequently, you could modify this file (and your startup disk) so that they will be permanently available (as long as the power doesn't go off, that is).

USING A RAM DISK WITH A HARD DISK

A RAM disk can be a great convenience even if you use a hard disk. Unless you have an AT or a hard disk with the AT's speed, RAM disks are still about ten times faster than hard disks. But if you use a hard disk, you probably don't want to load a particular set of files automatically because you don't always start up in the same application. Moreover, if you use a variety of applications, you probably don't always want the same size RAM disk. Indeed, there may be times when you'd rather not have a RAM disk at all. The programs shown in Listings 13.12 and 13.13 will allow you to change the size of your RAM disk or get rid of it entirely with a single command.

 Hint: If you use the JRAM Combo Disk, you do not need this program. The Combo Disk includes a program called MAKEDOS.COM. If you set your RAM disk to 0K, you can then type

MAKEDOS *NNN*

```
 1: ECHO OFF
 2: C:
 3: CD\
 4: IF NOT EXIST CONFIG.%1 GOTO gotit
 5: IF %1==320 GOTO do320
 6: IF %1==640 GOTO do640
 7: IF %1==192 GOTO do192
 8: IF %1==448 GOTO do448
 9: ECHO Syntax is RAMSIZE nnn, where nnn is 192, 320, 448, or 640.
10: GOTO end
11: :do320
12: IF NOT EXIST CONFIG.640 RENAME CONFIG.SYS CONFIG.640
13: IF NOT EXIST CONFIG.192 RENAME CONFIG.SYS CONFIG.192
14: IF NOT EXIST CONFIG.448 RENAME CONFIG.SYS CONFIG.448
15: RENAME CONFIG.320 CONFIG.SYS
16: GOTO warmboot
17: :do640
18: IF NOT EXIST CONFIG.320 RENAME CONFIG.SYS CONFIG.320
19: IF NOT EXIST CONFIG.192 RENAME CONFIG.SYS CONFIG.192
20: IF NOT EXIST CONFIG.448 RENAME CONFIG.SYS CONFIG.448
21: RENAME CONFIG.640 CONFIG.SYS
22: GOTO warmboot
23: :do192
24: IF NOT EXIST CONFIG.640 RENAME CONFIG.SYS CONFIG.640
25: IF NOT EXIST CONFIG.320 RENAME CONFIG.SYS CONFIG.320
26: IF NOT EXIST CONFIG.448 RENAME CONFIG.SYS CONFIG.448
27: RENAME CONFIG.192 CONFIG.SYS
28: GOTO warmboot
29: :do320
30: IF NOT EXIST CONFIG.640 RENAME CONFIG.SYS CONFIG.640
31: IF NOT EXIST CONFIG.192 RENAME CONFIG.SYS CONFIG.192
32: IF NOT EXIST CONFIG.448 RENAME CONFIG.SYS CONFIG.448
33: RENAME CONFIG.320 CONFIG.SYS
34: GOTO warmboot
35: :do448
36: IF NOT EXIST CONFIG.640 RENAME CONFIG.SYS CONFIG.640
37: IF NOT EXIST CONFIG.192 RENAME CONFIG.SYS CONFIG.192
38: IF NOT EXIST CONFIG.320 RENAME CONFIG.SYS CONFIG.320
49: RENAME CONFIG.448 CONFIG.SYS
40: :warmboot
41: YN              ^G  Have you saved the files on your RAM disk
42: IF NOT ERRORLEVEL 1 GOTO end
43: BASICA AUTOBOOT
44: :gotit
45: ECHO                You already have %1K of RAM in DOS memory.
46: :end
```

Listing 13.12 ▲ *RAMSIZE.BAT.*

where *NNN* is the amount of system memory that you want. You must then reboot the computer. It will leave the requested amount of system memory, and the remainder will be assigned to a RAM disk. However, this means that your RAM disk cannot have a default size. You must always reboot after startup in order to have a RAM disk of any size.

RAMSIZE.BAT is designed to be used with a hard disk and 640K of RAM. It gives you the choice of having 192K, 320K, 448K, or 640K of system memory. If you have 640K of system memory, there will be no RAM disk. If you choose any of the other amounts, the remaining memory will be assigned to a RAM disk. This is accomplished by having four versions of the CONFIG.SYS file on your root directory, each with a different RAM-disk configuration of the appropriate size. The one that is currently active is called CONFIG.SYS. The other three are all called CONFIG, but each has an extension that indicates the amount of system memory it will establish. Thus, for example, if you have 320K of system memory and a 320K RAM disk, your files will be called CONFIG.192, CONFIG.SYS, CONFIG.448, and CONFIG.640. (You could also put different things in the various CONFIG files—different size spooler buffers, for example, or additional device drivers when you have more system memory.)

To invoke the program, type

RAMSIZE *NNN*

where *NNN* is one of the four amounts of system memory for which you have CONFIG files. Although the program is quite long, its operation is simple. The basic technique is to rename the appropriate CONFIG file to CONFIG.SYS, rename the current CONFIG.SYS so that it has the correct extension, and automatically reboot the computer.

Here are the salient sections of RAMSIZE.BAT:

2–3: Logs you onto the root directory of the hard disk.

4: Checks to see whether a file named CONFIG.*NNN*

```
10 DEF SEG=&HF000:AB=&HE05B:CALL AB
```

Listing 13.13 ▲ *AUTOBOOT.BAS.*

exists. If it does not, then you already have the amount of system memory that you want, because the file that would create it is already named CONFIG.SYS.

5–8:   Checks the parameter that has been entered. If the parameter is correct, lines 5 through 8 direct execution to the appropriate routine.

9–10:   If the parameter is not a valid one, or no parameter has been entered, a message is displayed showing the correct syntax and the program ends.

Lines 11 through 16, 17 through 22, 23 through 28, and 30 through 34 are four virtually identical routines, one for each amount of system memory. Each one checks the various CONFIG file extensions to see which is missing. CONFIG.SYS is renamed so that it has the missing extension, and the file with the chosen system memory size is renamed CONFIG.SYS. Execution is then directed to line 37.

At line 37, you are asked whether you have saved your files on your RAM disk because line 40 will reboot the computer. If you answer with an N, the program ends, so you can save the files and reboot manually. If you answer with a Y, the computer reboots itself with the new CONFIG.SYS file active. This is accomplished by the one-line BASIC program shown in Listing 13.13.

WordStar Revivified

WordStar 4.0 contains several notable improvements over WordStar 3.3. One of the improvements is that it now can understand directory syntax. For this reason, WordStar 4.0 is much easier to use with a hard disk than earlier releases. However, it still uses overlays (four, to be precise), and it also reads and writes your working file often. Therefore, it can still benefit from the speed of a RAM disk.

In addition, DOS 3.2 and above have new facilities that make it easier both to find files and to copy files selectively. Thus, it can be used to accomplish those tasks we used JET for earlier.

The program WS4.BAT, shown in Listing 13.14, takes advantage of these new facilities. It's a simplified version of WSRAM.BAT, which appeared in Listing 6.7. We'll make the following assumptions about the way our system is set up:

- ▲ WordStar is on hard disk C, in a directory called \WORDSTAR, which is on the search path.
- ▲ The program file is called WS.EXE.
- ▲ Drive D is a RAM disk.
- ▲ WordStar has been configured using the WSCHANGE program to find the file WSMSGS.OVR on drive D.

The last point needs a bit of explanation. First, although WordStar 4.0 has four overlays, WSMSGS is the only one that is needed almost constantly. The others are used for printing, storing macros, and checking spelling.

Second, you can configure the program to find its overlays on a particular directory, by entering a path using WSCHANGE. However, the program always looks for a directory of the name you entered in WSCHANGE, no matter what disk is current. Thus, if you tell WordStar that WSMSGS.OVR is named D:WSMSGS.OVR, and the path you enter in WSCHANGE is \WORDSTAR, it will find that file only if it is on a \WORDSTAR directory in drive D.

```
 1: ECHO OFF
 2: IF NOT %2@==@ CD\%2
 3: XCOPY C:\WORDSTAR\WSMSGS.OVR D:\WORDSTAR>NUL
 4: IF %1@==@ SET FILE=NOFILE
 5: IF NOT %1@==@ SET FILE=%1
 6: D:
 7: CD \WORDSTAR
 8: IF EXIST C:%FILE% COPY %FILE%
 9: IF %FILE%==%NOFILE WS
10: IF NOT %FILE%==%NOFILE WS %FILE%
11: DEL *.BAK
12: DEL WSMSGS.OVR
13: REPLACE D:*.* C: /D
14: REPLACE D:*.* C: /A /P
15: C:
16: SET FILE=
17: CLS
18: DIR /P
19: DIR D:
```

Listing 13.14 ▲ *WS4.BAT.*

Now let's look at the program. To call the program, you enter a command of the form

WS4 *[FILENAME.EXT]* *[SOURCE]*

If you try to use wild-card characters in the name of the file to be opened (if you want to copy several files to the RAM disk at once), WordStar will give you an error message instead of opening a file. You must then open a file manually. (WordStar requires a specific file name.) *Source* is the name of the directory on drive C where the file is located. If you leave out the directory name, WS4.BAT will default to the current directory in line 2. You may leave out the file name if you want to create a new file. Here's how the rest of the program works:

3:	The XCOPY command creates a \WORDSTAR directory on drive D and copies the overlay file to it.
4–5:	If you do not specify a file name, the variable FILE is given the value NOFILE. Otherwise it takes the name of the file you entered on the command line.
6–7:	Makes the \WORDSTAR directory on drive D the current drive and directory, so you don't inadvertently copy other files you may have been using on the RAM disk in lines 13 and 14.
8:	If the file exists, copies it to the \WORDSTAR directory on drive D.
9–10:	If the file exists, opens it in WordStar; otherwise, calls WordStar.
11–12:	Deletes the files you do not want to update on the source directory.
13:	Updates any files that already exist on the source directory. (This will not work with PC-DOS, but the results may be acceptable without the /D switch.)
14:	Adds any new files you have created to the source directory, with your permission. This gives you the opportunity to copy new files to other directories after WS4.BAT ends, if you prefer.

15–18: A cleanup routine. Returns you to the source directory, elminates the environment variable, clears the screen, and shows you the directories, so you can be sure that you have copied all your files correctly.

If you specify a file name on the command line, and you have not yet created the file, you will get an error message in line 13. However, the file should be correctly copied to the hard disk by line 14.

S E N S I B L E
H A R D   D I S K
M A N A G E M E N T

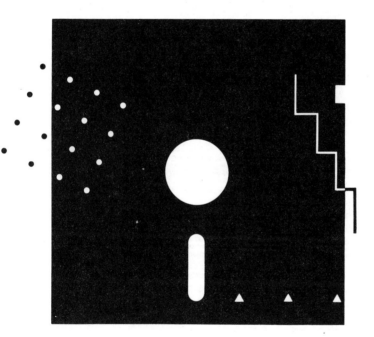

C H A P T E R

14

A HARD DISK CAN RADICALLY CHANGE the way that you use your computer. Your desk will no longer be cluttered with floppy disks, and the complex disk-shuffling setups we went through in the previous chapter all become a thing of the past. You will gain the advantage of their speed. Although nowhere near as fast as RAM disks, hard disks can load program overlays or read files three to ten times faster than floppy disk drives. Furthermore, you are not limited to 360K as a maximum file size for spreadsheets and databases.

The first generation of personal computer hard disks held ten megabytes, which is about as much as 27 floppy disks. Today, hard disks of 40 and 60 megabytes are not uncommon, and they are relatively inexpensive. You may wonder what you will do with so much storage. I did, too, until I got it. Now I find that I am constantly taking programs off the hard disk to make room for others that I use more often. If you are considering adding a hard disk to your system and wonder how large a disk you need, the answer is the same as for adding RAM: as large as you can afford. Once it's installed, it's there, and you will find a use for it.

BASIC ORGANIZING PRINCIPLES

Just imagine scrolling through a directory with thousands of file names in search of the latest version of a file you modified last Thursday, and you'll understand why it is essential to organize the storage space on your hard disk. Tree-structured directories will structure this space, but they do require some careful planning. Unless you have a program that displays a tree diagram of your entire disk, it's easy to forget which directories are subordinate to the main ones. If you take the time to plan the organization of your hard disk before you load it up with files, you can save yourself a lot of time and frustration.

There are four basic principles of organizing your hard disk. The first is

Don't nest your directories more than two levels deep.

If you can avoid it, don't even nest them more than one level. (Unfortunately, some programs virtually require you to use two levels of directories with a hard disk, and others create so many files that you can't find them unless you give them a separate directory.)

Not only does too much nesting make it hard to find your files, it also requires you to type inordinately long path names. The longer the command line argument, the more likely it is that you will make a mistake in entering the command. Even though you can execute a program on another directory with DOS 3.X, you still have to type the complete path, and the internal commands such as TYPE, COPY, and RENAME always require a complete path specification if the file is not on the current directory. Just think about typing

```
COPY \DATABASE\PROJRPTS\SMITH\APRIL\SLSFIGS.ASC
\WPFILES\SMITH\SLSFIGS.TXT
```

as a command, and you'll get the idea.

The second principle is

Don't clutter your root directory.

The root directory should contain only the files you need for starting your computer (and possibly not all of those) and other directories. These include COMMAND.COM, CONFIG.SYS and the device drivers that it loads, and AUTOEXEC.BAT and the startup files that it loads. Unless you work almost exclusively with a single software package or always start your day in a particular function, your root directory should simply be a jumping-off place.

Note: Many people argue that you should simplify your root directory even further, placing nothing on it but COMMAND.COM,

AUTOEXEC.BAT, CONFIG.SYS, and subdirectories. To accomplish this, you would place your configuration and startup files in a special, separate directory. I think it makes more sense to keep these files on your root directory. Having them there makes it easier to change your configuration as needed, for two reasons. First, you don't have to preface nearly every line in your CONFIG and AUTOEXEC files with a path name. Second, you can see immediately which files may be involved in your startup procedure.

The third organizational principle is

Don't give your subdirectory names extensions.

They just clutter up the syntax.

The fourth principle is a bit more complicated. Your hard disk should include the following directories:

▲ \DOS

▲ \BATCH

▲ \UTIL

All three of these directories, which are described in detail in the next section, should be on your search path, right after the root directory. In fact, you may find that you do not need the root directory on the search path at all—the SET COMSPEC statement, which DOS will place in the environment upon startup, will tell DOS where COMMAND.COM is located.

HARD DISK DIRECTORIES

The \DOS, \BATCH, and \UTIL directories can be your keys to a well-designed hard disk system.

The \DOS Directory

The \DOS directory should contain all the DOS external programs, except COMMAND.COM and any device drivers (ANSI.SYS, VDISK.SYS, and so on) that are used in your CONFIG.SYS file. The DOS files should be on a separate directory so that you know where to find them. By placing this directory on the search path, you can execute DOS external commands no matter what directory is current.

 Hint: If your DOS includes programs to set up or format the hard disk, omit them from the \DOS directory. Instead, execute them from the DOS floppy disk.

The \BATCH Directory

One of the more efficient ways to organize a hard disk is to keep each software package, with all its utilities (drivers, help files, overlays, and so on) in a separate directory. (Two other organizational structures—one suitable for those who work on many projects and one for a multiuser system—will be discussed later in the chapter.) If you choose this system, the \BATCH directory will simplify navigation around your hard disk.

 DOS 2.X

If you use DOS 2.X, this directory will contain a series of batch files of the form

```
ECHO OFF
CD \PROGDIR
PROGRAM %1 %2 %3. . .
```

where *PROGDIR* is the name of the directory on which the program is located and *PROGRAM* is the name of the program you are calling. This allows you to call any program from anywhere on your hard disk. (It does not, however, allow you to call programs on your hard disk from other drives—your floppy disk drive or your RAM disks. If you want to be able to do so, you must also include the drive specifier, on a separate line, before the CD command.)

 DOS 3.X

If you use DOS 3.X, the files on this directory will take the form

```
ECHO OFF
\PROGDIR\PROGRAM %1 %2 %3. . .
```

The preliminary step of making the program directory current should ideally not be necessary, because DOS 3.X lets you call an executable file with a full path name.

This ideal is not always achievable, however. As discussed below, under "Extending the Scope of the Path," some programs use several files, some of which they may not be able to find if called in this manner. To remedy the situation, you may have to set up some of the files as suggested for DOS 2.X. Alternatively, some combination of PATH and APPEND statements or path-extension software may overcome the limitations.

Create such files for each of your software packages that is not on the \UTIL directory, which is described in the next section.

You can make the batch files in the \BATCH directory more complex to automate your programs' startup procedures. For example, the FN.BAT file shown in Listing 14.1 is the batch file I use to start my accounting program using DOS 3.2. Here is a description of what this file does in addition to calling the program.

2:	Loads the relevant SuperKey macro file, which is made up of macros for the most common transactions, including variable fields for the amounts.
3:	Loads the version of SideKick with only the calculator and the ASCII table (I don't need the ASCII table, but you can't load the calculator without it).
4:	Makes the \ACCOUNTS directory the default directory.
5:	Copies the data files to the RAM disk.
6:	Calls the program. A SuperKey macro that closes all files and exits the accounting program also issues the command to clear the macros from memory and unload SideKick.

```
1: ECHO OFF
2: COMMAND /C KEY CPA/ML
3: COMMAND /C SK C
4: CD\ACCOUNTS
5: XCOPY C:\ACCOUNTS\*.DAT D:
6: FN D:
7: REPLACE D:*.DAT C: /D
8: DEL D:*.DAT
9: CD\
```

Listing 14.1 ▲ *FN.BAT.*

7:    The REPLACE command is used to copy only those files that have a more recent date and time than the originals back to the hard disk. Thus, only modified files are copied. (Note that this is possible only with MS-DOS, and not PC-DOS, since the PC-DOS version of the command does not have a /D switch. See below for an alternative in PC-DOS to the /D switch.)

8:    Erases the data files from the RAM disk.

9:    Makes the root directory current.

You may not need a batch file exactly like this one. However, it is an example of how you can use files on the \BATCH directory to automate procedures for any of your programs.

PC-DOS 3.2, 3.3

If you use PC-DOS, you can overcome the lack of a date switch by fiddling with the archive bit. Add the line

ATTRIB -A D:∗.DAT

between lines 5 and 6 of the batch file. This will clear the archive bit from the data files on the RAM disk. Then change line 7 to read

XCOPY D:∗.DAT C: /M

This will copy only matching files whose archive bit is set. Since the archive bit is set automatically when a file is updated, this command will copy only modified files.

Hint: You can think of the \BATCH directory as a series of AUTOEXEC files for different applications. Set up the files as though they were AUTOEXEC files to be used on a startup floppy disk for the application, but leave the background housekeeping to the true AUTOEXEC file on the root directory.

DOS 3.X

Even though DOS 3.X allows you to execute files on directories that are not current by including a full path specification, a \BATCH directory is still helpful for several reasons:

▲ It's much easier to invoke a program by entering a single command than by specifying a complex path. You can use the \BATCH directory to store files which contain nothing more than the path from the root directory to the program name.

▲ While you can invoke some programs (such as 1-2-3, dBASE II, and WordStar) from a directory other than the current one in DOS 3.X, these programs will not be able to find their overlays, drivers, and such, unless you are logged onto their directories. (Later in this chapter, we'll look at some software that can deal with this problem.)

▲ There are some RAM-resident programs (for example, SideKick and SuperKey) that can be called from any point in the directory structure once they are loaded, but cannot refer to their help files unless they are invoked from the directory in which the help files appear.

Warning: This last group of programs can find their help files if their directories are appended with the APPEND command *as a resident program,* or with a path extender. Placing the append list in the environment does *not* help.

The \UTIL Directory

The \UTIL directory contains your utility software, such as file-recovery programs, macro processors, desktop emulators, and file converters.

Like the \DOS directory, the \UTIL directory should contain the programs that you might want to use at any time, from any location. Some of these programs may require multiple directories or subdirectories.

Some utility programs (HomeBase, for example) create their own directory as a subdirectory of the root directory. They place a great many files in this directory and do not function properly if you place the files elsewhere, give the subdirectory a different name, or make it subordinate to a different directory. Other programs (such as SuperKey) may need access to so many different files that it becomes inconvenient to mix them in with other utility programs. Still others (such as The Norton Utilities) consist of so many files that you will have trouble finding them if they are included in a directory with many other files.

There are three possible solutions, or four if you have DOS 3.1:

▲ Create a separate directory for each collection of utilities.

▲ Create subdirectories to the \UTIL directory, and access them through the \BATCH directory.

▲ Create subdirectories to the \UTIL directory, and add these directories to the search path.

▲ Use DOS 3.1's SUBST command, as explained later in this chapter.

I prefer the second approach because it groups the files logically, but keeps the various utility packages separate from each other. This approach requires files such as KEY.BAT, shown in Listing 5.6. The only revision you need to make to that file is to change line 2 to

CD \UTIL\SUPERKEY

For SideKick and The Norton Utilities, files such as NU.BAT, shown in Listing 14.2, and SK.BAT, shown in Listing 14.3, are quite effective. These files make use of the %0 parameter, which we have not actually used before. As you may remember from Chapter 5, this is the original command itself. Thus, in calling The Norton Utilities, typing

NU

at a DOS prompt will call the main program. To call any of the subsidiary programs, type NU followed by the name of that program and any required parameters.

SK.BAT, which calls SideKick, works similarly. There are several versions of SideKick with different configurations. SKN.COM, for example, includes everything but the appointment calendar, and SKC.COM includes everything but the Notepad. To invoke the full setup, just type

SK

To invoke one of the smaller configurations, type SK followed by a space and the rest of the configuration name; for example,

SK N

If you typed SKN without the space, you would see the message

File not found

```
1: ECHO OFF
2: CD \UTIL\NORTON
3: IF %1@==@ GOTO main
4: %1 %2 %3 %4
5: GOTO end
6: :main
7: %0
8: :end
9: CD\
```

Listing 14.2 ▲ *NU.BAT.*

```
1: ECHO OFF
2: CD \UTIL\SIDEKICK
3: %0%1
4: BORDER
```

Listing 14.3 ▲ *SK.BAT.*

because there is no SKN.BAT file, and (presumably) SKN.COM is not on the search path (or appears in a directory that follows \BATCH on the search path). When you enter the space, the N is passed to the replaceable parameter %1. Since line 3 does not have a space between the parameters, the command line will be translated to read

    SKN

which invokes the configuration.

THE CONFIG.SYS AND AUTOEXEC.BAT FILES

As suggested in the previous chapter, you may want to have several different CONFIG.SYS files for different applications, or for installing different sets of device drivers. A file similar to RAMSIZE.BAT, shown in Listing 13.12, will allow you to switch between CONFIG.SYS files with a single command.

If some of the software that you install in your default configuration is incompatible with a particular application, you may also need to have several versions of an AUTOEXEC file. The DB3.BAT and NODB3.BAT files shown in Listings 5.4 and 5.5 illustrate one way of switching between AUTOEXEC files.

Your hard-disk AUTOEXEC file should take care of any basic house-keeping that you need to do before starting your work: reading the time from your real-time clock, deleting .BAK files, and setting your prompt, path, and APPEND list. In short, it does anything else you would normally do through an AUTOEXEC file on a floppy disk, except for actually starting the application (that's what the \BATCH directory is for).

In addition, there are some special features you may want to build into your AUTOEXEC file. Among them is an automatic backup system, which will be discussed later in the chapter. One point to keep in mind is that, despite the convenience of whatever RAM-resident programs you like to have at your fingertips, it may not always be a good idea to install them automatically. Some applications may require the additional RAM that these background programs use. Others may be incompatible with them. You may find it easier to load the RAM-resident packages from a batch file, rather than from the AUTOEXEC file.

THE SEARCH PATH

The considerations in setting a search path for a hard disk system are different from those for a floppy disk system.

What to Include on the Search Path

As suggested earlier, you should have your \DOS, \BATCH, and \UTIL directories on your search path. It's a good idea to include the drive specifier before each of the directories; for example,

```
PATH = C:\DOS;C:\BATCH;C:\UTIL
```

This way, the programs on these directories can be found even if you are logged onto a RAM disk or floppy disk. However, unless the commands in your batch files all include the drive specifiers, calling a batch file from the C:\BATCH directory while logged onto another drive may result in multiple

Bad command or filename

messages, as DOS vainly searches your current drive for files that are on the hard disk.

You probably also want your root directory on your search path, but you may prefer not to include the floppy disk drive. If you don't use this drive regularly, it's likely to be empty. If it's on the search path and you mistype a command, you may see the message

> Not ready error reading drive A:
> Abort, Retry, Ignore?

and (depending on your version of DOS) you may have to put a disk in the drive before your computer will speak sensibly to you again.

Should you put the software directories that you use often on the search path? That depends on both the version of DOS you use and the software you use. Programs that use ancillary files may not find them properly if you don't give the PATH command some help. Among the few exceptions are WordPerfect, Microsoft Word, and the unprotected version of Framework II. These programs can be called while you are logged onto any directory of any drive and will still find their subsidiary files if you have installed them correctly. In DOS 3.X, they can be successfully called from anywhere just by entering a full path name. They don't even need to be on the search path. Ideally, all software would be designed in this manner.

There are also some intermediate exceptions. The unprotected version of dBASE III PLUS can be called from anywhere if it is on the search path, but not by using a full path name. The same is true of WordStar 4.0.

On the other hand, if you use a DOS version that includes the APPEND command, you may be able to place most of your software on the search path if you also append the relevant directories. However, there are exceptions, and you can run into other problems if your path is too long.

Hint: So why do you want to be able to call your programs from anywhere in your system? If you work on more than one project at a time, consider how much easier it is to find your files if they are grouped logically by project, rather than mixed in with your software, or in directories subordinate to your software directories.

If you follow the installation suggestions included with many software packages, or in the DOS manual, you will have separate project or user directories subordinate to each program. Suppose you have a name-and-address database file subordinate to your database directory, and a form letter subordinate to your word-processor directory. Will you be able to complete a mailmerge with files that are five logical directories apart? If not, how many extra files will you have to create before you can complete the job? Answering these questions should make it clear why it's useful to place your software on the search path.

The Length of the Search Path

The length of the search path is also a consideration. The longer you make the search path, the longer DOS will look for a file that isn't on it before giving up. You can speed up the search considerably by increasing the number of buffers, but this may interfere with the efficiency of your other programs. You are also faced with the limitation that a DOS command cannot exceed 132 characters.

Moreover, if your search path gets too long you can run into the dreaded

Out of environment space

message. This is even more likely to happen if you also have a complex PROMPT string, and/or you place your list of appended directories in the environment.

There are two solutions. One is to use short directory names. Directories called \WP, \DB, and \SS, for example, use up a lot less of the environment than directories called \MSWORD, \DBASE, and \SCALC4, and are also easier to type. On the other hand, you may have trouble remembering what all your two-letter mnemonics stand for.

The other solution, explained in Chapter 8, is to increase the size of the environment with the SHELL command.

Extending the Scope of the Path

MS-DOS 3.2, DOS 3.3

If your DOS version includes the APPEND command, as discussed in Chapter 8, you can use it to help the PATH command run your programs. If your \LOTUS directory is both on the path and appended, for example, you can run it from your hard disk, although you'll still have to put the key disk in drive A. However, some programs don't take kindly to having their directories appended. The unprotected version of Framework II, for example, looks in every drive in your system before appearing on your screen if its directory is appended. Sometimes it never appears at all.

DOS 2.X; PC-DOS 3.0, 3.1

If your DOS does not include the APPEND command, programs known as *path extenders* can sometimes help. Generally, when you use a path extender, you include all directories for software that uses ancillary files in the search path and set up an additional command, either in the CONFIG.SYS or the AUTOEXEC file, that tells the path extender to use the same path. Sometimes you can safely leave out directories that do not include ancillary software files from the latter command. If you're lucky, the result will be that you'll be able to run all your software from any directory. If you're not, some peculiar things may happen, as detailed below.

SmartPath   Probably the easiest path extender to use is SmartPath, from Software Research Technologies. To invoke it, all you need to do is place the command

SPATH = ARGUMENT

in your AUTOEXEC file (*ARGUMENT* represents the same argument that you gave to the PATH command). If you include WordStar 3.3, 1-2-3, and dBASE II on the path, you can call these programs from any directory.

Unfortunately, some copy-protected programs refuse to load when SmartPath is active. They think it's DEBUG trying to break their copy-protection scheme.

Other programs get confused by SmartPath (and other path extenders as well). When ThinkTank's directory is an argument to SPATH, for example, the program searches through all the drives for its configuration file before freezing your keyboard and locking up the computer. (However, it behaves perfectly when its directory is appended with APPEND.)

To help you deal with such programs, you can type

SPATH OFF

at a DOS prompt. This does not remove SmartPath from memory, but it does keep it from functioning. You can turn it on again by issuing a new SPATH= command.

File Facility   Another less expensive program of the same type is File Facility, available through IBM Personally Developed Software. You load it after setting a path with the PATH command by typing

FILEFAC /I

This installs the current path as File Facility's search path for nonexecutable files. You can, however, install a different path after issuing this command by using the SET command and another command:

SET FF = [*DRIVE*]*PATH*;[*DRIVE*]*PATH*;...[*DRIVE*]*PATH*
FILEFAC /P

This path will then be used by File Facility instead of the one used by the PATH command. You can save the path used by File Facility at any time by issuing the command

FILEFAC /S

and restore the saved path by entering

FILEFAC /R

This can be very useful in some circumstances. For example, if you need a special search path for use with a single program, you can invoke the program with a batch file that first saves the default path, then uses SET and the /P switch to establish a new one. Finally, it should restore the original path with the /R switch when you exit the program.

File Facility has many other options as well, which are too complex to discuss here. To turn the program off (but not unload it from memory), type

SET FF =

DPATH + Plus   Probably the most powerful path extender is DPATH+Plus from Personal Business Solutions. The program disk includes four versions of the program, each with more extensive capabilities than the previous one. In its simplest form, DPATH+Plus does a bit more than the DOS 3.3 version of APPEND with the /X switch. For example, if you tell the program to include a directory called C:\MEMOS in its searches, a simple directory listing will show all the files on C:\MEMOS, as well as those on your current directory.

You can use DPATH+Plus along with the PATH command or in place of it. You can use it to replace the APPEND or the JOIN command, which is described below. (The caveats that apply to the JOIN command also apply to this use of DPATH+Plus.)

The more advanced versions of the program allow you to

▲ Direct all files with a given extension (or matching any wild-card pattern you specify) to a specific directory

▲ Change directories while a program is running

▲ Create aliases for file names, so that you can invoke programs that are not on its path

▲ Trace the program's activities, so you can debug the monster you have created

Needless to say, capabilities such as the more advanced options of File Facility and DPATH+Plus can be dangerous if used carelessly. You can, if you push your luck, create files on the wrong disk or erase a copy of a file in the wrong directory. File Facility, however, has some built-in safeguards against the latter disaster. A word to the wise is sufficient.

Extending the Path on the Fly

You already saw, in Chapter 9, how to use a batch file to restore your standard path after you have changed it. But what if you just want to add a directory to the path temporarily? The more sophisticated path extenders will let you do that, but suppose you don't want to use one?

It would be a real nuisance to use the SET command to view your current path, and then type in the entire thing again, adding one more directory to the end. Fortunately, an undocumented command makes it possible to overcome this limitation. As you know, the SET command displays the strings stored in the environment, and one of them is the PATH= statement. You can thus use the SET command to modify this string, by using a parameter of the form %PATH%. EXTPATH.BAT, shown in Listing 14.4, gives you a method for doing just this.

To use this program, type

**EXTPATH *PATHNAME*

```
1: SET PATH=%PATH%;%1
2: SET APPEND=%APPEND%;%1
```

Listing 14.4 ▲ *EXTPATH.BAT.*

where *PATHNAME* is the name of the directory you want to add to the path. Line 1 reads the value %PATH%, which represents your current path. Then it adds a semicolon and the path name you have entered. The effect is to add another directory to your path. Line 2 does the same for your list of appended directories. (This will work only if you originally established the list with the SET command.) Because ECHO is on, the result is displayed immediately. Note that you cannot use this technique on the command line. You *must* use a batch file, or it won't work. (Note that the %PATH% variable no longer works in PC-DOS 3.3.)

TWO OTHER TYPES OF DIRECTORY ORGANIZATION

If you work on a variety of projects, or share a computer with others, the software directory organization described earlier may not be the best one for you. Either the project or multiuser organization discussed here may be more suitable for your situation.

The Project Approach

For many purposes, it's a lot more practical to set up your directories so that all the files that relate to each of your projects are in a single directory. In such a structure, you maintain a single subdirectory for each project, in addition to your software directories. The document, graphics, database, spreadsheet, and any other files related to the project are kept in that directory. No data files are in, or subordinate to, your software directories.

The project organizational system is a lot more like normal filing systems than the usual hard-disk directory structure. You can use such a system if your software will permit you to organize your data in this manner (many programs will not) or if you can find a combination of SUBST commands and path-extension software that will force it to. With a program like SmartPath, you can log onto the directory for a particular project and call WordStar, 1-2-3, dBASE II, or PC Paint from there. This organization makes transferring data among applications a great deal less confusing, and you will find it easier to locate your files.

The Multiuser System

If your system is used by many different people, you may want to give each user a different directory, labeled with his or her name. However, like the project approach, you must overcome the limitations of your software to use this type of organization.

Grouping files in this manner will be much simpler than giving each user a subdirectory subordinate to the subdirectory that contains each software package, an approach recommended by many writers. The elaborate tree structures you see in some of the literature, suggesting three different users' subdirectories each to the WordStar, dBASE, and Lotus directories, each of which has further subdivisions by project or time period, are an invitation to frustration. You can end up with a disk cluttered by multiple copies of the same file in different stages of development, without a clue as to where the most current version is located. If each user adopts different file-naming conventions, the process can become well-nigh impossible.

Hint: If you must use an elaborate tree system, a public domain program called WHEREIS.COM may provide some help. It will give you the directory location of any file name matching the argument you give it (including wild cards), but you will still have to check each of the directories in order to see which copy of a file is the most recent. The FF external program from the Norton Utilities does the same thing.

SPECIAL HARD DISK NAVIGATION COMMANDS

DOS 3.1 and 3.2 introduced a number of new commands that can help you overcome design limitations inherent in some software. We'll look briefly at these various commands now. Earlier, DOS 2.0 introduced a command for the same purpose—the ASSIGN command. We'll look at this command now too.

Assigning One Drive Designation to Another

Some programs are designed specifically for single- or dual-drive systems and have the drive designators hard-wired into their code. To allow these programs to run comfortably on systems with more drives than they were designed for, the ASSIGN command was introduced in DOS 2.0.

This command lets you assign one disk drive to another. Say, for example, you have a program on your hard disk that expects its program files to be in drive A and its data files in drive B. You could place a data disk in drive A and type the command

ASSIGN B = A A = C

This would make your program (and your computer) think that the floppy drive was drive B and the hard drive was drive A.

To cancel a drive reassignment, type

ASSIGN

at a DOS prompt, with no parameters.

Note: Some aberrant versions of DOS will allow you to make successive reassignments with commands such as

ASSIGN B = A
ASSIGN A = C

In most versions, however, one ASSIGN statement cancels any previous ASSIGN statements.

ASSIGN has a number of risks attached to it. Suppose you have a program that runs only with an earlier version of DOS than the one installed on your hard disk. So you boot your computer with the floppy disk containing the program (and that version of DOS's ASSIGN command—you can't use external programs from one version of DOS with another—and issue the command

ASSIGN A = C

to get your computer to use drive C as drive A. At this point typing either

DIR A:

or

DIR C:

will give you the directory of drive C. However, since the version of the ASSIGN command you need to use to undo this assignment when you are finished is on the disk in drive A, you will not be able to access it. The only way out is to reboot your computer.

Moreover, if somehow you manage to get past this point and go on to other work, you could easily lose data or mess up your directory structure quite nicely by copying or erasing files on the wrong drive.

If there is any way you can avoid using the ASSIGN command, by all means do so. You may even be better off using DEBUG to go into the program code and eliminate all references to the drive specifiers A: and B:, replacing them with space characters. Better yet, if you have DOS 3.1 or later, you can use the JOIN and SUBST commands to make more efficient and less dangerous reassignments. If you don't have DOS 3.1 and you need to reassign drive specifiers, it's worth investing in an upgrade.

Treating a Directory as a Separate Drive

To get around the vagaries of the ASSIGN command DOS 3.1 added two new commands, SUBST and JOIN. Although somewhat safer than ASSIGN, they can also create quite a mess. The SUBST command allows you to treat a directory as though it were a separate disk. This can be very useful with programs that share with WordStar the trait of being unable to find their overlay files, device-driver files, or other files needed to function properly. (Among those programs are some releases of Lotus 1-2-3, the protected versions of the dBASE programs, and ThinkTank.) Instead of calling these programs from a subdirectory, you can use the SUBST command to "fool" DOS into thinking that the directories on which they reside are actually disk drives.

The syntax for the SUBST command is

    SUBST *DRIVE\DIRECTORY*

where *DRIVE* is the drive specifier you want to use and *DIRECTORY* is the directory to be regarded as a separate drive. As an experiment, while writing a portion of this book using the ThinkTank program and DOS 3.1, I used the SUBST command on both the program's directory and the directory where the files were located, using the following commands:

    SUBST A: \TANK
    SUBST B: \DOSBOOK

Everything worked as expected. ThinkTank behaved as though it were in drive A and was able, when told to, to open the file in the phantom drive B. Of course, at the same time, I lost access to the physical drives A and B—the floppy disk drives. (I could have avoided this problem by using E and F instead of A and B.)

This command has some peculiarities attached to it. A request for the display of a directory on the phantom drive you have created will display the volume label of the physical drive and what appears to be the root directory of the phantom drive. In this instance, for example, typing

DIR B:

resulted in a display that began with the lines

Volume in drive B is JK's TurboAT
Directory of B:

even though phantom drive B was a subdirectory named \TANK. If you attempt to give a volume label to the phantom drive it will relabel the *physical* drive of which the phantom drive is a part. Thus, for example, attempting to give the label TANK to the phantom drive would have resulted in the hard disk's label *JK's TurboAT* being replaced by the label *TANK*.

Typing SUBST without parameters displays a list of the substitutions currently in effect. In this instance, typing just SUBST produced the display

A: = > C:\TANK
B: = > C:\DOSBOOK

To undo a substitution, repeat the original command followed by a /D (for delete) switch:

SUBST A: \TANK /D

This command can be useful in many ways with programs that do not recognize path names. Using WordStar 3.3 again as an example, you could configure WordStar to find its overlays on drive F, for example, and run WordStar from a batch file that includes the command

SUBST F: \WORDSTAR

before the command that invokes the program. You can also use this technique to run programs on other directories using WordStar's Run a program command by substituting drive designators for the directories on which the programs appear. You might want to assign drive designators to your DOS and UTIL directories. If you include the command

SUBST G: \DOS

for example, you can format or copy a floppy disk while running Word-Star, without copying the FORMAT and DISKCOPY commands to WordStar's directory. These tricks can help with any program that does not take kindly to path syntax.

There is one additional fact you must take into account, however. DOS 3.X assumes a maximum of five drives in your system, labeled A through E. If you expect to use drive designations higher than E, you must include a LASTDRIVE command in your CONFIG.SYS file, as explained in Chapter 8.

Another use of the SUBST command is to shorten directory paths. Thus, for example, entering the command

SUBST F: \DBASE\SALES\INVOICES

would allow you to switch to the INVOICES subdirectory by typing

F:

While this will work, and seems tempting, you are better off using a batch file for this purpose, as described earlier in the chapter. The less the logical structure of your system departs from its physical structure, the less trouble you are likely to encounter.

Treating a Disk Drive as a Subdirectory

The JOIN command functions as the opposite of the SUBST command, letting you persuade DOS that a floppy disk drive, an additional hard drive, or a RAM disk is simply another directory on your hard disk. The syntax of the command is

JOIN *DRIVE1* [*DRIVE2*]*DIRECTORY*

where *DRIVE1* is the physical drive to be added to your main drive, *DIRECTORY* is the directory name by which you will refer to the physical drive, and *DRIVE2* is the designator of the main drive, which you must use if that drive is not current.

The following conditions must be in effect for the JOIN command to work:

▲ The subdirectory which is to substitute for the drive designation (the "host" subdirectory) must be one level below the root.

▲ The host subdirectory must be empty.

▲ The host subdirectory must not be current.

▲ Neither the host subdirectory nor the "guest" drive may be part of a network.

▲ The guest drive must not be current.

▲ Neither drive must be currently affected by an ASSIGN or SUBST command.

As an example, if you are logged onto drive C, and the conditions just described are all met, the following command would allow you to access drive B by referring to it as the directory \BDRIVE:

    JOIN B: \BDRIVE

If the directory does not exist when you issue the JOIN command, DOS will create it. As with SUBST, typing JOIN with no parameters displays the changes you have made:

    B: = > C:\BDRIVE

To restore normal access to your physical drive, type

    JOIN B: /D

The usefulness of this command is somewhat less obvious than that of the SUBST command. If you had a program that wanted everything on one drive, but recognized subdirectories, it could serve a purpose. However, I have never encountered such a program.

A Few Dire Warnings

 Warning: The ASSIGN, JOIN, and SUBST commands can all have consequences that are at best unpleasant and at worst dangerous. You can temporarily lose access to some of your data, overwrite files of the same name in different directories, and lock up your computer. In addition, the following commands will work erratically, unpredictably, or not at all when a JOIN, SUBST, or ASSIGN is in effect, or when one of the drives involved is part of a network:

▲ BACKUP

▲ RESTORE

▲ FORMAT

▲ DISKCOPY

▲ CHKDSK

▲ FDISK

Furthermore, none of these reassignment commands is safe to use when one of the others is in effect.

AUTOMATIC HARD DISK BACKUP

If you don't have backup copies of the files on your hard disk, you can lose everything on it when it fails. For this reason, it's essential to have some kind of regular hard disk backup system.

DOS includes the BACKUP and RESTORE commands for backing up hard disks and restoring the backed up files. A full ten megabytes takes about 25 minutes and 27 floppy disks to back up using the BACKUP command.

One alternative is to use an expensive tape backup unit, which will rapidly back up a hard disk virtually unattended, but the price is prohibitive for many users. On the other hand, there are ways to set up a backup system so that the procedure is almost painless, and there are some software packages that can simplify and speed up the process.

The BACKUP and RESTORE Commands

In DOS 2.X, the BACKUP command is used only to back up hard disks to floppy disks. In DOS 3.X, it may be used in other ways, which we'll explore shortly.

 Warning: The BACKUP command will abort the backup operation if it encounters an unformatted disk, so make sure that you have enough formatted floppy disks before you begin.

To back up an entire hard disk (assuming the hard disk is drive C) to floppy disks, log onto the root directory and type

BACKUP C:\A:/S

The /S switch tells the BACKUP command to back up subdirectories as well as the current directory. You will be prompted to change disks as each one becomes full. You should label them in numerical order, so you can find the files again.

As the backup process proceeds, the names of the files will be displayed on the screen. Therefore, it's a good idea to direct the output to the printer, so you have a record of which files have been backed up to which disks. If you direct the output to a file, you won't see the messages that tell you when to switch disks.

When a file has been backed up, its archive bit is cleared. Its format on the backup copy is somewhat different from the original, so before you can use the copy, you have to restore it with the RESTORE command. The file format created by the BACKUP command contains information about the subdirectory from which the file was backed up, so that the RESTORE command can place it on the same directory.

BACKUP Command Options   You need not back up an entire disk at once. You can specify a single directory or file to be backed up by using the form

BACKUP C:[*PATH*][*FILENAME.EXT*] A:

You can even use wild cards in the file names to back up a group of files.

As noted earlier, the /S switch backs up the subdirectories of the specified directory. There are three other switches for the BACKUP command:

▲ /M backs up only those files that have been created or modified since the previous backup (these files will still have their archive bit set).

▲ /A appends the files to the floppy disk. Normally, the BACKUP command erases all files on the backup disk before writing to it.

▲ /D:*mm*/*dd*/*yy* (date) backs up files created only on or after the date specified after the switch. (If you have nationalized your computer for a country other than the United States, use that country's date format.)

DOS 3.1

The DOS 3.1 BACKUP command also allows you to back up a floppy disk to another floppy disk, a floppy disk to a hard disk, or a hard disk to another hard disk (or to itself, if there is enough room). If you back up to a hard disk, the command creates a directory called \BACKUP, which will contain the backed up files. If your computer is part of a local area network, you can back up one hard disk to another through the network. See Appendix E for details.

MS-DOS 3.2, DOS 3.3

With MS-DOS 3.2 and DOS 3.3 new switches have been added to the BACKUP command:

▲ /L (log) automatically creates a file called BACKUP.LOG in the root directory, so that you need not redirect output to the printer, as suggested in Listing 14.6. This file will contain the date and time you started the backup, the complete path name of every file that has been backed up, and the number of the backup disk on which the copy appears. Additional backups will append the new information to the existing file.

▲ /T:*hh:mml* (time), where *l* can be replaced by *a* for a.m. or *p* for p.m., backs up only files created or modified later than the specified time.

Since the BACKUP command treats time and date independently, you should use the /D and /T switches together to back up files written after a specific point in time; for example,

BACKUP C: A:/S /D:12-31-87 /T:5:00p

DOS 3.3

DOS 3.3 added another new (and much-needed) switch to the BACKUP command. If you add the /F switch to your backup command line, the backup disks will be formatted if necessary. For this switch to work, FORMAT.COM must be in the current directory of the source disk or on the search path.

DOS 3.3 also made a major change in the way files are stored on the backup disk. Instead of one file per source file, there are now two files per backup disk: BACKUP.NNN and CONTROL.NNN. The first file

RESTORE Command Options You can restore single files, complete directories, directories plus their subdirectories, or entire disks. The syntax is the reverse of that for the BACKUP command:

RESTORE A: C:[*PATH*][*FILENAME.EXT*][/S][/P]

RESTORE has two optional switches—/S and /P. /S performs the same function as it does in the BACKUP command. If you add /P to the end of the command line, you will be asked permission before a file is restored, if the version on the hard disk is newer than the one on the backup copy, or if the hard disk file is marked read-only.

MS-DOS 3.2, DOS 3.3

Recent releases of DOS have added several new switches to the RESTORE command:

▲ /A:*mm-dd-yy* (after) restores only files created or modified on or after the specified date.

▲ /B:*mm-dd-yy* (before) restores only files created on or before the specified date.

▲ /E:*hh:mml* (earlier) restores only files created or modified earlier than the specified time.

▲ /L:*hh:mml* (later) restores only files created or modified later than the specified time.

Since the RESTORE command treats time and date independently, you should use the /B and /E or /A and /L switches together, to restore files written before or after a specific point in time, respectively.

Setting Up a Daily Backup System

The process of backing up a hard disk with the BACKUP command can be quite tedious. However, once you have backed up the entire disk, you can set up a system that backs up only the previous day's files as part of your startup routine. The simplest way is to issue the command

BACKUP C:\ A: /S/M/A

at a DOS prompt as soon as you boot up in the morning. This will back up all files that have been modified since the previous backup, on any subdirectory, and add them to the backup disk without wiping out its current contents.

 Warning: The only problem I have encountered is that, with some versions of DOS, you will be prompted to insert backup disk #1 in drive A, and when you do, you will be told that it is full. This happens only on the first attempt to back up the day's files after the entire disk has been backed up. You can avoid this bug by issuing the command without the /A switch the first day, and starting a second series of backup disks for your modified files.

Although it's easy to enter the BACKUP command daily, it's easier to forget about this step or just ignore it (until you've actually had a hard-disk failure). To make the backup system automatic, we're going to include it as part of the AUTOEXEC file. Of course, sometimes you have to reboot during the day, and you don't want to issue the BACKUP command every time you do—one backup a day is enough. So, this section of the AUTOEXEC file (which appears in Listing 14.5) will call a BASIC program (shown in Listing 14.6) that checks to see whether the system has already been backed up. If it has, a message to that effect is displayed, and execution is directed past the part of the AUTOEXEC file that handles the hard disk backup.

```
 1: CD \BASIC
 2: BASICA AUTOBKUP
 3: CD \
 4: IF EXIST BKUPTEST GOTO nobackup
 5: ATTRIB -A \WORDSTAR\*.BAK >NUL
 6: ATTRIB -A LASTBKUP
 7: ECHO  ^G^[[28CTurn on the Printer
 8: PAUSE
 9: COPY LASTCKUP PRN
10: BACKUP C:\ A:/S/M/A >PRN
11: CHKDSK /V \DOS\HARDDISK.DIR
12: GOTO continue
13: :nobackup
14: ECHO ^G^[[15C^[[7m The hard disk has already been backed up today. ^[0m
15: ERASE C:\BKUPTEST
16: :continue
```

Listing 14.5 ▲ *AUTOEXEC Code for Automatic Backup.*

```
10 CLS: KEY OFF: COLOR 15,3,3
20 LOCATE 3,25: PRINT "Checking date of last backup."
30 OPEN "C:\LASTBKUP" FOR INPUT AS #1
40 INPUT #1, LASTBACK$: CLOSE
50 TODAY$ = DATE$
60 OPEN "C:\LASTBKUP" FOR OUTPUT AS #1
70 PRINT #1, TODAY$: CLOSE
80 IF TODAY$ <> LASTBACK$ GOTO 100
90 OPEN "C:\BKUPTEST" FOR OUTPUT AS #2: PRINT #2:CLOSE
100 SYSTEM
```

Listing 14.6 ▲ *AUTOBKUP.BAS.*

The first steps, before you set up this system, are as follows:

1. Back up your entire hard disk.

2. Create a file on your root directory called LASTBKUP, containing the date in the form MM-DD-YYYY and nothing else.

3. Perform your first incremental backup on a fresh disk, using the command

   BACKUP C:\ A:/S/M

Let's look at the BASIC program first.

10: Sets up the screen. The colors are white text on a cyan background. You may leave out the COLOR statement.

20: Displays a message.

30–40: Opens and reads the file called LASTBKUP.

50: Sets up a variable called TODAY$, and assigns to it the value of the BASIC DATE$ function. This function returns the current date, in the form in which you entered it into the LASTBKUP file.

60–70: Writes today's date to the LASTBKUP file.

80–100: If today's date is the same as the date found when the file LASTBKUP was read in line 30, a new file, called BKUPTEST, is written. This file will be searched for by the AUTOEXEC file. If it exists, the backup will not be performed. If the dates are not the same, the BKUPTEST file is not created, so that the backup will be performed.

The section of code presented in Listing 14.5 should be placed in your AUTOEXEC file *after* you have set the date and time and established your path. Here is how the beginning section of the AUTOEXEC file works.

1–2: Logs onto the BASIC directory and then calls the AUTOBKUP program (presumably, the BASIC directory is not on your search path).

3–4: Changes back to the root directory and checks to see whether the BKUPTEST file exists. If so, execution is directed past the automatic backup routine, which ends at the label :nobackup in line 13.

5–6: These lines are optional. ATTRIB-A clears the archive bit of files that need not be backed up. It seems a bit excessive to back up files that are themselves backup files, and there is no need to back up the LASTBKUP file. If your DOS does not include the ATTRIB command, you can use CLRARC (from Computer Thaumaturgy) or UNMARK (from IBM Personally Developed Software) for the same purpose.

7–9: Prompts you to turn on the printer and waits for you to do so. Prints today's date (which is contained in the file LASTBKUP), so you know which files are backed up in each group.

10: Issues the incremental BACKUP command, and directs output to the printer, so that you will have a list of the files that have been backed up following the day's date.

11: Creates a file containing a list of all files currently on the hard disk, and places it in your \DOS subdirectory.

Hint: You can locate a file quickly by searching the file created in line 11 with the FIND filter. Since the CHKDSK /V command lists each file preceded by its complete path, you will know exactly where to find it. You may also want to clear the archive bit on the HARDDISK.DIR file before you perform the automatic backup, so that you don't have multiple copies of it on your backup disks.

12–16: If the hard disk has already been backed up today, displays a message to that effect. Erases the BKUPTEST file to be ready for the next time you boot up, and continues execution with whatever additional commands you want to include in your AUTOEXEC file.

Directories of backup disks written to by means of the BACKUP command can be read in the normal manner, even if the files on them cannot. Thus, you can find a given day's version of a particular file just by reading the directories of the backup disks.

Other Backup Considerations

As noted, files created by the BACKUP command cannot be used unless they are first restored. With early versions of BACKUP, you can restore only to a hard disk. If your hard disk crashes, you are out of work for the time being, unless you have additional backup copies of your files. The problem becomes even more complicated if you use a commercial hard disk backup program, some of which not only alter the files but use proprietary disk formats.

You don't want to leave yourself in this position (I assure you of this fact as I write on a borrowed IBM-PC while my Turbo AT is in the shop and all my software is backed up on 1.2MB disks). At the very least, you should keep installed copies of the software you use most often on 360K floppy disks.

DOS 3.2, 3.3

The easiest way to make these copies is to use the XCOPY command as soon as you install new software on your hard disk. Do it immediately, before your directory is cluttered up with other files. First make the new software directory current. Then place a formatted 360K floppy disk in drive A and enter

   XCOPY C: A: /M

The /M switch copies only files with the archive bit set and clears the archive bit, just like the /M switch to BACKUP. You need this switch because if your disk fills up, XCOPY will stop dead, unlike BACKUP. If this happens, you can enter the same command again, with a new disk, to back up the remaining files. You may then want to use the ATTRIB command to reset the archive bit before you do your next regular backup.

MS-DOS 3.2, 3.3

For backing up your data, the MS-DOS REPLACE command is the easiest way to go. You can back up each of your current data directories to a different disk. Use a batch file such as DATABAK.BAT, shown in Listing 14.7. It takes as a parameter the name of the data directory you want to back up, including the leading backslash.

This simple file does three things:

2:        Clears the archive bit of any backup files to ensure that they are not copied. You may need to change this line if your software uses a different extension for backup files. If it doesn't make backup files, you can eliminate this line.

3:        Copies only those files that are already on the backup disk and that have a later date than the copy on the backup disk. This ensures that the latest version of any existing files is on the backup disk.

4:        Copies only files that are not on the backup disk. This should, ideally, copy only files that you have created since the last time you ran DATABAK. If you keep other unrelated files on the same directory, add the /P switch so that you can select files to be added individually.

Software Solutions

There are several software packages that can make it even easier and faster to back up the files on your hard disk. We'll look at automated

```
1: ECHO OFF
2: ATTRIB -A %1*.BAK
3: REPLACE C:%1*.* A: /D
4: REPLACE C:%1*.* A: /A
```

Listing 14.7 ▲ *DATABAK.BAT.*

systems that use JET, which is part of the JRAM Combo Disk, a second package called FastBack, and the backup utility included with PC Tools.

PC-DOS 3.2, 3.3

Since PC-DOS's REPLACE command doesn't have a /D switch, you need a different command to complete this task. Your best bet, after clearing the archive bit on your backup files, is to use a command of the form

XCOPY C: A: /A/P/D:*mm-dd-yy*

where *mm-dd-yy* is today's date. The /D switch assures that the command will copy only files with today's date. The /A switch will copy only files with the archive bit set (newly created or modified files), but won't clear the archive bit as the /M switch does. Thus, they will still be copied during your next regular backup. The /P switch displays each file name meeting these criteria and the message

Copy this file (Y/N)?

so you can skip files not related to your project. If you have nothing on your data directories but files related to a single project, you can omit the /P switch.

Setting Up a Backup System with JET JET, as you have already learned, can copy files eight times faster than the DOS COPY command. Although it has some annoying quirks, it also has some powerful options. The following two files, JETBACK.BAT, shown in Listing 14.8, and JET-BACK.BAS, shown in Listing 14.9, are designed to overcome the former and take advantage of the latter. Like several other programs in this book, the basic technique is to use a batch file to call a BASIC program that creates the batch file that does the actual work.

The big disadvantage of JET compared with the BACKUP command is that it can back up only one subdirectory at a time. To use JET manually to back up an entire hard disk, you need to refer to a list of all your subdirectories (possibly a printout from the TREE command).

On the other hand, files backed up with JET can be used directly from the backup copies, without first being restored. JET's other advantages

```
 1: ECHO OFF
 2: IF EXIST DIRLIST GOTO continue
 3: TREE C:\ >TEMPLIST
 4: FIND "Path:" TEMPLIST >DIRLIST
 5: ERASE TEMPLIST
 6: :continue
 7: CD \BASIC
 8: BASICA JETBACK
 9: COMMANC /C JETTEMP
10: CD\
11: ERASE JETTEMP.BAT
12: CLS
13: ECHO ^[[17C^[[5;7m       Hard Disk Backup Completed       ^[[0m
```

Listing 14.8 ▲ JETBACK.BAT.

```
10 ON ERROR GOTO 500
100 CLS: KEY OFF: SCREEN 0,0,0: COLOR 10,0,2
110 GOSUB 400
120 PRINT "Place first backup diskette in drive A:"
130 PRINT "Strike any key when ready":A$=INPUT$(1)
140 OPEN "DIRLIST" FOR INPUT AS #1
150 OPEN "JETTEMP.BAT" FOR OUTPUT AS #2
160 PRINT #2,"ECHO OFF"
170 WHILE NOT EOF(1)
180 LINE INPUT #1, DIRNAME$
190 IF NOT INSTR(DIRNAME$,"Path:") GOTO 180
200 DIRNAME$ = RIGHT$(DIRNAME$,LEN(DIRNAME$)-INSTR(DIRNAME$,"Path: ")-5)
210 GOSUB 300                  'write entries to batch file
220 WEND
230 PRINT #2,"EXIT"
240 CLOSE: SYSTEM
297 '
298 '    *****  subroutine to write entries to batch file  *****
299 '
300 PRINT #2, "ECHO Backing up files from "; DIRNAME$; " directory"
310 PRINT #2, "ERASE C:"; DIRNAME$; "\*.BAK"
320 PRINT #2, "JET C:"; DIRNAME$; "A:" DIRNAME$ " /S/L"; OPT$
330 RETURN
397 '
398 '    *****  subroutine to choose partial or full backup  *****
399 '
400 PRINT "Back up only files changed since last backup?";:YN$=INPUT$(1)
410 IF YN$="y" OR YN$="Y" THEN OPT$="/J" ELSE OPT$=""
420 RETURN
500 RESUME NEXT
```

Listing 14.9 ▲ JETBACK.BAS.

include the following:

▲ JET can clear the archive bit, so that it can be used for incremental backups.

▲ If you ask JET to back up to a subdirectory and the subdirectory does not exist on the target disk, the program will create it.

▲ The /S switch forces JET to divide files and continue them on a subsequent floppy disk when a disk becomes full, to conserve space. BACKUP does this automatically. If you want to be able to use the files directly from the backups, leave this switch out of line 320 of the BASIC program.

JETBACK.BAT generates a list of path names, calls the BASIC program, executes the temporary batch file, and finally erases the temporary files and displays a message. The important lines are

3:     Sends the output of the TREE command to a temporary file.

4:     Passes the temporary file through the FIND filter to find all instances of

   Path:

The file produced by these lines has entries such as those shown in Figure 14.1. The information in this file will be used by the BASIC program to generate the second batch file. To make this program part of your daily startup procedure, insert it in place of lines 7 through 12 of Listing 14.5.

If you have already created a listing such as the one shown in Figure 14.1, line 2 directs execution to line 6, where the BASIC program is called. If you add a new directory, you should erase the old copy of DIRLIST.

```
---------- templist
Path:   \
Path:   \ACCOUNTS
Path:   \BASIC
Path:   \BASIC\COMPILER
Path:   \BASIC\COMPILER\LIBRARY
Path:   \BASIC\GRAPHICS
Path:   \BATCH
Path:   \DICT
Path:   \DOS
Path:   \DBASE
Path:   \FASTBACK
Path:   \LOTUS
Path:   \PAINT
Path:   \TANK
Path:   \TELECOM
Path:   \UNFILED
Path:   \UTIL
Path:   \UTIL\NORTON
Path:   \UTIL\SIDEKICK
Path:   \UTIL\SUPERKEY
Path:   \WORDSTAR
```

Figure 14.1 ▲ *Output of the TREE Command Filtered to Create a List of Paths.*

Here is a description of the significant portions of JETBACK.BAS.

180–190: Reads a line from the DIRLIST file. If the line does not contain the text "Path:", the next line is read. This skips any entries, such as the header and blank lines, that may not actually contain path names.

200: Rewrites the line so that the text "Path:" is removed from the beginning, leaving only a legitimate path name.

Hint: The result of line 200 should be a path name beginning with a backslash, but with no spaces at the beginning. However, some versions of DOS arrange the output from the TREE command slightly differently. If the file does not seem to be working properly, try adding the line

205 PRINT DIRNAME$

This will display the output on the screen. If there are spaces at the beginning, reduce the number at the end of line 200. If there is no backslash, or part of the path name is missing, increase it. Keep increasing or decreasing this number until DIRNAME$ produces a proper path name, with no leading spaces.

300: Displays a message telling which directory is being backed up.

310: Erases any .BAK files from the source directory. You may omit this line if you prefer.

320: Writes a line to the batch file. The instruction it writes tells it to back up the specified directory to the equivalent directory of the floppy disk, which JET will create automatically. The /L switch lists on the screen the names of all the files to be transferred before the transfer begins, and the /S switch forces it to split a file if the disk becomes full before the file is fully backed up.

400–420: Gives you the option of backing up the entire hard disk, rather than only those files that have changed since you last used this procedure. The /J switch clears the archive bit, so that the file will not be backed up on subsequent uses of the program unless it has been modified.

Setting Up a Backup System with FastBack   FastBack is a rather expensive software package whose sole purpose is to make speedy backups, and it does this quite well. As Figure 14.2 shows, it took only about 7½ minutes to back up about eight megabytes onto standard floppy disks. If you have a high-density drive, FastBack works even faster. The program uses its own disk format, so that you cannot even read the directory of the backup disks. However, it also creates a catalog showing which backup disk contains which file (including the date and time of the file's creation), and you can scan the entire catalog much more quickly (using the accompanying FRESTORE program) than you can load backup disks into the floppy disk drive. When you make subsequent incremental backups, the file names are added to the catalog, so that you can see which disk contains which versions of the files.

Like the BACKUP command, FastBack uses a special file format for its backup copies, so that they must be restored with the FRESTORE program before you can use them. However, this format is relatively compact—each disk holds about 421K of data, instead of 360K. Moreover, since the program uses its own unique disk format, you don't have to format your floppy disks in advance—FastBack will format them as it copies.

Listing 14.10 shows a revision of the code for the AUTOEXEC file for use with FastBack. Although it uses the same AUTOBKUP.BAS program as the original version, the AUTOEXEC file includes some changes to deal with FastBack's unique characteristics. Line 7 is the

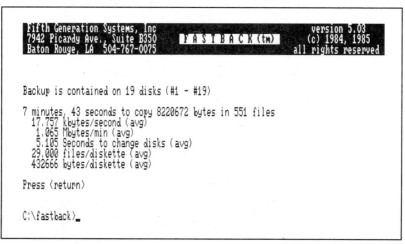

Figure 14.2 ▲ *FastBack Output Report Screen.*

line that actually calls the FastBack program (which must be in its own directory if the cataloging function is to work properly). The parameters answer the prompts that FastBack normally displays when it is called, as shown in Figure 14.3. Unfortunately, there is no way to redirect the output to the printer. However, the catalog is quite sufficient, and you can print it out as an ASCII file if you like.

The FRESTORE program also has some helpful features. It is one of very few backup/restore programs that automatically displays the entire catalog file when you restore. You can search through it for a specific file name or a wild-card pattern. You can also repeat the search to find the precise iteration of the file that you need. You can browse through the catalog a directory or a line at a time, and restore the whole disk, specific directories, or just selected files. If you wish, the program will ask your permission to restore a file if it already exists on the hard disk.

```
 2:  CD\BASIC
 2:  BASICA AUTOBKUP
 3:  CD \
 4:  IF EXIST BKUPTEST GOTO nobackup
 5:  CD\FASTBACK
 6:  ATTRIB -A CAT.BAK
 7:  FASTBACK C: \ Y *.* Y
 8:  COPY FASTBACK.CAT CAT.BAK
 9:  GOTO continue
10:  :nobackup
```

Listing 14.10 ▲ *AUTOEXEC Code for Use with FastBack.*

```
Which hard disk to copy from? (return for 'C:') c:

Which directory to back up? (return for '\') \

Back up subdirectories of C:\? (return for 'Y') y

Which files to back up? (return for '*.*') *.*

Skip files which haven't changed since last backup? (return for 'N') y_
```

Figure 14.3 ▲ *FastBack Prompts and Automatic Responses.*

FastBack does have two annoying features:

▲ If you abort the backup process, the catalog is erased. This is the reason for lines 6 and 8 of Listing 14.10. The batch file will automatically make a backup copy of the catalog, so that you can copy the backup to FASTBACK.CAT, the original catalog file, and begin again. (The ATTRIB command is included just to keep from cluttering up your backup disks.)

▲ The program that installs FastBack onto your hard disk checks your hardware very thoroughly. It performs a more sophisticated check of the DMA (direct memory address) chip than any other program, even the IBM hardware diagnostics. If it cannot use all of the chip's eight ports at once (no other program tests more than two at a time), FastBack operates no faster than the BACKUP command.

 Hint: Fifth Generation Systems, which markets FastBack, also sells a DMA-FIX board for $40. You can plug it in under your processor chip. I'd suggest ordering the program directly from Fifth Generation Systems, which offers a money-back guarantee.

Backups with PC Tools   If you find PC Tools congenial for its other facilities, you may want to use its backup and restore programs as well. These are the two external programs PCBackup and PCRestor. The backup program is as fast as FastBack once it gets started and stores data just as efficiently. To use it in place of FastBack with Listing 14.10 substitute the following lines:

```
7: ATTRIB -A LOG.BAK
8: PCBACKUP C: PATH = \ FILES = *.* /M /B
9: COPY PCBACKUP.LOG LOG.BAK
```

The PCRestor program is almost as friendly as FRESTORE. Although you can't automatically search the entire catalog for a file, you can search each directory by pressing a single key. In addition, it has a Verify option. This lets you compare the backups with the originals, directory by directory.

The one problem you may encounter is that if PC Backup encounters a bad sector on your target disk , it will abort. You will then have to start your backup series over, substituting a fresh disk for the faulty one.

Other Backup Software   Many other hard disk backup utilities are available. Most offer many more options than FastBack or PCBackup. Most notably, some will back up the files in readable form on DOS-formatted floppy disks. This can be a distinct advantage when your hard disk crashes or otherwise becomes unavailable. Some will back up from or to any DOS medium, like the latest version of the DOS BACKUP command. Most are at least a little bit faster than the BACKUP command. Many stress their flexibility in letting you decide exactly which files to back up and which to exclude. Among those I've looked at are Backup Master, Back-It, KeepTrack Plus, and Intelligent Backup.

They all work. In my experience, however, FastBack and PCBackup have three advantages that outweigh their single-mindedness about backing up everything that matches. First, they are very fast. Second, they operate with minimal attention. Third, no other utilities allow you to restore a single file as easily. If having usable backups or being able to exclude files from the backup procedure are more important to you than these considerations, by all means look into one of the others.

IMPROVING EFFICIENCY

There are quite a few ways you can make a hard disk more efficient. Several of them involve changes to the hardware itself and are beyond the scope of this book. Two others require additional software, and the third is available through DOS 3.3.

Optimizing File Layout

As you already know, when successive iterations of a file are written to disk, the file becomes fragmented. You can find how many chains a file comprises by typing the command

   CHKDSK *FILENAME.EXT*

This form of the CHKDSK command will display a report of the form

   C: *PATH* *FILENAME.EXT*
   Contains 2 non-contiguous blocks.

A command of the form

   CHKDSK *PATH*\ ***.***

will report on all files on the specified directory. Unfortunately, you cannot check file fragmentation on all subdirectories of a drive with a single command, although some DOS manuals imply that you can. For more details on CHKDSK, see Chapter 15.

DOS takes longer to read fragmented files. When a hard disk becomes filled with fragmented files, performance slows down considerably. Not only that, a fast backup program may not be able to find all of a file's chains in time to write them to disk, resulting in some infuriating problems. I promised you a less drastic solution than reformatting your hard disk.

The solution is a relatively new type of utility program that reorganizes your hard disk to make files contiguous. All of these programs will sort your directories and eliminate erased files from them, and will unfragment your files, leaving only one area of free disk space. I have never lost data while using of any of them. However, you should always do a full backup before running one of these programs for the first time, just in case it doesn't work on your particular combination of hardware.

Three of the unfragmenting utilities come with utility packages we've already looked at: Mace Utilities (which has hard disk preservation as its centerpiece), PC Tools (the external program Compress), and The Norton Utilities Advanced Edition (the SpeedDisk utility is not included in the regular edition). The first such program to appear on the market—Disk Optimizer, from SoftLogic Solutions—has recently been updated. In addition, a shareware program called DiskOrGanizer (DOG for short) has some advantages shared by none of the others.

These programs all work by finding the parts of your files, copying the files to a free area near the end of the disk, deleting the originals, and then copying the unfragmented files to the beginning of the disk. They differ most in their special features and in the order in which they arrange the files. All of them will refuse to move hidden files. This helps to preserve any copy-protected software on the disk.

▲ *Disk Optimizer* begins by placing all subdirectories at the beginning of the disk. Subsidiary directories appear immediately after their parent. Next, it places all files having extensions that match those in a list you create either at the beginning or the end of the disk. You select the extensions on the assumption that files having those extensions (.COM, .EXE, .PGM, and so on) do not change and therefore will not become fragmented. It will optionally do a fast unfragmenting, without reorganizing.

▲ PC Tools' *Compress* places COMMAND.COM first, followed by subdirectories, non-hidden system files, read-only files, and .BAT, .COM, and .EXE files, in their current order. All other files are sorted by date, in the default setting. Before you start, Compress offers you a choice of criteria by which all directories should be sorted.

▲ *Mace Utilities* places subdirectories first, followed by read-only files (presumably in their current order.) The documentation suggests that you make files that don't change (such as software) into read-only files. Like Compress, Mace Utilities gives you a choice of directory-sorting criteria. It works only on hard disks.

▲ Norton's *SpeedDisk* places subdirectories first and arranges the rest of the files in the order in which they appear in the directories. It does not sort directories, since the separate utility DirSort handles that function.

▲ *DiskOrGanizer* initially gives you a choice of four organization schemes: directory order, fast (unframenting without reorganizing), and two others. However, you can create a file called ORDER.DOG that tells it the precise order in which you want your files to appear. You must enter a separate line for each subdirectory and each file. Wild-card characters are not permitted. (The file is easy to create if you direct the output of CHKDSK /V to a file first and then edit that file.) While setup is tedious, creating ORDER.DOG allows you to do things like place all your overlay files near the beginning of the disk for fast access.

When using any of these programs, you should first unload any RAM-resident software from memory. If your computer has a switchable clock speed, set it at the slowest speed. And don't turn off the computer while the program is running. If you want to be extra cautious, you might uninstall any copy-protected software that is on your disk and reinstall it after the program finishes. Expect your first run of an unfragmenting program to take at least a half hour. Later passes may be considerably shorter.

Disk Caching

Another way to improve hard disk performance is to use a *disk-caching* program. This is a program that sets aside a section of memory to store information read from disk. As a rule, you read from the disk more often than write to it. Also, you often need to read information that you have recently read. If such information is stored in RAM, your program can use it much more quickly than is possible from reading a disk. Caching programs are especially helpful in decreasing the time it takes to read random database records.

Most caching programs do not intercept data that is written to disk—only data that is read. As a result, they are safer than RAM disks. They may also be faster. You usually have to specify the disks whose data you want intercepted by the cache.

Most expansion boards include a disk-caching program among their software utilities. Mace Utilities includes several caching programs: one for regular PCs; a second for ATs, to place the cache in extended memory; and a third to place the cache on an expanded memory board. Several other caching programs also offer these memory options. If you have one of these alternative types of memory in your system, you will probably want a caching program that uses it.

Keeping Track of Open Files

DOS 3.3

The latest release of DOS includes a FASTOPEN command. This is like a cache memory reserved especially for hard disk file and directory names. Each time you refer to a file, DOS places its name, and the names of all directories on the path to it, in the FASTOPEN buffer. This buffer is searched before DOS actually goes to disk. If the required names are in the buffer, DOS finds the file considerably faster than it would otherwise. When the buffer becomes full, old names are deleted on a first-in, first-out basis, and new ones are added.

As you might expect, this is another terminate-and-stay-resident program. It requires 35 bytes for each name it remembers. To install it, you call it once, with the command

    FASTOPEN *DRIVE:NNN DRIVE:NNN. . .DRIVE:NNN*

where *DRIVE* is a hard disk drive specifier and *NNN* is a number from 10 to 999. This number tells DOS how many file and directory names to remember from each disk. The default is 100 per disk. For maximum efficiency, you have to adjust this number so that it bears some realistic relationship to the number of files you are likely to open over, say, a couple of hours, and the degree to which you have nested your directories. Otherwise you waste memory and may not actually improve efficiency.

AN IRS LOG

If you are using a computer at home for both business and personal projects, you can get a tax deduction for part of your computer use. To do so, you must keep a log revealing the proportion of time that your computer is used for various purposes. JL.BAT, shown in Listing 14.11, will generate such a log.

JL (short for Job Log) is easy to use, but you must have some kind of clock driver that displays the date and time when you invoke it. Before you invoke a program, type

   JL *purpose invocation*

It then writes the purpose and the complete program invocation, including any necessary parameters, to a file called IRS.DAT. Next, it sends the output of the clock driver to that program, so that the time at which you begin a project is recorded. Finally, it invokes the program, passing the parameters to it in the last line.

To supplement this program, you need another program to log your quitting time. QUIT.BAT, shown in Listing 14.12, serves this purpose. If you use your computer all day, you can end this batch program with a line that calls the program to park the head of your hard-disk drive.

```
1: ECHO LOG-ON TIME: %1 %2 %3 %4 >> C:\IRS.DAT
2: CLOCK >> C:\IRS.DAT
3: %2 %3 %4
```

Listing 14.11 ▲ *JL.BAT.*

```
1: ECHO OFF:
2: CD\
3: ECHO LOG-OFF TIME: >> IRS.DAT
4: CLOCK >> IRS.DAT
5: ECHO ==================  >> IRS.DAT
```

Listing 14.12 ▲ *QUIT.BAT.*

An IRS Log in a Macro

If you have SideKick and SuperKey, you can use their special features to create an IRS log. The macro file JL.MAC, shown in Listing 14.13, will update a file called IRS.LOG in the SideKick Notepad. For this macro to work properly, the log must be a SideKick LOG file, distinguished by having

.LOG

in uppercase letters as its first line. When SideKick loads such a file, it automatically places the cursor at the end of the file as soon as it is loaded and enters the time and date.

To execute this macro, you must first have SideKick loaded. The first line of the macro automatically calls the SideKick Notepad, saves the currently open file (if there is one), and loads the IRS.LOG file from a directory called \UNFILED. SideKick automatically moves to the end of the file and enters the time and date.

The JL.MAC macro, in combination with the QUIT.MAC macro discussed below, creates a more-or-less columnar display, as shown in Figure 14.4. (It can't be perfect, because the Notepad doesn't let you set tab stops.) The columns are separated by two spaces, which should make it possible to transfer the resulting file into a spreadsheet or database program without mangling the data.

At the beginning of line 2, a backspace is issued to place the cursor at the end of the line with the new time and date. Then two spaces are entered to separate the columns. The command

<VFLD><VFLD>

sets up a variable-length field. In other words, it pauses for your input. It's up to you to remember to record the purpose for which you are using your computer. Line 3 saves the file and returns you to wherever you were working. Line 4 clears the macro from memory.

To enter the log-off time, load the macro file QUIT.MAC, shown in Listing 14.14. This file loads the IRS.LOG file into the Notepad, just as the JL.MAC file does, and enters the time and date on the last line. The tricky part is in lines 2 and 3. Line 2 moves the cursor to the beginning of the line and backspaces twice, to move the new time and date up to the end of the previous line. Line 3 adds two spaces, to separate the date from your notes in the center column. Next, it moves the cursor across the time to get to the date and deletes the date.

```
1: <BEGDEF><CTR><AUTO><SIDEKICK><F2><F3>c:\unfiled\irs.log<ENTER>
2: <BKS>   <VFLD><VFLD>
3: <F3>Y<SIDEKICK>
4: <CMD>MC<CMD><ENDDEF>
```

Listing 14.13 ▲ *JL.MAC.*

```
.LOG

09:24:55  1/15/1988   Intermediate project report  16:25:19

10:22:43  1/18/1988   Business Correspondence  12:27:05

13:26:32  1/18/1988   Intermediate project report  15:47:21

15:49:56  1/18/1988   Personal Correspondence  16:31:02

08:48:11  1/19/1988   Personal Correspondence  09:19:12       .

09:20:47  1/19/1988   Client Billing  11:49:34

12:56:03  1/19/1988   Intermediate Project Report  17:43:17

17:45:50  1/19/1988   Games  18:08:49
```

Figure 14.4 ▲ *The IRS.LOG File Created by JL.MAC and QUIT.MAC.*

```
1: <BEGDEF><CTR><AUTO><SIDEKICK><F2><F3>c:\unfiled\irs.log<ENTER>
2: <HOME><BKS><BKS>   <CtrlRGT><CtrlRGT><CtrlRGT><CtrlQ>y
3: <F3>Y<SIDEKICK>
4: <CMD>MC<CMD><ENDDEF>
```

Listing 14.14 ▲ *QUIT.MAC.*

If you have SuperKey, but do not have SideKick, you can use
SuperKey's date and time functions to create a similar file in your favorite text editor or spreadsheet program. Change line 1 of Listing 14.11 so
that it loads your preferred program editor and the file and includes the
command to move the cursor to the end of the file. Between lines 1 and
2, add the line

<CMD>FA<CMD> <CMD>FT<CMD><ENTER>

This calls SuperKey's date and time functions, respectively, entering
two spaces between the text that they create and placing the cursor on
the following line to print the first prompt. If you use a spreadsheet program, you might use macros to call the spreadsheet's date and time functions instead. This will spare you a great deal of frustration when the
time comes to do year-end arithmetic.

RECOVERING LOST FILES AND BAD DISKS

C H A P T E R

15

OW DO DISKS BECOME DAMAGED? On the back of almost any floppy disk envelope you will see an illustrated list of things you should not do to your disks. Putting your fingers through the oval-shaped hole may get grease on the magnetic medium. Placing magnets near floppy disks or storing them at temperatures that are too high or too low will scramble the data. Using pencils or paper clips on them, spilling coffee on them, or bending them will physically damage disks. You can inflict such damage unwittingly. You may be unaware that your monitor generates a magnetic field, and store disks too close to it. You may not be aware that your printer gets hot, and leave a disk underneath it by accident.

In addition to the disasters that can befall disks, there are also many ways you can damage your files. You can mangle a file by exiting a program improperly, leaving the file open on disk, which means that DOS won't know where the file ends. Frequent writing to a disk can sometimes leave you with a scrambled FAT (another reason to make frequent file-by-file backups).

DOS gives you two tools for dealing with lost or damaged files and with bad disks: CHKDSK and RECOVER. There are also some techniques you can use in DEBUG to recover or patch a damaged or erased file and to recover a file that has been left stranded in RAM. In this chapter, we'll discuss these methods of recovering files. We'll also take a look at some commercial software packages that can simplify the process and prevent or mitigate other disasters.

THE POWER OF CHKDSK

When you invoke the CHKDSK program with no parameters, it normally gives you a report of the following form:

```
NNNNNN bytes total disk space
   NNNN bytes in N hidden files
    NNN bytes in N directories
NNNNNN bytes in NN user files
NNNNNN bytes available on disk

NNNNNN bytes total memory
NNNNNN bytes free
```

The first part of this report refers to the disk, and the second part is about the computer's RAM.

Bad Sectors

If CHKDSK finds any bytes in bad sectors, the disk report will include a line of the form

```
NNNNN bytes in NN bad sectors
```

When this happens, the entire track on which a bad sector was found is recorded as defective in the FAT, so that DOS will not attempt to write to that track. You may think that this makes a disk safe to use, and to an extent it does. However, bad sectors have a nasty tendency to grow.

If you find that a floppy disk has bad sectors, you should immediately make a backup copy of its files and reformat the disk. Run CHKDSK again. If bad sectors show up after two or more attempts at reformatting, throw the disk away, or, if it has a warranty, return the disk to the manufacturer for replacement.

Lost Clusters

Sometimes CHKDSK will display the message

```
NNN lost clusters found in NN chains.
Write corrections to disk (Y/N)?
```

This means that parts of files, or complete files, are still recorded on the FAT, even though they have been erased from the directory (because you closed a file improperly or something else went wrong). Usually, such files do no harm, but they do take up valuable room on your disk.

If you invoked CHKDSK with no parameters and respond to this message with a Y, DOS will display

Errors found, F parameter not specified
Corrections will not be written to disk

If you invoked CHKDSK with a command of the form

CHKDSK /F

and you respond with a Y, each chain of lost clusters is written to a separate file, with a name of the form

FILE*NNN*.CHK

The first file is FILE0000.CHK, and each successive file is numbered consecutively.

These files will be listed in the disk's root directory, and you can use the TYPE command to view their contents. If they are parts of files that you previously erased, you can erase them again to free the disk space. If they are parts of files that you still need, you can rename them appropriately and, if necessary, concatenate them using the COPY command, as explained in Chapter 11.

If the recovered chains turn out to be program files, however, it is safer to erase the files and replace them with new copies from another disk. It is quite possible that a program recovered by this method will have errors in it, and even one incorrect byte in a program file can cause untold mischief.

Allocation Errors and Cross-Linked Files

If you see any of the following messages when you run CHKDSK, something is seriously wrong with your FAT.

B:*FILENAME.EXT*
Allocation error, size adjusted

B:*FILENAME.EXT*
Invalid cluster, file truncated

or

B:*FILE1.EXT*
Is cross linked on cluster *NNN*

B:*FILE2.EXT*
Is cross linked on cluster *NNN*

The first message means that the file size recorded in the directory is greater than the number of clusters assigned to the file. The second is the reverse case, in which case DOS shortens the file. The third message means that the FAT has recorded two different files as occupying the same cluster. If you see these messages, there may be some lost clusters as well.

These things are most likely to happen when your computer locks up while a file is open. They also mean that you have lost some data. When two files are cross linked, DOS doesn't know which file the cluster in question really belongs to. It arbitrarily assigns that cluster to one of the files.

Often, you will see both of these messages on a single pass of CHKDSK. Running CHKDSK with the /F option will allow you to eliminate or rescue the lost clusters, but it does nothing for the cross linked files. The only thing you can do is copy them to another disk and then delete them. You can later examine the copies and delete the extraneous information. If you are lucky, you may be able to recover some of the lost data, using methods described below.

WHEN TO USE RECOVER

There are two times when you might want to use the RECOVER command:

▲ When a file you need has been written to a bad sector

▲ When the FAT is so badly scrambled that DOS cannot find any of your files

Warning: RECOVER is a dangerous command. *Always* follow it with a file name unless your disk is completely unreadable. Using it without a file name will wipe out *all* the file names on a disk, even if it contains some usable files.

Recovering a Damaged File

If a file includes bad sectors, you can recover it with a command of the form

RECOVER *FILENAME.EXT*

This tells DOS to read the file one sector at a time and to rewrite the FAT excluding the bad sectors. You will lose part of your file, and if it is anything other than an ASCII file, the remaining part may still be useless. If it is a dBASE file, for example, the formatting information may be part of a bad sector, and the data will not appear in the proper fields.

There are several ways to deal with files with bad sectors:

▲ First, find out whether your application program can read the file at all. If so, and if it can write data to an ASCII text, comma-delimited, DIF, or other type of ASCII file, write the usable data to such a file. If you are familiar with the file format, you can then edit the result as an ASCII file in your word processor and read it back into the application program.

▲ If your application program uses Ctrl-Z as an end-of-file marker, you may be able to recover part of a file even if the data in the bad sectors are hopelessly mangled. Type

DEBUG *FILENAME.EXT*

to load the file into DEBUG. Use the Dump command to step through the file until you come to the damaged part. Then use the Enter command to place a Ctrl-Z (hex 1A) after the last coherent record. You should then be able to use the first part of the file.

▲ Mace Utilities includes a Remedy function which is much safer to use than the RECOVER command. It will actually try to read the data from the bad sectors and rewrite them to an undamaged part of the disk before locking out the bad sectors. Disk Optimizer will do something similar.

What to Do with a Scrambled FAT

Sometimes both copies of the FAT on a disk become so badly scrambled that DOS cannot find files. The files themselves may be quite intact, but they are useless if you can't find them. This is the only time when you should use the RECOVER command without a file name.

When you issue the RECOVER command with no parameters, the program systematically scans the disk and rewrites both the FAT and the directory. It enters each file in the directory with a name of the form

FILE*NNN***.REC**

All entries will be listed in the root directory. If you had more files on the disk than the root directory will hold (112 on a standard floppy disk), you will have to examine the recovered files and delete or copy some to another disk to make room in the directory. At the same time, you can rename those files that you recognize.

 Hint: At this point, the only way that you can distinguish files from one another without actually examining them is by the directory's listing of their length in bytes. This information may help you to find the one or two files that you absolutely must recover.

Software Solutions

If you need to recover data from a disk with a scrambled FAT, Mace Utilities can be a great help. Use the Remedy function. If one of the FATs is still intact, Mace will rewrite the scrambled one to match.

If Mace can't recover the FAT itself, you may still be able to recover at least some of the data. See if you can get Mace's Remedy function or Norton's NU /M function to read the disk at all. If it can, you can scan the disk for data and copy clusters that you need onto another disk as files. We'll look at these techniques in a bit more depth later in the chapter.

RECOVERING ERASED FILES

Many of us have experienced the nightmare of erasing the only copy of a vital file or wiping out an entire disk directory by mistyping a file specification that included wild cards. For example, when I was attempting to clean up a directory consisting almost entirely of batch files, I typed

ERASE ∗.BAT

instead of

ERASE ∗.BAK

DOS provides only the most limited facilities for recovering an erased file. Fortunately, there are several software packages that can do so quite effectively.

Warning: When you need to recover an erased file, *do nothing else to the disk that contains the file before you complete the recovery operation.* When a file is erased, the space it had occupied on disk is deallocated, and the next time you write to the disk, there is an excellent chance that part of the file's data will be overwritten. If you're too tired or frazzled to do the job when you discover the error, put the disk away and do it another time.

Recovering a File with DEBUG

If a file is one cluster or less (1K on a standard floppy disk, 2K or 4K on most hard disks), it's relatively simple to recover it using DEBUG. Since the FAT entry for the file does not contain pointers to any other clusters, all you have to do is get the file name back into the directory (see the section in Chapter 12 on rewriting directory entries).

When you erase a file, DOS changes the first byte of the file name in the directory to hex E5. You can recover the file by changing the E5 back to the file name's first character. Load the directory directly from disk using DEBUG, then browse through it using the Dump command until you see the name of the file that you want to recover. When you find the file name, use the Enter command to replace the E5 with the correct character. It is easiest to enter the value as the character itself (in uppercase) and inside quotation marks, rather than using the hex version of its ASCII code. Then write the directory sector back to disk. When you are finished, *immediately* copy the recovered file to a different disk. You should then run CHKDSK on the disk from which you recovered the file. This will probably shorten the recovered file to zero bytes. Erase it, and then copy the version that you saved onto another disk back onto the original.

You can recover an erased file that is more than one cluster long in DEBUG (if you can recognize it in DEBUG's format), but it's much more complicated. First, read the disk a cluster at a time until you see the beginning of the file. When you have the first cluster of the file, note the address where it ends. This should be hex 400, if your disk uses two-sector clusters.

Continue by reading clusters into memory at the *next* address (probably hex 401). Again, when you find the next cluster, note the ending address and continue reading at the next address.

When you have the complete file in memory, note the ending address. Now comes the tricky part. You started loading the file at address 100 hex, so you have to subtract 100 hex from the ending address to get the true length of the file. If it's any help, 100 hex is 256 decimal. Enter the length of the file in the CX register by typing

```
RCX
NNNNN
```

where *NNNNN* is the ending address less 100 hex. Use the name command to create a file to hold the data on another disk. Then write the data to the new file.

If the file is a text file, you may find it easier to write each cluster that you recognize to a separate file and concatenate them using the COPY command or with your word processor

If the erased file is a program, it's easier and safer to copy the file from the distribution disk or one of your additional backup copies. (Of course you made backups, didn't you?) If it's a data file, and it hasn't been updated recently, you may still be better off restoring it from a backup copy. But it seems inevitable that vital files get erased just when you finish updating them and before you have made a backup.

Software Solutions

The Norton Utilities (both versions), PC Tools, and Mace Utilities, all of which we've discussed in earlier chapters, have powerful file-recovery utilities. All of them have two recovery modes. In the quick mode, the program will attempt to find the file's data for you. In the manual mode, you select the data for the file a cluster at a time.

The success of the quick mode, as a rule, is in inverse proportion to the degree of fragmentation of the erased file. The programs will find the file's first cluster by reading the FAT. Then they'll assume that the rest of the file occupies the unallocated clusters that follow the first cluster, in the order in which they appear on the disk. If you have erased several files at once, you may have to use the manual method, unless you regularly use the RXBAK program from Mace Utilities, which we'll explore at the end of the chapter.

When you select the Unerase or Undelete function, the programs present you with a list of erased files from which to choose. Norton gives you a screen full of simple file names. PC Tools gives you a display similar to its normal directory display. Mace displays complete directory entries for all erased files on the disk. You can select from any of them by using the cursor. Next you have to supply the missing first character of the file name.

At this point, the programs diverge. Norton gives you a choice of letting it select the clusters for you, selecting them manually, or searching for data that should have been in the file. PC Tools gives you a choice of only manual or automatic selection. However, it tells you which files are good candidates for automatic recovery by placing an @ symbol next to their names.

Mace differs from the others in several important respects. First, its definition of quick undeletion is to undelete the file where it currently exists. Normally, it recovers the file to another drive of your choice. This is an excellent safety measure. It allows you to work with the deleted data a second time if the recovery is unsuccessful. Once you have decided whether to recover the file in place or to another drive, it begins displaying likely clusters. You can search for text by pressing F1. To switch to automatic mode, press the Ins key.

The other feature that makes Mace unique is its use of RXBAK. This program (like similar programs in Mace's competitors) maintains a second copy of the boot record, FAT, and root directory in another location on the disk. If you have updated this copy before deleting the file you want to recover, Mace, unlike its competition, can use RXBAK to help locate the file's clusters. (Central Point Software promises to include such a function in its next release of PC Tools, but it's not there yet.)

Mace also differs from the others in the way it displays a file's data. Both Norton and PC Tools use their byte editor's format to display the data. You can also switch to a text-only mode in both. Mace, on the other hand, displays the bytes in a block. Each byte is represented by the ASCII equivalent of the value it holds. You may find this display a bit more confusing than those of the other utilities.

As I said, all of the programs work reasonably well. You have the best chance of recovering a text file in those cases where you can reconstruct any missing pieces from their context. Files that include a great deal of formatting information, or internal pointers, may be much harder to recover. (For this reason, Mace includes a separate utility for dBASE files.) I was able to recover a 68K ThinkTank file that had 15 fragments with all three programs. However, when I undeleted a 100K Framework II file, Framework II couldn't read it. If you work extensively with spreadsheet or database programs, you may prefer to use Mace, because it uses a backup copy of the FAT to locate a complex file's clusters.

Hint: A point to keep in mind when using these programs is that to recover an erased file, you must have an erased file. If you have used the RECOVER command to save a damaged file, and the file ends up being too small, you may have to erase it, and then use your utility program to unerase it. Use the manual method to search for some text that you know was part of the file, but which did not appear in the recovered file. Include the sector among those to be unerased. That will reset the pointers. Finally, use CHKDSK to update the FAT.

RECOVERING FILES
FROM MEMORY WITH DEBUG

All or part of a file may be stranded in memory when one of the following things happens:

▲ Your program blows up.

▲ Your keyboard locks up, and you have to reboot.

▲ Your program responds to Ctrl-C, you have BREAK set to on, and you find yourself back at the operating system without having saved your file.

If your computer hasn't locked up, or if it can be warm-booted, you can probably recover the file. When you warm boot, memory is not actually erased—the operating system is simply reloaded, and the pointers to the beginning of available memory are reset. Thus, you can use DEBUG to get to the part of memory where the file is located.

Here is a step-by-step guide to recovering a file from memory using DEBUG.

1. Load DEBUG and the program that created the file. For example, if the file is a WordStar file, type

   DEBUG WS.COM

   with the appropriate drive and path specifiers.

2. Use the Dump command to step through memory until you have gone past the end of the program.

! **Hint:** You can skip a great deal of the program code if you check the directory first to see how long the program is, then convert the result to hex. A desk-accessory calculator that can make such conversions is extremely useful for this purpose. Start dumping at the resulting hex address.

3. When you see the beginning of the file, note its address.

4. Continue using the Dump command until you reach the end of the file. Note the address of the end of the file. Be sure that you include the final carriage-return/line-feed pair (0D 0A) as part of the file. You may want to insert a Ctrl-Z (1A) after the end of the file. If you do, the byte containing the Ctrl-Z will be the last byte of the file. Note the address where the Ctrl-Z is located.

5. Use the Move command to move the file to address 100. The syntax is

    M *start-of-file end-of-file* **100**

6. Calculate the number of bytes in the file (in hex) by subtracting the starting address from the ending address (a converting calculator is useful for this job, too).

7. If you used DEBUG as an assembler in Chapter 6, the rest of the procedure will be familiar. Enter the command

    RBX

    If the display reads

    :0000

    press Ctrl-C. Otherwise, enter a zero.

8. Enter the command

    RCX

9. Enter the length of the file in hex.

10. Name the file to which the data will be written using the Name command:

    N *FILENAME.EXT*

Do not use the name of an existing file unless you want it to be overwritten. You can include a drive and path specifier.

11. Enter W to issue the Write command. You should see the message

    Writing *NNNN* bytes

    where *NNNN* is the number you entered as the length of the file.

12. Enter Q to issue the Quit command.

Load the recovered file into the source program. If everything has proceeded as it should, your file will be intact. However, you may have to clean up the beginning and end of the file, especially if you missed the final carriage-return/line-feed pair.

RECOVERING FROM AN UNINTENTIONAL FORMAT

All three of the major utility packages include programs to help you unformat a hard disk. As you already know, this is possible only because DOS doesn't actually erase the data when it formats a hard disk. It just erases the FATs and the root directory. (There are some exceptions. Your DOS is an exception if it performs a read-write test after formatting a hard disk. But you don't want to format your hard disk just to find out.)

All the programs use essentially the same method to unformat a disk. Each contains a program that creates a backup copy of the boot record, the FAT, and the root directory elsewhere on the disk. The Norton Utilities Advanced Edition's FR (Format Recover) creates or updates the file FRECOVER.DAT. PC Tools' Mirror creates or updates two files, MIRROR.FIL and MIRORSAV.FIL. The latter is a small file that stores a pointer to the larger file's location on disk. Mace's RXBAK creates or updates a file called BACKUP.M_U. If it already exists, the old file is renamed to OLDBAK.M_U and retained.

You can ensure that the recovery file is reasonably current by including a call to the program in your AUTOEXEC.BAT file and in the batch files that call programs that create files.

If you do format your hard disk unintentionally, you must run a program that locates the backup file and then copies it to the proper position at the beginning of the disk. Unfortunately, you'll probably have to run that program from a floppy disk, because if it's on your hard disk, it will be lost along with everything else. With Norton, you run FR again. With PC Tools you run Rebuild. With Mace you run UnFORMAT.

Although the basic technique is the same for all three programs, there are enough differences to warrant a careful choice. Most obvious is the disk storage they require. Mace's BACKUP.M_U takes 81,408 bytes on my 30MB hard disk. With its backup copy, it uses 159K. FR doesn't make a backup copy, but FRECOVER.DAT takes 89,120 bytes, or 87K. MIRROR.FIL takes only 49,152 bytes, or 48K. Mirror saves some space by making only one copy of the FAT. The additional pointer file takes only one cluster, the very last one on the disk.

There is a risk associated with all of these programs. If your FAT has started to go bad and your recovery file already has a copy of the bad FAT, you won't be in any better shape than you were before. If this happens, you should reboot from a floppy disk whose AUTOEXEC file does not include a call to Mirror, FR, or RXBAK. You can then back up as much data as possible and reformat the disk.

This is one reason that Mace makes a backup copy of the file. You can emulate this function by copying (*not* backing up) the file to a floppy disk as part of your daily backup routine. In fact, it might be wiser to do so, because then you will have access to the file no matter what happens to your hard disk's FAT. Keep it on the same disk as your backup log.

There's a catch if you try to back up MIRROR.FIL, however. Mirror automatically marks the file as a read-only, hidden system file. Unless you have a utility to unhide it, the COPY command won't be able to find it. (PC Tools will do the job for you, but not with a simple command that you can include in a batch file. You could, however, invoke the program through a macro that performs all the keystrokes necessary to complete the task.)

If you're especially worried about your hard disk and can spare the overhead, Mace gives you some extra "bullet-proofing." First, there's a FORMAT-H program, which will soft-format a hard disk even if your DOS won't. (A companion program allows you to soft-format floppy disks.) Then there's the automatic backup copy of the rescue file. You can use a switch to keep RXBAK from making a backup. You can also have it create the latest copy on another drive (another way to back up the file automatically).

In addition, Mace's Remedy function can lock out bad sectors and move data to safe areas before any serious damage occurs, if you run it soon enough. When you run it, Remedy performs this function automatically. In contrast, you have to tell Norton's DT what to do at each stage. PC Tools' Compress program only lets you know whether bad sectors are present—it doesn't lock them out or rescue the data.

All of these programs work on floppy as well as hard disks. However, they will help you only when your FAT has gone bad. Unless you have used Mace's soft-format program to format the floppy disk, you cannot recover data from the newly formatted disk.

GETTING MORE FROM YOUR PRINTER

CHAPTER

16

UNDER NORMAL CIRCUMSTANCES, your printer can tie up a lot of
valuable computer time. The most obvious, and expensive, way to get
your computer back from your printer is to buy a *printer buffer*. This is a
piece of hardware that acts as a temporary storage area for any text
being sent to the printer.

There are, however, much less expensive ways to accomplish the
same thing. There are *print-queue* programs—one of which is included
with DOS—which keep track of a list of files to be printed and print
them from disk rather than from memory. There are also *print-spooler*
programs that create a printer buffer inside your computer's memory.

In this chapter, we'll look at DOS's PRINT.COM program before we
go on to examine some print-spooler software. We'll also examine ways
to change print modes on your printer without using a BASIC program
and see how to print graphics with DOS's GRAPHICS.COM program.

SETTING UP A PRINT QUEUE WITH PRINT

The basic function of DOS's PRINT.COM program is to set up a print queue, which is a list of files to be printed. In DOS 2.X, the utility of this program is extremely limited; in DOS 3.X, it is somewhat more useful.

DOS 2.X

In DOS 2.X, all that the PRINT command does is remember a list of files to be printed and print them from disk. It can print up to ten files, all of which must be on the current directory. You cannot change anything in a file once it has been placed in the print queue. The basic syntax of the command is

PRINT *FILE1.EXT FILE2.EXT FILE3.EXT . . . FILE10.EXT*

You can use wild-card characters in the file specifiers (but remember, only up to ten files will be stored in the queue). A small buffer is created in memory, so you have full access to your computer's other functions while each file is read from disk and sent to the printer. You can even log onto a different directory once you have issued the PRINT command. However, if you are printing from a floppy disk and switch disks in the drive that the PRINT command is using, the program will look for each file in turn, causing the printer to beep, print an error message, and issue a form feed for each file name in the queue until it comes to the end.

The first time you issue the PRINT command, the computer will display the message

Name of list device [PRN]

giving you the option of sending the files in the queue to another device. If you press Return, your files will go to your first printer port.

Options with the PRINT Command

Typing PRINT at a DOS prompt will display a list of the files in the queue. You can make changes to the queue once it is established by using the following switches in command lines at a DOS prompt:

▲ /T terminates all printing, including the file currently being printed. All subsequent files will be removed from the queue.

▲ /C, following a file name, cancels that file. If you enter other file names on the command line following the one with the /C switch, those files will be removed from the queue as well. For example

PRINT FILE3.EXT /C FILE7.EXT FILE10.EXT

will remove FILE3.EXT, FILE7.EXT, and FILE10.EXT from the queue, leaving the others undisturbed.

▲ /P, following a file name, adds that file. If you want to remove some files from the queue and replace them with others, follow the first of those to be added with the /P switch. For example

PRINT FILE3.EXT /C FILE7.EXT FILE11.EXT /P FILE12.EXT

will remove FILE3.EXT and FILE7.EXT from the queue, but add FILE11.EXT AND FILE12.EXT.

Limitations of the PRINT Command

One of the major shortcomings of the PRINT command—that it will print only from disk—leads to several other limitations. If your word processor does not have a print-to-disk function, there is no way that you can use the PRINT.COM program in conjunction with your word processor. Moreover, it ties up your printer in ways that can interfere with other jobs. For example, listing a BASIC program to the printer with the LLIST command or attempting to dump a screen with Shift-PrtSc will result in a

Printer not ready

message. The only way to get your printer back is to cancel the queue at a DOS prompt.

The second major shortcoming of the PRINT command—that it can print files only from the directory that is current when the command is issued—also leads to further complications. If you want to print files from various disks or directories, you must first copy them to a single directory, or print from one directory at a time. Moreover, as you already know, you cannot remove the disk that contains the files to be printed. In addition, the PRINT command can crash your system if it needs to access a disk at precisely the same moment as your foreground program does.

Enhancements in DOS 3.X

DOS 3.X

The PRINT command in DOS 3.X allows you to print files that are not in the current directory by specifying the path to the other directory. It also includes several new switches, each of which can have a parameter:

- ▲ /D:*device* allows you to specify the print device without waiting for a prompt. If you use this switch, it must appear immediately after the PRINT command, before any other switches or file names.

- ▲ /B:*size* allows you to specify the size of the print buffer. The default size is 512 bytes. A larger buffer—say 2,048 bytes—is considerably more efficient.

- ▲ /Q:*queuesize* allows you to specify the number of files to be placed in the queue, from 1 to 32. The default is still 10.

- ▲ /M:*maxtick* allows you to specify the number of ticks the computer should wait, in a range from 1 to 255. Your computer has an internal clock that ticks 18 times per second. Normally, the PRINT command will try for two of these ticks to send a character to the printer, and it will continue printing until this length of time is used up before returning control to the foreground program.

- ▲ /U:*busytick* specifies how many ticks the computer should wait until the printer is available before giving up its time to the foreground program. Again, the default is 2, and the range is from 1 to 255.

- ▲ /S:*timeslice* allows you to specify the maximum number of characters to be printed in the interval determined by the /M switch. Once the number of characters specified has been printed, control will be returned to the foreground program even if the time assigned by the /M switch is not used up.

PRINT SPOOLERS

If you bought a memory expansion board, a print spooler probably came with its software package. A print spooler, unlike DOS's PRINT.COM program, establishes a buffer in memory that intercepts anything being sent to the printer and stores it until the printer is ready to receive it.

The major limitations of print spoolers are two sides of the same coin: if you set aside too much memory for a spooler, you may not have enough left for your other programs. On the other hand, a print spooler that is too small can also cause problems. If your file is larger than your spooler buffer, your computer will not be available to you until the end of the file has reached the buffer.

The utility of spooler buffers also depends on your applications software. For example, if you use a word-processing program that formats text as it sends it to the printer, output from the program to the printer may be so slow that using a spooler buffer is not much of an advantage.

Let's look at a few commercial print-spooler packages and compare their advantages and disadvantages. These programs are all included in the same packages as the RAM-disk software discussed in Chapter 13.

QSPOOL

The QuadMaster III package includes several print spoolers, all of which are installed through the CONFIG.SYS file. They are among the easiest to use that I have encountered, and you can't beat the price.

Each spooler establishes a window that will tell you how full the spooler is (as a percentage). This window gives you the options of pausing the printing or flushing the buffer; flushing the buffer cancels any further printing from that buffer, unless your file is larger than the buffer. If so, the buffer will immediately fill up again. If you choose to pause the printing, the next time you open the window, you will have the options of flushing the buffer or resuming printing.

 Warning: When you use one of the QSPOOL spoolers in conjunction with SuperKey, opening the window when the spooler is empty will cause the keyboard to lock up.

You can install buffers for up to three parallel printers and a serial printer. You can thus have up to four printers running at the same time, while you have full access to your computer's other functions. Of course, you have to be careful to direct what you want printed on each printer to the appropriate port. When using a serial printer, you use the alternate program QSPOOLSR.SYS, with appropriate serial port parameters in the DEVICE= command. However, you must also use the MODE command to configure the port itself.

The package also includes a utility called QSWAP, which will swap the output of any two parallel ports.

The only major disadvantage of this package is that it takes up some system memory, which cannot be reassigned except by altering the CONFIG.SYS file.

JSPOOL

The JRAM Combo Disk includes a spooler called JSPOOL and two ancillary files called SPOOLCOM.COM and MAKEFILE.COM. They offer considerably greater flexibility than the QSPOOL buffers, but, unfortunately, require you to enter devilishly convoluted syntax. The big advantage of the JSPOOL package is that it will create its buffer either in system memory or on a RAM disk.

You install the driver through the CONFIG.SYS file in the usual manner. However, if you don't want to give up very much system memory, and don't always need a spooler buffer, you can configure the buffer for 129 bytes (the minimum size) and use the MAKEFILE program to create a buffer of any size on your RAM disk. If this small system-memory buffer is installed, you can turn an existing file on a RAM disk into a printer buffer, change the size of the buffer, or remove it entirely. If you wish, the buffer can be as big as your entire RAM disk. Once you are through with the buffer, you can use the MAKEFILE program again to remove it.

The SPOOLCOM program is used to send commands to the spooler. For example, typing

SPOOLCOM FLUSH

at a DOS prompt will empty the buffer.

JSPOOL's flexibility includes the ability to configure all the default settings of DOS 3.X's version of the PRINT command. It can also be configured for a serial printer.

Warning: The serial-port configuration described in the manual does not work. Instead of issuing the serial port parameters as part of the DEVICE= command in the CONFIG.SYS file, you must issue separate commands with the SPOOLCOM program. You can include them in your AUTOEXEC file, however. Moreover, you must not use the MODE command to configure the printer port.

On the negative side, JSPOOL behaves unpredictably (occasionally causing lockups) when other RAM-resident programs are present, and it may be unable to create a buffer on a RAM disk once you have actually begun working in an application. I have attempted to flush its buffer on occasion, for example, and have been greeted with a message implying that the number of characters still in it is greater than my entire RAM. It has the additional disadvantages that all spooler commands must be issued at a DOS prompt, and SPOOLCOM must be physically present in order to issue any spooler commands other than flushing the buffer (unless your application gives you access to other programs while it is running). You also need the MAKEFILE program on hand to change the size of the buffer or to create more than one.

The X2C Spooler

The spooler software included with the X2C board is, like the board, in a class by itself. The many marvelous features of the X2C spooler software include the following:

- ▲ It is loaded by way of a batch file or a DOS command, so that you need not include it in your setup for any given session.
- ▲ If you have expanded memory (above 640K), you can create the buffer in expanded memory.
- ▲ It is completely menu-driven; the menu is called by pressing a hot key of your choice.
- ▲ On-line help is readily available.
- ▲ A special window allows you to send escape sequences to your printer, even while another program is running, so that you can change type styles in the middle of a report.
- ▲ It includes commands that allow you to remove a file from the buffer.

The only problems that I have encountered with this program are that one of the applications programs I use generates a

Printer not ready

message when the spooler is installed; and that you can't close its windows by pressing the Esc key (as the documentation says you should) if you load it before SuperKey. (I have had no trouble with closing the windows when loading the spooler *after* SuperKey.)

CONTROLLING YOUR PRINTER'S TYPE STYLES

As you have no doubt already discovered, your printer manual expects you to control your printer by writing short BASIC programs to change the print pitch, type style, and whatever other aspects of the appearance of the printed output that can be controlled. Now that you know how to insert an Escape character into a batch file, you can easily control your printer through batch files instead of using BASIC.

Single-Line Commands

If you prefer command-line arguments to menus, you can create a series of one-line batch files, each of which issues a single printer escape sequence. For example, for an Epson printer, you could create a pair of files called CONDENSD.BAT and NOCOND.BAT. The first would contain the single line

```
ECHO ^O >PRN
```

to set the printer to print in condensed type. The second would contain the line

```
ECHO ^S >PRN
```

to return it to normal. You could create a whole series of files, with titles like ITALIC.BAT, NOITALIC.BAT, ELITE.BAT, WIDE.BAT, EMPHSIZE.BAT, and so on. If you have a hard disk, place them in your \BATCH directory. If you have a RAM disk, have them loaded automatically to your RAM disk from your startup disk.

On the other hand, if there is a single combination of type styles that you use regularly, you could place them all in a single line in your AUTOEXEC file. For example, the line

```
ECHO ^[2 ^[E ^[G >PRN
```

would automatically set the printer to six lines per inch, with emphasized, double-strike print. To clear it, you would have to either use a batch file to send ^ [@ to the printer (the CLEAR command for Epsons) or turn the printer off and on.

A Printer Command Menu

If you prefer a menu-driven approach to command-line arguments, Listings 16.1 and 16.2 illustrate a way to set up a menu of type styles for your printer. The codes are for an unmodified Okidata 92, but you can make the appropriate substitutions for your printer.

Listing 16.1, SETPRINT.BAT, makes use of many of the advanced features of DOS that we have covered in this book. To begin, it uses the CHOOSE.COM program from Chapter 6; then it uses the TYPE command to call SETPRINT.MNU, which appears in Listing 16.2. This file uses ANSI escape sequences to reassign the keys A through L to the function keys, as illustrated in Figure 16.1, so that the Ctrl-function and Shift-function keys can be used to issue the printer commands. The SETPRINT.MNU file also displays the menu screen itself. Codes are included for inverse video and highlighting on a monochrome display, and they will work quite well as black and white on a color display. You can change the escape sequences to add color if you wish.

SETPRINT.BAT displays a menu and allows the user to select as many escape sequences as desired. It does not include protection against issuing incompatible codes, however. Whoever uses the program will have to be aware that, for example, you can't have correspondence quality in condensed mode, or boldfaced correspondence-quality type. Here is how SETPRINT.BAT works.

3–17: Forms a loop for trapping responses to the CHOOSE command, created by the program in Chapter 6.

4: Resets the cursor to the same position after each time through the loop to keep the menu display from scrolling off the screen.

5: Invokes the CHOOSE program with the letters A through L as arguments. These keys will work as well as the function keys. However, the function keys make a relatively compact keypad for use with the menu, which is why the reassignments were made in the .MNU program.

18–50: A series of single-line escape sequences to be sent to the printer, each of which sends control back to the loop beginning at line 3.

```
 1: ECHO OFF
 2: TYPE SETPRINT.MNU
 3: :choices
 4: ECHO ^[[51;15f
 5: CHOOSE LKJIHGFEDCBA
 6: IF ERRORLEVEL 11 GOTO end
 7: IF ERRORLEVEL 10 GOTO reset
 8: IF ERRORLEVEL 9  GOTO 8lpi
 9: IF ERRORLEVEL 8  GOTO 6lpi
10: IF ERRORLEVEL 7  GOTO dpqual
11: IF ERRORLEVEL 6  GOTO corrqual
12: IF ERRORLEVEL 5  GOTO undlin
13: IF ERRORLEVEL 4  GOTO bold
14: IF ERRORLEVEL 3  GOTO wide
15: IF ERRORLEVEL 2  GOTO cond
16: IF ERRORLEVEL 1  GOTO elite
17: IF ERRORLEVEL 0  GOTO pica
18: :reset
19: ECHO ^X >PRN
20: GOTO choices
21: :8lpi
22: ECHO ^[8  > PRN
23: GOTO choices
24: :6lpi
25: ECHO ^[6  > PRN
26: GOTO choices
27: :dpqual
28: ECHO ^[0  > PRN
29: GOTO choices
30: :corrqual
31: ECHO ^[1  > PRN
32: GOTO choices
33: :undlin
34: ECHO ^[C  > PRN
35: GOTO choices
36: :bold
37: ECHO ^[H  > PRN
38: GOTO choices
39: :wide
40: ECHO ^_  > PRN
41: GOTO choices
42: :cond
43: ECHO ^]  > PRN
44: GOTO choices
45: :elite
46: ECHO ^\  > PRN
47: GOTO choices
48: :pica
49: ECHO ^^  > PRN
50: GOTO choices
51: :end
52: ECHO ^[[0;94;0;94p ^[[0;95;0;95p ^[[0;96;0;96p ^[[0;97;0;97p ^[[0;98;0;98p
53: ECHO ^[[0;99;0;99p ^[[0;100;0;100p ^[[0;101;0;101p ^[[0;102;0;102p
54: ECHO ^[[0;103;0;103p ^[[0;84;0;84p ^[[0;93;0;93p
```

Listing 16.1 ▲ *SETPRINT.BAT.*

51–54: When Shift-F10 is pressed, it indicates that the user is through making choices. Control is directed to this final module, which clears the key assignments.

```
SETPRINT.MNU
      1: ^[[2J
      2: ^[[0;94;65p ^[[0;95;66p ^[[0;96;67p ^[[0;97;68p ^[[0;98;69p
      3: ^[[0;99;70p ^[[0;100;71p ^[[0;101;72p ^[[0;102;73p
      4: ^[[0;103;74p ^[[0;84;75p ^[[0;93;76p
      5:
      6: ^[[2J ^[[3;17f ^[[0m
      7:
      8:                   ┌┌─────────────────────────────────────────┐
                           ‖  ^[[7m              SET UP PRINTER
^[[0m ‖                    ‖
      9:                   ‖├─────────┬──────────────────────┬────────┤
     10:                   ‖^[[7m CF1 ^[[0m3 Pica            ‖^[[7m CF2
^[[0m3 Elite       ‖
     11:                   ‖^[[7m CF3 ^[[0m3 Condensed       ‖^[[7m CF4
^[[0m3 Double-Wide ‖
     12:                   ‖^[[7m CF5 ^[[0m3 Boldface        ‖^[[7m CF6
^[[0m3 Underlined  ‖
     13:                   ‖^[[7m CF7 ^[[0m3 Corr. Qual.     ‖^[[7m CF8
^[[0m3 DP Quality  ‖
     14:                   ‖^[[7m CF9 ^[[0m3 6 lines/in.     ‖^[[7m CF10
^[[0m3 8 lines/in. ‖
     15:                   ‖├─────────┼──────────────────────┼────────┤
     16:                   ‖^[[7m SF1 ^[[0m3 Reset Printer‖^[[7m SF10
^[[0m3 Return to DOS ‖
     17:                   ‖├────────────────────────────────────────┤
     18:                   ‖^[[1mChoose settings, press Shift-F10 when
done^[[0m‖
     19:
```

Listing 16.2 ▲ *SETPRINT.MNU.*

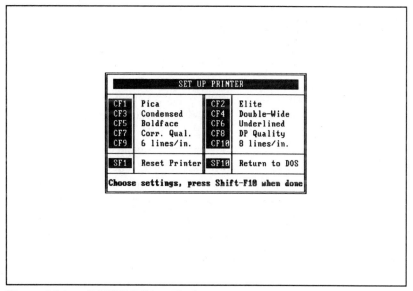

Figure 16.1 ▲ *SETPRINT Menu Display.*

If you find that the assignments are not properly cleared on your computer, you can try one of the following remedies:

▲ Place the assignment clearing codes in a separate text file, without the ECHO statements, and TYPE that file as the last line of the batch file.

▲ Place a blank line after each line of assignment clearings.

▲ If that doesn't work, place each assignment clearing code on a separate line.

The first of these three remedies is both the simplest and the most reliable.

This program is completely compatible with the DOSMENU program presented in Chapter 9, since none of the keys to which strings are assigned overlap. You could assign the string

SETPRINT

to a key in the DOSMENU program, and add it to the display screen. Then, after clearing the key assignments created by SETPRINT.MNU, add a line to SETPRINT.BAT that recalls DOSMENU.BAT.

Printing Graphics

The DOS external program GRAPHICS.COM allows you to dump graphics screens to your printer. This is another terminate-and-stay-resident program, so it takes up some system memory until you reboot. Once it is loaded, however, any time a graphics screen is on your monitor, pressing Shift-PrtSc dumps that screen dot-by-dot, so that you have a fully detailed reproduction of your screen. Most versions of DOS will print the screen sideways on the page, in large size.

The only problem you are likely to encounter with the program involves color. GRAPHICS has no problems with black-and-white screens, but it may interpret one color overlaid on another as black-on-black or white-on-white, so that you lose detail. If you intend to print a great deal of graphics, you might want to invest in some sort of paint program.

NATIONALIZING
YOUR
COMPUTER

17

BEGINNING WITH DOS 3.0, it has become possible to make your computer work comfortably in a variety of languages. New commands and files have been introduced to remap the keyboard so that it conforms to the standard typewriter layout in various countries. Additional files select national defaults, and tailor the screen and printer to match the remapped keyboards. This chapter explores in detail the tools provided by DOS for these purposes.

SELECTING NATIONAL DEFAULTS

The COUNTRY command allows you to select the form in which the computer displays the date and time, selects the decimal delimiter, and selects the currency symbol. This command is placed in the CONFIG.SYS file. In addition, you can use a standard DOS command to select one of five international keyboard layouts.

The country codes used in the COUNTRY command correspond to the country codes used in the international telephone system. DOS 3.0 includes five country codes, for the countries for which keyboard drivers are available. DOS 3.1 adds nine more countries and keyboards. If you do not add

COUNTRY = *NNN*

to your CONFIG.SYS file, your computer will default to the standard United States formats.

The country code affects not only the DATE and TIME commands, but the way dates and times are displayed in directory entries and the form in which you must enter dates and times as parameters to DOS commands. Figure 17.1 shows a directory display with the computer configured for Finland.

```
Volume in drive A is PC-DOS 3.30
Directory of A:\

COMMAND  COM    25307  17.03.87  12.00
CONFIG   SYS      250  29.07.87  16.53
NORMAL   BAT      512  26.06.87  14.06
ANSI     SYS     1678  17.03.87  12.00
APPEND   EXE     5825  17.03.87  12.00
ASSIGN   COM     1561  17.03.87  12.00
ATTRIB   EXE     9529  17.03.87  12.00
BACKUP   COM    31919  18.03.87  12.00
BASIC    COM     1063  17.03.87  12.00
BASIC    PIF      369  17.03.87  12.00
BASICA   PIF      369  17.03.87  12.00
BASICA   COM    36403  17.03.87  12.00
CHKDSK   COM     9850  18.03.87  12.00
COMP     COM     4214  17.03.87  12.00
COPY35   COM     2366  20.01.87  12.00
COUNTRY  SYS    11285  17.03.87  12.00
DEBUG    COM    15897  17.03.87  12.00
DISKCOMP COM     5879  17.03.87  12.00
DISKCOPY COM     6295  17.03.87  12.00
DISPLAY  SYS    11290  17.03.87  12.00
DRIVER   SYS     1196  17.03.87  12.00
EDLIN    COM     7526  17.03.87  12.00
EGA      CPI    49065  18.03.87  12.00
FASTOPEN EXE     3919  17.03.87  12.00
FDISK    COM    48216  18.03.87  12.00
FIND     EXE     6434  17.03.87  12.00
FORMAT   COM    11616  18.03.87  12.00
GRAFTABL COM     6128  17.03.87  12.00
GRAPHICS COM     3300  17.03.87  12.00
JOIN     EXE     8969  17.03.87  12.00
KEYB     COM     9056  17.03.87  12.00
KEYBOARD SYS    19766  17.03.87  12.00
LABEL    COM     2377  17.03.87  12.00
4201     CPI    17089  18.03.87  12.00
5202     CPI      459  17.03.87  12.00
LCD      CPI    10752  17.03.87  12.00
MODE     COM    15487  17.03.87  12.00
MORE     COM      313  17.03.87  12.00
NLSFUNC  EXE     3060  17.03.87  12.00
PRINT    COM     9026  17.03.87  12.00
PRINTER  SYS    13590  17.03.87  12.00
RECOVER  COM     4299  18.03.87  12.00
MORTGAGE BAS     6251  17.03.87  12.00
REPLACE  EXE    11775  17.03.87  12.00
RESTORE  COM     4299  17.03.87  12.00
```

Figure 17.1 ▲ *A Directory with Finnish Dates.*

```
SELECT     COM     4163   17.03.87   12.00
SHARE      EXE     8608   17.03.87   12.00
SORT       EXE     1977   17.03.87   12.00
SUBST      EXE     9909   17.03.87   12.00
SYS        COM     4766   17.03.87   12.00
TREE       COM     3571   17.03.87   12.00
VDISK      SYS     3455   17.03.87   12.00
XCOPY      EXE    11247   17.03.87   12.00
CONFIG     BAK      246   29.07.87   13.46
AUTOEXEC   BAT      374   29.07.87   12.50
TEMP       TXT      384   29.06.87   15.31
AUTOEXEC   BAK      384   29.06.87   15.31
FINNISH    BAT       62   29.07.87   13.46
          58 File(s)      611840 bytes free
```

Figure 17.1 ▲ *A Directory with Finnish Dates (continued).*

NATIONALIZING YOUR KEYBOARD

To nationalize the keyboard, DOS releases 3.0 through 3.2 include the files

KEYBFR.COM

KEYBGR.COM

KEYBIT.COM

KEYBSP.COM

KEYBUK.COM

These files load keyboard layouts for France, Germany, Italy, Spain, and the United Kingdom, respectively. Some versions of DOS have slightly different names for these programs, and some have keyboards for other countries. In addition, some MS-DOS versions include a Dvorak keyboard layout among their keyboard configuration files. To choose an alternate keyboard, type the command

   KEYB*CC*

where CC is the two-letter code for the country. If you want to use one of these layouts regularly, you should place this command in your AUTOEXEC file.

Once you load an alternate keyboard layout, you can always switch back to the default (United States) layout by pressing Ctrl-Alt-F1. Similarly, you can switch back to the alternate layout by pressing Ctrl-Alt-F2. However, you may not be able to make this switch when your software is active, especially if it takes over the function keys. Some RAM-resident programs may interfere with these toggle keys as well. You can enter the default characters of the punctuation and special-symbol keys by holding down the Alt key while pressing them.

For reference, the country codes for both nationality defaults and alternate keyboards appear in Table 17.1. Diagrams of some of these keyboard layouts appear in Appendix A. If you are interested in a nationality that does not appear in Appendix A, consult the DOS documentation.

Many European languages require accent marks. Some national keyboards produce accented characters by assigning them to the keyboard.

COUNTRY	COUNTRY CODE	KEYBOARD CODE
Australia	061*	US
Belgium	031*	FR
Denmark	045*	
Finland	358*	
France	033	FR
Germany	049	GR
Italy	039	IT
Israel	972*	
Norway	047*	
Spain	034	SP
Sweden	046*	
Switzerland	041*	FR, GR
United Kingdom	044	UK
United States	001	US

* Available in DOS 3.2 only

Table 17.1 ▲ *Codes for Nationalizing Your Computer in DOS 3.0–3.2.*

As you can see in Table H.1, many of the extended ASCII characters (above 127) are accented characters. The keyboard programs simply map these characters to positions on the keyboard.

However, some languages require additional accented characters. For these languages, the programs provide *dead keys*—keys that produce no character when struck, but place an accent mark over the next character, if an accent mark would be valid in the language. Some national keyboards also have keys that can produce three or four characters, instead of the usual two. These keyboards have the extra character symbols on the key cap, like the word *Break* on the Scroll Lock key. To produce these characters, you have to hold down the Alt, Ctrl, or Alt and Shift keys, while pressing the character key.

Displaying International Characters on a Color Monitor

If you use a color graphics adapter, you must use an extra command to be able to see the international characters. The GRAFTABL command is a small, memory-resident program that lets these characters show up on standard color monitors using a CGA card. If you have a monochrome, monographics, or EGA adapter, you do not need this command.

Be careful to use the GRAFTABL command only once each time you boot up. Each time you invoke the program it is loaded again. This serves no function and wastes memory.

The SELECT Command

PC-DOS 3.X

To simplify both creating boot disks and choosing a country, PC-DOS 3.X (and some computers' versions of MS-DOS 3.X) includes a SELECT command. This command takes two parameters: the numeric country code and the two-letter country symbol, which appear in Table 17.1. For example, to load the default formats for Spanish-speaking countries and the Spanish keyboard, you would type

SELECT 032 SP

The action of the SELECT command varies with the release of PC-DOS. All versions of the command create a bootable copy of the DOS floppy disk (or a bootable hard disk), but they do so by different means. If you have two floppy disk drives, it will make the copy in drive B. If you have one, you will have to swap disks.

 Warning: Do not use SELECT to nationalize your hard disk unless you also want to format it.

PC-DOS 3.0

When you invoke the SELECT command in PC-DOS 3.0, the DOS disk is copied using the DISKCOPY command. Next, a CONFIG.SYS file is written, including only the COUNTRY=*NNN* command. Finally, the following AUTOEXEC.BAT file is written:

```
PATH \;
KEYBCC
ECHO OFF
CLS
DATE
TIME
VER
```

PC-DOS 3.1

The PC-DOS 3.1 version of SELECT uses DISKCOMP to verify the copy before writing the CONFIG.SYS and AUTOEXEC.BAT files.

PC-DOS 3.2

The PC-DOS 3.2 version of SELECT does not use DISKCOPY. Rather, it first formats the target disk, then creates the AUTOEXEC and CONFIG files, and finally copies the files from the source using the XCOPY command. This means that if you already have a CONFIG.SYS or AUTOEXEC.BAT file on your source disk, your old file will wipe out the new one.

If you already have a CONFIG.SYS and AUTOEXEC.BAT file, the easiest way to nationalize your computer is to add the COUNTRY-=*NNN* command to your CONFIG file and the KEYBCC command to your AUTOEXEC file.

NATIONALIZING YOUR COMPUTER WITH PC-DOS 3.3

As of this writing, the only released version of DOS 3.3 is PC-DOS 3.3. The details of nationalizing a computer with this version of DOS are based on details of IBM hardware. Therefore a bit of history is in order. You can safely skip this section if you only want to know how to do it.

A Bit of History

IBM PCs sold outside the United States have key caps appropriate to the country in which they are sold. With previous releases of DOS, as you have seen, you had to load a special device driver to change the computer's defaults and another program to remap the keyboard so that the keys produced the characters shown on the key caps.

The keyboard remapping program used the standard MS-DOS character set as illustrated in Table H.1, with four exceptions. Slightly different character sets were used in computers sold for use in Norway or Denmark, Portugal, or French Canada. IBM referred to these character sets as *code pages*. These code pages were installed by using the appropriate country code.

Two types of IBM printers sold in these countries contained a special ROM chip that allowed the printers to print all the characters that the keyboard produced. IBM enhanced graphics adapters sold in these countries contained a similar chip so that EGA monitors could display the characters.

With PC-DOS 3.3, however, a new international font has become available. This font can be used with 11 different languages, including the four for which special fonts were originally provided. (For reference, the code page numbers associated with the various fonts appear in Table 17.2.) However, it will not accurately reproduce files created with the three alternate fonts provided with earlier versions of DOS or with the standard font. Therefore, some means had to be provided for switching between the old font and the international font. Thus was *code page switching* born. IBM wants you to use both your old font for reading files that you created with it and the new font for greater compatibility with other European languages.

The international font differs from the standard MS-DOS font only in the characters with ASCII codes of 128 or higher. Table H.5, in Appendix H, shows the high-range ASCII characters for the international font.

New Nationalizing Files and Commands

So much for the whys and wherefores. Now on to the whats. We'll get to the hows shortly.

To complicate nationalizing the computer, PC-DOS 3.3 now requires you to use up to 11 different files and a new DOS command, depending on your hardware. These are the files and brief descriptions of what they do:

▲ KEYB.COM is now the only keyboard-layout file. The two-character country code is now passed to the program as a parameter; for example, the code for Italy would be

   KEYB IT

There are now 17 different keyboard codes to choose from, as shown in Table 17.3.

▲ KEYBOARD.SYS contains the information that KEYB.COM needs to decide which characters to map to which keys. Despite its extension, it is *not* a device driver to be loaded in the CONFIG.SYS file. However, you must either keep it on the boot directory or specify the path to its location when you load the keyboard driver.

FONT	CODE PAGE NUMBER
United States	437
International	850
Portugal	860
French Canada	863
Norway and Denmark	865

Table 17.2 ▲ *Code Pages for Nationalizing Your Keyboard*

▲ COUNTRY.SYS contains the information for each of the countries supported (see Table 17.3) regarding date format, time format, capitalization conventions for accented characters, proper alphabetical order, and the character used as a decimal separator and the currency symbol. COUNTRY.SYS also contains information on which standard uppercase characters DOS will use in

COUNTRY	COUNTRY CODE	KEYBOARD CODE	OLD CODE PAGE	NEW CODE PAGE
Arabic	785	*	*	*
Australia	061	US	437	850
Belgium	031	BE	437	850
Canada (English)	001	US	437	850
Canada (French)	002	CF	863	850
Denmark	045	DK	865	850
Finland	358	SU	437	850
France	033	FR	437	850
Germany	049	GR	437	850
Israel	972	*	*	*
Italy	039	IT	437	850
Latin America	003	LA	437	850
Norway	047	NO	865	850
Portugal	351	PO	860	850
Spain	034	SP	437	850
Sweden	046	SV	437	850
Switzerland (French)	041	SF	437	850
Switzerland (German)	041	SG	437	850
United Kingdom	044	UK	437	850
United States	001	US	437	850

* Not available

Table 17.3 ▲ *Nationalizing Codes for DOS 3.3.*

file names when accented characters from the keyboard are used to enter the name. It is used to support the COUNTRY= command in CONFIG.SYS.

▲ DISPLAY.SYS, unlike COUNTRY.SYS, *is* a device driver, loaded through the CONFIG.SYS file after ANSI.SYS. It allows you to display international characters on EGA and LCD monitors and the new PS/2 displays. It in turn calls

▲ EGA.CPI for EGA monitors and PS/2s, or

▲ LCD.CPI for LCD monitors. (CPI stands for *code page information.*)

▲ PRINTER.SYS performs a similar function for the two IBM printers that can print international characters. It calls either

▲ 4201.CPI for the IBM ProPrinter, or

▲ 5202.CPI for the IBM QuietWriter III printer.

▲ NLSFUNC.EXE (for *national language support function*) is a RAM-resident program that prepares areas of memory to handle the alternate fonts. It can also call COUNTRY.SYS if you forget to include the COUNTRY= command in CONFIG.SYS.

▲ MODE.COM, our old friend, is now used to prepare specific code pages for use by the devices supported by DISPLAY.SYS and COUNTRY.SYS.

The new DOS internal command is CHCP, which stands for *change code page.* It is used to switch between two fonts that you have already set up using device drivers, NLSFUNC.EXE and MODE.COM.

Of course, if you use a color graphics adapter, you must still use GRAFTABL to be able to see any of the international characters.

Setting Up a National Keyboard

Now that we know what we're up against, let's get our computer to speak Finnish. You can try some other language if you like. Just use the appropriate country code, keyboard code, and code page numbers from Table 17.3. To see which keys will produce which characters for seven selected languages, consult Appendix A.

We'll assume the following:

▲ You have an EGA and an EGA monitor.

▲ You bought your equipment in the United States.

▲ You have an IBM ProPrinter.

▲ All your device drivers are in the root directory on drive C.

We'll begin with the CONFIG.SYS file. You'll need to install ANSI.SYS, the country code, the display driver information, and the printer driver information. Along with whatever else you put in your CONFIG.SYS file, you'll have to include the following code:

```
DEVICE = ANSI.SYS
COUNTRY = 358 COUNTRY.SYS
DEVICE = DISPLAY.SYS CON = (EGA,437) DISPLAY.SYS
DEVICE = PRINTER.SYS LPT1 = (4201,437) PRINTER.SYS
```

The first line loads ANSI.SYS. The second line establishes the nationality defaults for Finland. The third line tells DOS that the display device you will use is an EGA, with a ROM character generator using the United States character set. Similarly, the last line tells DOS that you have a ProPrinter (model 4201) with the same character ROM. If the files you need to use are not on the boot directory, you can include drive and path specifiers before the file names.

You can do a great deal more with these commands, but first let's complete our experiment. Now that DOS knows about your devices, you have to actually get the computer to produce the characters you want from the proper keyboard. The file FINNISH.BAT, shown in Listing 17.1, will do the rest of the job.

This program assumes that all the necessary files (NLSFUNC.EXE, KEYB.COM, KEYBOARD.SYS, MODE.COM, EGA.CPI, and 4201.CPI) are either in the current directory or on the search path.

```
1: ECHO OFF
2: NLSFUND
3: KEYB SU
4: MODE CON CP PREP=((850)EGA.CPI)
5: MODE LPT1 CP PREP=((850)4201.CPI)
6: CHCP 850
```

Listing 17.1 ▲ *FINNISH.BAT.*

Here is what this program does:

2:    Loads NLSFUNC, which prepares the computer to deal
      with code pages.
3:    Invokes the keyboard program, with the code for Finland.
4–5: Prepares the international font (code page 850) for use by
      the EGA and the printer, respectively. CP PREP is short
      for *codepage prepare*, which you can use if you prefer. After
      these commands execute, you will see the message

MODE Prepare Codepage function completed

6:    Makes the international font current.

You should see the screen jump when this command is executed, as it
jumps to another page of video memory. You'll also notice that some
characters look different. Uppercase O's, for example, will have
straighter sides than usual, and the slashed zero will be replaced by one
with a dot in the center. You'll find that the = key and the] key are now
dead keys. They place umlauts or grave accents over the vowels.

To return to your computer's native mode, type

CHCP 437

and press Ctrl-Alt-F1. Although currency symbols and date and time
formats will still be Finnish, your keyboard and screen should behave as
though they were in the United States again.

More Arcane Syntax

If you bought your computer in one of the four countries that uses a special character ROM chip, or if you want to do some other strange
things, you need slightly different values in the commands shown
above. In particular, DISPLAY.SYS and PRINTER.SYS have other
options, none of which you can use if you use a monochrome or regular
color monitor.

The full syntax for DISPLAY.SYS is

**DEVICE = DISPLAY.SYS CON = (*TYPE*,[*PAGE*],[*#PAGES*],
[*SUBFONTS*])**

These parameters refer to the following options:

▲ *TYPE* is the type of display adapter. Use EGA for the EGA and
for PS/2 computers, or LCD for computers with an LCD display.

You can also use MONO or CGA as parameters here, but they don't do anything.

▲ *PAGE* is the number of the code page included in the adapter's character ROM chip. This will depend on its country of purchase. See the last column in Table 17.3 for the most likely suspect.

▲ *#PAGES* is the number of additional code pages you want to use. Acceptable values range from 0 to 12, with the default being 2 for the EGA and PS/2, and 1 for LCD monitors. If you want to look at all five code pages supplied with PC-DOS 3.3, set this value to 5.

▲ *SUBFONTS* refers to the EGA's ability to display more than 25 rows of 80 characters. It accomplishes this by creating smaller-than-normal character cells. The font of characters for each size cell is called a *subfont*. The default is 2 for the EGA and PS/2 computers and 1 for LCD monitors. It's none too clear how you get your computer to use these fonts. Presumably, some software makes use of them, and they need to be loaded if your software needs them.

PRINTER.SYS has a similar range of parameters. The full syntax is

```
DEVICE = PRINTER.SYS
LPTN = (TYPE,[PAGE],[PAGE2,...PAGEN],[#PAGES])
```

The parameters refer to the following options:

▲ LPTN is the parallel port to which the printer is attached.

▲ *TYPE* is the type of printer. The ProPrinter is 4201, the Quiet-Writer III is 5202.

▲ *PAGE* is the code page built into the printer's ROM. Some printers have two such pages, in which case both should be specified.

▲ *PAGE2,...PAGEN* represents the additional code pages you want to prepare for the printer. If you have specified two in the previous parameter, you cannot add any code pages here.

▲ *#PAGES* is the number of additional pages that can be prepared. The default is 0, the maximum is 12. A buffer in memory has to be set aside for each additional page.

If you have more than one printer that is compatible with the

PRINTER.SYS command, you can set up code pages for both with a single command line; for example,

```
DEVICE = PRINTER SYS LPT1 = (5202,850,5)
LPT2 = (4201,437,2)
```

There are a few tricks to using the code page parameters for MODE as well. First, the code pages you name as parameters must be valid for the country specified by the COUNTRY= command. In most countries, the code page in ROM is 437, which means that the only valid code page parameter is 850. If your code page in ROM is something other than 437, then you can have two parameters: 850 plus the other code page for your country.

APPENDIX A

INTERNATIONAL
KEYBOARD
LAYOUTS

T HE FOLLOWING DIAGRAMS show the keyboard layouts for PC, PC-XT, and AT computers for seven national keyboards. (Since the PC/AT and XT are not available for the Netherlands, the Enhanced PC and Convertible are shown for that country.) Dead keys are shaded.

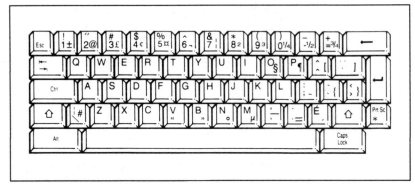

Figure A.1 ▲ *French-Canadian Keyboard: PC and PC/XT.*

Dead Keys: ´ ` ^ ¨ ˛

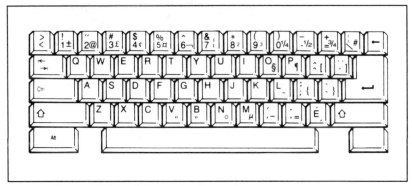

Figure A.2 ▲ *French-Canadian Keyboard: AT.*

Dead Keys: ´ ` ^ ¨ ˛

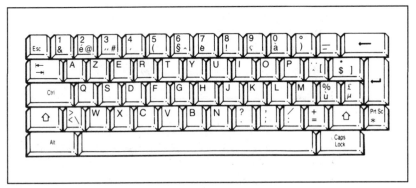

Figure A.3 ▲ *French Keyboard: PC and PC/XT.*

Dead Keys: ¨ ´ ^

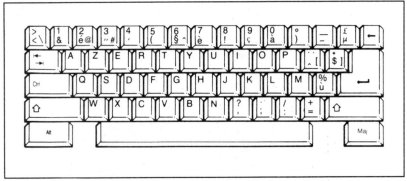

Figure A.4 ▲ *French Keyboard: AT.*

Dead Keys: ´ ¨ ^

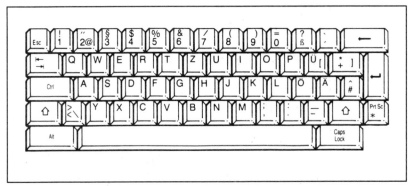

Figure A.5 ▲ *German Keyboard: PC and PC/XT.*

Dead Keys: ´ `

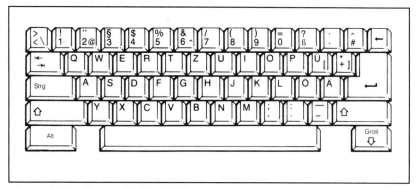

Figure A.6 ▲ *German Keyboard: AT.*

Dead Keys: ´ `

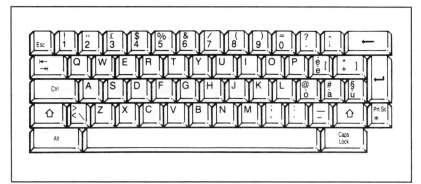

Figure A.7 ▲ *Italian Keyboard: PC and PC/XT.*

No Dead Keys

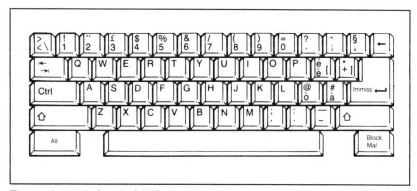

Figure A.8 ▲ *Italian Keyboard: AT.*

No Dead Keys

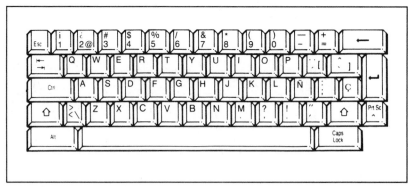

Figure A.9 ▲ *Latin American Keyboard: PC and PC/XT.*

Dead Keys: ¨ ´ ` ^

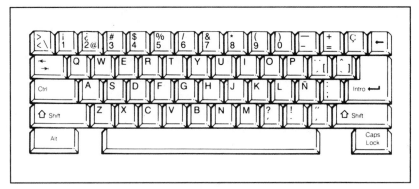

Figure A.10 ▲ *Latin American Keyboard: AT.*

Dead Keys: ¨ ´ ` ^

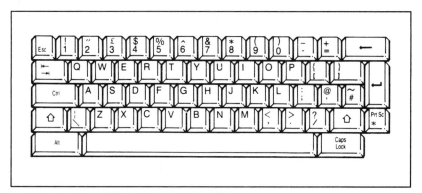

Figure A.11 ▲ *U.K Keyboard: PC and PC/XT.*

No Dead Keys

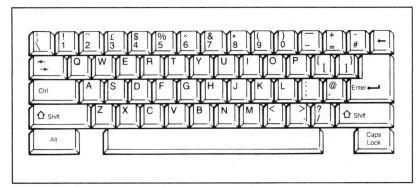

Figure A.12 ▲ *U. K. Keyboard: AT.*

No Dead Keys

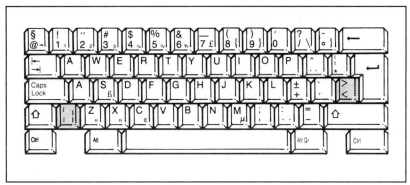

Figure A.13 ▲ *Dutch Keyboard: Enhanced PC.*

No Dead Keys

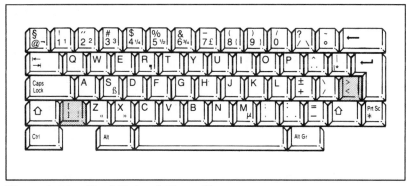

Figure A.14 ▲ *Dutch Keyboard: Convertible.*

No Dead Keys

A P P E N D I X B

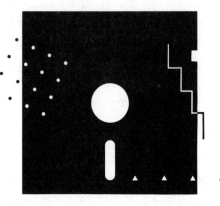

A N S I   E S C A P E
S E Q U E N C E S

GRAPHICS DISPLAY

The codes in Table B.1 establish the foreground and background colors on a color display. On a monochrome monitor, they establish the attributes of the displayed text. The syntax is

^ [[N;...;Nm

where N is any value from Table B.1.

Any number of values may be included in a single escape sequence, as long as they are separated by semicolons. However, there must not be a semicolon between the final value and the terminating code m. Note

COLOR	FOREGROUND	BACKGROUND
Black	30	40
Blue	34	44
Green	32	42
Cyan	36	46
Red	31	41
Magenta	35	45
Yellow	33	43
White	37	47

VIDEO MODES	PARAMETERS
All attributes off	0
High-intensity text	1
Underlined text*	4
Blinking text	5
Inverse video	7
Concealed text	8

*Available in monochrome only.

Table B.1 ▲ *Graphics Display Codes.*

that the code for blue text will result in underlined text on a monochrome monitor (if the background is black), and the codes for black text on a white background will appear as inverse video on a monochrome monitor.

VIDEO MODE

The codes in Table B.2 are used to establish the video mode. They are equivalent to specific parameters to the MODE, SETUP, or CONFIG command. The syntax for establishing the video mode is

^ [[= Nh

or

^ [[= Nl

where N is any value from Table B.2.

WORD WRAP

To establish word wrap on the screen (the default setting) use the sequence

^ [[?7h

VIDEO MODE	CODE	EQUIVALENT MODE COMMAND
40 × 25 black & white	0	MODE BW40
40 × 25 color	1	MODE CO40
80 × 25 black & white	2	MODE BW80
80 × 25 color	3	MODE CO80
320 × 200 color graphics	4	MODE COGR
320 × 200 black & white graphics	5	MODE BWGR
640 × 400 high-resolution graphics	6	MODE HIGR

Table B.2 ▲ *Video Modes.*

To eliminate word wrap, so that lines longer than 80 characters are truncated, use the sequence

[[?7l

CURSOR POSITIONING

The escape sequences in Table B.3 establish the position of the cursor on the screen.

ESCAPE SEQUENCE	EFFECT
^[[row;columnH	Moves the cursor to the specified row and column. When no parameters are given, places the cursor in the home position.
^[[row;columnf	Has the same effect as the H terminating code.
^[[rowA	Moves the cursor up the specified number of rows.
^[[rowB	Moves the cursor down the specified number of rows.
^[[columnC	Moves the cursor forward the specified number of columns.
^[[columnD	Moves the cursor backward the specified number of columns.
^[[s	Records the position of the cursor at the time the escape sequence is issued.
^[[u	Restores the cursor to the position recorded by ^[[s.
^[[2J	Clears the screen, and places the cursor in the home position.
^[[K	Erases from the current cursor position to the end of the current line.
^[[row;columnR	Reports on the screen the position of the cursor at the time when the escape sequence was issued.

Table B.3 ▲ *Escape Sequences for Positioning the Cursor.*

REASSIGNING KEYBOARD FUNCTIONS

Keyboard functions can be reassigned by inserting the decimal ASCII code (or the extended ASCII code from Table H.3) for the key to be defined, followed by the new value for the key, expressed either as an ASCII code or a string in quotation marks. To have the string end in a carriage return, end the sequence with ASCII code 13. Extended ASCII codes are prefaced with a 0 and a semicolon. The new value is separated from the old value by a semicolon, and each ASCII value or string is separated from the others by semicolons. The sequence is terminated with a *p*. Table B.4 shows some examples.

To clear key assignments, you must assign them to themselves. For example, to clear the assignments illustrated in Table B.4, issue the following escape sequences:

        ˄[[65;65p
        ˄[[72;72p
        ˄[[0;68;0;68p

ESCAPE SEQUENCE	EFFECT
˄[[65;80p	Pressing shifted A displays an uppercase P.
˄[[72;"Help";13p	Pressing shifted H displays the word Help, followed by a carriage return.
˄[[0;68;"DIR B:";13p	Pressing F10 issues the command DIR B:.

Table B.4 ▲ *Sample Key Reassignment Codes.*

APPENDIX C

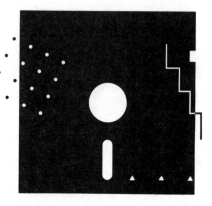

SOURCE CODE FOR ASSEMBLY-LANGUAGE PROGRAMS

T HE YN AND CHOOSE programs are presented in Chapter 6, along with two methods of entering these assembly-language programs. The source code for YN.ASM is shown in Listing C.1, and the source code for CHOOSE.ASM appears in Listing C.2.

```
;-------------------------------------------------------------------
;FILENAME: YN.ASM
;FUNCTION: Prints a message entered on the DOS command line followed
;          by the prompt '(Y/N)'.  Waits for keyboard input.  Returns
;          1 if 'Y' or 'y' is typed, 0 if 'N' or 'n' is typed.
;To create YN.COM using Microsoft or IBM macro assembler:
;        Type    MASM YN; (semicolon required)
;        Type    LINK YN; (semicolon required)
;        Type    EXE2BIN YN.EXE YN.COM
;AUTHOR  : Joe Campbell 2/6/86
;-------------------------------------------------------------------
PROG    SEGMENT BYTE    PUBLIC
ASSUME  CS:PROG,CS:PROG,SS:PROG
ORG 100H
yn      PROC    NEAR
        ;;
        mov     bx,81H                  ;point at command line tail in PSP
        add     bl,BYTE PTR [DS:80H]    ;add number of chars in tail
        mov     BYTE PTR [bx],'$'       ;put string terminator at end of tail
        mov     dx,82H                  ;now point DX at tail, minus space
        call    printit                 ;display message on screen
        mov     dx,OFFSET ynmsg
        call    printit
again:
        mov     ah,7                    ;DOS keyboard input function
        int     21H
        and     al,0DFH                 ;make upper case
        cmp     al,'Y'
        mov     cl,1                    ;return code temporarily in CL
        je      exit
        cmp     al,'N'
        mov     cl,0                    ;return code temporarily in AH
        jne     again
exit:
        mov     dx,OFFSET crlf          ;create newline on screen
        call    printit
        xchg    cl,al                   ;return code to CL for return to DOS
        mov     ah,4CH                  ;return to DOS with error code in AL
        int     21H
ynmsg:  DB      ' (Y/N)?$'
crlf:   db      0DH,0AH,'$'

printit:
        mov     ah,9
        int     21H
        ret
        ;;
yn      ENDP
prog    ENDS
END     yn
```

Listing C.1 ▲ *Source Code for YN.ASM.*

```
;--------------------------------------------------------------------
;FILENAME: CHOOSE.ASM
;FUNCTION: Compares keyboard character to characters on DOS command
;          line, ignoring their case.  Returns an error code based on
;          the character's position relative to the END of the command
;          line list.  For example, if the command line were ABCDEF,
;          typing A would return 5, while typing F would return a 0.
;To create CHOOSE.COM using Microsoft or IBM macro assembler:
;          Type   MASM CHOOSE;        (semicolon required)
;          Type   LINK CHOOSE;        (semicolon required)
;          Type   EXE2BIN CHOOSE.EXE CHOOSE.COM
;AUTHOR  : Joe Campbell 2/6/86
;--------------------------------------------------------------------
PROG      SEGMENT BYTE    PUBLIC
ASSUME    CS:PROG,CS:PROG,SS:PROG
ORG 100H
choose    PROC    NEAR
          cmp     BYTE PTR [DS:80H],0    ;exit if nothing on command line
          je      onlist
          dec     BYTE PTR [DS:80H]         ;adjust count for space
                  ;;raise command line to upper case
          mov     bx,82H
          xor     cx,cx                  ;clear CX
          mov     cl,BYTE PTR [DS:80H]   ;number of bytes on command line ...
cmdloop:
          and     BYTE PTR [bx],0DFH     ;raise to upper
          inc     bx
          dec     cx
          loop    cmdloop
                  ;;
          cld
          mov     ax,ds                  ;set up ES:DI for SCASB
          mov     es,ax
again:
          mov     di,82H
          xor     cx,cx                  ;clear CX
          mov     cl,BYTE PTR [DS:80H]   ;number of bytes on command line ...
          mov     ah,7                   ;DOS keyboard input function
          int     21H
          and     al,0DFH                ;upper
          cmp     al,'A'
          jb      again
          cmp     al,'Z'
          ja      again
cmploop:
          scasb                          ;"CMP AL, [ES:DI]"
          je      onlist
          loop    cmploop
          jmp     again                  ;not on list, back to keyboard
onlist:
          dec     cl                     ;adjust cardinal to ordinal
          mov     al,cl                  ;AL = ordinal for return as ERRORCODE
          mov     ah,4CH
          int     21H
                  ;;
choose    ENDP
prog      ENDS
END       choose
```

Listing C.2 ▲ *Source Code for CHOOSE.ASM.*

APPENDIX D

ACCESS GUIDE TO UTILITY SOFTWARE

Computer Thaumaturgy DOS Utilities, Set A

Computer Thaumaturgy, Inc.
1212 Miami Valley Tower
40 W. Fourth Street
Dayton, OH 45402-1828
Suggested retail price: $30
(Often available for $5)

Disk Optimizer 2.0

SoftLogic Solutions
530 Chestnut Street
Manchester, NH 03101
(800) 272-9900
Suggested retail price: $49.95

Disk OrGanizer (DOG)

SoftGAMs Software
1411 10th Avenue
Oakland, CA 94606
Registration fee: $20

DPath + PLUS

Personal Business Solutions, Inc.
P. O. Box 757
Frederick, MD 21701
(301) 865-3376
Suggested retail price: $49

Fastback V5.14

Fifth Generation Systems
7942 Picardy Avenue #B-350
Baton Rouge, LA 70809
(800) 225-2775
In California (213) 439-2191
Suggested retail price: $179
May require DMA-FIX board: $40

File Facility

IBM Personally Developed Software
P. O. Box 3280
Wallingford, CT 06494
(800) IBM-PCSW
Suggested retail price: $19.95

HomeBase 2.5

Includes:
    Power Menu
    Dr. DOS

Brown Bag Software
2105 South Bascom Ave. , Suite 164
Campbell, CA 95008
(800) 323-5335
Suggested retail price: $89.95

JRAM Combo Pack

Includes:
    JBOOT and JDRIVE RAM-disk software
    JET fast copy program
    JSPOOL print spooler

Tall Tree Systems
1032 Elwell Court
Suite 124
Palo Alto, CA 94303
(415) 964-1980
Suggested retail price: $60

Keyworks

Alpha Software Corp.
30 B Street
Burlington, MA 01803
(617) 229-2924
Suggested retail price: $99.95

Mace Utilities 4.10

Paul Mace Software
400 Williamson Way
Ashland, OR 97520
(800) 523-0258
(503) 488-0224
Suggested retail price: $99

The Norton Utilities, Release 4.0 and Advanced Edition

Peter Norton Computing
2210 Wilshire Boulevard
Santa Monica, CA 90403
(213) 453-2361
Suggested retail price:
Release 4.0: $99.95
Advanced Edition: $150

PC Tools R3.23

Central Point Software
9700 S.W. Capitol Highway
Suite 100
Portland, OR 97219
(503) 244-5782
Suggested retail price: $39.95

PolyWindows DeskPlus

Polytron Corp.
P. O. Box 787
Hillsboro, OR 97123
(800) 547-4000
Suggested retail price: $84.95

ProKey V4.0

RoseSoft Inc.
4710 University Way N. E., #601
Seattle, WA 98105
(206) 524-2350
Suggested retail price: $130

Quadmaster III

Includes:
  QSPOOL multiple-printer print spooler
  QSWAP printer-port switcher
  QDISK RAM-disk driver

Quadram Corp.
4355 International Boulevard
Norcross, GA 30093
(404) 923-6666
Suggested retail price: $10

Ready!

Living Videotext, Inc.
2432 Charleston Road
Mountain View, CA 94043
(415) 964-6300
Suggested retail price: $99

SideKick V1.5

Borland International
4585 Scotts Valley Drive
Scotts Valley, CA 95066
(800) 255-8000
In California (800) 742-1133
Suggested retail price: $84.95

SmartKey V5.1, SmartPath

Software Research Technologies, Inc.
3757 Wilshire Boulevard, #211
Los Angeles, CA 90010
(213) 384-5430
(800) 824-5537
Suggested retail price:
SmartKey: $49.95
SmartPath: $29.95

SuperKey V1.11

Borland International
4585 Scotts Valley Drive
Scotts Valley, CA 95066
(800) 255-8000
In California (800) 742-1133
Suggested retail price: $69.95

X2C Extended Memory Board
with Non-Volatile RAM

Franklin Telecom
23141 Verdugo, Suite 104
Laguna Hills, CA 92653
(714) 859-6531
Suggested retail price: $469 for board; $39 for nonvolatile RAM

Public-Domain Software and Shareware   Mention is made in the book of two
types of noncommercial software: *public-domain software* and *shareware*.
Public-domain software comprises programs that have been released to the
public at no cost by their creators. The programs may or may not be
copyrighted, but you are free to use them, copy them, and give them away.

Shareware refers to programs that you may *obtain* for free, but which
you are expected to pay for if you use. Such programs are copyrighted
and are the property of their authors. They are released to the public on
the assumption that you have the right to try it before you buy it. Generally, a license fee establishes you as a registered user and gets you a
printed manual (in place of a disk file) and access to upgrades. Sometimes you even get a commission if someone registers a copy they got
from you.

You can obtain these types of programs at most user's groups. They are
also available on many electronic bulletin boards, from which they can
be downloaded by modem. In addition, several mail-order companies
will sell you disks full of public-domain and/or shareware programs for a
nominal fee.

APPENDIX E

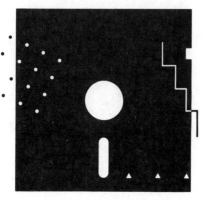

NETWORKING FEATURES OF VERSIONS 3.2 AND 3.3

E ACH VERSION of DOS has contained some new commands, absent in earlier versions. Perhaps the most significant of the new additions introduced in version 3.1 are commands—or enhancements to commands—that allow DOS-based computers to operate as part of a local-area (token-ring or broad-band) network.

NETWORK FEATURES OF DOS 3.1 AND 3.2

When your computer is hooked up to a local-area network (LAN), any computer on the network that has a hard disk or a printer can be set up so that other computers on the network can access them. Setting up a network involves a great deal more than a few DOS commands. You need special network boards installed in each computer, cables to connect them, and software capable of managing the network. In addition, some person must be designated as the network manager. For a complete discussion of setting up and using LANs with DOS-based computers, see *Operating the IBM PC Networks* by Paul Berry (SYBEX, 1986).

The most obvious advantage of a network is that it allows you to share files, such as large databases or spreadsheets, which must be updated frequently. Having the file located on a single computer while allowing access to it by different computers can do a great deal to ensure the integrity of the data. It prevents multiple copies of the file from floating around, each with different revisions. It also allows all those who need access to that file to have it.

Networks and Files

When access to a file is shared, different users can actually use the same file at the same time. This creates the risk of a "deadly embrace"—the situation that occurs when one user tries to read a record that is being modified by another user at the same time. To prevent this, a file or a record can be *locked* while it is in use. Thus, a file can be

- ▲ shared by several users, each with exclusive access to a record, by means of record locking.

- ▲ shared by several users without exclusive access.

- ▲ used exclusively by a single user anywhere in the network, by means of file locking.

Some programs are designed to be used with networks. However, since LANs are relatively new, the vast majority are not. When a program is not designed for use on a network, a file can be shared only if it is opened on a read-only basis (something established through the network software). Otherwise, only exclusive (locked) use is possible.

Granting Access

In order for someone else to be able to use files on your hard disk or to use your printer, you must enter the command

SHARE

There are two switches to the SHARE command:

▲ /F:*NNNN*, where *NNNN* is a number of bytes, designates the amount of memory to be used to record the information that DOS needs to keep track of file-sharing operations. For each shared file, you must assign enough bytes to include the full name of the file, including its extension, plus 11. If you do not use the /F switch, the default is 2,048 bytes.

▲ /L:*NN*, where *NN* is a number of locks, designates how many people may have exclusive use of a portion of a file.

Access Levels

Most network software is menu-driven, so that you can establish your position on the network by responding to a series of prompts. When the network is installed, you access the menus by typing the network command

NET

at a DOS prompt. If you are a server or messenger, you can also hit the *Network-request key* (Ctrl-Alt-Brk) to bring up network menus. The menu gives you the option of setting the level of access to the resources on your computer. There are five levels of access:

R   Allows opening the file for reading only.

RW   Allows opening the file for reading or writing.

W   Allows opening the file for writing only. This may result in the file being overwritten completely if the program that uses the file writes to it from the beginning.

WC   Allows write-only access, but also allows the user to delete the file or create a new one.

RWC   Includes all three types of access: read, write, and create or delete.

When the network is loaded, you access a directory on another computer (provided that it has been opened for sharing) as if it were a drive on your own computer. Each computer on the network has a name. You would use the network command NET USE to assign a drive designation to the directory on the computer whose files you want to use. When a directory is opened for sharing, all directories subordinate to it will also be opened. Thus, to make an entire hard disk available, the root directory must be given a name and opened. Say the computer whose files you want to use is given the network name CENTRAL, and its root directory is \MAIN. You would first use the command

NET USE F: \\CENTRAL\MAIN

(The two backslashes indicate a network directory, rather than one on your own computer.)

Then, say, to access the dBASE directory of the CENTRAL computer, you would just type

F:\DBASE

The PERMIT Command

The PERMIT command is supplied with the network software. It allows a computer that does not have a hard disk to share a disk or directory with other computers on the network. However, it also grants exclusive use of your computer to the computer to which permission is granted. In other words, the PERMIT command makes one of your floppy disk drives an appendage of some other computer, and you can no longer use your computer at all. From the point of view of the remote user, however, using this drive is no different from using any other drive to which access is permitted.

The syntax of the PERMIT commmand is

PERMIT *resourcename remotename specialname* [*/access*]

where *resourcename* is the drive and/or path to which you are permitting access; *remotename* is the network name of the computer that you are allowing to use your drive; and *specialname* is a secret name, known to both you and the the operator of the remote computer. The final parameter is one of the five access modes described previously, preceded by a slash.

You can regain control over your computer in one of two ways. Either the person who is using your computer remotely can issue the command

NET USE [*drive*] /D

where *drive* is the virtual-drive designator being used for your computer. Alternatively, you can press Ctrl-Break on your own keyboard.

Sharing Printers

You can attach several printers of different types to a single computer, each with a special network name. If you do, that computer can handle all printing operations. This has the advantage of allowing all of the computers on the network access to several different types of printers. However, such a setup has two serious drawbacks:

▲ It virtually requires that one person be permanently on hand at the computer to which the printers are attached. This person will have to take care of such matters as restocking the printers when they run out of paper, replacing ribbons, unjamming print heads, and preventing all the other nasty things that printers do when you decide not to watch them.

▲ All print jobs are placed in a single print queue even though the text may be sent to different printers. This may result in long delays in waiting for printed output. If you are a real technical wizard, you might be able to find some way of using QSPOOL's four spoolers in conjunction with a network to overcome this limitation.

Setting the Number of Open FCBs

Some software structures its files in records of a uniform length. Many such programs make use of a DOS feature called the *file control block*, or FCB. This block contains information on the name, length, and structure of the file, and it is used to keep track of the location in the file that is being accessed by the program. It is also used in creating, reading, writing to, and deleting files.

Normally, there is no limit to how many file control blocks can be open. However, if you are sharing files through a network, an additional command is needed in the CONFIG.SYS file. This command tells DOS how many file control blocks (that is, how many files) may be open at one time, and how many of those files cannot be closed automatically by DOS if a program tries to open more than the specified number. The syntax of the command is

FCBS = *N,M*

where N is the number of files that can be open at one time, and M is a number, smaller than N, of files that DOS cannot close automatically. The default for the number of open files is four, and for the number that cannot be closed, the default is none.

Setting the Number of Drives

When the network is loaded, virtual drives up to N can be specified without any special commands. However, if you need to refer to more than 14 drives (including virtual drives that you may create with the SUBST command, as well as network drives), you can add a LASTDRIVE= command to the CONFIG.SYS file. The command

LASTDRIVE = Z

will allow you to refer to up to 26 drive designations.

APPENDIX F

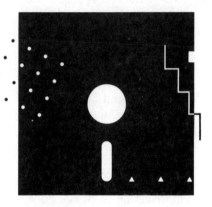

CREATING A
TRUE ASCII
PRINTER
DRIVER FOR
WORDSTAR 4.0

I F YOU WANT TO use WordStar 4.0 to create files that contain extended ASCII characters, such as the border characters found in some of the files in this book, you must make some changes to the ASCII printer driver. The driver supplied with WordStar precedes each high-order ASCII character with an Escape character and follows it with a Ctrl-\. This makes the characters displayable in WordStar, but it sure makes a mess of your screen when you display files containing them at a DOS prompt.

First, enter the file WSASCII.PAT, shown in Listing F.1. Next, you must use WSCHANGE to patch the ASCII printer driver with this file. Type

  WSCHANGE *FILENAME*

where *FILENAME* is the name you use for WS.EXE. Make the following series of menu selections:

1. **B   Printer**
2. **C   Printer driver lib**
3. **D   Change printer driver data**
4. **A   Select a driver**

Enter the number for the driver named ASCII. It will vary, depending on how many drivers you have kept in your library. Select

  E   Driver auto patcher

When asked for a file name, enter

  WSASCII.PAT

WSCHANGE will do the rest. Just keep pressing X until you see the prompt

  Are you through making changes? (Y/N)

and then press Y.

```
XCHAR=00,01,02,03,04,05,06,07,08,09,0A,0B,0C,0D,0E,0F
=10,11,12,13,14,15,16,17,18,19,1A,1B,1C,1D,1E,1F
=80,81,82,83,84,85,86,87,88,89,8A,8B,8C,8D,8E,8F
=90,91,92,93,94,95,96,97,98,99,9A,9B,9C,9D,9E,9F
=A0,A1,A2,A3,A4,A5,A6,A7,A8,A9,AA,AB,AC,AD,AE,AF
=B0,B1,B2,B3,B4,B5,B6,B7,B8,B9,BA,BB,BC,BD,BE,BF
=C0,C1,C2,C3,C4,C5,C6,C7,C8,C9,CA,CB,CC,CD,CE,CF
=D0,D1,D2,D3,D4,D5,D6,D7,D8,D9,DA,DB,DC,DD,DE,DF
=E0,E1,E2,E3,E4,E5,E6,E7,E8,E9,EA,EB,EC,ED,EE,EF
=F0,F1,F2,F3,F4,F5,F6,F7,F8,F9,FA,FB,FC,FD,FE,FF
```

Listing F.1 ▲ *WSASCII.PAT.*

If you use the same printer driver library for all your versions of Word-Star, you need do this only once. If you have created several different libraries, you will have to repeat the procedure for each version of WordStar that uses a different library.

APPENDIX G

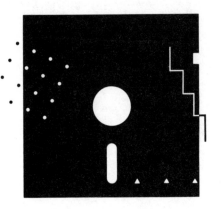

CREATING A KEYBOARD FOR BOX AND BORDER CHARACTERS

I F YOU WOULD LIKE to create an alternate keyboard for typing box and border characters, you can do it by patching one of the keyboard-layout files from DOS 3.0 through 3.2. This appendix will show you how to do this and how to use the resulting program.

This procedure will work *only* with versions 3.0 through 3.2, because earlier versions don't have keyboard-layout files, and version 3.3 uses a different method for altering keyboard layouts. Also, your DOS version's keyboard-layout files must be .COM files, not .EXE files. However, once you have created the file, you may be able to use it with other versions of DOS.

The file BOXKEYS.DEB, shown in Listing G.1, will replace many of the characters on the keyboard with box and border characters in the KEYBUK.COM program from PC-DOS 3.2 *only*. To use it, type the file exactly as listed. Next, be sure that KEYBUK.COM and BOXKEYS.DEB are on the current directory and DEBUG is on the search path. Then type the command

DEBUG<BOXKEYS.DEB

As you can see in the program listing, BOXKEYS.DEB is a script file. It uses the Enter command (E) to replace characters in the original file with the hexadecimal values for the new characters.

If all goes as it should, DEBUG should create BOXKEYS.COM for you. You can load it as you would any other keyboard-layout file. Make sure that you don't have a RAM-resident program loaded that uses Ctrl-Alt for its hot keys. You will need these keys to switch between the new layout and the normal one. (See Chapter 17 for a full explanation of keyboard layouts.)

```
N KEYBUK.COM
L
E 9AB DA C2 BF D5 D1 B8
E 9B2 DF
E 9B4 B0 B1 B2
E 9B9 C3 C5 B4 C6 D8 B5 DE DB DD
E 9C7 C0 C1 D9 D4 CF BE
E 9CE DC
E 9D7 B3 C4 BA CD
E 9E5 C9 CB BB D6 D2 B7
E 9F3 CC CE B9 C7 D7 B6
E A01 C8 CA BC D3 D0 BD
N BOXKEYS.COM
W
Q
```

Listing G.1 ▲ *BOXKEYS.DEB.*

The correspondence between the keys and the new characters is shown in Figure G.1. One advantage of rewriting one of the DOS keyboard programs is that it allows you to assign new values to both upper- and lowercase characters, as we have done with the first six keys on the left side of the bottom three rows. You can't do that with a macro processor, because most of them assign values to keys, rather than to characters.

If you have PC-DOS 3.1 or 3.0, you can create this program by substituting the appropriate addresses shown in Table G.1 for those in the second column of Listing G.1.

Figure G.1 ▲ *Keyboard Character Set Created by BOXKEYS.COM.*

PC-DOS 3.1	PC-DOS 3.0
662	592
669	599
66B	59B
670	5A0
67E	5AE
685	5B5
68D	5BD
69C	5CC
6AA	5DA
6B8	5E8

Table G.1 ▲ *Entry Addresses for PC-DOS 3.0 and 3.1.*

If you have some other version of DOS, you may still be able to create these files. You will have to find the entry addresses yourself. Begin by entering the command

DEBUG KEYBUK.COM

Then search for the familiar keyboard layout. Type

RCX

to see how long the file is, press Ctrl-C, and then enter

S 0 L *NNNN* "asdfg"

where *NNNN* is the length of the file as shown in the CX register. When you find it, display a section of code so that you can see all four keyboard rows in upper- and lowercase, as shown in Figure G.2. The characters you need to replace are shown in boldface. You will have to count from the starting address of each line to find the correct address for each new character. In this example, the entry addresses would be

>3C4D
>3C54
>3C56
>3C5A
>3C69
>3C70
>3C79
>3C87
>3C95
>3CA3

```
XXXX:3C40   32 33 34 35 36 37 38 39-30 2D 3D 08 09 71 77 65    234567890-=..qwe
XXXX:3C50   72 74 79 75 69 6F 70 5B-5D 0D FF 61 73 64 66 67    rtyuiop[]..asdfg
XXXX:3C60   68 6A 6B 6C 3B 27 60 FF-5C 7A 78 63 76 62 6E 6D    hjkl;'`.\zxcvbnm
XXXX:3C70   2C 2E 2F FF 2A FF 20 FF-1B 21 40 23 24 25 5E 26    ,./.*. ..!@#$%^&
XXXX:3C80   2A 28 29 5F 2B 08 00 51-57 45 52 54 59 55 49 4F    *()_+..QWERTYUIO
XXXX:3C90   50 7B 7D 0D FF 41 53 44-46 47 48 4A 4B 4C 3A 22    P{}..ASDFGHJKL:"
XXXX:3CA0   7E FF 7C 5A 58 43 56 42-4E 4D 3C 3E 3F FF 00 FF    ~.|ZXCVBNM<>?...
```

Figure G.2 ▲ *Keyboard Characters Shown in DEBUG.*

APPENDIX H

ASCII TABLES

ASCII	PRINTS	HEX		ASCII	PRINTS	HEX
0 *		0		32 **		20
1	☺	1		33	!	21
2	☻	2		34	"	22
3	♥	3		35	#	23
4	♦	4		36	$	24
5	♣	5		37	%	25
6	♠	6		38	&	26
7	•	7		39	'	27
8	◘	8		40	(	28
9	○	9		41	)	29
10	◙	A		42	*	2A
11	♂	B		43	+	2B
12	♀	C		44	,	2C
13	♪	D		45	–	2D
14	♫	E		46	.	2E
15	☼	F		47	/	2F
16	►	10		48	0	30
17	◄	11		49	1	31
18	↕	12		50	2	32
19	‼	13		51	3	33
20	¶	14		52	4	34
21	§	15		53	5	35
22	▬	16		54	6	36
23	↨	17		55	7	37
24	↑	18		56	8	38
25	↓	19		57	9	39
26	→	1A		58	:	3A
27	←	1B		59	;	3B
28	∟	1C		60	<	3C
29	↔	1D		61	=	3D
30	▲	1E		62	>	3E
31	▼	1F		63	?	3F

*Nonprintable character   **Space

Table H.1 ▲ *MS-DOS Printable ASCII Characters.*

ASCII	PRINTS	HEX		ASCII	PRINTS	HEX
64	@	40		96	`	60
65	A	41		97	a	61
66	B	42		98	b	62
67	C	43		99	c	63
68	D	44		100	d	64
69	E	45		101	e	65
70	F	46		102	f	66
71	G	47		103	g	67
72	H	48		104	h	68
73	I	49		105	i	69
74	J	4A		106	j	6A
75	K	4B		107	k	6B
76	L	4C		108	l	6C
77	M	4D		109	m	6D
78	N	4E		110	n	6E
79	O	4F		111	o	6F
80	P	50		112	p	70
81	Q	51		113	q	71
82	R	52		114	r	72
83	S	53		115	s	73
84	T	54		116	t	74
85	U	55		117	u	75
86	V	56		118	v	76
87	W	57		119	w	77
88	X	58		120	x	78
89	Y	59		121	y	79
90	Z	5A		122	z	7A
91	[	5B		123	{	7B
92	\	5C		124	:	7C
93	]	5D		125	}	7D
94	^	5E		126	~	7E
95	_	5F		127	⌂	7F

Table H.1 ▲ *MS-DOS Printable ASCII Characters (continued).*

ASCII	PRINTS	HEX	ASCII	PRINTS	HEX
128	Ç	80	160	á	A0
129	ü	81	161	í	A1
130	é	82	162	ó	A2
131	â	83	163	ú	A3
132	ä	84	164	ñ	A4
133	à	85	165	Ñ	A5
134	å	86	166	ª	A6
135	ç	87	167	º	A7
136	ê	88	168	¿	A8
137	ë	89	169	⌐	A9
138	è	8A	170	¬	AA
139	ï	8B	171	½	AB
140	î	8C	172	¼	AC
141	ì	8D	173	¡	AD
142	Ä	8E	174	«	AE
143	Å	8F	175	»	AF
144	É	90	176	░	B0
145	æ	91	177	▒	B1
146	Æ	92	178	▓	B2
147	ô	93	179	│	B3
148	ö	94	180	┤	B4
149	ò	95	181	╡	B5
150	û	96	182	╢	B6
151	ù	97	183	╖	B7
152	ÿ	98	184	╕	B8
153	Ö	99	185	╣	B9
154	Ü	9A	186	║	BA
155	¢	9B	187	╗	BB
156	£	9C	188	╝	BC
157	¥	9D	189	╜	BD
158	₧	9E	190	╛	BE
159	ƒ	9F	191	┐	BF

Table H.1 ▲ *MS-DOS Printable ASCII Characters (continued).*

ASCII	PRINTS	HEX	ASCII	PRINTS	HEX
192	∟	C0	224	α	E0
193	⊥	C1	225	β	E1
194	┬	C2	226	Γ	E2
195	├	C3	227	π	E3
196	─	C4	228	Σ	E4
197	┼	C5	229	σ	E5
198	╞	C6	230	μ	E6
199	╟	C7	231	τ	E7
200	╚	C8	232	Φ	E8
201	╔	C9	233	Θ	E9
202	╩	CA	234	Ω	EA
203	╦	CB	235	δ	EB
204	╠	CC	236	∞	EC
205	═	CD	237	ø	ED
206	╬	CE	238	∈	EE
207	╧	CF	239	∩	EF
208	╨	D0	240	≡	F0
209	╤	D1	241	±	F1
210	╥	D2	242	≥	F2
211	╙	D3	243	≤	F3
212	╘	D4	244	⌠	F4
213	╒	D5	245	⌡	F5
214	╓	D6	246	÷	F6
215	╫	D7	247	≈	F7
216	╪	D8	248	°	F8
217	┘	D9	249	·	F9
218	┌	DA	250	·	FA
219	█	DB	251	√	FB
220	▄	DC	252	ⁿ	FC
221	▌	DD	253	²	FD
222	▐	DE	254	■	FE
223	▀	DF	255 '		FF

Table H.1 ▲ MS-DOS Printable ASCII Characters (continued).

ASCII Value	Control Character	Hex Value	Keyboard Equivalent	Device Control Effect
00	NUL	00	Ctrl-@	Null
01	SOH	01	Ctrl-A	
02	STX	02	Ctrl-B	
03	ETX	03	Ctrl-C	
04	EOT	04	Ctrl-D	
05	ENQ	05	Ctrl-E	
06	ACK	06	Ctrl-F	
07	BEL	07	Ctrl-G	Beep
08	BS	08	Ctrl-H	Backspace
09	HT	09	Ctrl-I	Tab
10	LF	0A	Ctrl-J	Linefeed
11	VT	0B	Ctrl-K	Cursor home
12	FF	0C	Ctrl-L	Form feed
13	CR	0D	Ctrl-M	Carriage return
14	SO	0E	Ctrl-N	
15	SI	0F	Ctrl-O	
16	DLE	10	Ctrl-P	
17	DC1	11	Ctrl-Q	
18	DC2	12	Ctrl-R	
19	DC3	13	Ctrl-S	
20	DC4	14	Ctrl-T	
21	NAK	15	Ctrl-U	
22	SYN	16	Ctrl-V	
23	ETB	17	Ctrl-W	
24	CAN	18	Ctrl-X	
25	EM	19	Ctrl-Y	
26	SUB	1A	Ctrl-Z	
27	ESC	1B	Ctrl-[or Esc	Escape
28	FS	1C	Ctrl-\	Cursor right
29	GS	1D	Ctrl-]	Cursor left
30	RS	1E	Ctrl-^	Cursor up
31	US	1F	Ctrl-_	Cursor down

Table H.2 ▲ *ASCII Control Codes and Their Effects.*

The codes in Table H.3 must be preceded by an ASCII 0 (null); for example, for F10 use 0;68. The numerical order of the codes for alphabetic characters follows the keyboard layout, rather than their order in the alphabet.

KEY OR CHARACTER	CODE
Null	3
Shift-Tab	15
Ctrl-PrtSc	114
Alt –	130
Alt-1	120
Alt-2	121
Alt-3	122
Alt-4	123
Alt-5	124
Alt-6	125
Alt-7	126
Alt-8	127
Alt-9	128
Alt-10	129
Alt-=	131
Alt-A	30
Alt-B	48
Alt-C	46
Alt-D	32
Alt-E	18
Alt-F	33
Alt-G	34
Alt-H	35

Table H.3 ▲ *Extended ASCII Codes.*

Alt-I	23
Alt-J	36
Alt-K	37
Alt-L	38
Alt-M	50
Alt-N	49
Alt-O	24
Alt-P	25
Alt-Q	16
Alt-R	19
Alt-S	31
Alt-T	20
Alt-U	22
Alt-V	47
Alt-X	45
Alt-Y	21
Alt-Z	44
FUNCTION KEYS	
F1	59
F2	60
F3	61
F4	62
F5	63
F6	64
F7	65
F8	66
F9	67

Table H.3 ▲ *Extended ASCII Codes (continued).*

F10	68
Shift-F1	84
Shift-F2	85
Shift-F3	86
Shift-F4	87
Shift-F5	88
Shift-F6	89
Shift-F7	90
Shift-F8	91
Shift-F9	92
Shift-F10	93
Ctrl-F1	94
Ctrl-F2	95
Ctrl-F3	96
Ctrl-F4	97
Ctrl-F5	98
Ctrl-F6	99
Ctrl-F7	100
Ctrl-F8	101
Ctrl-F9	102
Ctrl-F10	103
Alt-F1	104
Alt-F2	105
Alt-F3	106
Alt-F4	107
Alt-F5	108
Alt-F6	109
Alt-F7	110

Table H.3 ▲ *Extended ASCII Codes (continued).*

Alt-F8	111
Alt-F9	112
Alt-F10	113
CURSOR KEYPAD KEYS	
Home	71
Cursor-Up	72
PgUp	73
Cursor-Left	75
Cursor-Right	77
End	79
Cursor-Down	80
PgDn	81
Ins	82
Del	83
Ctrl-Home	119
Ctrl-PgUp	132
Ctrl-Cursor-Left	115
Ctrl-Cursor-Right	116
Ctrl-End	117
Ctrl-PgDn	118

Table H.3 ▲ *Extended ASCII Codes (continued).*

213	209	184		214	210	183	
╒	╤	╕		╓	╥	╖	
198	216	181		199	215	182	
╞	╪	╡		╟	╫	╢	
212	207	190		211	208	189	
╘	╧	╛		╙	╨	╜	
201	203	187	205	218	194	191	196
╔	╦	╗	═	┌	┬	┐	─
204	206	185	186	195	197	180	179
╠	╬	╣	║	├	┼	┤	│
200	202	188		192	193	217	
╚	╩	╝		└	┴	┘	

Table H.4 ▲ *Box and Border Characters*

ASCII	PRINTS	HEX		ASCII	PRINTS	HEX
128	Ç	80		160	á	A0
129	ü	81		161	í	A1
130	é	82		162	ó	A2
131	â	83		163	ú	A3
132	ä	84		164	ñ	A4
133	à	85		165	Ñ	A5
134	å	86		166	ª	A6
135	ç	87		167	º	A7
136	ê	88		168	¿	A8
137	ë	89		169	⌐	A9
138	è	8A		170	¬	AA
139	ï	8B		171	½	AB
140	î	8C		172	¼	AC
141	ì	8D		173	¡	AD
142	Ä	8E		174	«	AE
143	Å	8F		175	»	AF
144	É	90		176	░	B0
145	æ	91		177	▒	B1
146	Æ	92		178	▓	B2
147	ô	93		179	│	B3
148	ö	94		180	┤	B4
149	ò	95		181	╡	B5
150	û	96		182	╢	B6
151	ù	97		183	╖	B7
152	ÿ	98		184	╕	B8
153	Ö	99		185	╣	B9
154	Ü	9A		186	║	BA
155	¢	9B		187	╗	BB
156	£	9C		188	╝	BC
157	¥	9D		189	╜	BD
158	₧	9E		190	╛	BE
159	ƒ	9F		191	┐	BF

Table H.5 ▲ *High-Order ASCII Characters for the International Character Set (Code Page 850).*

ASCII	PRINTS	HEX		ASCII	PRINTS	HEX
192	L	C0		224	α	E0
193	⊥	C1		225	β	E1
194	τ	C2		226	Γ	E2
195	⊦	C3		227	π	E3
196	–	C4		228	Σ	E4
197	+	C5		229	σ	E5
198	⊧	C6		230	μ	E6
199	‖	C7		231	τ	E7
200	⊾	C8		232	Φ	E8
201	⊓	C9		233	θ	E9
202	⊥	CA		234	Ω	EA
203	⊤	CB		235	δ	EB
204	⊩	CC		236	∞	EC
205	=	CD		237	ø	ED
206	⧈	CE		238	∈	EE
207	⊥	CF		239	∩	EF
208	⊔	D0		240	≡	F0
209	⊤	D1		241	±	F1
210	π	D2		242	≥	F2
211	⊔	D3		243	≤	F3
212	⊾	D4		244	⌠	F4
213	⌐	D5		245	⌡	F5
214	π	D6		246	÷	F6
215	‖	D7		247	≈	F7
216	+	D8		248	°	F8
217	⌐	D9		249	•	F9
218	⌐	DA		250	·	FA
219	█	DB		251	√	FB
220	▪	DC		252	ⁿ	FC
221	▌	DD		253	²	FD
222	▐	DE		254	■	FE
223	▪	DF		255		FF

Table H.5 ▲ *High-Order ASCII Characters for the International Character Set (Code Page 850) (continued).*

P R O G R A M I N D E X

I N D E X

Selections from The SYBEX Library

DOS

The ABC's of MS-DOS
Alan R. Miller
224pp. Ref. 395-3
This plain-language guide for new or intermediate users treats everything from first start-up to customizing the system for day-to-day use. Includes useful utilities, plus tips on avoiding traps and recovering from errors.

Mastering DOS*
Judd Robbins
450pp. Ref. 400-3
This four-part, in-depth tutorial addresses the needs of users at all levels. Topics range from running applications, to managing files and directories, configuring the system, batch file programming, and techniques for system developers. A major book.

The MS-DOS Handbook (Second Edition)
Richard Allen King
339pp. Ref. 352-X
Two reference books in one, with separate sections for the programmer and the user. Topics include disk, screen and port control, batch files, networks, MS-DOS/PC-DOS compatibility, and more. Covers version 3.

MS-DOS Power Users Guide, Volume I (Second Edition)*
Jonathan Kamin
397pp. Ref. 345-7
Tips, techniques and programming utilities for high-performance systems. Configuring the system, redirecting I/O, disk, file and directory structures, hard disks, RAM disks, batch programming in depth, and the ANSI.SYS device driver.

Performance Programming Under MS-DOS
Michael J. Young
400pp. Ref. 420-8
Practical techniques for maximizing performance in MS-DOS software by making best use of system resources. Topics include functions, interrupts, devices, multitasking, memory residency and more, with examples in C and assembler.

The ABC's of PC-DOS*
Alan R. Miller
250pp. Ref. 438-0
A beginner's guide to PC-DOS for users of the IBM PC and compatibles – everything from working with disks and files, to using built-in commands, customizing the system, recovering from errors, and adding some handy utilities.

Essential PC-DOS (Second Edition)
Myril Clement Shaw/ Susan Soltis Shaw
332pp. Ref. 413-5
An authoritative guide to PC-DOS, including version 3.2. Designed to make experts out of beginners, it explores everything from disk management to batch file programming. Includes an 85-page command summary.

The IBM PC-DOS Handbook
Richard Allen King
340pp. Ref. 368-6
A guide to the inner workings of PC-DOS 3.2, for intermediate to advanced users

and programmers of the IBM PC series. Topics include disk, screen and port control, batch files, networks, compatibility, and more.

OTHER OPERATING SYSTEMS AND ENVIRONMENTS

Programmer's Guide to GEM
Phillip Balma/William Fitler
504pp. Ref. 297-3
GEM programming from the ground up, including the Resource Construction Set, ICON Editor, and Virtual Device Interface. Build a complete graphics application with objects, events, menus, windows, alerts and dialogs.

Programmer's Guide to TopView
Alan R. Miller
280pp. Ref. 273-6
A guided tour through every features of the TopView multitasking, windowed, operating environment for the IBM PC, with programming techniques and examples showing proper use of system resources. Includes assembly-language programming.

Power User's Guide to Hard Disk Management
Jonathan Kamin
315pp. Ref. 401-1
Put your work, your office or your entire business literally at your fingertips, in a customized, automated MS-DOS work environment. Topics include RAM disks, extended and expanded memory, and more.

Programmer's Guide to Windows
David Durant/Geta Carlson/Paul Yao
645pp. Ref. 362-7
This high-level structured tutorial covers every aspect of effective Windows programming using the Software Development Kit routines. Includes scores of sample programs in C, and complete reference material.

Introduction to UCSD-p System
Charles W. Grant
300pp. Ref. 061-X
This book explains how to enter a Pascal program in the computer, edit it, store it on a file and then manipulate files.

The CP/M Handbook
Rodnay Zaks
320pp. Ref. 048-2
The definitive introduction and reference guide to the CP/M and MP/M operating systems, for users at all levels. With tutorials on file handling, PIP and the editor, programming information, and a complete reference section.

Mastering CP/M
Alan R. Miller
398pp. Ref. 068-7
An advanced guide to using, altering and adding features to CP/M, with an introduction to macro programming and a useful macro library. Full details on BIOS and BDOS operations, and the 8080 and Z80 instruction sets.

The CP/M Plus Handbook
Alan R. Miller
248pp. Ref. 158-6
Easy-to-read chapters show readers how to use the transient commands, take advantage of the features of the system editor, speed up operations with the automatic file search path, and get the most out of CP/M Plus.

SPREADSHEETS AND INTEGRATED SOFTWARE

The ABC's of 1-2-3 (Second Edition)
Chris Gilbert/Laurie Williams
245pp. Ref. 355-4
Online Today recommends it as "an easy and comfortable way to get started with the program." An essential tutorial for novices, it will remain on your desk as a

valuable source of ongoing reference and support. For Release 2.

Mastering 1-2-3
Carolyn Jorgensen
466pp. Ref. 337-6
Get the most from 1-2-3 Release 2 with this step-by-step guide emphasizing advanced features and practical uses. Topics include data sharing, macros, spreadsheet security, expanded memory, and graphics enhancements.

Lotus 1-2-3 Desktop Companion (SYBEX Ready Reference Series)
Greg Harvey
976pp. Ref. 385-6
A full-time consultant, right on your desk. Hundreds of self-contained entries cover every 1-2-3 feature, organized by topic, indexed and cross-referenced, and supplemented by tips, macros and working examples. For Release 2.

Power User's Guide to Lotus 1-2-3*
Pete Antoniak/E. Michael Lunsford
400pp. Ref. 421-6
This guide for experienced users focuses on advanced functions, and techniques for designing menu-driven applications using macros and the Release 2 command language. Interfacing techniques and add-on products are also considered.

Lotus 1-2-3 Book of Style*
Tim K. Nguyen
350pp. Ref. 454-2
For users of 1-2-3 who want a definite and comprehensive guide to writing 1-2-3 spreadsheets in a stylistically correct and acceptable way. Lots of examples show how to create models that are powerful and efficient, yet easily understandable.

Mastering Lotus HAL
Mary V. Campbell
342pp. Ref. 422-4
A complete guide to using HAL "natural language" requests to communicate with 1-2-3—for new and experienced users. Covers all the basics, plus advanced HAL features such as worksheet linking and auditing, macro recording, and more.

Simpson's 1-2-3 Macro Library
Alan Simpson
298pp. Ref. 314-7
Increase productivity instantly with macros for custom menus, graphics, consolidating worksheets, interfacing with mainframes and more. With a tutorial on macro creation and details on Release 2 commands.

Data Sharing with 1-2-3 and Symphony: Including Mainframe Links
Dick Andersen
262pp. Ref. 283-3
The complete guide to data transfer between Lotus products (1-2-3 and Symphony) and other popular software. With an introduction to microcomputer data formats, plus specifics on data sharing with dBASE, Framework, and mainframe computers.

Mastering Symphony (Third Edition)
Douglas Cobb
840pp. Ref. 470-4
A complex program explained in detail. Includes version 1.2 with the new Macro Library Manager. "This reference book is the bible for every Symphony user I know...If you can buy only one book, this is definitely the one to buy." —IPCO Info

Focus on Symphony Macros
Alan Simpson
239pp. Ref. 351-1
An in-depth tutorial guide to creating, using, and debugging Symphony macros, including developing custom menus and automated systems, with an extensive library of useful ready-made macros for every Symphony module.

Focus on Symphony Databases
Alan Simpson/Donna M. Mosich
398pp. Ref. 336-8
Master every feature of this complex system by building real-life applications from the ground up—for mailing lists, inventory and accounts receivable. Everything from creating a first database to reporting, macros, and custom menus.

Better Symphony Spreadsheets
Carl Townsend
287pp. Ref. 339-2

Complete, in-depth treatment of the Symphony spreadsheet, stressing maximum power and efficiency. Topics include installation, worksheet design, data entry, formatting and printing, graphics, windows, and macros.

Andersen's Symphony Tips and Tricks (Second Edition)
Dick Andersen/Janet McBeen
321pp. Ref. 342-2

Hundreds of concise, self-contained entries point the way to optimal use of Symphony features, including troubleshooting tips. Covers all five Symphony modules, plus macros and the command language, and Release 1.1.

Mastering Framework II
Douglas Hergert/Jonathan Kamin
509pp. Ref. 390-2

This business-minded tutorial includes a complete introduction to idea processing, "frames," and software integration, along with its comprehensive treatment of word processing, spreadsheet, and database management with Framework.

Advanced Techniques in Framework: Programming in FRED
Alan Simpson
320pp. Ref. 246-9

This introduction to the FRED programming language is for experienced Framework users who need to expand their word processing, spreadsheet, graphics, and database management skills.

Mastering Enable*
Keith D. Bishop
350pp. Ref. 440-2

A comprehensive, practical, hands-on guide to Enable 2.0 integrated word processing, spreadsheet, database management, graphics, and communications—from basic concepts to custom menus, macros and the Enable Procedural Language.

Mastering Q & A
Greg Harvey
399pp. Ref. 356-2

This hands-on tutorial explores the Q & A Write, File, and Report modules, and the Intelligent Assistant. English-language command processor, macro creation, interfacing with other software, and more, using practical business examples.

Mastering SuperCalc 4
Greg Harvey
311pp. Ref. 419-4

A guided tour of this spreadsheet, database and graphics package shows how and why it adds up to a powerful business planning tool. Step-by-step lessons and real-life examples cover every aspect of the program.

Also:
Mastering SuperCalc 3
Greg Harvey
400pp. Ref. 312-0

Understanding Javelin PLUS
John R. Levine
Margaret Levine Young
Jordan M. Young
558pp. Ref. 358-9

This detailed guide to Javelin's latest release includes a concise introduction to business modeling, from profit-and-loss analysis to manufacturing studies. Readers build sample models and produce multiple reports and graphs, to master Javelin's unique features.

ACCOUNTING

Mastering DAC Easy Accounting*
E. Carl Merrifield
400pp. Ref. 442-9

This hands-on tutorial shows you how to run your own business accounting system from start to finish, using DAC Easy Accounting. Ideal for non-accounting professionals.

DATABASE MANAGEMENT

Mastering Paradox
(Second Edition)
Alan Simpson
463pp. Ref. 375-9
Comprehensive treatment of Paradox versions 1.0 and 1.1 from database basics to command file programming with PAL. Topics include advanced queries and reports, automatic updating, and managing multiple data tables.

Mastering Reflex
Robert Ericson/Ann Moskol
336pp. Ref. 348-1
A complete introduction to Reflex: The Analyst, with hands-on tutorials and sample applications for management, finance, and technical uses. Special emphasis on its unique capabilities for crosstabbing, graphics, reporting, and more.

dBASE III PLUS Programmer's Reference Guide
(SYBEX Ready Reference Series)
Alan Simpson
1056pp. Ref. 382-1
Programmers will save untold hours and effort using this comprehensive, well-organized dBASE encyclopedia. Complete technical details on commands and functions, plus scores of often-needed algorithms.

The ABC's of dBASE III PLUS
Robert Cowart
264pp. Ref. 379-1
The most efficient way to get beginners up and running with dBASE. Every 'how' and 'why' of database management is demonstrated through tutorials and practical dBASE III PLUS applications.

Mastering dBASE III PLUS:
A Structured Approach
Carl Townsend
342pp. Ref. 372-4
In-depth treatment of structured programming for custom dBASE solutions. An ideal study and reference guide for applications developers, new and experienced users with an interest in efficient programming.

Also:
Mastering dBASE III: A Structured Approach
Carl Townsend
338pp. Ref. 301-5

Understanding dBASE III PLUS
Alan Simpson
415pp. Ref. 349-X
A solid sourcebook of training and ongoing support. Everything from creating a first database to command file programming is presented in working examples, with tips and techniques you won't find anywhere else.

Also:
Understanding dBASE III
Alan Simpson
300pp. Ref. 267-1

Understanding dBASE II
Alan Simpson
260pp. Ref. 147-0

Advanced Techniques in dBASE III PLUS
Alan Simpson
454pp. Ref. 369-4
A full course in database design and structured programming, with routines for inventory control, accounts receivable, system management, and integrated databases.

Also:
Advanced Techniques in dBASE III
Alan Simpson
505pp. Ref.282-5

Advanced Techniques in dBASE II
Alan Simpson
395pp. Ref. 228-0

Simpson's dBASE Tips and Tricks (For dBASE III PLUS)
Alan Simpson
420pp. Ref. 383-X

A unique library of techniques and programs shows how creative use of built-in features can solve all your needs—without expensive add-on products or external languages. Spreadsheet functions, graphics, and much more.

Simpsons's dBASE III Library
Alan Simpson
362pp. Ref. 300-7

A goldmine of techniques and ready-made programs to expand the off-the-shelf power of dBASE. Includes tutorials on command file programming, plus routines for finance, statistics, graphics, screens, oversize databases, and much more.

Expert dBASE III PLUS
Judd Robbins/Ken Braly
423pp. Ref. 404-6

Experienced dBASE programmers learn scores of advanced techniques for maximizing performance and efficiency in program design, development and testing, database design, indexing, input and output, using compilers, and much more.

Understanding R:BASE System V
Alan Simpson
499pp. Ref. 394-5

This complete tutorial guide covers every R:BASE function, while exploring and illustrating the principles of efficient database design. Examples include inventory management, mailing list handling, and much more.

Also:
Understanding R:BASE 5000
Alan Simpson
413pp. Ref. 302-3

Power User's Guide to R:BASE System V*
Alan Simpson
350pp. Ref. 354-6

A tutorial guide to structured programming in R:BASE, including system design, pro-cedure files, performance issues and managing multiple data tables. With complete working systems for mailing list, inventory and accounts receivable.

GENERAL UTILITIES

The ABC's of the IBM PC
Joan Lasselle/Carol Ramsay
143pp. Ref. 102-0

Hands-on experience—without technical detail—for first-time users. Step-by-step tutorials show how to use essential commands, handle disks, use applications programs, and harness the PC's special capabilities.

Business Graphics for the IBM PC
Nelson Ford
259pp. Ref. 124-1

A complete guide to business graphics programming in IBM PC BASIC. Sample programs illustrate line, bar, and column charts, logarithm and scatter graphs, how to rotate, size and move graphs, printing, plotting and more.

Mastering ThinkTank on the IBM PC
Jonathan Kamin
350pp. Ref. 327-9

A business-minded tutorial on "idea processing" with ThinkTank—from first outlines to advanced features. Examples include logging sales calls, maintaining a resume, and creating a marketing plan. With complete reference sections.

Power User's Guide to SideKick*
Albert Holt
250pp. Ref. 371-6

A goldmine of tips and uses of SideKick and SuperKey with custom programming and popular applications, including 1-2-3, dBASE, WordStar and Crosstalk XVI. Includes discussion of interrupts, compatibility, programming issues, and commonly wanted patches.

How to Get the Programs in This Book

If you'd rather not type in the listings in this book, they are all available on disk from the author. The disk also includes several utility programs which are in the public domain and are supplied free. Among them are utilities that perform the following operations:

▲ Rename directories

▲ Move files from one directory to another without copying them

▲ Display a clock and toggle-key indicators on the screen

▲ Create a command stack

▲ Display directories in sorted order

▲ Locate a file name on any directory

To obtain a copy of the disk, complete the order form below, and return it with a check or money order for $20 in U.S. funds. (California residents please add appropriate sales tax for your county. Overseas orders please add $1.00.)

You will receive a disk by first-class mail. I cannot accept telephone orders or credit cards, nor can I send disks by any other delivery system.

Kamin Consulting Services
3985 Lyman Road
Oakland, CA 94602

Please send me a copy of the companion disk for *MS-DOS Power User's Guide, Volume 1.*

Name _____

Address _____

City/State/Zip _____

Enclosed is my check or money order.
(Make check payable to *Kamin Consulting Services*.)
Price includes postage within the United States.

This offer is made solely by the author, and SYBEX assumes no responsibility for any defect in the disk or program.

SYBEX Computer Books are different.

Here is why . . .

At SYBEX, each book is designed with you in mind. Every manuscript is carefully selected and supervised by our editors, who are themselves computer experts. We publish the best authors, whose technical expertise is matched by an ability to write clearly and to communicate effectively. Programs are thoroughly tested for accuracy by our technical staff. Our computerized production department goes to great lengths to make sure that each book is well-designed.

In the pursuit of timeliness, SYBEX has achieved many publishing firsts. SYBEX was among the first to integrate personal computers used by authors and staff into the publishing process. SYBEX was the first to publish books on the CP/M operating system, microprocessor interfacing techniques, word processing, and many more topics.

Expertise in computers and dedication to the highest quality product have made SYBEX a world leader in computer book publishing. Translated into fourteen languages, SYBEX books have helped millions of people around the world to get the most from their computers. We hope we have helped you, too.

For a complete catalog of our publications:

SYBEX, Inc. 2021 Challenger Drive, #100, Alameda, CA 94501
Tel: (415) 523-8233/(800) 227-2346   Telex: 336311